Maritime Trade and State Development in Early Southeast Asia

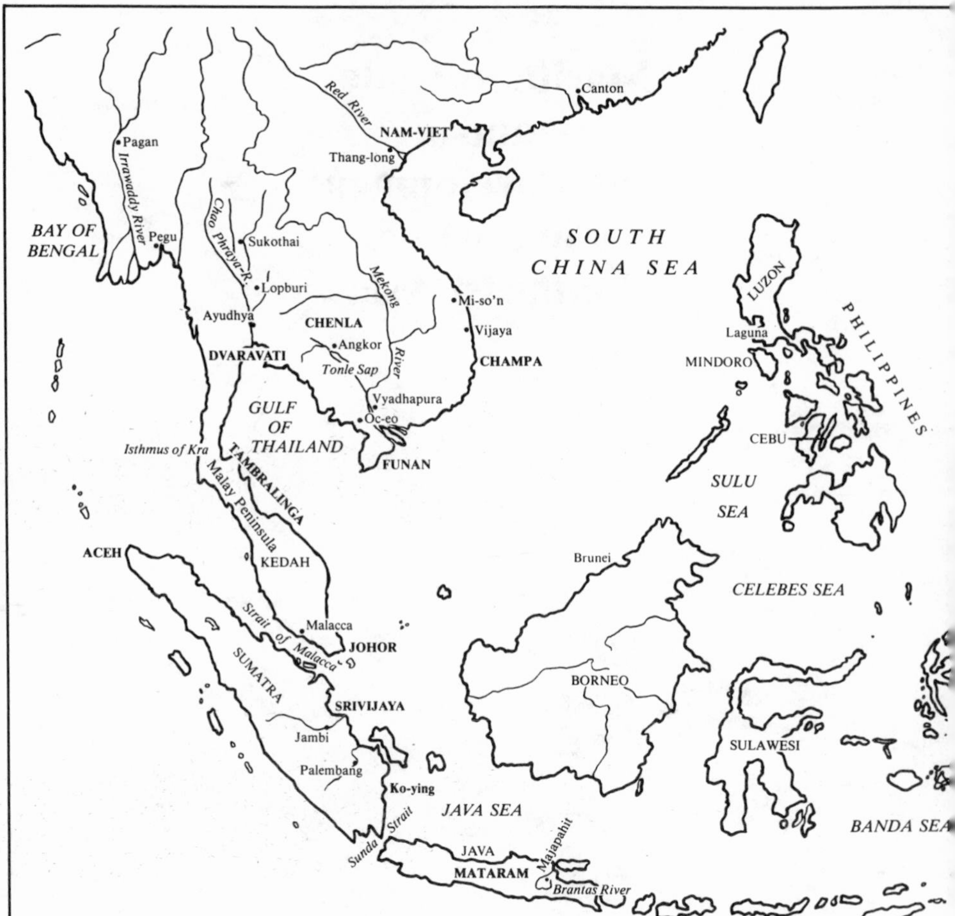

CLASSICAL SOUTHEAST ASIA

Maritime Trade and State Development in Early Southeast Asia

Kenneth R. Hall

UNIVERSITY OF HAWAII PRESS • HONOLULU

Library of Congress Cataloging in Publication Data

Hall, Kenneth R.
Maritime trade and state development in early Southeast Asia.

Bibliography: p.
Includes index.
1. Asia, Southeastern—Commerce—History. 2. Asia, Southeastern—History. I. Title.
HF3790.8.H35 1985 382.'0959 84-22777
ISBN 0-8248-0843-6
ISBN 0-8248-0959-9 (pbk.)

To

Randy, Janie, and Jason

Contents

Maps

Figures

List of Photographs

Preface

Research in the premodern history of Southeast Asia has been limited by a paucity of sources, a fact that has discouraged many from undertaking further study of the pre-1500 era. There is, for instance, a total absence of a local chronicle tradition until after the eleventh century. The bulk of the available local sources for Southeast Asia's early history are the inscribed stones and metal plates through which religious institutions and political elites presented their idealized view of early Southeast Asian society. When historical events or individuals are mentioned at all, it is to illustrate that the proper order of the universe is maintained by the subordination of those in the secular realm to those who are concerned with the universe's harmony. To overcome the ambiguities, distortions, and voids in these sources, historians have looked to external references that reflect the visits of foreigners to Southeast Asia, for example, the accounts of Western travelers (including Arabs) and Chinese pilgrims, and to the records of diplomatic contact between Southeast Asian states and the great civilizations of India and China. Among the latter the Chinese dynastic chronicles have been the most useful.

Early scholarship on Southeast Asian history in the West was the product of well-trained Dutch, French, and British historians whose research was an extension of their countries' colonial experience. They tended to focus on external forces that shaped Southeast Asia. Furthermore, these historians concentrated on the religious and political aspects of the epigraphic and literary sources and thus were especially concerned with the reconstruction of dynastic chronologies. Working from this base, modern historians have begun to reexamine the sources critically in order to filter out information useful for the reconstruction of social and economic history. They have also attempted to balance the picture of outside forces by focusing equally on indigenous responses. And in the past fifteen years archaeological research in Southeast Asia has become sufficiently sophisticated to begin to supply these historians with new data.

To appreciate these advances and new orientations, one might make a comparison of George Coedès' impressive works *The Making of Southeast Asia* or *The Indianized States of Southeast Asia* with O. W. Wolters' *Early Indonesian Commerce* and *The Fall of Srivijaya in Malay History.* Coedès was synthesizing early twentieth-century Western history of Southeast Asia, much of it done by Coedès himself, and work that was concerned with Indian culture as the basis for state development. Wolters, on the other hand, focused on the activities of those Southeast Asians who responded to the presence of traders and other foreigners —on their own initiative—by optimizing their opportunities. Unlike Coedès, however, Wolters and other recent scholars have normally examined specific areas within the region without coming to terms with the general regional patterns that characterize Southeast Asia's early history.

But in his extended essay *History, Culture, and Region in Southeast Asian Perspectives,* Wolters summarizes his perceptions of features common to the various early Southeast Asian societies he has researched. To demonstrate the validity of studying Southeast Asia as a regional unit, Wolters stresses the linkages and cultural dialogue among Southeast Asian peoples who shared a "common ocean." Like Coedès, Wolters is concerned with the role foreign culture (Indian or, in the case of Vietnam, Chinese) assumed in the process of societal development; but in contrast to Coedès, Wolters is more sensitive to the indigenous elements that shaped the "localization" of foreign forms.

This study also puts Southeast Asia on a large canvas and treats areas not previously brought together for treatment along comparative lines. By bringing together new theoretical constructs and recent archaeological finds and interpretations it attempts two things: to ask new questions of old sources and to integrate the histories of individual civilizations to demonstrate general regional patterns. It is intended to stimulate and encourage further study of Southeast Asia's premodern era.

Chapter 1 introduces Bennet Bronson's model of riverine exchange and statecraft and postulates a hierarchical and integrated marketing system that reflects the pattern of trade and state relations characteristic of the wet-rice civilizations of mainland Southeast Asia and Java. Chapter 2 describes trade during the era of the Roman Empire. It integrates archaeological evidence with Roman and Chinese texts to examine the expansion of the international maritime trade in the first century of the Christian era. It looks at why the Funan state grew and the increasing volume of trade from India to the Isthmus of Kra, from the isthmus to Funan's coastal realm on the lower Vietnam coast, and from there to China.

Chapter 3 emphasizes the dual nature of Funan's success as both a maritime depot and wet-rice producer and begins to demonstrate the descriptive value of the models of statecraft introduced in chapter 1. Reevaluating the evidence concerning Funan, a realm whose authority by the third century A.D. had spread from lower Vietnam across modern Thailand and Cambodia's coasts to the upper Malay Peninsula, the demise of Funan is explained by the development of a route around the Malay Peninsula and the subsequent emergence of new trade depots in Sumatra and Java around the fifth century. The sources for Funan's history include archaeological, epigraphic, and Chinese dynastic records, and a new look at them establishes that although Funan was not the well-integrated political system the Chinese believed it to be, it was nevertheless important because of the cultural forms it evolved, forms that anticipate later riverine and wet-rice plain political systems.

Chapter 4 analyzes the rise of Śrīvijaya and its rule over the Strait of Malacca from the sixth through the eleventh centuries and argues that Śrīvijaya was essentially a Sumatran state. By examining in detail the earliest epigraphy of the Śrīvijaya state, one finds that Śrīvijaya's coastal depots had elaborate systems of statecraft that integrated the depots with their hinterland and also separated international traders from those hinterland people who actually produced the commodities that the depot-based rulers collected and sold. Their success depended not simply on outside traders but more importantly on their ability to see the value of and to use selected items of Indian statecraft to consolidate their rule locally and thus control the hinterland as well.

Chapter 5 argues that pre-tenth-century Javanese polities, contemporaries of Śrīvijaya, were ritually based and were evolving market systems but were not the centralized states described by many historians. The chapter reevaluates the epigraphic and archaeological remains of pre-tenth-century Java and the studies of this evidence by Dutch and Indonesian scholars and explains why the regionally based Javanese elites were unable to develop a higher form of political integration until the Javanese court was established in eastern Java during the late tenth and early eleventh centuries.

Chapters 6 and 7 describe the development of systems of socioeconomic integration in the mainland civilizations of Angkor and Champa. Surveying Khmer (Cambodian) and Sanskrit epigraphy from the Angkor realm, chapter 6 examines the development of Khmer temple networks and their role in the evolution of the Angkor-based polity. Discussion of

Khmer wet-rice plain statecraft in the Angkor era from the ninth through the early thirteenth centuries is continued in the following chapter, where it is compared to the statecraft practiced in the Cham realm of the southern Vietnam coast. The chapter surveys Cham historical records but concentrates on two Arab inscriptions that provide the only concrete references to merchant activity in this area. It also draws upon Vietnamese chronicle references to enhance understanding of the impact of the maritime community upon the Cham state.

Chapter 8 studies archaeological remains; Burmese, south Indian, and Khmer epigraphy; and early Thai and Malay chronicles to analyze transitions in early Southeast Asian statecraft. In the eleventh and twelfth centuries the mainland states of Burma, Thailand, and Cambodia withdrew from the main international route into their own regional commercial networks. Their withdrawal was accompanied by a Theravāda Buddhist revival and helps to explain why these areas were not on the routes that Islam traveled—and why Islam's later importance in Southeast Asia was confined to the peninsula and the islands. It also notes the new Java-dominated trade in the archipelago and the emergence in the thirteenth century of new riverine states on the north Sumatra coast.

Chapter 9 examines epigraphic and literary records of the east Java-based Majapahit state that rose to prominence in the late thirteenth century. Since the kings of Majapahit were among the first to transform a pre-1300 classical tributary system into a more highly integrated, centralizing state, its history serves to demonstrate regional trends that persisted into the sixteenth century.

In romanizing Southeast Asian languages, I have employed the practice currently favored in the Southeast Asian country under study. Chinese words and names appear according to the Wade-Giles system rather than the currently fashionable Pinyin system; Sanskrit and Tamil words and names appear with diacritics appropriate to each and are written in the form currently used by most Indologists.

Acknowledgment is extended to the University of Michigan Center for South and Southeast Asian Studies, Elmira College, Tufts University, the American Institute of Indian Studies, the National Endowment for the Humanities, and the American Council of Learned Societies, who in various periods financed my research and the preparation of this book. Southeast Asia's history was introduced to me by Robina Quale at Albion College, Constance Wilson at Northern Illinois University, and John K. Whitmore at the University of Michigan, who has continued to be an invaluable critic. I studied Indonesian languages under David H. deQueljoe at Northern Illinois University; Madhav Deshpande introduced me to Sanskrit at the University of Michigan; and William Gedney provided suggestions on the translation of early Khmer.

My interpretation of Southeast Asia's early history has been shaped by my contact with numerous colleagues in the United States and in Southeast Asia. While teaching in New York, I benefited from O. W. Wolters' comments. I have tested my ideas on the members of the faculty and student body at Elmira College, the State University of New York at Binghamton, Tufts University, and North Adams State College. David K. Wyatt of Cornell University, Robert Van Niel of the University of Hawaii, George W. Spencer of Northern Illinois University, Lynda Shaffer of Tufts University, and John Villiers, director of the British Institute in South-East Asia (Singapore) generously provided criticism of the preliminary manuscript. Damaris A. Kirchhofer of the University of Hawaii Press patiently guided the preparation and publication of the final draft. My wife Lynne has endured the various ups and downs over five years as the manuscript took shape and finally went to press. To all these as well as many others too numerous to individually name I extend my thanks.

I stress that my view of Southeast Asia's early history is still evolving and in no way does this study represent a final depiction of early Southeast Asian history. I acknowledge that the noted paucity of sources makes my translations of Southeast Asian epigraphy and interpretations of other currently available sources subject to instant revision when new archaeological discoveries are made. Until such new information allows a definitive analysis, other historians' translations and interpretations that disagree with mine are equally plausible. I have purposely structured the text to make the modern historiography of Southeast Asia's past accessible to a wider audience. The chapters that follow are intended to solicit discussion, and I encourage others to test my hypotheses in their own studies of Southeast Asia's early history.

1

Trade and Statecraft in Early Southeast Asia

The subject of this book is the interaction between Southeast Asian peoples and foreign cultures that was the consequence of the strategic position of the Southeast Asian archipelago along the major premodern maritime route connecting East and West. Under examination are the classical centers of power that emerged between the first and early fourteenth centuries A.D. and the problems their leaders encountered in ruling their domains. Two forms of classical states are examined: the riverine coastal states of the Indonesian archipelago, the Malay Peninsula, and the Philippines and the lowland wet-rice states of the mainland (Burma, Thailand, Cambodia, Laos, and Vietnam) and of Java.

The book approaches the sources of Southeast Asia's classical era with the tools of modern economic history and highlights the role that international trade in Southeast Asia played in the evolution of classical civilizations. The view taken here is that Southeast Asia's response to international trade was a reflection of preexisting patterns of exchange. Well-developed internal socioeconomic and political networks existed in Southeast Asia before significant foreign economic penetration took place; with the growth of interest in Southeast Asian commodities and the refocusing of the major East-West commercial routes on the region during the early centuries of the Christian era, internal conditions within Southeast Asian states changed to accommodate the increased external contacts. The juncture of the trade routes and the existing or developing forms of exchange and state polity in Southeast Asia suggests the way this adjustment was made.

An early type of exchange involved highland hunters and gatherers who exchanged their goods and services with lowland cultivators; for example, trade between groups that practiced swidden (slash and burn) and *sawah* (wet-rice) cultivation.[1] Another type of early exchange network was characterized by trade between hinterland populations and coastal peoples; the hinterland people supplied local agricultural or forest products that were in turn dispensed to international traders. Coastal-based traders returned goods of foreign origin or specialized services (for example, "moneylending") to the hinterland producers. In a third variant, foreign merchants established a coastal base and then worked from this base to organize the necessary trade mechanisms that allowed them to extract local products from the hinterlands. In contrast to some views that identify this last pattern of interaction as most characteristic of Southeast Asia's premodern age,[2] this study contends that direct contact was unusual and that Southeast Asia's interaction with foreign merchants was the result of indigenous initiative and response to opportunities that already existed.

In this book, as in other studies by Western historians, there is a tendency to impose Western values on ideas of what constituted advanced civilizations in early Southeast Asia. Urbanization and the development of state systems are considered signs of advancement. The great urban centers of Angkor (Cambodia) and Java with their massive stone edifices thus become standards for comparison. But were the nonurban yet focused classical societies less valid as being "advanced" or "civilized," and was it necessary for an advanced civilization to leave impressive temple complexes?[3]

In partial response to this dichotomy, the focus here is on political integration rather than on political centralization. The evolution of Southeast Asian societies needs to be understood on their terms. An approach to this understanding can be made by looking at instances of cultural transition and continuity that took place whether or not there was outside stimulation or the development of a highly centralized polity—that is, a state in which a bureaucratic center dominated and effectively integrated its subordinate population centers under its elaborate system of administration, justice, and protection. The states of Southeast Asia's classical age are not depicted as highly bureaucratic polities, even in the case of the prosperous Cambodian and Javanese wet-rice realms. Rather this study analyzes why a higher degree of political centralization was not possible, despite the opportunities for economic development and consequent political innovation afforded by participation in international trade.

Statecraft in Indianized Southeast Asia

An examination of Southeast Asia's geography reveals two dominant patterns. The island world is characterized by numerous river systems that flow from interior highlands to the ocean, a feature that has had significant impact upon the island world's social and economic evolution. Over time people settled among these various river systems, populations becoming concentrated only in the broad delta regions at river mouths. This diffusion of the population had important implications for the island realm's political systems, as those who attempted to govern the island world found it necessary to bring multiple river systems under their authority in order to implement their political hegemony. Because it was impractical to control an entire river system, a pattern more common than complete political subjugation emerged—the establishment of partial hegemony through direct rule of only coastal plains and river mouths. By controlling the river mouth it was possible to influence movement up and down a river system. A river-mouth ruler was able to utilize his control over the riverine communications network to forge various alliances with upriver groups.

In contrast to the geographical inaccessibility of the island world caused by the multiple river system pattern, Southeast Asia's mainland along with a small number of island locales is dominated by major river systems with corresponding broad river plains, which are relatively flat, fertile, and extremely productive agriculturally. These river plains were conducive to the development of population centers by those seeking to cultivate rice in the rich soil of the plains. Rice plain population centers also proved easier to dominate politically than the more diffused population centers of the multiple river system geography. Southeast Asia's great political systems of the past all had a geographical base in a fertile rice plain: for example, Pagan in the Irrawaddy River plain of Burma, Angkor near the Tonle Sap in Cambodia, and the Vietnamese state in the Red River basin of Vietnam.

In the island world this great plain geographical pattern is found in central Java and again in the Brantas River basin of eastern Java. As on the mainland, population centers and great states developed in both regions. While the majority of the island world shared a multiple river system geography and thus what may be characterized as a riverine political system, the rich-soiled rice plains of central and eastern Java allowed the development of a higher degree of social and political integration than was possible elsewhere in the island world.

The problem of defining what constituted a classical Southeast Asian "state" may be approached by a careful description of the statecraft—the management of state affairs—of the riverine and wet-rice plain systems. Based on Western and Chinese prejudices that equate advancement with the evolution of elaborate state systems, successful Southeast Asian wet-rice civilizations of the mainland and Java are assumed to have become centralized polities.[4] Historians have also minimized the level of integration between the coast and hinterland of the riverine states.[5] The wet-rice states were not as centralized as most Western historians have believed, however, and the riverine states were not as isolated from their hinterlands as previously thought. Indeed, the two systems were not totally unrelated, as the mainland states had both a wet-rice aspect and a coastal international trade sector that enhanced the economy of the hinterland. Thus, the two were not at opposite poles but were part of a continuum. In both, local statecraft was organized to control people not boundaries. Indeed, manpower was the basis of political power.

Classical Southeast Asia was generally underpopulated. Would-be rulers competed among themselves to attract the manpower necessary for them to assume power. The continued existence of a state and its management polity—that is, a state in which a bureaucratic center dominated and effectively integrated its subordinate population centers under its elaborate system of administration, justice, and protection—depended on the ruling elite's ability to control population centers. The control a state claimed and its actual control over people, however, were quite different.[6] The "core" of the domain was that area of land, usually near the capital, that was administered directly by the state's central administration. The king was usually a major landholder in this core, but the landholding rights of others—normally rights to a share of the produce from the land under their authority rather than ownership in the modern sense—were also protected.[7] "Peripheral areas," those areas bordering the core, were in a tributary relationship to the state. Although the state might claim to have administratively annexed these areas, its real control was minimal, as local elites remained in power while paying homage to the center. Although the records of monarchs might be widely distributed, the wording employed in engraved inscriptions found in areas outside the state's core domain, where the ruler's power was not direct, honored the authority of the strong local elite. It was through the support of such leaders of local populations that the ruler could command the loyalty of population centers peripheral to the state's core.

Classical states showed little capacity to absorb the populations of regions beyond their core. People of various regions could be brought under the state's control, yet, although a regional population might be engulfed by a state even for several centuries, with the decline of that state, this same group of people was capable of reemerging with its local traditions intact—a pattern not unique to Southeast Asia. The key to a center's control over manpower was its ability to form political alliances with the locally based elite. A ruler, acting from a center of authority, fragmented his potential enemies by reaching agreements with the leaders of local population centers, and these potential opponents became subordinate allies of the state. In return for their patronage of the state's monarch, the local elites enjoyed enhanced status in the eyes of their followers, and the allied population received the protection afforded by the state's armies and shared in a successful state's prosperity.

Early historiography of the classical period depicted the capitals of Southeast Asian states as a social pyramid, with the monarch and his elite on top having little personal contact with the people below. In this view local populations were subjugated, continually exploited, and generally in awe of the elite who resided in the state's capital.[8] A more intense interaction and interdependency existed between state centers and their subordinate populations, however. In some cases the rulers of classical states even appointed their own clan members to administer key "provinces." In Java, for instance, classical states were divided into numerous regional provinces *(watĕk),* each governed by provincial chiefs *(rakrayān)* who were often the sons of the states' monarchs.[9] In the Sumatra-based state of Śrīvijaya certain areas of the realm in the Strait of Malacca were ruled by chiefs *(dātu),* some of whom were relatives of the king, while others were ruled by *dātu* of nonroyal background. The distinction between the powers of the two is not entirely clear, although it appears that the Śrīvijaya monarch was quite willing to accept strong local leaders as his subordinate *dātu.*

Śrīvijaya, Java, and other classical Southeast Asian states merged traditional indigenous symbols of divinity and power with Indian cosmological symbolism and religious theory to form an ideological basis for their kingship. The blending of indigenous and Indic traditions is seen, for instance, in the universal significance of the mountain in the three mainland wet-rice states. In Cambodia, "Mount Mahendra" became the home of the *devarāja* in the cult of Jayavarman II in the early ninth century—a cult that extensively subordinated worship of local deities to the king's worship of Śiva (see chap. 6). As the traditional abode of ancestor spirits, the mountain was already considered sacred by indigenous tradition. By incorporating the external god Śiva, who was known in Indian philosophy as the "Lord of the Mountain" and for his association with fertility, the king's position was reinforced. It remained for Cambodian kings to associate themselves with this mountain and thereby symbolize their ability to guarantee the flow of life-power from the realm of the ancestors to their subjects. In Burma, the various *nat* spirits were integrated into a similar cult that also came to be focused on a "Lord of the Mountain," the Mahagīri spirit of "Mount Popa." In Vietnam, kings were regarded as descendants from the union of the *nāga* (water) spirit and a maiden who resided on the mountain inhabited by the mountain spirit. The necessity of this process of incorporating indigenous folk belief is well shown in the case of Vietnam, where one reason for the failure of the early Sino-oriented elite of the upper Red River Delta to form a lasting state was their unwillingness to integrate local folk traditions into their Confucian ideology.[10]

The early Southeast Asian monarch's powers were bestowed through ceremony. The royal court, its activities, and its style recreated a world of the gods—in theory, a heaven on earth. Here all greatness and glory were concentrated. By successfully fulfilling his role as the hypothetical focus of all sanctity and power, the king maintained the orderliness of the world. The king's court attempted to develop ritual links to its subordinate centers of power by integrating local religious cults into a state religious system, whereby the subordinate centers imitated the ritual style of the royal center.[11] Local deities and, of most consequence, local ancestor worship were blended into the state's religious ceremony. The state made great use of Indian (or, in the case of Vietnam, Chinese) ceremony, performed by religious specialists or elites who assumed the role of priests. These state ceremonies, however, were built on traditional beliefs of how spirits and ancestors were to be manipulated to guarantee the prosperity of the living. Indic or Sinic patterns were thus utilized to enhance local religious views to the advantage of the elite, whose ritual magic was presented to their subjects as being greater than that of earlier practice.

The state elite's patronage of the Hindu and Buddhist traditions from India brought them into a wider universe of symbols and attachments and provided an Indian framework for their statecraft. Southeast Asian kings utilized Sanskrit vocabulary, described the world in the idiom of Hindu and Buddhist thought, and sponsored art and architecture that expressed the Hindu and Buddhist world views.[12] Royal monuments were cosmological symbols redefining the boundaries of time and space to the advantage of the state's elite. A vast and orderly cosmos was substantiated by the most advanced mathematical astronomy of the time and was the foundation for Hindu and Buddhist thought.[13] States were patterned on the order of the cosmos and linked the sacred and secular orders. A ruler and his capital were at the center of the universe; cosmological and magical symbols expressed royal power. In the Hindu and Buddhist concepts of state the ruler facilitated the establishment of a secular society that was more nearly in harmony with the natural cosmic order *(dharma)*. In a successful state, society was harmonious as well as prosperous. The most effective ruler did not force conformity by use of physical might *(daṇḍa)* but achieved success due to his righteous victory *(dhammavijaya/dharmavijaya)* and continued peaceful leadership. The just ruler was the *cakravartin* ("universal monarch"), whose illustrious

A major river system: the Irrawaddy in Burma.

Paddy fields, eastern Java.

Dry-field agriculture. Pagan, Burma.

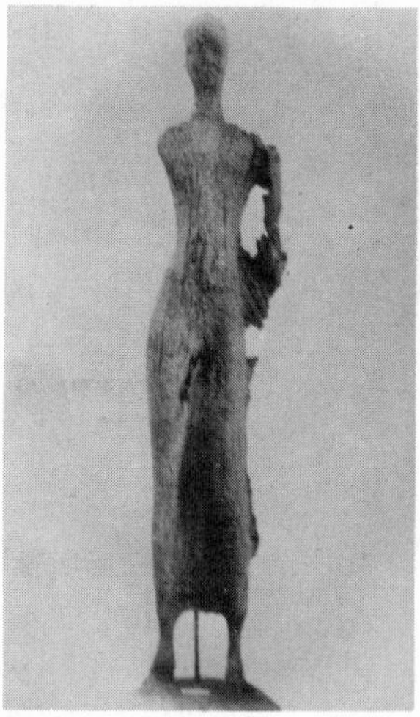

Wooden Buddhist statue from Oc-èo. Photo courtesy Truong Buu Lam.

Roman coin from Oc-èo. Photo courtesy Truong Buu Lam.

moral force uplifted his subjects and established the secular conditions necessary for the attainment of their salvation.[14]

Summarizing their perceptions of the Hindu and Buddhist traditions, early Southeast Asian rulers fused these cosmological principles with Indic topographical formulas (*maṇḍala*—a "contained core") that provided a design for the integration of clan or lineage-based groups into more complex centralized polities. In the Indian philosophical tradition a *maṇḍala* was a sacred diagram of the cosmos that was normally depicted in art as a geometric construct of encompassed circles and rectangles. The worldly *maṇḍala* (state) in early Southeast Asia was defined by its center, not its perimeter, as there was no notion of a firm frontier.[15] Subordinate population centers surrounding the center were variably drawn to participate in the ceremony of the state system. To encourage their participation, the personal and regional cults practiced in the state's regions were assembled at the center. One theoretically moved from the mundane world toward the spiritual one by approaching the sacred axis from one of the four quarters (defined by the points of the compass). The devotee/subject was to become caught up in a psychological state that grew in intensity as he was drawn to this sacred core of the universe and its "world mountain" (normally a central temple complex) that joined the celestial powers with the fertile soils of the earth.

While in a theoretical sense the king's only duty was thus to maintain the world order—to promote prosperity and to facilitate passage to the realm of the ancestors—in practice his duties sometimes involved the application of customary law regarding land and labor. In an inscription from central Java dated 860, for example, state administrators were asked to intervene in a local dispute when the village elders and a certain individual, who represented a religious foundation (temple), could not resolve the method of repaying a considerable debt owed to the local community. In this case the state administrators ruled in favor of the local community.[16] However, since Southeast Asian epigraphy does not contain many references to the adjudication of local disputes, one may assume that the state normally remained above such conflicts during the classical age, discouraging all but major disputes from clogging the state's administrative system. This policy encouraged the continuity of local custom, which the state generally left untouched as long as it was not disruptive to state harmony.

The effective ruler also took an interest in his state's economic activity. In addition to being the ideological center of the state, the royal capital was the economic center of the monarch's domain. The economic resources of the state's core were very important to its ability to maintain power. Rulers of wet-rice states therefore attempted to increase the agricultural output of their core. Under state supervision the construction of water tanks and irrigation systems were undertaken, and economic development in general was encouraged. In Java, for example, to develop economically peripheral lands, reward loyal followers, and extend the control of the throne, royal land grants known as *sīma* ("freehold") were given.[17] Although such land was considered to be outside the administrative authority of the king—freeing it from royal demands for taxes and service—a ceremony dedicating the *sīma* land grant emphasized that the grantee was expected to remain loyal to the Javanese state. This ceremony involved an oath in which the grantee pledged his loyalty, and it culminated with the pronouncement of a curse by a religious official threatening those present who were not loyal to their monarch.[18]

Although different in nature, the economic center of the Śrīvijaya maritime state was functionally similar to those of the wet-rice producing states. It served as a locus for economic redistribution, fulfilling roles both as a trade entrepôt and as the central treasury for a series of ports. A downriver port on the edge of the Sumatra hinterland, the Śrīvijaya capital was more vulnerable to attacks from outsiders as well as to the rebellions of its hinterland inhabitants than the land-based states that were established inland well away from the coast. Yet the capital's economic control over its disparate subject population—upriver tribesmen and coastal sea nomads—was similar to that of the land-based states. Because it was difficult to control directly tribal producers who were distant from the capital, the Śrīvijaya state relied on either physical force or alliance relationships, symbolized by an oath administered to state subordinates, to establish and maintain its economic hegemony in peripheral areas. While a royal navy of sea nomads maintained the capital's position as the dominant port on the Sumatra coast, a network of alliances with its hinterland tribesmen allowed a flow of goods from the interior to the ports—giving Śrīvijaya its economic and thus its political strength.

The classical political systems, whether wet-rice or riverine, attempted to draw the resources of their realms—in the form of tribute, talent, men, and goods—to their centers. Central Javanese states, for instance, expected both taxes in kind and labor service from their subjects (see chap. 5). Inscriptions report that rulers of eastern Java's states received specified shares of local products such as rice and cloth, as well as goods supplied regularly by traders such as spices, ceramics, and cloth of foreign origin. Resources acquired from a state's own core, when added to tribute extracted from politically subordinate peripheral areas, supplied the centers with large quantities of wealth. This wealth was in turn redistributed to maintain loyalty to the state. One type of investment was the regional construction of large temple complexes that emphasized the state's theoretical powers. Often such construction was financed by the transfer of the royal right to a share of local products and labor to a community, and the community applied this designated income to finance local temple construction and the temple's maintenance. In such instances the royal investment also provided for economic development in the vicinity of the temple, and the construction of elaborate temple complexes promoted the growth of an indigenous artisan class.[19]

Payments to various state armies and administrators were important revenue outlays of the state. Military power was essential in the process of concentrating as many resources as possible at the center. Military strength allowed the state to "protect" its subordinate territories—whether in theory or in fact—which in turn facilitated the establishment of the state's economic base, the administration of oaths, and the formulation of the various royal cults. To insure the flow of revenues that supported the classical state, a system of record keeping was initiated and in the more developed wet-rice states a council was formed to handle it. This royal administrative council, concentrated at the center, was composed of a small group of administrators who were generally literate and capable of dealing with a variety of matters.[20] Periodically they were sent out individually or as members of a mobile royal retinue traveling from place to place within the realm to act on disputes that could not be solved locally or on affairs that were considered to be in the state's interest.[21] These state administrators also participated in the various state ceremonies. In a system of statecraft in which ritual links were a vital tool of integration, it was essential that the ritual at the center be performed by an elite who knew how to conduct the required ceremonies properly.[22]

To achieve political integration, the leaders of a classical Southeast Asian state had to diversify the state's economy as well as manipulate a set of symbols that would distinguish them from other elites in the state. Therefore, the ruling elite of a coastal-based state who had ambitions of political grandeur, for example, had to make their state a leader in the externally focused international trade sector. To accomplish this, they had to establish their economic and political authority over upriver populations as well as over the maritime-oriented inhabitants of the coastal enclave. To depend only on the redistributions—the allocation of rewards and resources that served to help integrate the society—derived from facilitating trade in a coastal enclave with limited upriver ties made a coastal-based riverine political system vulnerable to the fluctuations of international trade. If revenues derived from international trade diminished, political and economic alliances that depended on the redistribution of trade goods could no longer be sustained. As the maritime trade diminished, the state's maritime allies might turn to open piracy to maintain their personal livelihood, thereby further destroying the coastal center's viability by discouraging international traders from navigating the state's waters.

Likewise a state too dependent on income derived from its wet-rice plain base was also limited in its development potential. The rice plain state elites of both Java and Angkor shared land control with rival landed elites and institutions. Some of the competing institutions had been created by the state's elite to reinforce the state's legitimacy. For example, temples and temple networks were heavily endowed with economic resources by various classical-era rulers. Initially this patronage returned merit and bestowed superior status on the state elite, but over time the continued endowment of temples could have left the temples with income rights exceeding those of the state. A network of temples could—and in the case of the Burmese state of Pagan did[23]—use their wealth and their control over large segments of the state's land and labor to influence state policy.

Since income derived from the land was the major source of a rice plain-based elite's ability to exercise political sovereignty, providing the would-be ruler with material as well as "symbolic" capital with which to construct alliance networks, a successful sovereign had to have either immense personal prowess or greater economic resources at his personal disposal than did potential sovereigns from other elites within the realm. It was only when those claiming sovereignty in a rice plain state became more actively involved in external commercial affairs that the authority of the state leaders and their court relative to competing regionally based elites and institutions became more secure. Economic leadership in the commercial sector provided a new source of income for wet-rice plain monarchs and in turn enhanced their political accomplishments. Development of an international trade sector also promoted the prosperity of the wet-rice sector, providing new markets for local rice production and facilitating the expansion of wet-rice agriculture, which then stimulated the development of a more integrated political and economic order.

Structures of Trade in the Classical Southeast Asian World

Two models may be used to explain the ways that external trade came into contact with existing and developing internal forms of exchange. One reflects the riverine political system, in which upriver exchange networks connected with foreign trade at coastal centers through the agency of river mouth rulers who shared trade-derived prosperity with the interior. The second model attempts to show how trade was conducted in the river plain realms of the Southeast Asian mainland and Java. Contact with foreign merchants was similar to that in the riverine states. Trade gravitated toward the coastal centers, and the trade's profits were redistributed to emphasize the ruler's hegemony. But the geography of a rice plain economy held greater potential for the evolution of an integrated and hierarchical system of market exchange, which was capable of facilitating political and social integration. In both economic systems the potential for conflict with foreigners was minimized because trading activities were confined to the coastal ports, where business was transacted by indigenous merchants who supplied the rice, pepper, and other products the foreign seafarers desired.[24]

Riverine and Rice Plain Exchange Networks

Figure 1 gives a diagram of exchange in decentralized Southeast Asian riverine political systems.[25] In this model, an economic system's trade "center" *(A)* is a coastal base located at a river mouth. Points *B* and *C* are secondary and third order centers located at upstream primary and secondary river junctions. Point *D* identifies distant upstream centers, the initial concentration point for products originating in more remote parts of the river watershed. Points *E* and *F* are the ultimate producers—the nonmarket-oriented population centers of the hinterland and upland or upriver villages whose loyalty to the marketing system dominated by

Figure 1
Riverine System Exchange

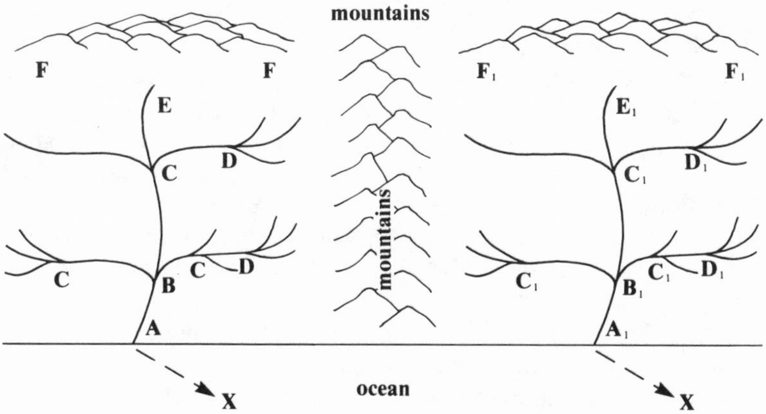

Adapted from Bennet Bronson, "Exchange at the Upstream and Downstream Ends: Notes Toward a Functional Model of the Coastal State in Southeast Asia," 42.

A is minimal. A_1 represents a rival river-mouth center and its marketing system. A_1 can compete for the loyalty of *E* and *F* as well as for trade with *X,* an overseas center that consumes the exports and supplies imports for *A* and A_1.

This riverine marketing system is integrated by coercion, where practical, or can be directly administered or colonized by *A*. *A* holds the loyalty of its marketing system by exacting oaths and/or tribute or through exercising its ability to select or confirm local leadership. *A* must also compete with *B* to establish and maintain dominance over the hinterland network. *A* relates to *B* and the other upriver centers via emphasis on traditional mechanisms of alliance but also depends on *X* as a consumer of local products or as a supplier of foreign luxury goods and as the source of the entire network's prosperity. *X,* though, can likely acquire goods from each of several *A*s, concentrating upon a coastal center where foreign merchants can acquire the best quality or the best deal, or ideally both. *X* can shift its trade to a rival *A* without regard for the acute economic or political hardships suffered by a center temporarily deprived of trade, or *X* can even attempt to deal directly with the interior centers of supply. Points *A* and A_1 are thus natural enemies, and it is in the interest of one or the other to establish political hegemony over the other. In this instance *A*'s control of A_1's entire marketing network is not even necessary.[26] As long as *A* controls A_1, *A* will dominate the flow of trade goods to and from A_1's river mouth. *A*'s dominance over B_1 could also conceivably accomplish this same objective.

This riverine system model can be applied to the Śrīvijaya maritime state as documented in the early seventh-century inscriptions discussed in chapter 4 (see map 4).[27] Initially Śrīvijaya's center was in the Palembang area of Sumatra, a point at the intersection of several river systems upriver from the coast, a strategic position that allowed Śrīvijaya's rulers to dominate commerce flowing upriver and downriver from its harbor. Palembang's control over its hinterland was based on its own physical might, but was especially dependent on an oath of allegiance that was administered to the state's subordinate elites, inculcations, the systematic redistribution of wealth from the royal treasury, alliances with local chieftains *(dātu),* and even the assignment of royal princes to leadership positions in the hinterland. Śrīvijaya's marketing network was based more upon alliances and the common sharing of the wealth derived from foreign trade than on direct coercion. The Śrīvijaya monarch was recognized as the source of the system's prosperity.

Palembang's natural enemy was Jambi, a rival coastal center dominating the Batang Hari River system. Consequently, one of the Śrīvijaya ruler's first expeditions of conquest was against Jambi in A.D. 682. Śrīvijaya's victory over the rival river-system center and subsequent victories over other river-mouth centers on the Sumatran, Malayan, and western Javanese coasts guaranteed Śrīvijaya's control over the flow of goods within the Strait of Malacca and as well from the region into the international trade route.

The riverine system model implies that the riverine system was by nature impermanent, and indeed some historians believe that Śrīvijaya as a political entity was characterized by a shifting center. The Śrīvijayan "capital" may have initially been on the Musi River system but in the eleventh century was at Jambi and was likely focused on other riverine centers in the Strait of Malacca region at times in between.[28]

Chinese dynastic records document this internal competition among the various Malay river systems. Numerous river-mouth centers sent tribute missions to the Chinese court in hopes of receiving recognition as a "preferred" trade partner of the Chinese.[29] Such recognition would seemingly have reinforced a riverine center's ability to trade not only with the Chinese but also to assume a special position in trade with Western merchants who would stop in the Southeast Asian archipelago on their way to China.

While the riverine system diagram provides a model for the understanding of trade relationships within the island world, the geography and historical records of the river-plain realms of the mainland and Java do not lend themselves to this analysis. The second model (see fig. 2) better characterizes the commercial networks in the rice plain economies of Java and the Southeast Asian mainland. Although discussion of the model in this chapter is specific to Java, the model is intended to illustrate the rice plain states' trade structure in general, and it will be applied to the rice plain states of the mainland in subsequent chapters.

Contemporary Javanese inscriptions portray networks of clustered villages called *wanua* as the most important units of local integration in the pre-Islamic Javanese hinterland. These village networks are generally viewed as units of social and political integration; what is not understood is how the indigenous village networks provided for the flow of goods from coastal ports to village cluster markets. Merchants who had external ties and who were encouraged by Javanese monarchs had a role in providing this commercial linkage.[30] Such encouragement may be seen, for example, in the royal grants to merchants that freed them from royal tax assessments on their transactions within specified village cluster markets.[31] However, the village clusters may be equally understood as local marketing networks whose nucleus was in every instance a periodic market, identified as *pkĕn* in Javanese inscriptions.

In pre-Islamic Java, *pkĕn* village markets operated on a five-day

Figure 2
Marketing in Pre-European Java

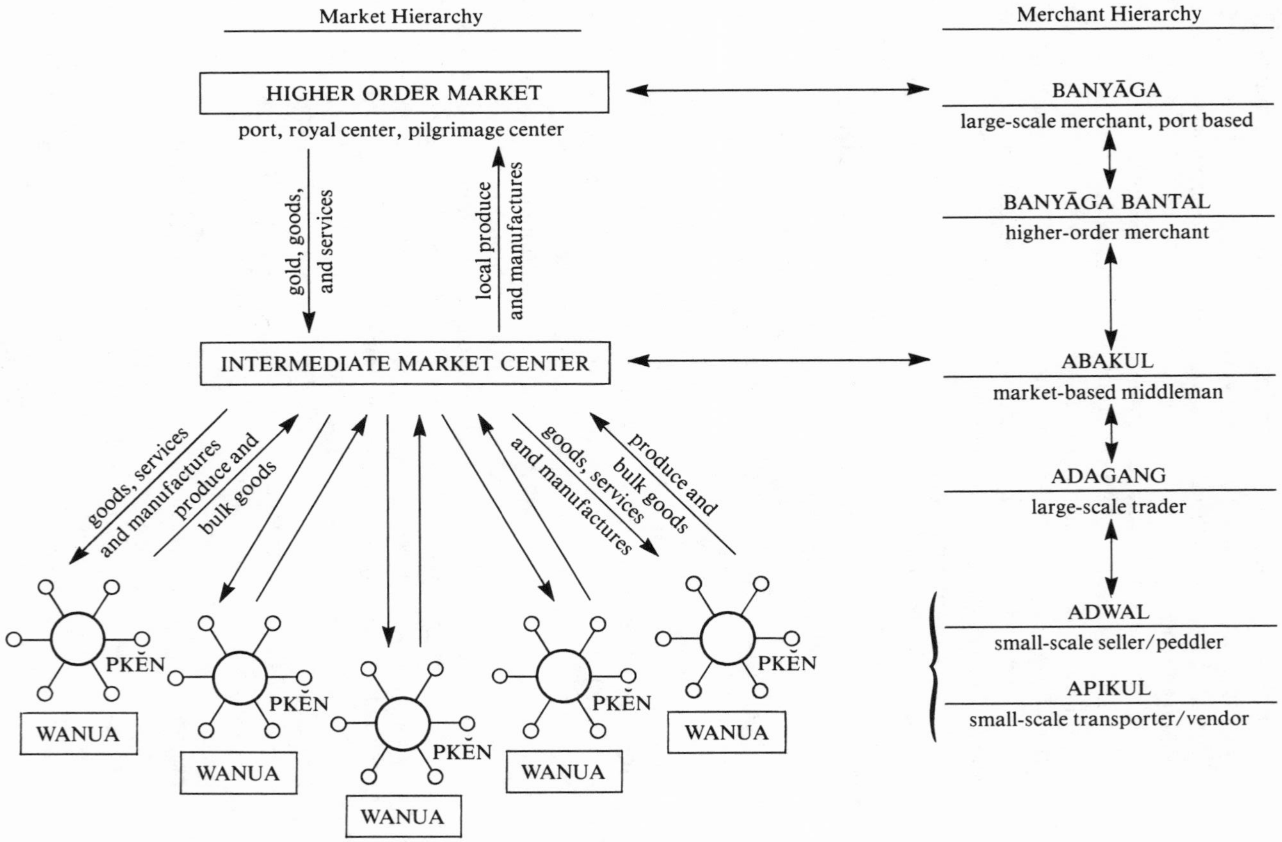

weekly cycle; itinerant merchants circulated among groups of tightly knit village clusters within this cycle. Figure 2 shows the resulting hypothetical marketing hierarchy. At the base of the marketing system were the *wanua,* local village clusters ("communities of exchange") that converged at a market center *(pkĕn)* where the village cluster's inhabitants gathered once every five days. The *pkĕn* markets were centers of local exchange. Market participants included farmers and artisans who sold their products and who purchased local goods or those commodities transported to the market by itinerant peddlers.[32] To facilitate easy access for the population, a *pkĕn* marketplace would have to have been located within walking distance of the homes of the village cluster's inhabitants, thus dictating the *pkĕn* market's position near the geographical center of the village cluster. A local official controlled access to the marketplace, collected taxes on goods offered for sale, and in general represented the village cluster's interest in dealings with the itinerant peddlers.[33]

These itinerant peddlers, identified in the inscriptions by the titles *adwal* and *apikul,* linked village clusters horizontally into marketing networks composed of multiple *wanua* communities of exchange. Peddlers circulated among *pkĕn* markets and made their travels conform to the indigenous marketing cycle—or the local marketing cycle conformed to the travels of the peddlers. In either case the various village-cluster communities of exchange were integrated into market cycles, which allowed one *wanua* community's *pkĕn* market to hold its transactions on a certain day of the week and others one each on the other four. A band of roving peddlers could thus have potentially served five *wanua* communities, participating in a different *pkĕn* market every day and trading in each village cluster once every five days.

The peddlers and their *pkĕn* market networks, in turn, were integrated by intermediate full-time market centers. Unlike the *pkĕn* markets, the intermediate centers of exchange had permanent shops or at the minimum a market that met every day. Such centers were inhabited by *adagang,* "large-scale traders," who conducted both a retail and wholesale trade, as well as groups of artisans.[34] Also based in the intermediate center were *abakul,* "market-based middlemen," who were the key to the natural flow of commodities between village clusters and the intermediate market center. Both serviced the needs of the *pkĕn*-focused itinerant peddlers, supplying goods of various sorts in exchange for local products acquired by the peddlers on their circuit. *Abakul* were wholesale specialists who traded in bulk for local production, especially for the rice, salt, beans, and dyes that figure so prominently in lists of Java's major exports.[35]

Goods acquired by *abakul* intermediate traders were transmitted to *adagang,* the large-scale traders, who in turn transferred goods to "higher order" merchants, identified by the title *banyāga bantal,* who connected the intermediate marketing centers to higher order markets that were inhabited by *banyāga,* "large-scale and seafaring traders"—"those who encircle the sea, those who travel throughout the sea."[36] These higher markets were major commercial centers integrating the various networks of exchange below them and were normally located during this age at coastal ports rather than at a royal center or a major pilgrimage center—the negotiation of major commercial transactions would have been inappropriate to such sanctified urban centers.[37] It is noteworthy that *banyāga* do not appear in lists of those participating in *pkĕn* market exchange, implying that there was a hierarchy of merchant and marketing activity within the early Javanese economy. *Banyāga* were clearly functioning only at the topmost levels of the marketing system, integrating the intermediate and local levels of commercial exchange to the "foreign" realm of trade. In the Javanese plains, free of physical constraints on the movement of goods from the hinterland, a number of small, periodic market centers connected to intermediate and higher order centers of exchange by a hierarchy of specialized and large-scale traders thus expedited the natural flow of goods destined to be sold to seafarers.

Javanese kings, especially in the post-tenth-century era of eastern Javanese dominance, played a key role in facilitating trade.[38] They encouraged and legitimized the incursions of port-based traders *(banyāga)* into the Javanese hinterland to collect specified amounts of produce. The royal stance in relation to the trade is reflected in an inscription that elaborates five royal instructions on the conduct of trade, quality control, and the use of standards and approved weights and measures at warehouses and rice granaries.[39] In the tenth century, according to one inscription, a Javanese ruler removed royal taxes from twenty vessels and the shippers of goods of twelve different classes—a total of 135 vessels were operating from one north coast port, reflecting a sizeable trade.[40] Another tenth-century inscription records a royal grant to encourage settlement along the river and roads leading to an eastern Java port to lessen the danger to merchants and coastal people from banditry.[41] Development of a port in eastern Java under royal patronage is also shown in an eleventh-century royal project that dammed the Brantas River to "reduce the threat of flooding to benefit shiphandlers, pilots, and gatherers of goods at Hujung Galah, including ships' captains, and merchants *(banyāga)* originating from other islands and countries."[42] Royal charters were granted to port-based merchants, and late in the era of eastern Javanese hegemony port-based merchants were even employed as royal tax collectors in areas near their port. This was a further means of facilitating the movement of goods from the hinterland, or it may also be viewed as an attempt by the Javanese monarch to penetrate local political autonomy. The use of foreign tax collectors may also indicate internal political instability, revealing the political system's need to depend on foreigners to support the king's authority.

It is important to remember that the centralization of trade constituted not only a convenience for all participants but also served as a mechanism for minimizing the penetration of the hinterland by outsiders. Control of the activities of higher order merchants strengthened the social cohesion of the local village cluster communities of exchange by protecting the interests of indigenous merchants and producers. For a river plain state desiring to participate in the international commercial networks, the aid of foreign merchants and seafarers was a necessary source of extended economic contacts with China and India. Indeed, eastern Javanese inscriptions reflect considerable interaction with a south India-based international trade consortium.[43] The use of seafarers as maritime allies was a double-edged sword, however. These allies could be a source of support or a serious threat to the political system's stability if they chose to act independently of the ruler's authority. There was always the potential for a port community to initiate a successful challenge to the state's authority. The port could do this by establishing its autonomy from royal control or by undermining royal authority by supporting one royal faction against another. Further, successful trade made the coastline vulnerable to naval attack. Southeast Asia's early history is full of references to maritime raids, one of the most famous being the 1292 maritime expedition of the Mongols against Java. Most Javanese ports therefore had fortified enclosures that were under the charge of the port's merchant community.

Thus foreign merchants and seamen who were beneficial to a ruler's ambitions could also destroy his state. Merchants and seafarers of foreign origin are described in Cham epigraphy from the southern Vietnam coast as "demonic" and "vicious," and are justifiably seen as "a threat to established order" (see chap. 7). To protect itself, and to remain consistent with the essentially inner focus of the Javanese state, the Javanese royal capital was situated well within the Javanese hinterland. Merchants and seafarers of foreign origin were confined to coastal ports where the potential danger of their commercial activities could be isolated. Local marketing networks and merchants provided the intermediary links to supply their needs and demands for goods. Ultimately, with the coming of more powerful foreign traders in the sixteenth century, penetration beyond these ports became possible, with disastrous consequence to the traditional Javanese way of life.

Maritime Trade in Early Southeast Asia: Zones and Eras

Premodern maritime exchange in Southeast Asia was transacted in five commercial zones (see map 1). The first zone encompassed the northern Malay Peninsula and the southern coast of Vietnam and was the first to openly solicit and facilitate East-West trade during the last millennium B.C. In this age Southeast Asia was regarded by foreign seamen as an intermediate and virtually unknown region lying between the riches of India and those of China. The initial agents of foreign contact were Malayo-Polynesian sailors who made voyages to as far west as the African coast and to China in the east.[44] Passage through Southeast Asia by international traders became important in the second century A.D. as the central Asian caravan routes, the previously preferred connecting link between East and West commercial networks, were disrupted by internal strife. During the second and third centuries the transport of goods shifted to the sea, and shipping flowed along a maritime route between the southeastern coast of China to the Bay of Bengal via a land portage across the upper Isthmus of Kra. Merchants' transit through Southeast Asia followed ports on the western edge of the Mekong Delta, said by the Chinese to have been under the authority of the early Southeast Asian state of Funan.

It is unlikely that the same group of sailors made the complete journey from the Middle East to China or vice versa, in part due to the seasonal nature of the monsoon winds, which were critical to navigation. Westerly winds from the southern Indian Ocean begin in April and peak in July. In January the wind flow reverses direction as the northeastern monsoons bring easterly winds. This means that voyagers had to wait at certain points until the next season's winds could take them to their destinations. Because the complete transit from one end of the route to the other was not possible within a single year, sailors found it expedient to travel only one sector of the route. One group would make the trip between Middle Eastern ports and India, and another made the Bay of Bengal voyage to the Isthmus of Kra, where their goods were transported across the isthmus and shipped from the Gulf of Thailand to the lower Vietnam coast. There commodities from the West were exchanged for those of the East. Another group of sailors then made the voyage from Funan to south China.[45] By the time fleets arrived in Funan ports, those ships traveling the China leg of the route had already gotten underway. Initially no local Southeast Asian products were exported from Funan's ports.

During this second- and third-century era a second commercial zone emerged in the Java Sea region. This Java Sea network was chiefly involved with the flow of gharuwood, sandalwood, and spices such as cloves among the Lesser Sunda Islands, the Moluccas, the eastern coast of Borneo, Java, and the southern coast of Sumatra. The development of a commercial center, known in Chinese records as Ko-ying, on the northern edge of the Sunda Strait region, was critical in connecting the riches of the Java Sea region with the international route.[46] The Sunda Strait location was ideal as a point at the end of the Java Sea where the flow of commerce within the Java Sea and beyond Java could be concentrated. Likewise a Sunda Strait entrepôt offered easy access to Funan and its international clientele. Malay sailors initiated the transport of spices from Ko-ying to Funan. They also began to supplement Eastern and Western products with products from the forests of the Indonesian archipelago. Ko-ying well represents the indigenous response to the potential for trade provided by the new maritime activities.

By the early fifth century the southern Sumatra coast assumed an additional importance, due in part to Java Sea spices. The principal East-West maritime route shifted from its upper Malay Peninsula portage to a nautical passage through the Strait of Malacca, making direct contact with the northwestern edge of the Java Sea.[47] The Strait of Malacca thus became the third zone of Southeast Asian commerce, and its center on the southeastern Sumatra coast soon became the focal point for Malay trade in western Borneo, Java, and the eastern islands, as well as the upper Malay Peninsula and its hinterland, the Chao Phraya and Irrawaddy river systems.[48] O. W. Wolters described southeastern Sumatra as a "favored coast" that aided the flow of commerce, marketing its own Sumatra forest products and Java Sea goods and utilizing Malay ships and crews to connect indigenous exchange networks with the international route.[49]

Under the Śrīvijayan maritime state, which dominated strait commerce until the early eleventh century, a pattern of riverine statecraft emerged built on alliances with Malay coastal populations and balanced by an expanding inland power base.[50] In the eyes of the Chinese, Śrīvijaya was the perfect trade partner. It was able to keep goods moving into south China ports by servicing vessels voyaging through the Southeast Asian archipelago. Śrīvijaya's ports were utilized as centers of exchange for those ships traveling over but one segment of the maritime route or as ports of call for ships awaiting the appropriate monsoon winds to take them to their destination. Śrīvijaya also successfully protected the South-

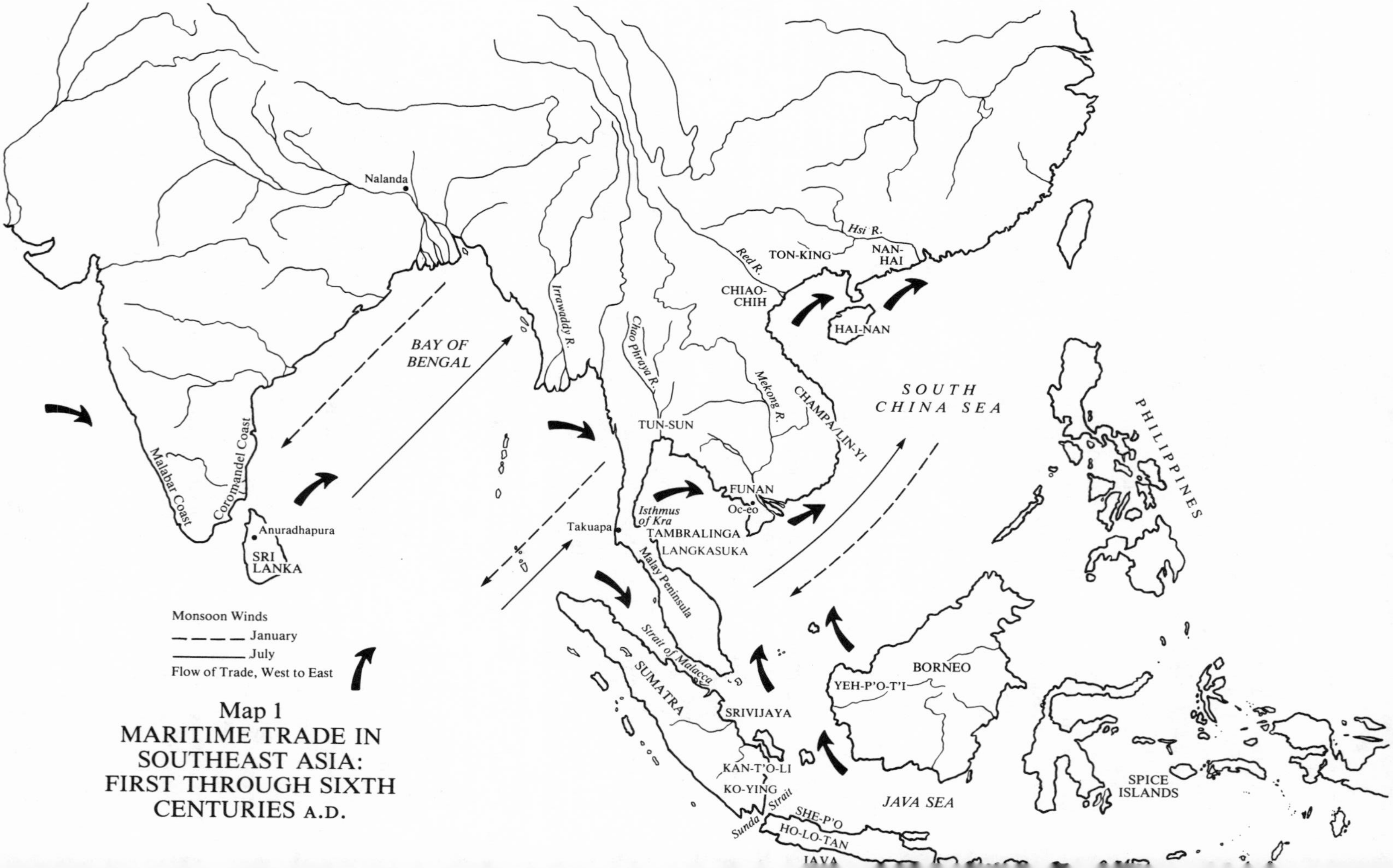

Map 1
MARITIME TRADE IN SOUTHEAST ASIA: FIRST THROUGH SIXTH CENTURIES A.D.

east Asian zone of the international commercial route from piracy. In recognition of Śrīvijaya's power the Chinese granted the maritime state preferred trade status, suggesting that those who utilized Śrīvijaya's ports were given preferential treatment when entering Chinese ports. Wolters argued that this Chinese connection was critical to Śrīvijaya's prosperity and that Śrīvijaya's power was dependent upon the fluctuations of the Chinese economy.[51] When trade with China's ports was prosperous, Śrīvijaya thrived. But when China's ports periodically closed, the economic repercussions were disastrous to Śrīvijaya's political authority. With declining trade revenues Śrīvijaya was unable to maintain the loyalty of its seafarers, who shifted their energies to open piracy.

The Śrīvijayan era of economic hegemony came to an abrupt close in 1025, when the south Indian Cōḷa dynasty successfully attacked the Malacca region's ports and shattered Śrīvijaya's authority over the strait. This raid began a two-century restructuring of the patterns of Southeast Asian maritime trade. In this era not only Indian but also Chinese and Arab traders began more openly to penetrate Southeast Asia's markets, moving more directly to the sources of commercial goods. Foreign merchants began to regularly travel into the Java Sea region to acquire spices, a movement that encouraged the development of Javanese ports on the northern and eastern Java coasts as trade intermediaries and as ports of call for foreign merchants from the West. The destruction of Śrīvijaya's hegemony also allowed the reemergence of the southern Vietnam coast as a commercial power, as coastal centers in the Cham domain became more prominent ports of call on the way to China.

The relationship of the plain-based and internally focused Javanese state to the outside world changed radically during the eleventh and twelfth centuries. During the eighth and ninth centuries the Javanese capital and the territory under its control had been situated in and around the Kedu Plain of central Java, to the south of the Merapi-Perahu mountain range. After the removal of the Javanese state's political center to the lower Brantas basin of eastern Java in the tenth century, and the subsequent consolidation of the eastern and central Javanese plains under one authority, Javanese rulers began to take a more active interest in overseas trade. This change was in part due to the shift of the royal center to the Brantas River basin and in part to the increasing economic potential that direct interaction with the maritime traders provided.[52]

Not only was this the era of Śrīvijaya's demise, it also coincided with a significant increase in the volume and economic importance of trade with China during the reign of China's Sung dynasty. At the same time that the Java Sea zone flowered as a commercial power during the eleventh and twelfth centuries, the penetration of Chinese seamen from the north through the Sulu Sea to acquire the products of the Spice Islands brought the development of the Philippines and northern Borneo as the fourth Southeast Asian commercial zone. Chinese traders established trade bases in the Philippines during this era. To distribute imports and to gather the forest products the Chinese traders desired, an intensive and extensive network of native trade evolved in this age, and it stimulated major changes in Philippine society.[53] The archaeological remains of early Laguna, Mindoro, and Cebu society especially document the rapid growth of trade centers, as people from the interior and other islands congregated around ports fortified with brass artillery—to protect against the piracy rampant in this region's sea channels—in response to the opportunities and demands afforded by foreign trade.[54]

The growing interest among the mainland powers at Angkor and Pagan in directly participating in international trade activities resulted in the development of a fifth Southeast Asian trade region, in the Bay of Bengal, during the post-Śrīvijayan age. Bay of Bengal regional trade encompassed the mainland political systems and the former Śrīvijayan domains on the upper Malay Peninsula and the northern and western coasts of Sumatra and made contact with the international route in southern India and Sri Lanka. Meanwhile, southern Sumatra and the lower Malay Peninsula remained the principal Southeast Asian landfall for the international traders. Arab traders focused their contact on the Kedah coast of the lower Malay Peninsula and shifted their activity from Palembang to Jambi on the southern Sumatra coast in the late eleventh century.

By the thirteenth century Southeast Asia's internal trade was back in the hands of Southeast Asians, as foreign merchants found it once again more expedient to deal with Southeast Asia-based intermediaries at major international entrepôts rather than attempting to deal directly with the people who controlled the sources of supplies. This was due in part to the growing efficiency exhibited by Southeast Asians in capably providing goods for the foreigners at selected ports. As opposed to the Śrīvijaya era, when trade was dominated by a single Malay state and its ports, by the thirteenth century all five Southeast Asian maritime zones had become prosperous and independent economic networks, not as competitors for maritime dominance but representing an overall commercial prosperity within Southeast Asia. The strongest of the island realm's political systems, Majapahit, was centered in east Java. Javanese rulers facilitated the Java Sea spice trade but found no need to dominate the ports of the Strait of Malacca as Śrīvijaya had in the earlier age.[55] The Javanese established a loose hegemony that saw the emergence of new ports; among them were northern Sumatra ports that depended heavily upon commercial interaction with Arab and Indian seamen.[56]

Java's limited control over the strait region is also linked to the rise of strait piracy. The eventual establishment of Malacca at the end of the fourteenth century was a result of initiatives given out by the Chinese Ming dynasty to fill what they perceived to be the absence of a major political power in the area that could be depended on to contain piracy, which was jeopardizing the steady flow of commerce into Chinese ports.[57] By the 1430s, however, Malacca's prosperity depended less on Chinese support and more on interaction with Javanese merchants and Javanese commercial networks. The Javanese controlled the island traffic to and from the strait and used Malacca as a trade intermediary through which to market Javanese rice and Java Sea spices.

A new era of Southeast Asian commerce unfolded after Portuguese entry into the strait region in 1511. Not only did the Europeans take over Malacca, but they also penetrated the Javanese sphere in the eastern archipelago, attempting to break Java's hold on the spice trade. Over the next four hundred years the Portuguese and other Europeans who followed attempted to impose their direct control over the sources of products and to eliminate the indigenous intermediaries who had controlled trade in Southeast Asia since its inception. Although the Europeans' attempts to monopolize Southeast Asia's trade failed, they did successfully open the archipelago to a variety of competing groups, both Eastern and Western. By the seventeenth century ports on Java's north coast, which had emerged as independent economic centers during the decline of the Majapahit state, were destroyed by the emerging inland power at Mataram in central Java. This victory effectively internalized Javanese commerce and ended the remaining control of Javanese merchants over the Java Sea trade. Henceforth control over the international trade was assumed by others. In the Strait of Malacca, in Aceh on the northern tip of Sumatra, and in Johor on the southern Malay Peninsula, there emerged successors to Malacca and the Javanese; and in the eastern archipelago Malay seamen in Brunei and Sulu assumed control over the regional and Chinese trade with the Spice Islands.

The waxing and waning of states in various parts of Southeast Asia were directly tied to shifting international trade routes, just as trade routes shifted in response to local power configurations and local initiatives. The following chapters discuss this pattern of growth and decline in detail.

2

The Development of Maritime Trade in Asia

International maritime trade in Asia developed in stages. It first became prosperous along the Middle East–to–India route, expanding after Rome established its *Pax Romana* in the first century of the Christian era and corresponding to a diffusion of knowledge among sailors of Greece and the Roman Orient on the use of the monsoon winds for navigation. When Westerners reached India in the first century they found that a regular maritime route connected India to the Malay Peninsula. Malay seamen and Indian and Arab traders routinely made the voyage from India's eastern coast or Sri Lanka to Southeast Asian ports, which provided access to China's rich markets. In the earliest era of maritime trade, ships from Indian ports touched land on the upper western coast of the Malay Peninsula, their trade goods were portaged across the Isthmus of Kra to the Gulf of Thailand, reloaded on ships, and transported along the coast to ports on the western edge of the Mekong Delta, most notably to one identified by archaeologists as Oc-èo in the Funan realm. The Funan state, based on the lower Vietnam coast, dominated trade in this sector of the commercial route until the fifth century. From Funan ports goods were transported to ports in south China.

Traders of the Roman Empire eventually joined the ships on this route, and Western maritime contacts were extended beyond India and Sri Lanka to Sumatra and other commercial centers at the western end of the Java Sea, which in the post-Funan age came to replace the Malay Peninsula and mainland as the locus of international trade in Southeast Asia. The full development of the maritime route by international traders making regular use of the Strait of Malacca and the South China Sea came in the late fourth and early fifth centuries. By the fifth century commercial intercourse between East and West was concentrated in the maritime route.

As a consequence, during the first five centuries of the Christian era international trade in Southeast Asia became well defined, regular, and prosperous as trade relationships were extended to include new members and products. This expansion of trade in turn stimulated significant transitions in Southeast Asian economic and political organization. Once the route was established through the region interaction between Southeast Asian peoples and foreign merchants was inevitable; the peoples of the region were also exposed to foreign cultures and ideas. Initially, the role of Southeast Asia's ports in the international trade was simply to provide facilities for foreign merchants who were passing through on their way to China or India or laying over until the next season's winds allowed a return voyage. Coastal states on the edges of settled hinterlands served as commercial entrepôts, providing suitable accommodations for sailors and traders, food, water, and shelter, and storage facilities and marketplaces, thus facilitating the exchange of Eastern and Western goods.

Soon, however, Southeast Asian merchants began to market their own spices and aromatics as substitutes for foreign commodities and then built upon this substitution to market other indigenous products. Demand for Southeast Asian products was quickly established when spices from Indonesia's eastern archipelago began to flow out of the Java Sea region to international markets in the fourth and fifth centuries. The new marketing opportunities required more formal political and economic relationships between hinterland populations and coastal commercial communities than had hitherto been necessary, however. The international trade thus acted as an impetus to state-building efforts in the region.

The Expansion of Roman Trade in the Indian Ocean

In the seventh century B.C. goods from India were imported into Babylon along two well-traveled commercial routes.[1] The preferred overland route crossed the mountains of Central Asia. By the fourth century B.C., however, Aramaic inscriptions from the Middle East begin to record an active maritime trade along the coast, with goods being carried by sea from India's northwestern coast to Saleucia in Mesopotamia via the Persian Gulf and the Tigris River. Alexander the Great's admiral, Nearchus, after employing local pilots to explore the Indus River and commissioning a fleet of thirty oared galleys, used the same coastal route to transport Alexander's troops from India to Mesopotamia in 321 B.C.

Very early maritime contact between Middle Eastern and Asian ports was characterized by coastal shipping rather than by transocean voyages. There was apparently little knowledge or use of the seasonal monsoon winds until the first century A.D., except by Malay seamen who were sailing between the Indonesian archipelago and Madagascar. Early Middle Eastern literary references speak colorfully of six-month voyages during which "trained birds" were used to guide ships to land; sailors navigated by the stars and by watching the flight of birds. The small-oared galleys that made these voyages tried to stay within sight of land as they hopped from port to port between Mesopotamia and India.

Western markets for goods transported along this coastal route were at first limited because of political fragmentation in the West; the real blossoming of maritime trade between East and West awaited a stable Western market. This peaceful setting was provided after the consolidation of Roman rule. Rome's political growth heralded a demand for luxury goods, among them spices, scented woods, resins, and cloth from the East, which substantially encouraged the expansion of Indian Ocean shipping. Technical advances soon followed as innovations in Western ship construction provided sailing rigs capable of undertaking voyages with larger loads and ultimately promised a means of using the ocean monsoon wind currents, thus enabling navigators to make transoceanic voyages.

The discovery and excavation of the Arikamedu site near Pondicherry on the southeastern coast of India in the late 1940s and early 1950s gave dated proof of the existence of an expanding maritime trade network connecting East and West.[2] Arikamedu was a trade station, an emporium or entrepôt, complete with harbor, warehouses, and merchant residences, which served as a center for the exchange of goods coming from East Asia and the West. Reaching its zenith between A.D. 23–96, Arikamedu was a port of call for convoys of oceangoing merchants during the trading seasons. In the early months of the year merchants would arrive from the West via the northeast monsoon and would depart for home on the southwest monsoon by early summer; seamen would arrive from Southeast Asia shortly thereafter and would leave on the northeast monsoon around the first of the year. Arikamedu was also the permanent residence of the Western merchants known in Indian literature as *yavana*. Archaeological excavations at Arikamedu have shown that its exports to the West included pepper, pearls, gems, muslins, tortoise shell, ivory, and silk. Imports from the West were coral, lead, copper, tin, glass, vases, lamps, wine, and coined money.

Unfortunately, Arikamedu and one or two other south Indian sites stand alone as the major sources of archaeological evidence of this first-century trade. Literary sources are ample, however, particularly those from Rome itself. The earliest of these sources, the *Geography* of Strabo (63 B.C.–A.D. 21), records the growth of the Asian trade, contrasting the smallness of the trade in earlier times to the significant expansion experienced during the reign of the emperor Augustus (27 B.C.–A.D. 14). While formerly only twenty ships passed annually through the Strait of Bab el Mandeb from the Red Sea into the Indian Ocean, now ships were departing for Asia in convoys of 120 from the upper Red Sea port of Myos Hormos alone.[3]

Perhaps the richest of the classical sources is the *Periplus of the Erythrean Sea,* written between A.D. 40 and 75, the work of an anonymous sailor who had actually made the voyage from Rome to the ports of western India.[4] The *Periplus* sailor's handbook lists commodities worth exporting to and bringing back from India and is also a definitive guide for sailing to and from India's western or Malabar Coast, with extensive descriptions of the harbors and ports encountered on the way. The *Natural History* of Pliny the Elder (A.D. 23–79), primarily a scientific treatise, provides useful details on Indian ports and most notably makes an exaggerated claim that there was a serious drain of Rome's precious metals to India to pay for the luxury trade.[5] Works by the Egyptian Claudius Ptolemaeus (Ptolemy, A.D. 100–170) offer a comprehensive list of ports and inland centers of second-century India.[6] Of particular interest is his reference to one emporium and one royal residence per Indian maritime district. When compared to first-century works, Ptolemy's compilation shows a growing knowledge of the trade routes and documents the expansion of trade into new regions. Especially noteworthy is his knowledge of the Coromandel or eastern coast of India, of which nothing is said in the *Periplus.*

Roman trade interest focused on two commodities that India offered: Malabar pepper and cloth, both Indian and Chinese. Pliny eloquently described Roman demand for Indian pepper:

> It is quite surprising that the use of pepper has come so much in fashion, seeing that, in other substances which we use, it is sometimes their sweetness and sometimes their appearance that has attracted our notice; whereas, pepper has nothing in it that can plead as a recommendation to either fruit or berry, its only desirable quality being a certain pungency; and yet it is for this that we import it all the way from India! Who was the first to make trial of it as an article of food? And who, I wonder, was the man that was not content to prepare himself by hunger only for the satisfaction of a greedy appetite?[7]

Prior to the first century, the coast-hopping trade made northern Indian ports the most expedient destination for Western vessels. Spices from Malabar were carried north by Indian coastal fleets where they were exchanged for commodities from the West. According to the *Peri-*

Map 2
MAJOR FIRST-CENTURY MARITIME ROUTES

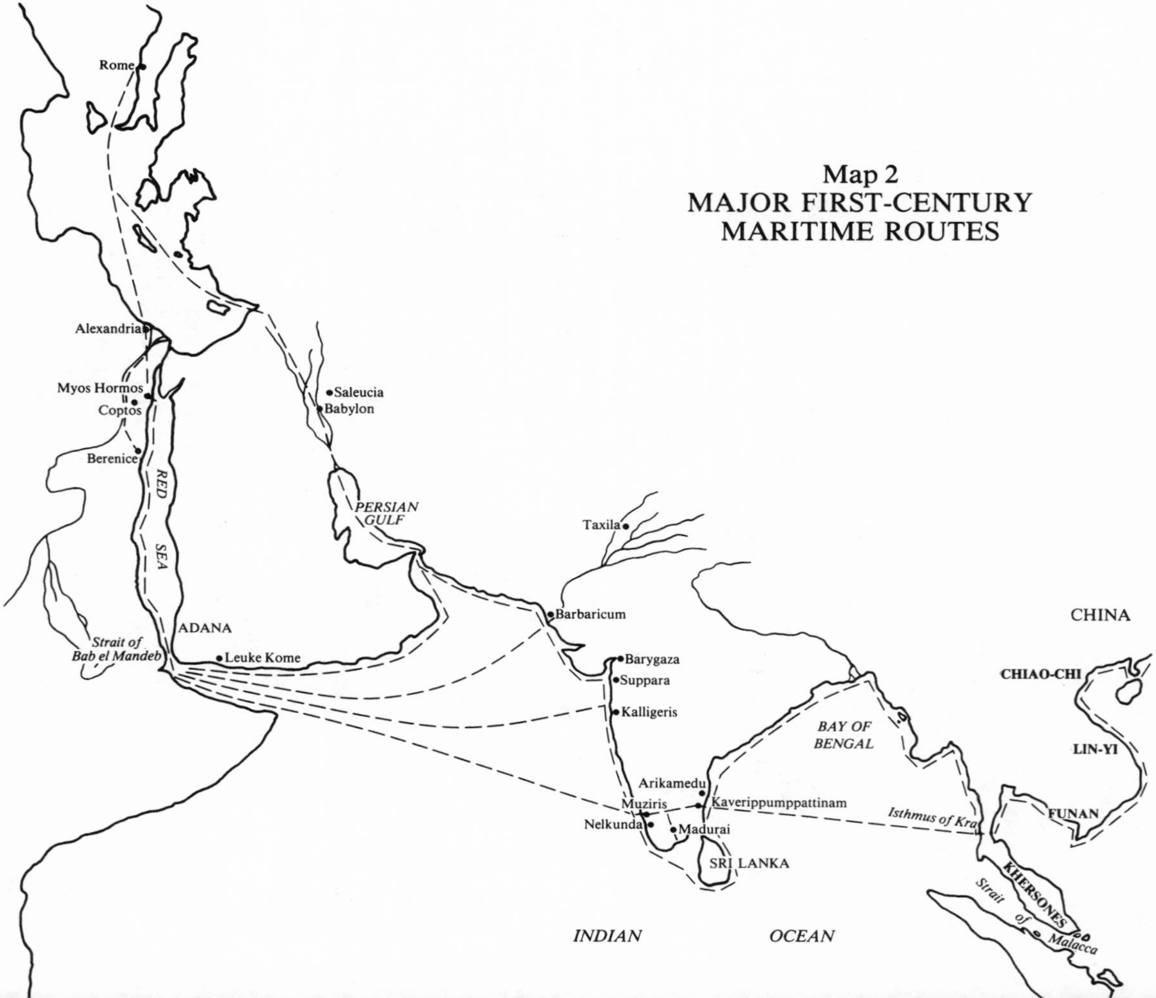

plus, Barygaza in present-day Gujarat was the most important destination of the coastal galleys. The overland caravan route between India and China also terminated in Barygaza in that period, further heightening this port's significance as an international center of trade. Finished Chinese silk cloth carried overland through Central Asia was transported down from Taxila in the north, partly via a highway built several centuries before, where it was exchanged for Arabian frankincense, "a product always more highly valued in China than India."[8] Another route was used for the transport of Chinese silk threads from Taxila south to Barbaricum at the mouth of the Indus River. From there the yarn was carried by sea to Arabia, where it was used in the manufacture of embroidered and silk-shot fabrics. This route down the Indus is described in the *Periplus* as less important "owing to the character of the tribes living on the lower reaches [of the river]," reminding readers that political instability in a port area was a serious impediment to commercial development.[9]

Pliny detailed the change in this pattern. Of primary importance was the discovery of the monsoons, known in Rome as the *Hippalos* winds, which made possible direct travel first between Arabia and the Indus River ports; later a shorter route in both distance and time from Arabia to Kalligeris, south of present-day Bombay, was developed. In the first century A.D. yet shorter direct voyages were made to the Malabar ports themselves. It is believed that the monsoon winds were known in the West before Roman expansion but that they were a well-kept secret of Arab (Parthian) commercial middlemen and their Indian trade agents.[10] For this reason, the profitable spice trade was until then exclusively in the hands of Arab merchants. The *Periplus* attributes the discovery of the monsoons to the Roman sailor Hippalos, thus the common Roman reference to the *Hippalos* winds, and informs us that in the time of the *Periplus*' author Roman ships began crossing from North Africa to southern Malabar Coast ports. With knowledge of the monsoon winds there came a change in ship construction. Multi-oared galleys were replaced by sailing ships, and a new rigging system, perhaps a Persian innovation, allowed ships to sail closer to the wind.

The Western termini of Roman ships were the Red Sea ports of Myos Hormos and Berenice, from which Indian goods were transported overland by caravan to the Nile and then by boat to Alexandria (see map 2).[11] Apparently to break the Arab monopoly on the India trade and ensure its control of ports with access to the Indian Ocean, Rome began to exert its authority over the Red Sea region during the first century. The *Periplus* reports that a Roman military garrison was established at Leuke Kome, a small-vessel port at the mouth of the Red Sea populated by Arab seamen, to collect a duty of 25 percent of all imports. Meanwhile trade at the "official" Roman ports in the Red Sea was being charged only a 3 percent duty.[12] It may be logically concluded from this account that the Roman government was forcing the India trade merchants to patronize Rome's "preferred" ports and not those of the Arab merchants. This action was quite similar to practices the Romans had observed in India during the same period.

There appear to have been treaty relationships between Roman merchants and the Indian ports. The *Periplus* uses the phrase *nomimom emporium* ("lawful market") with respect to Kalligeris.[13] Ptolemy singles out sixteen coastal towns as emporia from the Indus to the Ganges (e.g., Muziris emporium, Podouke emporium), which apparently were the principal commercial centers of each maritime district, each having been assigned special legal provisions for trading. The *Periplus* states that local markets on the west coast between Barygaza and Malabar could be visited only under the supervision of the rulers of the area.[14] At Kalligeris, the rulers had cancelled, or at least obstructed, rights conferred on traders by their predecessors to the extent of seizing Greek ships upon arrival. Guards were placed on board an offending ship, which was then taken to the "official" port at Barygaza.

Various Western literary sources imply that an international port in order to be successful in these times had to offer a neutral meeting ground for a cosmopolitan population. It was not enough for a port to offer goods from its own hinterland or from regions farther afield. The international merchant groups active in the port region had to feel a sense of security, but the "protection" provided had to be carefully regulated so that the visiting merchants did not feel threatened or abused. If an inland-based political power put too many restraints on the traders they would have shifted their operations to another port that allowed them more freedom to transact their business.

The *Arthaśāstra,* the classical north Indian treatise on statecraft, describes in general terms the trade transacted in the international markets found on the coasts during these times and makes a distinction between commerce conducted in the fortified cities of the interior and that taking place in those designated centers for international exchange known as *pattana*.[15] *Pattana* markets were administered by three royal officials. Market exchange was coordinated by a "supervisor of markets," whose chief function, according to the *Arthaśāstra,* was to keep merchants and artisans from cheating their customers. When commodities of distant origin came into the marketplace the supervisor of markets called in the "director of trade," an expert in determining prices, who then fixed a price on the foreign commodities after calculating the investment, production, duty, interest, rent, and other expenses that contributed to the fair price of such items. This director of trade was normally subordinate to a "commissioner of ports," whose duty it was to set regulations for the port town. In the terminology of the *Arthaśāstra,* a *pattana* was an emporium, a place officially designated by local rulers as a legal center for the exchange of goods that arrived by boat or caravan.

The formal international trade agreements concerning emporia were subject to continuous negotiation. Access to Indian markets by foreign merchants had to be arranged with local authorities before the merchants were allowed to participate in local commerce. The reverse might also be true, that is, that ports sought out the merchants for trade, since embassies negotiating such treaties were to be found moving from East to West. Two Indian delegations to Augustus Caesar were recorded in 25 B.C. and 21 B.C., which coincides with the entry of Roman traders into the Indian markets and the circumvention of Arab sailors and other intermediaries who had monopolized the India traffic prior to that time.[16]

We know from the *Periplus* that Barygaza was India's greatest port during the first century chiefly because of its cloth trade and as a result had become the principal point of contact between the Western and Eastern commercial realms. Most of Barygaza's exports were sent there from other commercial centers and included onyx-stones, porcelain, cottons, silk cloth, and peppers. Barygaza's imports from Roman ports were wines from the Italian peninsula, brass, copper, tin, lead, coral, cloth goods, white glass from Arabia, gold and silver specie ("which brings a profit when exchanged for native specie"),[17] perfumes, and a steady supply of luxuries for the local king. The commercial dominance of Barygaza over other hinterland and coastal centers on the subcontinent is emphasized in the *Periplus.* Local ports such as Suppara (Sopara) and Kalligeris were said to be subservient to Barygaza. But the *Periplus* also notes the emergence of Nelkunda and Muziris (Cochin) on the Malabar Coast as ports of trade outside Barygaza's sphere of influence. These were the ports where Roman vessels could acquire pepper without dealing through Barygaza middlemen.

Rome's discovery of the monsoons was critical to the emergence of south Indian ports as independent centers of trade, free from Barygaza's economic dominance. The Malabar Coast pepper supply was sufficient to attract Western ships, and once direct trade with the West was established these ports became dominant over their own commercial network. Chinese silk and goods that had been transported overland to the Malabar Coast from the southeastern regions of the subcontinent—pearls, ivory, cloth goods, and jewels—were also available to Roman ships anchoring in south Indian ports. In exchange Roman ships traded great quantities of specie, cloth, white glass, copper, brass, tin, lead, and wine —essentially the same commodities that they traded at Barygaza.[18]

The author of the *Periplus* had nothing to say of India's eastern coast and beyond. Ptolemy was the first knowledgeable authority in the Roman realm on the geography of India's Coromandel Coast, and it appears that his information was largely new to his readers.[19] Classical Tamil literature from south India describes the emporium of Kaverippumppattinam, an east coast terminus for both overland and coastal trade in the first centuries of the Christian era. Kaverippumppattinam had a huge warehouse to which were taken large quantities of articles obtained from numerous places.[20] The excavations at Arikamedu substantiate this literary reference. The distribution and concentration of Roman coin hoards across the southern part of the subcontinent indicate that an overland route was preferred during the first century, with caravans of merchants crossing from the Malabar Coast to the Kaveri River. The traders of the Roman Orient left circumnavigation of the subcontinent to Indian merchants and their smaller vessels.[21] Whether these commercial centers were reached by land or by sea, however, it is clear that they were part of the developing India-Rome trade network by the mid-first century.

The study of Roman coin hoards found in India further substantiates these contacts. Of sixty-eight coinage finds throughout the entire subcontinent, no fewer than fifty-seven were discovered in the south, and of these fifty-seven all but a few stray Roman coins were found in hoards located inland between the western and eastern coasts. These are invariably of gold or silver content; coins of Augustus (27 B.C.–A.D. 14) and Tiberius (A.D. 14–37) predominate.[22]

According to the *Periplus,* first in importance among first-century imports carried by Western merchants to the Malabar Coast ports were gold and silver coins. Pliny noted that India absorbed some 55 million gold coins *(sesterces)* annually, and further stated that 100 million *sesterces* were taken to India, China, and Arabia combined.[23] It is interesting that most recovered Roman coins have been either pierced for suspension or mutilated by a cut across their obverse, which implies that Indians used this coinage as bullion rather than as currency. Roman coins, it seems, were weighed out in exchange for goods, a fact that explains the existence of the south Indian hoards. As subdivided and stamped subunits of precious metal, coins undoubtedly facilitated the Indian trader's accounting and also benefited him in his dealings with his customers; that they were widely recognized units of value no doubt made it easier for the trader to negotiate his various transactions with numerous population centers that would have had no other common unit of exchange.

The flowering of Roman trade in the Indian Ocean during the first century A.D. not only had important implications for Rome but was also of significance to the development of political and economic centers in southern India. Recent scholarship views this commercial growth as a critical stimulus to the evolution of south Indian statecraft. Former tribal chiefs are seen seizing the opportunities offered by the growing trade to organize the flow of trade goods out of the hinterland and into the coastal ports, expanding their political hegemony in the process.[24] This thesis may well be valid, for it is during this era that the earliest south Indian states begin to appear. Corresponding to this political development and in response to the demand for local commodities, new hinterland commercial and political centers evolved. It is no coincidence that the most illustrious hinterland urban center of that time, the Pāṇḍya capital of Madurai, was strategically located at the center of a major cotton producing and weaving region and was as well directly linked to the major caravan route between the western and eastern coasts of southern India.[25]

Initial Maritime Contacts with Southeast Asia

Early references to trade with Southeast Asia are rather ambiguous. Indian literature from the first centuries A.D. refers to Southeast Asia in general as Yāvadvīpa or Suvarṇadvīpa, the "Golden Island" or "Golden Peninsula." The *Rāmāyaṇa,* India's great classical-era epic poem about Rama's attempts to rescue his wife, who had been abducted by the king of Sri Lanka, records seven kingdoms on the "Gold and Silver Islands" beyond Sri Lanka. The Buddhist *Jātaka* fables from popular literature mention Indian merchants who went to Southeast Asia in search of wealth. Ptolemy, writing in the mid-second century, uses Yāvadvīpa, "the Golden Peninsula," in describing the lands beyond India. He makes it quite clear that few Roman sailors were making the passage to Yāvadvīpa, and indeed Indian evidence indicates that not many Indian sailors were making the passage either.

Chinese records provide a more satisfactory yet still incomplete view of the burgeoning Southeast Asian commerce. Substantial references to Western trade began to appear in official Han sources in the last decade of the first century. By 111 B.C., the Han dynasty had extended its control into southern China, and Han emperors, following the lead of the illustrious emperor Han Wu-ti (140–87 B.C.), who is believed to have encouraged the development of the Central Asian caravan route, came into control of Canton, a coastal city with strong commercial interests. During a break in Han rule in A.D. 9–25, the southern part of China had become a haven for refugees escaping from the turmoil in the north, among them northern aristocrats, who further encouraged the development of Canton as a commercial center. These aristocrats, now resident in the south, constituted a growing market for Western goods.

The term *Ta-ch'in* was used by the Chinese to refer to the Roman provinces in the Middle East stretching from Syria to Egypt. From these western regions "precious and rare objects of all foreign countries" were said to come.[26] A Han history text dating from A.D. 125 vaguely describes Ta-ch'in's trade with the northwestern coast of India. Profit to Ta-ch'in's traders from this trade was said to be tenfold, but "honest."[27] Ta-ch'in products reaching China included glass, carpets, rugs, embroideries, piece goods, and precious stones. Among these, manufactured goods—notably glassware in the form of imitation jewelry and ornaments of colored glass—were especially valued.[28]

There are several reasons for the growth of maritime trade during the first century. First, historians have theorized that gold became difficult to acquire during this time.[29] Due to internal disturbances in the Central Asian steppe region, caravan routes from Central Asia no longer provided gold from Siberian deposits, one of the major sources of the precious metal in the Asian world in earliest times. Since gold was the medium of Asian trade, enabling commercial exchanges between merchants of disparate cultures, new sources had to be found to cover trade imbalances. The demand for Roman gold coinage increased accordingly until the emperor Nero (A.D. 54–68) responded to inflation by debasing the gold content in Roman coinage, which quickly brought decreasing interest among Eastern traders in accepting Rome's coins in commercial transactions.[30] The emperor Vespasian (A.D. 69–79) made an official attempt to stop the unfavorable flow of gold coins away from Rome.[31] As a consequence, Indian merchants began looking toward the mythical wealth of the "Islands of Gold" with keen interest and embarked on a major effort to secure these riches.

Second, the quest for gold coincided with the revolution in boat construction and navigation techniques. By the first century Western ships were being built with fore and aft rigging that greatly increased sailing efficiency. Ships of considerable size came into use, some with the capacity to carry six to seven hundred tons of cargo. Pliny wrote of a 75-ton ship making the ocean crossing.

Third, the first century marked a great age of Buddhism in South Asia. Buddhism did not view commercial activity as negatively as did the

Hindu tradition. Its spread during this time was tied to the evolution of the new Mahāyāna Buddhist school in northern India. Under the patronage of rich Indian merchants, Buddhist monks who instructed the lay community split with the monks of the Theravāda school, who observed the more elitist "Way of the Fathers." The popular worship of the Mahāyāna sect was practiced in great public shrines rather than in the seclusion of monasteries. Less scholastic and not as concerned with self-attainment, Mahāyāna developed the concept of compassion and of assisting others to salvation as symbolized by the Bodhisattva, the "Buddha-to-Be" who postponed his own ultimate salvation to remain among mortals as a spiritual guide. The Mahāyāna school can be viewed as a response to a dynamic and expanding world, a world intimately connected to commerce. Buddhist tales (*Jātakas*) thus came to deal extensively with the activities of common men, including their economic activities, normally ignored in Hindu literature. In these tales the pursuit of wealth, as long as it was not accomplished at the expense of others, was not seen as evil but was considered natural to man. Indian Ocean seamen were particularly devoted to the Buddha Dīpamkara, the "Calmer of the Waters."[32] Significantly, a number of outstanding Dīpamkara statues associated with this era are distributed throughout the Southeast Asian archipelago.[33]

By the sixth century Buddhism would become especially important to the Chinese, and Southeast Asia played a key intermediary role between South Asia, the source of Buddhism, and China. Buddhist monks passed along the international sea route and by a land route through Burma; Chinese monks traveled to India to acquire deeper understanding of their faith; and Indian monks journeyed to China to share their knowledge with Chinese patrons. As early as the third century an urban community on the edge of the Red River Delta in Vietnam had become a center of Buddhism, with at least twenty temples and over five hundred monks in residence. By the seventh-century voyage of the Chinese pilgrim I-ching, it was viewed as an important stopping point prior to one's entry into China, not only because it was a commercial entrepôt but also because it had become an important religious center for Buddhist pilgrims.[34]

The Sumatran state of Śrīvijaya was also in that age considered a "must" stop for pilgrims. Śrīvijaya, like Vietnam, seems to have been able to fit into the more egalitarian Buddhist world order. I-ching reported that an international community of a thousand monks studied at the capital of the Śrīvijaya monarch in 671. Those who traded with the Chinese and Indian markets in the name of the Śrīvijaya ruler could claim prestige appropriate to those who came into contact with this great patron of the Mahāyāna Buddhist school. Mahāyāna Buddhism thereby allowed Southeast Asian realms that followed the Vietnam and Śrīvijaya examples prestige in the channels of religious communication, raising their status above the "barbarian" image normally held by the Chinese of Southeast Asians and providing the basis for intellectual as well as commercial interaction among the states that participated in the international maritime route.

A fourth reason for the growth of maritime trade through Southeast Asia was Chinese interest, which broadened after the disintegration of the Han dynasty between A.D. 190 and 225. With trouble in Central Asia along the old caravan route and political strife in northern China, there was an increasing need for a southern maritime link between East and West.

Western diplomatic missions to China traveled overland until A.D. 160, when suddenly missions from northern India began to arrive by sea reflecting Central Asian upheaval that must have effectively closed the overland route. The south China based Wu dynasty (A.D. 220–264) encouraged the import of Western textiles (mainly Indian cotton), tree resins, coral, pearls, amber, glassware, jewelry, and other manufactures. A group of traders appeared on the south China coast in A.D. 166 claiming to be envoys from the Roman emperor Marcus Aurelius Antoninus; in 226, Ta-ch'in merchants from the West visited the Wu court. They were questioned extensively by the emperor Sun Ch'uan himself, who sent an official to accompany them on their return voyage.[35] Lu Tai, Wu governor of a Chinese province in northern Vietnam, was assigned a special role in advertising south China's interest in this trade, sending envoys "to the South." When envoys from the lower Vietnam coastal states of Funan and Lin-yi paid official visits in 226 and 231, respectively, Lu Tai was congratulated by the emperor for his "meritorious performance." In 240, Wu envoys were dispatched to Funan's ports to view firsthand the nature of trade with the West—and seemingly as well to evaluate whether conquest down the coast beyond the Red River Delta would be worthwhile.[36] These envoys' reports not only provided important information on Funan but also on Ta-ch'in and northern Indian commercial centers.

K'ang T'ai, one of the envoys, informed his emperor that the kingdom of Funan was a prosperous realm from which great merchant ships departed for China and India. Funan's authority stretched beyond the lower Mekong Delta to the upper Malay Peninsula. After a major naval expedition in the early third century, Funan had assumed authority over many of the trade centers on the Malay coast, thereby consolidating its dominance over the flow of commerce through Southeast Asia. By the early fourth century, however, significant changes were taking place on the international route that resulted in the demise of Funan and other northern peninsula commercial centers.

The Fifth-Century Transition

In the second half of the fourth century the Chin dynasty in China lost access to the Central Asian caravan routes. While in the third century the south China-based Wu elite had depended totally on the maritime route for luxury goods from the West, the Chin elite had been able to balance their needs, receiving goods from both the maritime and overland networks. However, with the loss of access to the caravan route they too began to encourage the further development of the sea passage. Of greatest consequence to Funan was the reaction of would-be Southeast Asian entrepôts south and east of the Malay Peninsula to the new commercial initiatives by the Chinese. Chinese efforts to expand the volume of trade along the sea route had met with an immediate response from a number of Sunda Strait coastal centers that had already been trading directly with India but indirectly with China via Funan's ports. These commercial rivals quickly seized the opportunity to trade directly with China.

Records of direct commercial and maritime contact between the Java Sea region and China show that by the fifth century Funan's role as the principal commercial power in the Southeast Asian world was being seriously eroded. In 430, the ruler of the western Java kingdom known to the Chinese as Ho-lo-tan/t'o petitioned the Chinese court seeking protection for his ships that sailed on a regular basis to China.[37] The significance of this embassy is that it documents the fact that direct voyages were being made from the Sunda Strait region to China across the South China Sea, bypassing Funan.

The Sunda Strait state known to the Chinese as Ko-ying was described in sixth-century Chinese records as having been previously cut off from China. "For generations" Ko-ying had traded with China via Funan. Nevertheless, Ko-ying had evolved during the Funan era as a terminus for shipping using the Strait of Malacca, a point of departure for trade between India and the Spice Islands of the eastern archipelago.[38] At Ko-ying's trade depots Indian merchants acquired the forest products and spices of the archipelago in exchange for pearls, gold, jade, areca nuts, glassware, and horses. In the fifth century, however, Ko-ying's economic position was challenged by the western Java commercial center of Ho-lo-tan/t'o, and ultimately both were replaced by a new southeast Sumatra commercial center, Kan-t'o-li, and its successor, the Śrīvijaya state, as the dominant maritime power in the western Java Sea realm.

Evidence that Funan was being bypassed in favor of a Strait of Malacca and South China Sea passage comes first from the Buddhist pilgrim Fa Hsien. Fa Hsien had traveled from China to India overland but returned by sea from Sri Lanka in A.D. 413–414. His description of the return voyage provides a vivid picture of the sea passage from Sri Lanka to Southeast Asia:

> [I] took passage on board a large merchant vessel, on which there were over two hundred souls, and astern of which there was a smaller vessel in tow in case of accidents at sea and destruction of the big vessel. Catching a fair wind [i.e., the monsoon], [we] sailed eastwards for two days; then [we] encountered a heavy gale, and the vessel sprang a leak. The merchants wished to get aboard the smaller vessel; but the men on the latter, fearing that they would be swamped by numbers, quickly cut the tow-rope in two. The merchants were terrified, for death was close at hand; and fearing that the vessel would fill, they promptly took what bulky goods there were and threw them into the sea. . . . The gale blew on for thirteen days and nights, when [we] arrived alongside an island, and then, at ebb-tide, they saw the place where the vessel leaked and forthwith stopped it up, after which [we] again proceeded on [our] way. This sea is infested with pirates, to meet whom is death. The expanse is boundless. . . .[39]

After sailing through the Strait of Malacca, Fa Hsien landed at a trade depot known to the Chinese as Yeh-p'o-t'i, believed to have been located on the west coast of Borneo. From there he might have been expected to go to Funan, for archaeological evidence from the presumed site of Yeh-p'o-t'i, notably carved sacrificial posts known as *yūpa*s, substantiate a Borneo cultural link to Funan, indicating as with other archipelago coastal centers that early interactions between these depots and the Chinese and Indian commercial markets had been funneled through Funan's ports.[40] Yet Fa Hsien went directly from Yeh-p'o-t'i to Canton, a voyage of fifty days under normal conditions.

An Indian prince and Buddhist monk, Guṇavarman, also sailed from India to Southeast Asia in the early fifth century, landing at the Javanese trade depot of She-p'o. He departed from there with the intention of making an intermediate stop in a Lin-yi (Cham) port on the lower Vietnam coast before entering China. The winds were unfavorable, however, and the merchant ship on which he had taken passage sailed nonstop for China.[41]

Indigenous elites in early Southeast Asian coastal centers found that the increased volume of international trade during this era afforded them with other opportunities as well. Local leaders came to recognize that facilitating trade could be useful in reinforcing their sovereignty vis-à-vis potential rivals and subordinates. Successful rulers could organize the flow of local products from their hinterlands to their courts, sell the products themselves or receive a share of the profits from others' sales, and assess fees on international merchants who came to trade for the products in their ports. Income from this trade amounted to a significant supplement to the income a landed or tribal elite already received from lands they held. Exotic goods and additional income from trade also enhanced an elite's capacity to implement their gift-giving "ritual sovereignty" (discussed later in this chapter), thereby increasing their alliance capital. Southeast Asian rulers thus found it in their personal interest to control local contact with the international trade routes. Rulers consequently took great interest in the collection and redistribution of wealth derived from trade. This wealth, as well as foreign luxury goods acquired on the coast, was shared with supporters to reinforce the status of the monarch and his subordinate elite. The development of new state systems was thus in part due to an elite's successful manipulation of external and indigenous commercial networks to expand their authority vis-à-vis competing elites.

As noted in chapter 1, by the fifth century the southern coast of Sumatra had become a "favored coast," serving the archipelago as well as hinterland systems that had formerly been within the Funan sphere of influence. The new importance of this favored coast was partially due to the expanding Chinese market for Southeast Asian products. Chinese overtures encouraged river-mouth centers in the Java Sea region to send their products directly to Chinese ports. Chinese initiatives also stimulated competition among the emerging trade depots for dominance over neighboring river-mouth centers.

Commercial centers on the Sumatran coast near the Sunda Strait enjoyed a strategic location between the riches of the Java Sea region and China. Their coastal and hinterland networks were easily mobilized to provide manpower and goods for the China trade. Malay ships and crews transported Sumatran products and Java Sea spices to China and brought back Chinese goods. Soon coastal rulers began to use these same seamen to police the Strait of Malacca, for piracy was a plague to shipping in this area. Once it was brought under control, maritime contacts between Sumatran ports and India expanded. Ships from India began sailing south through the strait instead of landing on the upper Malay Peninsula and sending their goods by land across the Isthmus of Kra. Trade depots vied for political supremacy over rival river-mouth centers on the coasts of southeastern Sumatra, northwestern Java, and southwestern Borneo, all the while maintaining and facilitating the movement of goods between Chinese, Indian, and other Southeast Asian markets.

With this transition to the sea passage through the Strait of Malacca, Funan's ports became peripheral to the mainstream of international commerce. To participate in international trade, Funan's traders had to travel to other trade depots, just as previously Southeast Asian seafarers had to come to Funan to carry on their exchanges.

The China Trade

Who provided passage from Southeast Asia's ports to China and India in the first centuries of the Christian era? Early Chinese records make it clear that Malay ships and seamen based in Southeast Asia, identified by the term *K'un-lun,* sailed the route between Southeast Asia and China.[42] Until the eleventh century no Chinese ships made the voyage on a regular basis, and until the sixth century Persian ships went no farther east than Sri Lanka. There is disagreement, however, on who provided the passage from South Asia to Southeast Asia.

Many Western historians initially thought that Indian seamen in Indian-made ships developed the route. In reiterating this view, one has recently argued that Southeast Asian seamen were not capable of building the great ships making the voyage.[43] Indians duplicated in shipyards along the Indian coast the more advanced Persian ships, and Indian sailors, most of them Buddhists, then sailed the vessels with their international passengers and cargoes to the "Land of Gold." Opposing this position, other historians now believe that it was not Indians but Southeast Asians piloting K'un-lun ships from the Southeast Asian archipelago to India and back who provided this early linkage for international merchants,[44] which would make Southeast Asian seamen responsible for opening the entire sea route from India to China. They point to Western accounts from this age that record voyages by Malay seafarers as far west as the African coast and draw the conclusion that if Malay ships could reach Africa, they could reach India.

When the need for a maritime route increased, these seamen were able to turn their maritime skills to financial gain. Because Western traders at this time were primarily interested in exchanging Western goods for Chinese products, access to the ports of south China was a critical factor that allowed Malay seamen to expand their Western trade. By securing Chinese commodities and transporting them to Southeast Asian and South Asian trade depots, Southeast Asian seamen eliminated the need for Western ships to venture beyond South Asia.

Malay seamen, however, were not only facilitators of international trade; they could be a serious obstacle as well. They had the potential to be shippers or pirates. Chinese records report that "merchant ships of the barbarians" (K'un-lun) were used to transfer Chinese envoys to their destinations in the archipelago, and that these seamen profited equally from the trade and from plundering and killing people.[45] Herein the Malay seamen's duality is fully recognized. The Chinese considered Southeast Asia to be generally unstable politically and a potential threat to the efficient flow of commercial goods into China. The Chinese government in its dealings with Southeast Asian states was not as much interested in having its political legitimacy and dominance recognized—there was no need to annex the southern regions since the Chinese ruling elite was sure that the southern barbarians would eventually become part of the Chinese cultural realm—as it was in establishing commercial goals as the basis of relationships. The Chinese thus looked for a strong, dominant state in the area that would be able to maintain trade and prevent plundering by the sea pirates based in Southeast Asian waters.

The Chinese apparently favored consistency, preferring not to shift alliances from one state to another. They would recognize one state and attempt to maintain a tributary relationship with it. If the state stopped sending envoys to the Chinese court the Chinese would try to reestablish contact with the state before granting official recognition to another. Southeast Asian states in a tributary relationship with China received nothing from the Chinese but recognition of their legitimacy and trading status. Appeals for direct military aid or patronage were generally ignored.[46] Southeast Asian states did capitalize on Chinese recognition, however, to attract trade to their ports. Chinese support bestowed on them a legitimacy that contributed to their rise. Traders who frequented a "legitimate" coastal trading center seem to have been given preferential treatment in their trade with China. The Malay seamen who provided shipping for goods and merchants saw the potential for acquiring great wealth in the China trade and joined forces with the legitimized states. They turned to policing rather than pirating the sea channels and in return for their loyalty shared in the trade-derived prosperity.

So critical was Chinese recognition that any coastal trade depot wishing to prosper sent a tribute mission to the Chinese court. According to one historian's analysis of these political missions, which were dutifully recorded by Chinese scribes, when they were few it meant stability in the area, that is, when one trade depot's authority over the sea lanes was unchallenged.[47] Periods of internal dissension and political turmoil are reflected, on the other hand, by numerous tribute missions, as various coastal commercial centers competed for the preferred status the Chinese could bestow. For example, in the era of Funan's supremacy, Funan ports were officially recognized by the Chinese court and sent few tribute missions. But by the fifth century, when the pattern of trade was shifting from Funan to the Sunda Strait region, numerous tribute missions from the former economic subordinates of Funan appeared at the Chinese court soliciting favorable trade relationships. Funan attempted to regain Chinese favor, sending both tributary missions and trade envoys to the Chinese court, but the Chinese, fully aware of the transition taking place in trading patterns, chose to ignore the Funan initiative and to give official recognition instead to the ports of a southeastern Sumatra state as well as to those of Funan's neighbor, former vassal, and mortal enemy, the Cham state of Lin-yi.

The Impact of Trade on State Development in South India and Southeast Asia

Over the years historians have examined the possible roles of Brahman priests, Kṣatriya warrior-adventurers, or Vaiśya traders from India in spreading Indian civilization along the emerging maritime routes to developing Southeast Asian states. While some have postulated wholesale colonization by Indian exiles,[48] others have maintained that "Indianization" was wholly created by Southeast Asians themselves, by summoning Brahmans to their courts and creating a thin veneer of Indianized customs.[49] Indeed, the historical records provide no evidence of Indian colonies, Indian conquest, or direct Indian control. The adoption of Indic culture appears to have been voluntary on the part of the Southeast Asians, although some segments of a Southeast Asian society may well have had Indian cultural forms imposed upon them by an indigenous elite. Since the process did not merely occur once or twice but on numerous occasions between the third and fourteenth centuries A.D., in riverine coastal centers as well as in hinterland wet-rice plains, questions of who brought the Indian civilization are better refocused to ask how and why Southeast Asians chose to adopt the Indic culture.[50]

In response to these questions of how and why, a comparative examination of expanding international commercial contacts in southern India and Southeast Asia may provide a basis for understanding transitions in Indian Ocean commercial patterns and also contribute to an understanding of early south Indian and Southeast Asian political organization. South India is different from northern India historically and ethnically: the relationship of south India to northern India is in some ways parallel to the relationship of Southeast Asia to northern India—the differences are differences of degree. The historical issues confronting the scholar of early Southeast Asian civilization are similar to those raised by southern Indian civilization. Both areas developed state systems by integrating north Indian Sanskritic ideology with existing cultural forms. Thus by coming to terms with the process of state formation in southern India, whose history is far better documented than that of early Southeast Asia, one may acquire a conceptual perspective that can be tested and applied on a comparative basis to Southeast Asia; that is, the understanding of one in many ways facilitates the better understanding of the other.

The study of south Indian history suggests that while early south

Indian monarchs were in general introspective, their interest in promoting trade and in the development of institutions and organizations to enable the efficient flow of products into and out of their ports was stimulated by the potential revenue to be gained from cesses on luxury goods brought in by seafaring merchants. Between the sixth and fourteenth centuries—the height of classical Southeast Asian civilization and also the golden age of early south Indian civilization—the Coromandel Coast was under the rule of the Pallava and Cōḷa dynasties. Their royal style required the conspicuous display of grandeur; seeing the benefits to be derived from a positive attitude toward commerce, these rulers structured their relationships accordingly with those who participated in the trade.[51]

In Pallava and Cōḷa times agricultural settlements were spreading inland from the coast along river valleys.[52] Clusters of villages inhabited by a settled agrarian population were surrounded by various nonagrarian areas occupied by tribal peoples. The village clusters were dominated by a local landholding elite. In this multicentered system of power, direct control by a royal house extended only to the village clusters located near the base of royal power. Beyond the royal centers dynastic rulers were limited in their ability to mobilize material and human resources.

A village cluster tried to preserve local resources for its own use, which created tensions between local and higher levels of political authority on the issue of who was to receive what share of the local agricultural surplus. A strong community was able to retard the flow of goods to a political center. The dynastic rulers sometimes found it necessary to undertake military campaigns, not to conquer territory but to take plunder to offset the villagers' unwillingness to share their surplus.[53] Often a ruler's desire for personal glory was at odds with the amount of revenue he could peacefully extract from his own domain. As a result royal armies were frequently turned loose into the field where they sustained themselves on the resources of conquered territories.

As an alternative to the use of force, south Indian kings attempted to institutionalize and regularize their relationships with landholding elites. Particular emphasis was placed on the peaceful consolidation of the population through the royal bestowal of legitimacy on certain local rulers, a theory of legitimacy that drew heavily on Brahmanical Hindu thought. The network of alliances that south Indian kings constructed was acted out in ceremonies of "ritual sovereignty."[54]

Ritual sovereignty stressed the consolidation of the society under the royal ideology of legitimacy. The integration of semiautonomous agrarian units into a state system centered upon the king, who functioned as the ritual center—a political, cultural, and social reference rather than an all-powerful authority. By endowing temples, temple ceremonies, and settlements of Brahman-dominated villages in strategic locations,[55] a king could be viewed as expressing his concern for social morality and the spiritual welfare of the realm. It added merit to the royal house when the state endowed a temple with land and funded ceremonies to the perpetual memory of the king. The record of such endowments was inscribed for eternity in the stone of the temple walls. Each inscription reflected the kingly style: long Sanskrit and Tamil eulogies composed at the court were included in the prologue of royal inscriptions throughout the realm. Brahmanical terminology, an important element in the claim of royal legitimacy, was grafted onto existing institutions. Local deities were incorporated into "respectable" pantheons. Local temples and pilgrimage centers were patronized by royalty and gained added luster through the association. Religious patronage was intended to raise the king's status in the eyes of the subject population. Royal inscriptions encouraged this recognition, noting the prosperity the king had brought to his domain. Royal eulogies undoubtedly represented an attempt to diminish the visibility of local elites while increasing that of the king, but there was no similar effort by kings to eliminate or disperse the local centers of power.

Locally entrenched agrarian elites had to be willing to recognize royal suzerainty, however. On the one hand, the king with his superior might could physically eliminate or replace local rulers; on the other hand, the king could defend them against local or outside threats. Aside from the threat of force, the most important legitimizing factor in gaining their cooperation was that south Indian kings were patrons of Sanskritic tradition, which provided an ideological justification for the landed elites' claim to hold superior status vis-à-vis other members of the agrarian order. They also allied themselves with south Indian kings in order to draw upon the dynastic rulers' religious networks and symbols, normally concentrated in temples, thereby enhancing their status by being seen as certified patrons of the royal cults.

In return the king received the fealty of the elites and their subordinates. Sometimes this relationship was formalized by the flow of local cesses into the king's treasury. Such cesses were often immediately returned in the form of royal patronage of local temples. In other instances, locally raised troops might fight as loyal followers of a king in a military campaign and in return share in the spoils of victory. The king's spiritual prowess was also enhanced by local support for royal temples. Notables made gifts to the temples, financed holy ritual in the king's name, or subordinated local temples and their cults, which were supervised by the local elite, to those of the central royal temples.[56]

The political synthesis of Sanskritic culture in south India provides a meaningful parallel to that which took place in Southeast Asia. Notably, Hindu and Buddhist Sanskritic culture provided the basis for south Indian as well as Southeast Asian ritual sovereignty. The adoption of Sanskritic culture was encouraged by leaders in both areas because of its potential as a source of political and social cohesion. Sanskritic culture was not imposed through the conquest of south India or Southeast Asia by northern Indians nor was it due to the mass migration of north Indian elites to the south. Sanskritic ideology was adopted because of the advantages it offered to an emerging indigenous agrarian-based elite, who emulated the Hindu model of kingship and order in which in theory the monarch relied on virtue rather than force to extend his sovereignty. South Indian as well as Southeast Asian monarchs who sought alternatives to violence by which to force the landholding elites into submission depended instead upon ritual kingship to integrate their realm. They promoted alliances rather than relying on the threat of physical retribution.

Revenues generated from maritime commerce reinforced alliance networks. They supplemented local revenue collections and were redistributed by successful monarchs to reinforce the ties formed through their ritual sovereignty. The sea trade described earlier was thus a stimulus to state development. Local chiefs in southern India and Southeast Asia developed their coastal ports to serve the needs of the international trading community. In exchange they garnered income from various port cesses. This revenue in turn increased their wealth such that they were able to transform material benefits into political advantage. For instance, a local leader with an income sufficiently higher than that of his fellow chiefs and tribesmen could expand his manpower base by soliciting the support of rival chiefs and/or their followers. This base of support could then be used to protect or provision the port—for example, to police the sea channels against piracy, stabilize the hinterland, guarantee the flow of food for visiting merchants, or assure the delivery of the local products desired by traders. Followers shared in their chief's success as a facilitator of international trade through direct redistributions of profits. Rulers also cultivated their followers' loyalty by subscribing to north Indian Sanskritic religious tradition, which reinforced the chief's spiritual prowess, putting his magic above that of his followers.

Indic cultural forms were indeed important to evolving Southeast Asian states as an ideological base for their expanding sovereignty. In the chapters to come we shall look at how these cultural forms were introduced into and influenced the development of specific states.

3

The "Indianization" of Funan, Southeast Asia's First State

We have seen that the growing importance of the maritime route through Southeast Asia had a significant impact on the political and economic systems of the region. Just what that impact entailed can perhaps better be observed by examining in detail the earliest known Southeast Asian political entity, Funan.

As noted in chapter 2, when in the 240s the first Chinese envoys on record traveled to Southeast Asia to explore the nature of the sea passage at the behest of the Wu dynasty, it was to Funan on the southern Vietnam coast that they went. From the reports filed by K'ang T'ai and Chu Ying, the origins of Funan become intelligible.[1] K'ang T'ai's report provides a contemporary glimpse of the prosperous state, informing his emperor that the people of Funan

> live in walled cities, palaces, and houses. . . . They devote themselves to agriculture. They sow one year and harvest for three. . . . Taxes are paid in gold, silver, pearls, and perfumes. . . . There are books and depositories of archives and other things. Their characters for writing resemble those of the Hu [a people of Central Asia who used a script of Indian origin].[2]

Among the coastal centers in the vicinity of the upper Malay Peninsula that quickly developed to service the growing numbers of merchants traveling the sea and overland Isthmus of Kra route were ports on the lower Vietnam coast said by the Chinese to have been under Funan's authority. Archaeological remains at Oc-èo, the site of one such Funan port, show that the coast was occupied in the early first century A.D. by Malay fishing and hunting groups.[3] Already building their own ships, these seamen recognized that the location of their coast in relation to the new international route across the Isthmus of Kra would enable them to provide passage for Indian and Chinese goods. Soon Oc-èo was booming. Port facilities were constructed, including buildings for storing goods and hostelries for merchants laying over until the next season's monsoon winds would allow their return voyage.[4]

The archaeological data from Oc-èo also indicate that the evolution of the Funan port as a commercial center for maritime trade was ultimately connected to a parallel or previous development of Funan's agricultural base. A vast water management system that at some point included elaborate hydraulic projects allowed the Funan land-based population to produce multiple rice harvests annually—supplying sufficient surplus to easily feed foreign merchants resident in Funan ports and to provision their ships.[5] It is unclear, however, whether this water management system required either a new level of technological competence and/or a central leadership for its construction.[6] It would seem that the hydraulic projects (discussed later in this chapter) did not appear until later and that Funan's early agricultural development was based on flood-rice cultivation, for which the Funan region (unlike others) was most suited. Thus Funan's rise had two sources: the development of an advanced agrarian system (possibly including the drainage of coastal swamps) and its strategic location opposite the Isthmus of Kra. To determine whether Funan's emergence was the consequence of indigenous development or the result of a significant input of foreign expertise, especially Indian, it is necessary to examine Funan's earliest history.

The Origin of Funan

According to Chinese sources the founding of the Funan state took place in the first century A.D., and its origin is suggested by a local legend. In that age a female ruler is said to have led a raid on a merchant ship, whose passengers succeeded in fending off the raiding party and landing. One of the travelers was a man from a country "beyond the seas." This man drank water from the land and then married the local ruler, thereby becoming "king" over her domain. At the time of their marriage Funan consisted of several settlements, principally along the Mekong, each of which was under the authority of its own local chief. The first "king" of Funan and his wife not only assumed the right to rule but assigned their son the right to rule over seven of these population centers; the remainder of the domain they retained under their own authority.[7]

The basic elements of this legend are reiterated elsewhere in Indian and Southeast Asian folklore—the marriage between the foreigner, bearing the Indian name "Kauṇḍinya,"—a great Brahman, and a local *nāga* princess, daughter of the ruler of the water realm.[8] This legend is broadly used to symbolize the union of Indian and indigenous cultures, Kauṇḍinya representing elements of Indian culture and religions and the *nāga* princess symbolic of local ways and indigenous fertility cults. The marriage myth may be an attempt to explain not only the penetration of Indian culture into Southeast Asia, but also the origin of Southeast Asian kingship. Historians have not, however, been in agreement on its interpretation.

One classic account of the process symbolized in the Kauṇḍinya myth is provided in this early twentieth-century historical reconstruction:

> The true picture must have been something like this: two or three Indian vessels sailing together eventually arrived [there]. The newcomers established relations with the chiefs of the country, earning favor with them by means of presents, treatment of illnesses, and amulets. . . . No one could use such procedures better than an Indian. He would undoubtedly pass himself off as of royal or princely extraction, and his host could not help but be favorably impressed.[9]

These Indians are then seen uniting in marriage with the daughters of the local chiefs as the basis for converting the rulers and their population to Indian ways. Because the local population had no equivalent vocabulary or understanding to deal with the social, moral, and religious innovations the foreigners wished to undertake to uplift the native population, it was necessary for the Indians to use their own terminology. Indian culture soon engulfed the more primitive local civilization, as the local population became subjects of an Indianized state.

This theme of Indians traveling to Southeast Asia and presiding over a cultural transformation is carried to the extreme by several Indian historians who have argued that large numbers of South Asians not only migrated to but also colonized Funan and other early centers of civilization in Southeast Asia.[10] In opposing the colonization theories, while not denying the role of Indians in stimulating the formation of early Southeast Asian states, Justin van Leur was the first among modern historians to stress the active role of Southeast Asia's indigenous rulers in forging the initial linkage.[11] Many historians hold that Indian traders were the precursors and agents of the cultural transformation.[12] Van Leur, however, reasoned that traders would have been incapable of transmitting most of the more subtle concepts of Indian thought. Rather, local rulers, having learned of Indian culture through their interaction with Indians on the maritime route, recognized the advantages to them of certain elements of Indian civilization and drew from the Indian tradition for their own benefit by encouraging the migration of Brahman clerks to help them administer their realms.

George Coedès denied a Southeast Asian initiative and argued that Indian Brahmans, or other Indians claiming to belong to the Indian upper caste, were behind much of this interaction.[13] He suggested that in some instances Indians imposed their authority over a local population, in others they strengthened the power of the local chief, and in yet others they intermarried with members of the local elite to legitimize the new high-caste status of the "Hinduized" rulers.

Arguing against Coedès' emphasis on the role Indians may have played in the change, O. W. Wolters stressed the idea of a mutual sharing process in the evolution of Indianized statecraft in Southeast Asia.[14] The initial contact with and knowledge of Indian cultural traditions came through Southeast Asian sailors. Southeast Asian rulers, recognizing that Indian culture provided certain opportunities for administrative and technological advantages vis-à-vis their rivals, followed up on these contacts. The Indianizing of their realms was not due, then, to commercial pressures (i.e., a desire to convert in order to facilitate trade with Indian merchants). The early era of trade contact was one of adaptation and learning—an "apprenticeship"—when rulers of states like Funan were curious about Indian and other foreign cultural traditions and were in the habit of looking overseas to their own benefit. The initiative was Southeast Asian, not Indian; and it was a slow process of cultural synthesis, not one of rapid imposition of Hinduism made possible by a massive influx of Brahmans, that was responsible for the Indianization of Southeast Asia.[15]

Wolters has further proposed that a significant obstacle in understanding the Indianization process is that historians have tried to depict Funan and other early Southeast Asian political entities as unified kingdoms. He argues that the difficulty in dealing with the "Hinduization" of early Southeast Asian states is that they cannot be assumed to be "states" in the modern sense but must be viewed as tribal societies that from time to time produced certain chiefs who were able to mobilize sufficient military power, family networks of relatives and their allies, and marriage alliances to other chiefs' groups to impose their hegemony over neighboring chiefs.[16] Such overlordship was of temporary duration and was made possible by the formation of a coalition of those who supported the adventurer seeking hegemony. To the successful candidate and his coalition went the rewards of victory. Those who wished their local authority to remain undisturbed would hasten to have it confirmed by the new overlord. Only the Chinese viewed early Southeast Asian states as unified kingdoms with continuous dynastic lines holding "thrones," which was consistent with their knowledge of their own historical experience of kingship and dynastic succession. There was, however, no indigenous sense of kingdom and its supraterritorial demands on loyalty among the Southeast Asians themselves. Kingship derived from personal abilities and meritorious acts, not because of a claim of descent from a royal lineage. Although an overlord might speak of his descendance from ancestors who were remembered for their accomplishments, kinship was not critical to the promotion of authority. Political reality was that of temporary overlordships shifting from this to that group. One group's leader replaced another, not by a usurpation of the throne, but by demonstration of leadership, often through a renewal of tribal warfare that would then produce another era of short-lived unity. A kingdom was no more than a territorial measurement of those people allied to and acknowledging a leader's authority.

In Wolters' view, statecraft in early Southeast Asia was characterized by personal achievement. Local belief supported the idea that some people (chiefs) could be superior to others, that there was an uneven distribution of both secular and spiritual prowess. An individual's heroic secular accomplishments confirmed his spiritual superiority. Wolters documents strong concerns over death in early Southeast Asia.[17] Through worship of the dead, ancestors who had achieved eminence in life were recognized; personal achievements in an individual's lifetime earned him ancestor status. Just as one sought alliances with those of superior prowess in life, so too one desired a personal bond to "ancestors of prowess," who it was believed could bestow material and spiritual substance on devotees. Those who achieved greatness in life thereby demonstrated that their contact with the ancestors was greater than that of others of their generation.

When an individual established a relationship with a successful leader he confirmed his own bond with the ancestors. Homage to one's leader was thus a gesture of obedience to the ancestors. A subject validated his own potential to become an ancestor of prowess by sharing in his leader's continuous achievement. One important role of an overlord was thus to support his followers' hopes for a superior death status. The successful chief carefully recognized his followers' achievements and meritorious deeds by bestowing material (e.g., titles and wealth) and spiritual (e.g., ritual and death status) gifts on those whose secular performances on his behalf were noteworthy. He was thereby able to influence his supporters' stature in this life as well as their hopes for recognition after death.

Wolters' thesis is that the Indic religious tradition had certain teachings that were supportive of the efforts of chiefs to distinguish themselves as secular and spiritual superiors. As noted, heroic accomplishments demonstrated an individual's superior prowess, which in turn was the ideal of ascetic achievement. After consolidating his position by force, the successful Southeast Asian chief began to practice Hindu asceticism, further demonstrating spiritual superiority. Achievement exemplified one's close relationship not only with the ancestors but also with Hindu gods. Specifically, Wolters notes early patronage of the god Śiva. In early mainland inscriptions Śiva was depicted as a patron of asceticism and as the lord of the universe. Men of achievement became recognized as Śiva's spiritual authorities on earth, and since Śiva's authority over all that exists was absolute, their powers on earth had no limit. The accomplished leader thus partook of divinity. Relationships with such a leader thus not only linked followers to the society's ancestors but also established a relationship with an Indian divinity who reigned over the universe.[18]

Wolters concluded that Southeast Asia's early rulers did not try to develop state institutions but instead initiated religious cults that allowed their followers to draw from a leader's spiritual relationship with both the ancestors and a universal deity. Early Southeast Asian society thus rallied behind spiritually endowed leaders who were supported by a blend of local and Indian cultural symbols and values. Such leaders were able to use these symbols and values to mobilize local populations for various intraregional adventures.

If these different interpretations are synthesized for the purpose of undertaking an analysis of Funan's political development, it may be concluded that the entrepreneurial activities of traders of various cultures stimulated the local rulers to selectively adopt Indianized patterns for their own purposes. Funan chieftains oversaw the initial commercial transactions with foreign traders as the instigators and organizers of Funan's ports and served as mediators between the traders and the local Malay population. As the international trade through ports such as Oc-èo developed and increased in volume, Funan's rulers were subjected to a range of experiences beyond those of their land-based subordinate populations. They were exposed to new perceptions of the world, new life goals, and became especially aware of new organizational possibilities. The local ruler became a cultural broker, as well as the principal beneficiary of profits directly derived from the commercial route. The rewards included ceremonial regalia, beads, textiles, wealth (precious metals/ "cash") that could be shared with clients, and other items useful to a chief attempting to stress his superiority over other similar indigenous rulers. The chief thus had a vested interest in the continuation and expansion of the system that was evolving. Since his own society's norms restricted his ambition, he was forced to rise above the indigenous system in order to assume a more illustrious personal status, one closely associated with the Indian model of divine kingship.

This synthesis may also be applied to the Funan origin myth. In this age the volume of international maritime commercial traffic between India and China was increasing and various coastal rulers in Southeast Asia were competing to attract merchant ships to their ports. The transformation of a coastal center into an international port depended on a local ruler's initiative in organizing his supporters to facilitate this trade. First a port facility had to be built. Second, a center had to establish itself as a purveyor of the goods desired by international traders. In the case of Funan this was initially done by providing superior facilities or, if necessary, by using force to build up a supply of both Chinese and Western goods in its ports. Funan chiefs formed working alliances with the Malay seagoing population, who could facilitate the flow of trade by serving as transporters of goods and policemen over the sea channels or could plunder merchant ships, if that proved more profitable.

In the Funan origin myth, a local chief (a female, denoting the importance of women in Funan society prior to Funan's adoption of "Indianized" statecraft, in which males normally assumed leadership roles) led a band of Malay seamen from the Funan coast against a passing merchant ship. This is symbolic of initial efforts to bring shipping to Funan's ports by force or it demonstrates an early pirate stage in Funan's development. Interestingly, the attack was said to have been beaten off by the ship's travelers, explaining why the use of force was not always successful. Piracy rejected, only with the marriage of the local ruler and the ship's traveler was the prosperity of Funan guaranteed. The marriage of the local princess and the foreigner therefore represented a pact, a promise that in the future Funan would be willing to deal more positively with foreign merchants—in other words, a better way for Funan to become prosperous had been found.

Thus the Funan origin myth may not in any way document an actual marriage between a native princess and a foreign traveler, as it is usually interpreted. Instead of symbolizing the "Indianization" of Funan, the legend more validly symbolizes a marriage of interests—the establishment of Funan as a major Southeast Asian trade center, its ports serving international shipping—and reflects the actual evolution of Funan's power.

In order to develop into a thriving entrepôt in this age, a port had to present a cosmopolitan character. The Kauṇḍinya myth suggests that Funan's ports became such a neutral meeting ground, where foreign merchandise could be peaceably exchanged. Funan rulers offered international merchant groups active in their ports a sense of security, but protective measures were carefully regulated so that visiting merchants did not feel threatened.[19] If too many restraints were placed on the traders they would have shifted their operations to other ports that allowed them more freedom to transact their business.

Funan's origin myth as it appears in Chinese sources specifies that the foreign traveler drank the water of the land before his marriage to the local princess. This is possibly an allusion to the construction of the Funan hydraulic system, described by archaeologists, by which Funan drained saltwater from the land near the coast to increase its agricultural productivity. Since the establishment of a system of water management is associated with the founding of the Funan state and appears to be specifically attributed to the foreign traveler, many historians have concluded that the application of foreign technology, the presence of foreign supervisors, or the corresponding development of a foreign component within Funan statecraft was critical to the expansion of Funan's agrarian base.

The history of Funan's hydraulic projects is subject to controversy. Air surveys of the Funan region show a network of skillfully laid out channels between the Bassac estuary and the Gulf of Thailand—hundreds of canals, estimated to cover 200 kilometers, connecting at least a dozen urban centers whose populations lived in houses built on stilts within great earthen ramparts. The Funan realm was criss-crossed by canals that could have provided an internal transport system as well as water control. Although Louis Malleret believed that the canal network was constructed to drain salt out of the land, preventing the waters of the sea from flowing back into the Bassac estuary, his detailed presentation and analysis of archaeological remains were inconclusive as to whether its purpose was irrigation or land drainage. Further, Malleret dated the construction of the works to the fifth or sixth centuries, a period corresponding—as will be shown in this chapter—to the demise rather than to the origin of the Funan state.[20]

Based on K'ang T'ai's description of Funan residents sowing seed one year and harvesting the next three years, I. W. Mabbett argued that Funan agriculture was characterized by rain-fed cultivation. Mabbett holds that K'ang T'ai's report does not provide evidence that an intensive irrigation system existed in the third century and that even if such a system existed, it does not necessarily mean that Funan had developed into a densely populated and highly integrated state system.[21]

This view is in part substantiated by a Cham inscription that records the Funan origin myth and stresses that wet-rice agriculture was an indigenous development. Contrary to the Chinese account of the myth noted above in which a foreigner (Kauṇḍinya) is credited with the draining of

Funan's swamplands, in the Cham version the father of the local princess —a chief who enjoyed the protection of the *nāgas*—gave his daughter and Kauṇḍinya a dowry at their wedding, making the Funan area suitable for habitation by "drinking up the water that covered it" and thus allowing the local population to farm the lands of the Mekong Delta.[22]

A 1980 study of the development of irrigation systems in the Mekong Delta region by W. J. van Liere also supports the indigenous development thesis, finding that the area around Funan's archaeological remains was ideally suited for early flood-rice cultivation.[23] The study shows that cultivators avoided the lower Vietnam coast because of its dense mangrove vegetation and because in numerous areas of the Mekong Delta region dense evergreen and mixed deciduous forests required too much labor to clear. However, the zone associated with Funan at the delta's edge was a floodplain covered by savanna vegetation, which was more readily farmed.[24] Further, in this area of the upper delta backswamps kept out saltwater and retained the fresh water run-off of the monsoonal rains, making usable water available year round. The gentle flood patterns of the area—a rapid rise of water, but not too deep, and a gradual water drain-off—were ideal for simple wet-rice cultivation. Local broadcast rice cultivation, as opposed to more elaborate irrigated wet-rice cultivation, required no leveling or bunding of fields nor, due to the area's natural flood regulators, was there need to dig canals for irrigation or drainage. Simple water management and broadcast cultivation systems were capable of producing a substantial rice surplus that could have supported a rapid population increase. Interestingly, van Liere has demonstrated that the area that extended inland from the Oc-èo region on the coast to the hinterland surrounding Funan's capital city of Vyādhapura was ideal for broadcast rice cultivation. But his study further notes that as the early broadcast rice civilizations of the Mekong Delta region matured, it was not unusual for them to construct water reservoirs to store large quantities of water for the dry season, which when circulated through a new network of irrigation canals produced more substantial multiple rice crops—adding credence to Malleret's thesis that Funan's wet-rice irrigation projects were constructed in the fifth and sixth centuries.[25]

The various versions of the Funan origin myth and K'ang T'ai's report all emphasize a developed agrarian sector as a key factor in Funan's general prosperity. While the Funan origin myth first deals with sea contacts, its secondary focus on the land reflects the dual nature of the Funan domain. Not only was Funan's success the result of its interaction with the sea, but its wealth was equally due to its agrarian base. The impetus for initial or further agrarian development came from the maritime sector, when merchants and seamen putting in at Funan's ports demanded food during their layover periods. This demand for rice created a need for a rice surplus that had to be supplied by Funan's agrarian population —given the undesirability or improbability of importing rice, which would have required merchants to devote an inordinate part of their ship cargo space to food.[26] While the construction of an irrigation or drainage system would have facilitated greater productivity, Funan's terrain initially allowed the land-based population to produce sufficient rice to supply seamen stopping at its ports. A portion of the trade revenues were in turn reinvested in the development of hydraulic projects that expanded Funan wet-rice cultivation. Regardless of where the technology came from—whether it was local or foreign—the evolution of Funan's water management system was stimulated by foreign demand. Agrarian development or the agricultural potential in Funan thus contributed to Funan's growth as an international entrepôt.

The Funan origin myth describes the early Funan domain as being comprised of several settlements, each ruled by its own chief. This reinforces Wolters' thesis that early Southeast Asian states, including Funan, derived their power from control over manpower.[27] According to the myth, the first Funan king assumed direct rule over a specific sector of land, assigning his son seven "centers," or subordinate chiefdoms to supervise. The seven subordinate population centers were thus ruled indirectly, their loyalty questionable beyond their personal ties to the Funan ruler/chief. The Funan ruler drew income from two sources to use in establishing his supremacy over his fellow chiefs. Revenues collected in Funan ports—usage fees collected from those taking advantage of port facilities—flowed directly into the royal treasury. These revenues were used to expand the Funan economic base not only in the commercial sector—upgrading ports—but in the agrarian sector as well. More sophisticated hydraulic projects could be undertaken, thus making more land fit for cultivation and expanding the economic potential of the agrarian core. This added potential in turn allowed the Funan ruler to support a larger manpower base. Initially, then, Funan's might was derived from local tribesmen who both cultivated and went to war on behalf of their chiefs, and who shared in the Funan ruler's prosperity.

The Rise of Funan as a "State"

The process of economic transformation that was taking place in Southeast Asia at the time Funan was expanding its hegemony was marked by a transition in mechanisms of exchange.[28] In a less complicated tribal existence, reciprocity—a sharing process among family, community, and religious groups—maintained the social unit. According to geographer Paul Wheatley, Southeast Asia prior to the expansion of the maritime route in the first century was "occupied exclusively by societies whose most advanced level of political organization was the chiefdom and among whom the instrumental exchanges characteristic of a reciprocative mode of integration dominated."[29] Except for the Red River Delta region of northern Vietnam, which came under Chinese political authority and was thus subjected to the sudden imposition of an external tribute system, the exchange mechanisms of most of Southeast Asia were only gradually transformed. Entrepreneurial advances associated with international commerce created social imbalances within societies like that of Funan, with the result that the indigenous economy was transformed and political entities based on redistributive exchange emerged. Redistribution is here defined as the allocation of rewards and facilities by an individual (a tribal chief) or a small group (a tribal, merchant, or religious elite) for the purpose of integrating that society. In the case of Funan, the initial efforts of the ruler to subordinate other chiefs and thus to integrate the society under his authority included ritualized redistributions of the wealth derived from foreign trade.[30]

Wheatley holds that several Southeast Asian societies (he does not consider Funan to be one of these) went beyond this level of integration, developing strong "mobilizative sectors" in their economies. Such "mobilization-oriented economies" he views as having developed organizational mechanisms for the acquisition, control, and disposal of resources in pursuit of collective goals, most of which were political. While in the "redistributive economy" the resources of the realm "naturally" flow to a center to be redistributed for the benefit of all, in the "mobilizative economy" impersonalism takes hold. Tribal gifts are transposed into tribute and agricultural surplus is taxed by state administrators to support a court. Tribesmen are not only replaced as warriors by a royal army paid from a central treasury but are also demoted from cultivators to peasant status, becoming less personally involved in the affairs of their former chief.[31] Their chief is transformed into a divine king, his legitimacy defined no longer by tribal tradition but by elaborate Sanskrit ritual—his hut has become a palace, the tribal spirit house a temple, the local spirit stone a powerful *liṅga* (the symbol of Lord Śiva's powers of fertility), and the tribe's village the center of the king's rule over the villages of other tribes, as these villages and their tribesmen are integrated into a state.[32] With the development of the institutional structures necessary to administer this expanded political realm, Wheatley maintains, a society's old reciprocity networks were overlaid with redistribution and mobilization systems, as in some way all sectors of the state inevitably interacted with the new order.

That Wheatley does not believe this process occurred in Funan raises the question as to whether Funan can be categorized as a "state." Wolters holds that it cannot be. Recent studies concur but see the Funan region as an important early Southeast Asian cultural center. Some even argue that reference to "Funan" should be avoided until historians reach a better understanding of what Funan was. Nevertheless, archaeological evidence does suggest that Wheatley's economic transformation process, which he considers critical to early Southeast Asian state development, can be discerned in Funan's history as well.

The degree of integration that occurred in the Funan realm can best be measured by a comparison of Funan's archaeological remains with those from the Chansen region of central Thailand.[33] Chansen's archaeological remains provide a contrast between cultural developments in early central Thailand and those in the Funan realm and also demonstrate the impact of Funan on early central Thailand civilization. While the Oc-èo area's sites show a high degree of uniformity and economic integration in the Funan age, those of contemporary central Thailand do not. Archaeological remains there make it difficult to speak of extensive regional economies or political development until the seventh century (although there is previous evidence of subregional integration and development), but the similarity of the evidence from the Funan sites is indicative of a higher level of regional, economic, cultural, and political integration.

The canal network connecting Funan's population centers, surrounded by earthworks and moats, which has been seen in archaeological air surveys, is considered to have been critical both to Funan's irrigation agriculture and to riverine communication within the Funan realm.[34] Archaeological remains from Oc-èo include an abundance of items that reflect its commercial prominence: ceramics, jewels, gold rings, merchant seals, and tin amulets with symbols of Viṣṇu and Śiva. Roman materials that date to the second through fourth centuries are highlighted by glassware fragments, a gold coin minted in the reign of Marcus Aurelius, A.D. 161–180 (see page 8), and a gold medal of Antoninus Pius dating from A.D. 152. Imports from China include a bronze mirror dating from the Later Han dynasty (first to third centuries) and several Buddhist statuettes from the Wei period (A.D. 386–534).[35]

In addition to these objects of Western and Eastern origin, there is ample evidence of local craft production. Glass beads, possibly a local application of Western glass technology, are abundant in the Oc-èo excavations. More impressive, however, are numerous molded and engraved tin plaques (a craft not known to have been practiced elsewhere in that time).

Local adaptation of Indian religious art is evident in the sculpture and stone architecture found in Funan's core area. While Indian stonecarvers in this early era normally sculpted statues that were part of wall reliefs or were backed or enclosed by a stele or a wall, Funan sculptors developed their own free-standing style that is first evinced in two wooden standing Buddhas, believed to date to the fifth century, that were miraculously preserved in the mud near Binh-hoa (see page 8). This sculptural expression reached its height in the early sixth century when several stone Viṣṇu and Buddhist statues discovered at Phnom Da were produced, which have impressed one art historian with their "delicate and graceful [bodies], soft and smoothly rounded, with muscles indicated only slightly, but yet with astonishing sensitivity, so that one feels the swing of a body in motion, or the balance of a gently bending body at rest."[36] The sexless style of this statuary is characteristic of later Southeast Asian Buddhist sculpture, which was seemingly modeled on that of Funan's craftsmen.

Also demonstrative of local initiative is a building ("K") among those excavated at Oc-èo where local architects constructed a temple that was modeled on the rock sanctuaries that were popular in south and central India during the late Gupta period (fifth and sixth centuries). The crafting of this brick and granite temple in an area with no rock or cliffs demonstrates the power of local technology; the skill by which the granite slabs were held together especially shows the local control of technique. Such artistic initiative impressed the Chinese court, which received several stone Buddhist statues that the Indian monk Nāgasena brought from Funan in the late fifth century. In 503 a Funan monarch sent the Chinese emperor a coral statue of the Buddha and an ivory stupa.[37]

In central Thailand the principal evidence for an early indigenous consolidation is not only the distribution of various local pottery types, of which each has its own character, but also the number of trade goods from external sources, especially those from Funan, which have their own distinctive and consistent markings. These archaeological data imply that the growth of Funan civilization spurred the state-building process in central Thailand, as the flow of trade goods into the region supplied the demand of an emerging foreign-oriented elite class who came to emulate Funan.[38]

The archaeological evidence substantiates Wheatley's thesis that there was a pattern of simultaneous economic and political integration. Furthermore, it shows that Funan was not an exception to it. External trade was a likely stimulus to local trade, and the growth of domestic commerce promoted the need and the desire for a higher degree of economic integration. The need for economic integration in turn necessitated the exercise of authoritative control over areas of potential conflict, the management of the economic resources of the domain, and the ability to support an increased population in the area.

Wolters considers that one of the key factors that constitute a state is continuity from ruler to son. It was suggested earlier that the seven chiefs initially allied with the Funan ruler under the authority of his son were in part drawn to the Funan ruler by their desire to participate in his rapidly expanding economic base and prosperous redistribution network. The threat of conquest was another likely pressure, however, since the Funan ruler's wealth could be used to mobilize more troops for his band of armed supporters. In this sense the first Funan ruler, in appointing his son overlord of the seven subordinate chiefs, made an attempt more sophisticated than the use of force to integrate these centers into Funan and as well to provide a foundation—a manpower base—for his son when it came time, after his death, for the son to assume the throne. Chinese sources are vague on this succession, but in their view there was continuity among early Funan rulers through the second half of the second century.[39]

Through an analysis of other early developing centers of mainland civilization (to allow reconsideration of the limited sources for Funan's history), it was found that the Kauṇḍinya-*nāga* myth was commonly used by later Khmer rulers of Cambodia as the basis for the construction of their royal genealogies.[40] The Khmer domain was ruled by a "royal family" whose members were descended authentically, whether by fact or by law, from "Funan" rulers, who were themselves descended from the original Kauṇḍinya. This demonstration of the importance of the Funan legacy to Khmer kingship adds credence to the proposition that the Funan region manifested a level of cultural if not political integration beyond the tribal level.

Other studies have found that Funan was a cultural axis as well as a commercial center connecting three early Southeast Asian cultural realms. One cultural zone extended from lower Burma (Chin-lin) to Funan and was inhabited by developing Mon-Khmer and Pyu civilizations.[41] A second zone extended from Funan north up the Vietnam coast and comprised what was to become the domain of the Cham and Vietnamese civilizations. Funan also had contacts with a third zone, extending from Funan into the Java Sea cultural realm with its Malay populations.[42] Ideas from Funan were introduced into the three zones via the principal networks of communication, the trade routes that connected the developing population centers of the mainland and the Indonesian archipelago.

Evidence from archaeological, linguistic, and literary sources, then, support the conclusion that Funan may best be understood as the first Southeast Asian "state." Clearly, the Funan region was an economic center, with an economic base that supported a more sophisticated level of political integration than was indicated previously in the area. This integration was achieved through the attempts of Funan's first ruler to build a continuous manpower base, subordinating local chiefs to his authority as well as to that of his chosen successors. The resulting "royal family" that appears in later Khmer genealogies, said to be descended from the original Kauṇḍinya, is evidence of a continuity associated with higher levels of political integration. More elaborate cultural forms evolved within the Funan realm; over a period of time preexisting indigenous cultural and ethnic diversity were synthesized with external ideology to create a new syncretic higher-order cultural base.[43] The Funan region also served as the locus of contact between various regional and local marketing systems and the higher-order international marketing network. It was in Funan's ports that attempts were first made to substitute the exchange of Southeast Asian goods for those of foreign origin.[44] Through these economic ties Funan's political, economic, and cultural advancements spread into other areas of Southeast Asia.

Let us examine the early history of Funan to explore the character of this first state and the process of economic, cultural, and political diffusion as it relates to the Indianization of Southeast Asia.

The Extension of Funan's Hegemony

In the Chinese account of Funan's early history, during the second half of the second century a ruler known to the Chinese as Hun P'an-huang, a descendant of the original Kauṇḍinya, was said to have enjoyed a long reign, further consolidating his state's hold over local chiefs by sowing dissension among them. Having thus fragmented their unity, he attacked and conquered these chiefs. He then sent his sons and grandsons to rule directly over their political centers.[45]

By the late second-century reign of Hun P'an-huang the original seven subordinate tribal centers and others as well were being incorporated into the area directly ruled by the Funan monarch, as the pattern of Funan statecraft began to emerge. The origin myth stipulates that these victories were the consequence of dissension among the ruler's enemies, the use of his ever-increasing wealth either to bribe or at least to create envy among his rival chiefs' followers, and his exploitation of weaknesses in the local political systems. With the potential for united resistance among his opponents weakened, the Funan ruler was able to extend his hegemony over them. His sons and grandsons, his direct kin—those whose personal loyalty he depended upon—were sent to rule over the former rivals, who were then integrated under Funan's direct control.

K'ang T'ai's third-century report to the Chinese emperor also supplies information on Hun P'an-huang's conquests. It relates that Hun P'an-huang captured large elephants while on hunting expeditions into the jungle and, while domesticating the elephants, brought about the submission of many "countries" whose lands he hunted upon. This tale of the hunting king relates to the origin of Funan's capital of Vyādhapura, "the city of the hunter king."[46] The Funan name is itself a derivative of the Khmer *phnom (bnam)* or "mountain"; Funan's rulers were known as *kurung bnam,* "kings of the mountain."[47] According to Chinese records the sacred mountain of Funan was located inland 500 *li* (200 kilometers) from the sea, which is almost exactly the distance from the Ba Phnom mountain to the site of Oc-èo's remains, adding authenticity to the Chinese accounts.[48] Vyādhapura was constructed adjacent to the sacred mountain Ba Phnom. Because the Funan state and its rulers derived their name from this mountain, it is therefore reasonable to date the origin of a Funan state to the conquests of Hun P'an-huang and the establishment of his capital city Vyādhapura, named in his honor. Vyādhapura was strategically placed to establish the cosmological and supernatural base that substantiated the legitimacy of future Funan rulers. By localized Indian tradition, the mountain was the repository of supernatural powers that were dispensed by Funan monarchs to benefit their subjects.[49] The mountain symbolized the ruler's authority, and from it, as from the monarch himself, came the domain's prosperity. This contact with the supernatural enhanced the superior status of Funan rulers and further encouraged adjacent populations to submit to the Funan monarch.[50]

During the early third century the rulership of Funan passed to a great general, known to the Chinese as Fan Shih-man, who was selected to rule by the people of Funan after the death of Hun P'an-huang's son. In dealing with records of Fan Shih-man's reign, one first notes that the legend of Fan Shih-man's succession to the throne stressed that he was selected by Funan's subjects. The shift of leadership to someone who was not a direct relative of Hun P'an-huang would seemingly have raised questions of legitimacy. Such a problem was apparently alleviated by taking the issue "to the people," in a process whereby Fan Shih-man was nominated to rule principally because he had sufficient military power to impose his hegemony over Funan's tribal chiefs. Fan Shih-man's legitimacy was thus based on his past success as a leader and his position as the head of a sizable body of troops. Likely Fan Shih-man could have easily seized power with or without the validation of a council of chiefs or tribal elders representing the people of Funan. Whatever the circumstances of his succession, Fan Shih-man assumed power with the approval of Funan's population.

Building upon this "vote of confidence," Fan Shih-man soon embarked on a campaign to extend Funan's authority. He first consolidated Funan's hold over the Mekong Delta, annexing territory northward up to the mouth of the Tonle Sap and then subjugating the Cham domain to the south on the north edge of the delta.[51] Having thus secured his mainland base, Fan Shih-man next took a naval expedition against the upper Malay coast, utilizing the Malay seamen of his ports. This campaign was clearly an attempt to assume direct authority over the trade centers on both sides of the peninsula, from the Isthmus of Kra region to Burma, thereby solidifying Funan's dominance over the flow of commerce through Southeast Asia. His conquest of the Malay coast is described by the Chinese envoys:

> [Fan Shih-man] attacked and conquered the neighboring kingdoms. All recognized themselves [as] his vassals. [As a result] he took the title of "Great King of Funan." Then he had great ships built and crossing the immense sea he attacked more than ten kingdoms, [including] . . . Tun-sun. He extended his territory 5,000 or 6,000 li [2,000 miles]. Then he wished to subdue the country of Chin-lin [lower Burma]. But he fell ill [and died].[52]

Fan Shih-man's key conquest on the Malay Peninsula was an entrepôt known to the Chinese as Tun-sun. K'ang T'ai reported that Tun-sun was a "state" where:

> There are five kings [who rule Tun-sun] who all acknowledge themselves vassals of Fu-nan. The eastern frontier of Fu-nan is in communication with Tong-king [the Red River Delta of Vietnam], the western with India and Persia [i.e., Tun-sun's domain encompassed both sides of the Malay Peninsula]. All the countries beyond the frontier [beyond the Chinese frontier, i.e., Southeast Asia] come and go in pursuit of trade because Tun-sun curves around and projects into the sea for more than 1,000 li [roughly 333 miles]. The Gulf of Siam is of great extent and ocean-going junks have not yet crossed it direct [i.e., ships were navigating from Malay Peninsula ports to Funan's ports on the lower Vietnam coast sailing close to the coast rather than directly crossing the Gulf of Thai-

land]. . . . At this mart East and West meet together so that every day great crowds gather there. Precious goods and rare merchandise—they are all there. . . .[53]

The Tun-sun polity was concentrated in a city some ten *li* from the sea. Among the "five kings" (chiefs) who shared the rule over the northern peninsula, the ruler of Tun-sun was dominant. After Fan Shih-man's conquest all the chiefs transferred their loyalty to Funan. Resident in Tun-sun were a thousand "Indian Brahmans," who were receiving the daughters of the local population in marriage, which encouraged the Indians to stay. There were also some five hundred families of "Persian" origin—likely Western merchant families.[54]

At the time that Fan Shih-man embarked on his sea expedition, sailors voyaging from the Malay Peninsula to China via the South China Sea hugged the coastline. K'ang T'ai reported that the passage from Tun-sun to Funan took thirty days, and this was the reason it did. Ships navigated close to the coast rather than sailing directly across the Gulf of Thailand to Funan's ports. Ships seldom ventured into the open sea before the fifth century. Funan already dominated the coastal route between the Malay Peninsula and China at this time. For it to totally dominate Southeast Asian trade, including the Malay Peninsula transit—which was Fan Shih-man's ambition—Funan needed to acquire a base on the Malay Peninsula. Tun-sun, already established as a cosmopolitan center of commerce on the peninsula's upper east coast and a terminus for the Isthmus of Kra portage, was a well-chosen victim for Fan Shih-man's superior naval power.[55]

Described by the Chinese envoys as a loose confederation of five chiefs whose territories stretched from coast to coast, Tun-sun was representative of other settlements on the northern Malay Peninsula that had developed because of and depended upon the transpeninsular portage of commercial goods. In addition to Tun-sun, there were Langkasuka in the Pattani region, Tāmbraliṅga in the area south of Chaiya on the east coast, and Takuapa on the west coast, all believed to have been major Malay entrepôts during this early age of commercial development (see map 3).[56] Fan Shih-man's conquest of Tun-sun not only gave Funan a solid position on both sides of the Gulf of Thailand, it also allowed the Funan monarch to extend his dominance over these other entrepôts, which were river valley-based political entities that, like Tun-sun, were no more than loose tribal confederacies. A more broadly based polity had evolved in Funan by this time with an agrarian system that stabilized the revenue flow of its rulers. Funan's political and economic potential far exceeded that of the more simple tribal societies of the isthmus, which

Map 3
SOUTHEAST ASIA IN
THE FUNAN AGE

depended almost entirely on trade revenues to finance their statecraft. Funan thus had a distinct advantage in attracting the loyalty of the Malay sea populations of the gulf. Funan's rulers were able to supply a steady income and the promise of prosperity to Malay seamen. They provided Funan with a naval force like that which Fan Shih-man used on the peninsula and protected the sea lanes between the Malay Peninsula and southern China.[57]

The conquest of Tun-sun and the acquisition of a peninsula base had other than purely economic significance for Funan, however, for it was after Fan Shih-man's reign that Funan statecraft began to exhibit signs of stronger Sanskritic influence. Chinese sources imply that the likely source of Funan's new Indian mannerisms were the conquered peninsula entrepôts, which had a substantial Indian character prior to their takeover by Funan. Tun-sun was not the only peninsula center having an Indian element in its population. P'an P'an, an entrepôt indicated by Chinese sources as being south of Tun-sun that was also conquered by Fan Shih-man, was said to have been inhabited by "numerous Brahmans [who] have come from India to seek wealth by serving the [local] king, with whom they are in high favor."[58] The most dramatic consequence of the presence of these Indians as far as Funan was concerned appears to have been the growing use of Sanskrit in Funan; the first known Sanskrit inscription in Funan was issued shortly after Fan Shih-man's death in the third century.[59]

Although Indian vocabulary came to be used in the conduct of state affairs, Indian cosmology and statecraft had little significance at the time in the actual workings of Funan's political system, as evinced in the transfer of power to Fan Shih-man's successor. When Fan Shih-man's son attempted to assume the Funan throne after his father died he was put to death by a ruler the Chinese sources knew as Fan Ch'an, son of Fan Shih-man's sister, whose claim to the throne was based upon his recognition as a war chief by two thousand men.[60] As with Fan Shih-man's succession to the throne, control over manpower was still the most important variable in determining legitimate succession in Funan.

One of the most important incidents of Fan Ch'an's reign according to K'ang T'ai occurred when the envoy called Chia Hsiang-li came from India buying and selling and told the Funan monarch all about India, of which Fan Ch'an was said to have been ignorant.[61] It is remarkable that the Funan ruler could be ignorant about India when Indian traders should have been following the route to China via Funan for a century. Fan Ch'an's limited knowledge of the trade route west of the Isthmus of Kra, however, is testimony to the local character of Funan's early statecraft and the absence of a true Indian presence that might have stimulated Indianization in a significant way. The account gives credence to the belief that Southeast Asian seamen, not Indians, dominated the ocean east of the Malay Peninsula during the early Funan era. It was during Fan Ch'an's reign that regular diplomatic contact between Funan and both India and China was said to have been established. More because of commercial interests than political ambition, Fan Ch'an sent a relative to India to gather information and to solicit trade. Embarking from Takuapa, Fan Ch'an's envoy sailed to the mouth of the Ganges on the Bengal coast. From there he traveled inland some 7,000 *li* (roughly 2,333 miles) up the Ganges until he reached the court of a Kushāna prince. This prince was so impressed with the visit that he sent back a present of four horses to Fan Ch'an. Later in his reign Fan Ch'an also dispatched Funan's first official embassy to China.

The politics of Funan were still dominated by warring factions in the mid-third century when Fan Ch'an was killed by another of Fan Shihman's sons (an infant at the time of his father's death), who had assembled a band of supporters. This son had taken refuge—"living among the people"—during Fan Ch'an's reign and "was able to collect good soldiers of the country" from among them.[62] These soldiers were the kinsmen of his mother who, when the opportunity arose, had mobilized their own allies to support a new bid for hegemony. This son was in turn assassinated by a man the Chinese sources identify as Fan Ch'an's "general" Fan Hsun, yet another chief with his own manpower resources, who assumed the Funan throne around A.D. 240.

It was during Fan Hsun's long reign in the middle of the third century that Funan commercial prosperity reached its zenith. The Wu envoys K'ang T'ai and Chu Ying visited Funan around 240 and made their extensive reports on Fan Hsun's domain and its history, depicting Funan as a wealthy political domain whose rulers supplemented their income from the land with the taxes paid by foreign merchants—"gold, silver, pearls, and perfumes. . . ."[63] An Indian vocabulary was in use and there is evidence of Indian technological influence, but political theory and religious philosophy in Funan were still strongly indigenous in character. Not for another two hundred years, until the mid-fifth century, do Chinese and indigenous sources denote any significant Indianization. Then a sudden departure from indigenous patterns occurred that was in some way related to the takeover of the Funan throne by a new line of monarchs.

Political Transitions in Fifth-Century Funan

The dynastic line that came to ascendancy in Funan in the fifth century may have originated in the more Indianized peninsular center known to the Chinese as P'an P'an, which came under Funan's authority during Fan Shih-man's reign. The Chinese record of Fan Shih-man's conquests stressed that P'an P'an's rulers were patrons of Indian Brahmans, as if this were quite different from the practice of Funan's rulers. The succession to the Funan throne of this new line was reported by the Chinese:

> The people of Funan heard of him [the ruler of P'an P'an]. The whole kingdom rose with joy. They came to him and chose him king. He changed all the rules according to the custom of India.[64]

Was this "second Kauṇḍinya," as this ruler is known by some historians, from P'an P'an, or was he actually of Indian origin?[65] The strongly Indian character of Funan's fifth-century statecraft has been thought to have been the work of an Indian Brahman or a ruler who patronized Brahmans and gave them a significant role in the creation of a new ideological base for Funan's political system.[66] The only definite evidence of Indian Brahmans resident in Southeast Asian courts, however, is post-eighth century in date.[67] Although Brahmans may well have influenced the new Funan polity, it is not necessary to trace the origin of this transition all the way to India; rather, the changes that occurred reflect an internal evolution in Funan's dynastic system and are best understood within an indigenous context.

The Chinese report of the fifth-century Kauṇḍinya suggests that the people of Funan had become embroiled in another succession dispute or some other internal disharmony between regional armed factions. As a consequence a chief having his base in P'an P'an was either invited by Funan's clan elders to restore internal order or a P'an P'an-based chief and his supporters seized power directly. The report makes it clear that the new ruler felt it was necessary to establish the legitimacy of his line by imposing substantially new patterns of state administration upon Funan —changing all the rules according to the custom of India. If there was indeed a succession of P'an P'an's ruling line to the Funan throne, then the administrative style introduced would likely have been synthesized with earlier Funan practice, producing a more Indian character to Funan's state. It was from this era onward that Sanskrit came into widespread official usage. An Indian dating system became standard. Worship of Indian deities, especially official worship of the Śiva-*liṅga* Maheśvara and icons of the Mahāyāna Bodhisattva Lokeśvara and the Lord Viṣṇu, was systematized and extended. The Sanskrit honorific title -*varman* was added to the names of rulers. There was also an attempt to consolidate and construct an official genealogy for Funan's royal line elaborately tracing the origin of Funan monarchs to the marriage of the first Kauṇḍinya and the *nāga* princess. All of these changes reflect a significant attempt to redefine the basis of legitimacy and especially to elevate more distinctly the prestige of the Funan ruler above that of his subordinate chiefs. As shown in Chinese records, pre-fifth-century succession to Funan's throne was dependent on the candidate having royal blood, designated by the Fan clan prefix before his name, and on having enough armed supporters to guarantee "election" by a group of clan elders (chiefs).[68]

P'an P'an was more extensively Indianized than Funan because of its intense direct interaction with Indian merchants. The story of Fan Ch'an and the Indian merchant who visited Funan and informed him about India, related above, implies that there was little opportunity for Funan monarchs to acquire firsthand information about India; that is, that few India-based merchants were visiting Funan ports but were instead concentrating their activities in the maritime zone between India and the Malay Peninsula entrepôts. This is further evidence that Malay seamen from Funan were shipping goods between the Malay Peninsula and the southern Vietnam coast, and likely between southern Vietnam and China ports as well. In P'an P'an as well as in other Malay Peninsula entrepôts that facilitated the international trade, Indianization was a means of elevating the status of the indigenous rulers both in the eyes of their own people and with the visiting Indian merchants whose presence was essential to continuing prosperity. Funan's reasons for Indianization were quite different. Funan began to refocus its statecraft in the fifth century because it needed to develop an agrarian base as the principal source of royal revenue collections. Indianized statecraft became extremely useful in the transition from the earlier maritime focus to one in which the prosperity of the agrarian sector was the most essential contributing factor to the state's continuation.

The thesis that there was a fifth-century dynastic crisis and resulting transition is substantiated in other sources. First, Chinese court records report Funan embassies to China in 268, 286, and 287, a period marking the fall of the Wu dynasty and its replacement by the Chin.[69] Applying O. W. Wolters' thesis that embassies to the Chinese court were sent only in times of upheaval, these three embassies in the third century guaranteed continued commercial interaction between Funan and southern China under the new Chin rulers.[70] Apparently the effort was successful, for Funan did not send another embassy until 357. Fifth-century embassies reached China in 434 and again in 484, dates corresponding to the era of political transition in Funan. Since the succession to the Funan throne by the P'an P'an ruler would have taken place around the date of Funan's 434 embassy, it may be viewed as being sent by Funan's new rulers to renew the Chinese commercial relationship.[71]

Second, an inscription dated 478 issued by a Funan prince named Guṇavarman, who is believed to have been the second Kauṇḍinya's grandson, is even more telling: Guṇavarman's father, King Jayavarman (son of Kauṇḍinya) was said to have ruled over a domain "conquered in the mud." George Coedès believed that this passage symbolized the recovery of land accomplished by the draining of Mekong Delta swamps. This association fits well with the fifth- and sixth-century dates assigned to the Oc-èo area canals by Malleret. But Funan's wet-rice system clearly predated the fifth- and sixth-century dates Malleret (and Coedès) gave to the Funan irrigation system. As noted earlier, a network of tanks and canals for irrigated wet-rice cultivation was not necessary to support Funan's earliest agricultural needs—which were satisfied by broadcast cultivation—and are best seen as a product of later Funan society.[72]

In light of evidence of a fifth-century dynastic crisis, the "conquered in the mud" statement may better be understood as reflecting an actual war that took place in Funan's ricelands in the Mekong Delta. Chinese reports support this interpretation, further relating that during the mid-fifth century a Funan prince fled to the Cham kingdom known as Lin-yi, based north of the Mekong Delta on the Vietnam coast, where he ultimately became the king of the Chams. This prince has been thought to have been a second son of King Jayavarman who was forced to flee after he failed in an attempt to usurp his father's throne.[73] Chinese accounts record this second son's name as Fan Tang, employing their name for the old Funan royal clan, when the Chinese officially recognized his rule over Lin-yi in 491.[74] If Fan Tang was the son of King Jayavarman, as Coedès has proposed, the use of the Fan prefix in his name would suggest that Jayavarman and his son Guṇavarman, as well as the second Kauṇḍinya, although all taking Indian titles, were in fact regarded by the Chinese as being members of the indigenous Funan royal line.

It should be remembered that Fan Shih-man and other Funan kings had traditionally sent direct relatives to rule over conquered territories or had intermarried with the families of these territories. Thus P'an P'an in the early fifth century was likely under the rule of a kin group of the Funan royal family. P'an P'an's fifth-century rulers would therefore not have been "foreigners," but blood relatives of the line holding the Funan throne. If one accepts that there was a dynastic crisis at this time, then it is not unreasonable to believe that the P'an P'an line became the dominant lineage group in Funan's political system.

Once on the throne, the P'an P'an rulers would have begun to change the character of Funan's statecraft, as discussed above. These innovations—the use of Indian vocabulary, worship of Indian deities, and presence of "Brahman bureaucrats"—more clearly distinguished the Funan monarch from other Funan elites in the state polity. This new organization was intended to avert the factional competition for the throne that was characteristic of the earlier era. It is likely that Funan's old elites were not entirely pleased with their diminished status, however. Thus a civil war between Funan's new rulers and those of the old order could well have taken place, and Fan Tang may well have taken part. Although the new Funan line was able to retain its authority and continue to Indianize the state, under Fan Tang's leadership a rival faction might have left Funan to take refuge in Lin-yi, where they waged war "in the mud" to establish their independence from Funan.[75] In Lin-yi this rival Funan faction would have posed a continuing threat to the new rulers of Funan. The imposition of an Indianized style of rule may also have been a necessary step in distinguishing the Funan rulers from their rivals, now operating from self-imposed exile in Lin-yi.

Third, by the fourth century significant changes were taking place in the international trade route that had profound impact on Funan. As was seen in chapter 2, by the second half of the fourth century the Chin dynasty no longer had access to the central Asian caravan routes and was forced to turn its attention to the maritime route. Southeast Asian trade centers beyond the Malay Peninsula responded to Chinese initiatives, significantly Ho-lo-tan/t'o in western Java and Ko-ying in the Sunda Strait.[76] From Chinese records it is clear that both these centers were trading directly with China, rather than through Funan's intermediary ports, by the fifth century. The Isthmus of Kra portage had fallen into disuse, and ships leaving Sri Lanka and India were sailing via the Strait of Malacca directly to ports on the western edge of the Java Sea, which were closer to the source of the Indonesian archipelago spices that were beginning to find an international market.[77] One of Funan's early advantages as a commercial center was its ability—without wet-rice irrigation technology—to produce surplus rice to provision passing seamen and traders. By the time the route began to change, other Southeast Asian population centers—notably in Java—employed wet-rice drainage and irrigation techniques that allowed them to produce multiple wet-rice crops and provision the increasing numbers of passing traders.[78]

The Buddhist pilgrim Fa Hsien and the Indian prince Guṇavarman provide the first evidence that the Isthmus of Kra passage had been abandoned and Funan was being bypassed in the fifth century. Fa Hsien sailed directly from Yeh-p'o-t'i on the Borneo coast to Canton without stopping at any Funan port.[79] Guṇavarman likewise went nonstop to China from She-p'o, a trading center on the north Java coast.

Both the accounts of Fa Hsien and Guṇavarman and corresponding Chinese evidence substantiate a fifth-century transition in the maritime patterns of Asian trade. Whether this refocusing of the international trade was directly responsible for Funan's dynastic crisis is not certain, but it had profound consequences for Funan in the future. The shifting of the commercial shipping route to the Strait of Malacca and the subsequent omission of stops at Funan's ports denied the Funan rulers important revenues. Deprived of this major source of royal income, the ruler as well as his followers, including subordinate chiefs and their supporters, found their prosperity diminished. Such a decline in royal income could well have touched off a dynastic crisis as rival claimants, promoting their ability to restore Funan's prosperity, attempted to gather enough supporters to seize the throne.

Because of the shift in the trade route, diplomatic interaction between Funan and China declined. Apart from the 434 embassy, Funan's only other recorded contact with China in the fifth century took place around 484, when King Jayavarman sent a group of merchants to Canton to solicit Chinese trade. The Indian Buddhist monk Nāgasena accompanied them on their return, and then was sent back to the Chinese court to plead for Chinese aid against the Chams. Nāgasena's comments to the Chinese emperor do not reflect the existence of regular interaction between Funan and China and hint at growing instability in Funan politics. Nāgasena reported that Funan was "ceaselessly invaded by Lin-yi and has [therefore] not entered into relations with [the Red River Delta region]. That is why their embassies so seldom come."[80]

Embassies from the Chinese emperor were sent to three Indonesian coastal centers in 449 to confer titles on the rulers of these "states," but significantly, no similar action was taken by the Chinese to recognize the ruler of Funan, their old trade partner. Under normal conditions the Chinese tried to maintain established commercial relations with Southeast Asian states and did not actively seek out new ones.[81] The lack of attention to Funan implies that the Chinese fully recognized by 449 that Funan's ports were no longer the most important source of international trade but had been replaced as the dominant force in Southeast Asian commerce by Java Sea entrepôts.

In 491, the Chinese court bestowed an important title upon Fan Tang, ruler of Lin-yi, proclaiming him "General Pacifier of the South, Commander-in-Chief of the Military Affairs of the Seashore, and King of Lin-yi."[82] This, coming after Nāgasena's 484 appeal on Funan's behalf for Chinese aid against the Chams, reflects the low opinion the Chinese had of Funan at that time, and when considered in light of the 449 initiatives indicates that, to China, Lin-yi had become the more important trade ally by the late fifth century. It should be remembered that when Guṇavarman traveled from the Javanese entrepôt of She-p'o to China in the mid-fifth century his ship was originally to have made an intermediate stop on the Cham coast, not at Funan (see chap. 2). This may mean that calling in a Cham port had become routine in the voyage between Java Sea centers and China. The title bestowed upon Fan Tang put more emphasis on Fan Tang's role as protector of the Cham seacoast than on his role as Lin-yi's monarch. In his report to the Chinese emperor Nāgasena related that he had been shipwrecked on the Cham coast, where his possessions had been stolen. The fact of his reporting the theft to the Chinese court and the Chinese investiture of Fan Tang as "Commander of the Seashore" show that Fan Tang was now held responsible for curtailing acts of piracy on the lower Vietnam coast.

The 430 petition of Ho-lo-tan/t'o to the Chinese court seeking protection for its ships sailing from the western Javanese coast to China provides more evidence of Funan's diminished status along the trade routes. Following a route similar to that from She-p'o, voyagers from Java to China, to avoid the navigational hazards associated with the Paracel reefs south of Hainan Island, sailed within range of the Cham coast of lower Vietnam.[83] Here, it would seem, fifth-century Javanese shipping was threatened by piracy. This piracy was either the result of Funan's attempts to retain its control over the maritime channels by forcing ships to utilize its ports as intermediaries or because Funan's decline as a major commercial center had forced its Malay maritime colony to resort to piracy. Perhaps Funan's loss of revenue meant that it could no longer pay enough to Malay sailors, for whom piracy proved more lucrative.

Fan Tang's investiture by the Chinese court may be seen as a response to the instabilities precipitated by Funan's impending commercial demise.[84] The Chinese interest in Southeast Asia was clearly to keep the flow of goods moving into south China's ports. Despite the fact that throughout the third and fourth centuries Lin-yi had, with Funan's aid, continually harassed the Chinese Ton-king (Chiao-chi) province in the Red River Delta to the north, the Chinese emperor in 491 found himself able to overlook this past misbehavior and resulting inconvenience when bestowing the "Commander" title upon Fan Tang.[85]

It is thus apparent that by the mid-fifth century Funan was no longer a major trade center. One further likely consequence of Funan's commercial demise was the shift of the seagoing population in its ports to more prosperous Cham ports. By 431, Lin-yi's ruler was capable of pulling together a force of over one hundred ships to pillage the northern Vietnam coast.[86] When Fan Tang and his faction from Funan took control of Lin-yi, this relocation of population was given further impetus. Fan Tang, by maintaining the old style of Funan statecraft in Lin-yi, at least initially, established a certain amount of continuity in the relationship of his state and the sea trade. Significantly, Fan Tang's move to the Cham domain and the growth of Lin-yi's maritime prominence coincide in Chinese eyes, making this reconstruction plausible.

Thus, while Funan was more concerned with reorganizing its internal administrative structure at this time, in part due to the loss of its dominance over trade, Lin-yi's ports were in the meantime becoming more involved as intermediaries in the trade. When in the latter half of the fifth century Funan's ruler was trying to reattract traders to his ports, Lin-yi's ports had already assumed a strong commercial position on the southern Vietnam coast as a result of their more strategic geographical proximity to the now restructured international maritime route that went through the western part of the Java Sea before turning northward toward China. This fact was acknowledged by the Chinese in their 491 eulogy of Fan Tang.

The Demise of Funan

The failure of Funan's attempt to reclaim a significant role in the international trade—including the ill-fated 484 appeal to the Chinese—marked the collapse of Funan as a major international entrepôt. Funan's vassals began to break away and establish their own independent identities as centers of trade. Not only the Chams, but numerous river valley centers on the Malay Peninsula coast began sending tribute missions to the Chinese court in order to solicit favorable trade relationships with the Chinese.

Without the prosperity of the previous age, Funan rulers withdrew their civilization inland, concentrating their rule in the ricelands of the upper Mekong Delta. The virtual elimination of trade-derived revenues forced them to internalize to better maximize revenue collections from their agrarian economic base. Concomitantly, Funan statecraft took on a more Indian character. The Indian pattern of statecraft, with its focus on the land, was more effective in dealing with the economic situation Funan found itself in.[87] It may be that when the new Funan rulers "changed all the rules according to the custom of India," it was in response to political and economic expediency.

Prior to the era of political transition in Funan, a ruler's capacity to extract revenues from rural clan and tribal subordinates had been constrained by the basic premise of Funan statecraft—reciprocal alliance—which was inherently unstable. The court's limited revenue demands on its agrarian sector were also due to the fact that Funan ports produced sufficient revenues to allow ample redistributions to loyal supporters as well as to finance the royal court and its projects. In light of the need in the fifth century to depend more on the agrarian sector for revenues, it is significant that the archaeological evidence of Funan's hydraulic projects has been dated to exactly this period, when expansion of the state's agrarian base beyond earlier wet-rice system development became critical. As noted earlier, the hydraulic projects would have indeed made possible both the expansion of Funan's agrarian sector and the concentration of manpower on lands under the direct authority of Funan's rulers and thereby allowed the production of an even greater rice surplus.

Indian celestial deities provided the sacro-religious legitimacy that Funan's rulers required. Funan monarch worshiped the Śiva-*liṅga* Maheśvara and stressed the *liṅga* as the source of the land's fertility, although this was in effect a synthesis with existing fertility and ancestor cults, thus giving indigenous beliefs legitimacy and more clearly focusing the local fertility and ancestor cults on the monarch. By this time, the Funan monarch was known in inscriptions as the "king of Vyādhapura,"[88] who personally received benefits of the god Maheśvara's power, which he then bestowed on the entire population. The king, also the patron of knowledge, promoted Indian intellectual discourse as his court became the cultural and intellectual center of his realm. The king was the personal benefactor of a number of "Brahmans," who conducted Indian rituals, and he called on "Indians," those who had become students of Indian civilization, to assist him in the efficient administration of the royal court and the ricelands that by the end of the fifth century provided most of the court's income. This intellectual elite's prominence was also due to their ability to read and write Sanskrit, which allowed them to serve as an administrative elite in the ruler's developing court bureaucracy.[89]

By the sixth-century reign of Rudravarman (514–539), the capital had been moved from Vyādhapura to Angkor Borei. The nearby mountain of Phnom Da became the locus of Rudravarman's worship of Viṣṇu and seems to have replaced the Śiva-focused Ba Phnom as the sacred center of the Funan realm. This may have been the result of a succession dispute. Chinese records describe Rudravarman as a usurper, born of a concubine, who after the death of his father King Jayavarman murdered the rightful heir, Guṇavarman, and seized the Funan throne.[90] As a usurper, Rudravarman might well have refocused the Funan cults of legitimacy on Viṣṇu.[91]

Ultimately, the effort to reorganize the state did not succeed, however. By the mid-sixth century Funan was severely weakened by internal power struggles. Recognizing Funan's internal crisis, its neighbors applied increasing pressure. The Chams moved to fill the power void in the lower

Mekong Delta and the peoples of the Khmer domain known to the Chinese as Chen-la began to move against Funan from modern Thailand and Cambodia to the north.[92] As a result in part of Lin-yi's preoccupation with petty wars against its northern Red River Delta neighbors, the Funan domain was ultimately conquered by Chen-la. The Khmers were thus responsible for the final demise of Funan, either destroying or failing to maintain its hydraulic networks. Funan's lands were depopulated as cultivators shifted their labor to more productive and secure lands. What remained of the agrarian population moved either by choice or by force to the Khmer rulers' developing economic base in the Tonle Sap area to the north. Largely depopulated, the hydraulic system laid to waste, and no longer subject to administrative supervision and financial support from a central authority, Funan's ricelands quickly reverted to swamp and jungle.[93] The former Funan Mekong Delta domain declined as the centers of Cham and Khmer authority became the focal points for civilization on the mainland, the Chams controlling the southern Vietnam coast and the Khmers building a great agrarian civilization at Angkor.

Both these peoples traced their lineage to Funan and based their evolving polity on the Indianized patterns of statecraft developed by Funan rulers. While Funan rulers had begun to bridge the gap between tribal politics and Indianized statecraft, it remained for the Chams and especially the Khmers to develop the mainland Southeast Asian classical state to its fullest.

4

Trade and Statecraft in Early Śrīvijaya

With the decline of Funan, the Chinese sought to establish commercial relationships with other Southeast Asian entrepôts capable of maintaining the flow of East-West trade. As was noted previously, early Southeast Asian trade centers were responsive to the fluctuations of the international markets, especially those of China. The opening and closing of Chinese markets constituted a "rhythm of trade" that is reflected as well in the pattern of tribute missions sent to the Chinese court from Southeast Asia.[1] Frequent missions from many states represented times of political and economic competition during which states solicited Chinese patronage. Few missions indicated periods of relative stability—that is, the Chinese recognized one state that dominated others. In times when China was particularly interested in the trade—when Canton came under the control of a new, stable imperial government—various Southeast Asian centers attempted to become the dominant entrepôt of the region. One such state to emerge was Śrīvijaya.

The state of Śrīvijaya dominated maritime commerce passing through Southeast Asia between A.D. 670 and 1025. In the fifth century when the international trade route shifted to a sea passage through the Strait of Malacca and Funan lost its strategic position, a number of new commercial centers had arisen on the southeastern Sumatra and northwestern Java coasts to take advantage of the trade. Śrīvijaya was able to gain control of the seas in the strait region, put down piracy and competition, establish a cosmopolitan center on the southeast coast of Sumatra, and attract the support and patronage of China. Chinese trade with the Malay Peninsula and beyond came to be focused on Śrīvijaya's ports, and the principal peninsula entrepôts of earlier East-West trade became secondary and were brought into the sphere of Śrīvijayan control.[2] The ports of Śrīvijaya furnished supplies, local products, Chinese and Western goods, storage facilities, and living accommodations for passing traders waiting out the monsoon season.

The name "Śrīvijaya" came to enjoy a certain prestige in Chinese and Indian markets; to trade in China, a merchant would wish to deal in the name of the Śrīvijaya ruler. Using this prestige, Śrīvijaya was able to build an empire by blending the naval power and commercial skill of coastal ports with the land-force potential of the interior populations. As opposed to other ancient ports of trade that were politically and economically peripheral to land-based empires, the Śrīvijaya state was equally dependent on its ability to organize hinterland trade and local contact with international traders. In return the local communities of this hinterland and coast reaped such benefits as subsidized religious ceremonies, social pageantry, and wars (which brought the promise of booty), as well as the underwriting of the construction of public and religious edifices.

Śrīvijaya was once thought of as a "federation of trading ports on the fringe of large areas of forest, . . . not a state with territorial boundaries, but a series of interlocked human relationships among harbor principalities and pirate lairs based on patronage, loyalty, and power."[3] According to this reconstruction there were three zones of dependencies: the Malay Peninsula, where Śrīvijaya's dominance was not continuous; the north and the northeast coasts of Sumatra, which supplied raw materials for international trade; and the east coast and island area near Palembang in southeastern Sumatra, which became the heartland of the state's power. This heartland was supported by a group of seminomadic Malay seamen whose power was measured in the number of ships under their control. It was believed that a Southeast Asian harbor area such as Palembang could have—with the support of these Malay seamen—established autonomy within its own domain and then spread its influence outward along the seacoast to encompass other similarly structured harbor ports. Surrounding the developing port zones were tribal peoples of the interior who supplied the ports with raw materials but were in general feared. For example, the central Sumatran port of Jambi did not attempt to collect taxes from the population outside its own town boundaries.[4] In this analysis such ports had no need for an agrarian base. The local ruler looked elsewhere for his revenues—essentially to the sea.

An emphasis on the maritime aspect of Śrīvijaya, while in the main correct, tends to neglect the important relationship between the Śrīvijaya ports and their hinterland. For instance, the Kedukan Bukit inscription found near Palembang reports that on 23 April, A.D. 683, the king of Śrīvijaya embarked in a boat to go on a *siddhayātrā* (a quest for supernatural prowess), and that on 19 May he conducted an army from one place and arrived at another. This army consisted of about two hundred sailors and two thousand foot soldiers and was said to have the potential to reach twenty thousand in strength.[5] Since so large a force of fighters must have been recruited from a land-based population rather than from port-based seamen (who contributed two hundred sailors), this inscription does not indicate a lack of interaction between the port city and its hinterland, but rather the opposite.

Limited archaeological research conducted in the Palembang area as well as in its river estuaries provides evidence of a Śrīvijaya hinterland from which such troops could have been recruited.[6] Remains from the Śrīvijaya period indicate that Śrīvijaya's culture penetrated deeply into the interior not only along the rivers that flowed to its capital at Palembang, a downriver rather than a seacoast port, but also along those that flowed through other contemporary downriver and seacoast commercial centers on the island of Sumatra, the Malay Peninsula coast opposite it, and the numerous islands that lay between.[7]

Both Arab and Chinese documents record that Śrīvijaya was the source of forest products and aromatics, yet its principal ports on the southeastern Sumatra coast were not strategically located to exercise direct control over the source of these rich natural resources from north and central Sumatra.[8] These products were important enough to the international commercial community, however, that the center of trade would have shifted to other ports in central and northern Sumatra if Śrīvijaya had failed to supply the demand. By neglecting to examine Śrīvijaya's relationship to its hinterland, historians have left the impression that there were no formal political alliances that generated the flow of products to Śrīvijaya's ports. Yet the nature of the trade required a regular, ongoing relationship with the hinterland to allow goods from the interior to reach the ports. Foreign sources are generally ambiguous when describing the Sumatra interior, suggesting that visiting merchants did not make direct contact with this area. Thus it may be assumed that goods flowed into Śrīvijaya's ports either as part of a tribute system in which subordinate chiefs were required to supply the Śrīvijaya ports with marketable commodities or that Śrīvijaya came to control an indigenous trade network in which people of the interior exchanged forest products they had collected for the imported goods that were available in coastal ports.

There are two primary sources for the study of early Śrīvijaya statecraft. One is an extremely generalized Arab account of the redistribution of gold bars dredged from the Palembang harbor at the death of a *mahārāja*.[9] The Arab geographers Ibn Khurdādhbih (writing in 846) and Abū Zaid (writing in 916) both spoke of the custom of Śrīvijaya *mahārājas* communicating with the sea.[10] Daily, the *mahārāja* propitiated the ocean by throwing a gold brick into the water, saying, "Look, there lies my treasure," and thereby demonstrating his debt to the sea. The greatness of a deceased king was measured by the number of gold bars retrieved from the water. These were divided first among the royal family, then among the military commanders, and what remained were given to the king's other subjects. While providing little elaboration of these "class" distinctions, the Arab account is consistent with the second of the primary sources—the various epigraphic records left by Śrīvijaya rulers.

The inscriptions left by the Śrīvijaya state, most of which have come from the late seventh-century period, are the second major source. Among these the majority have been recovered from the Palembang area (see map 4). The earliest of the dated Old Malay inscriptions, the Kedukan Bukit (683) and Talang Tua (684) inscriptions, as well as two epigraphic fragments, were discovered near Bukit Seguntang—the highest point in the area—on the southern edge of the present-day city of Palembang.[11] A second group of inscriptions was collected north of the city at Sabokingking. These include the Telaga Batu inscription (ca. 686), the most detailed among the late seventh-century Old Malay inscriptions, and three contemporary epigraphic fragments.[12] Edited versions of the Telaga Batu inscription have also been found at Kotakapur on the island of Bangka, off the east coast of Sumatra, Karangbrahi on the Batang Hari River system (upriver from modern Jambi), and Palas Pasemah on the southeastern Sumatra coast adjacent the Sunda Strait.[13] In addition to these late seventh-century records, a Śrīvijaya inscription was found on the Karimum Besar Island in the Riau Archipelago in the Strait of Malacca, and there are two inscriptions from Nakhọn Si Thammarat on the east coast of the Malay Peninsula, one dated 775 that records the dedication of a Buddhist monastery by the Śrīvijaya monarch.[14]

The Telaga Batu inscription has served as the main source for the analysis of Śrīvijaya's government. J. G. de Casparis provided a complete and accurate translation of the Telaga Batu inscription but stopped short of using it to speculate on the system of statecraft established by Śrīvijaya's early rulers or the similarities between this system and the indigenous pattern of Sumatran culture.[15] The discussion of early Śrīvijayan history that follows will explore the possibilities of such an analysis of this and other Śrīvijayan inscriptions.

The Śrīvijaya Monarch as a Traditional Chief

It is useful to approach the ruler of Śrīvijaya as a product of his own culture, that is, as a Malay *dātu* or chief. In the earliest period of Śrīvijaya's

THE DISTRIBUTION OF
SEVENTH-CENTURY INSCRIPTIONS
AT PALEMBANG

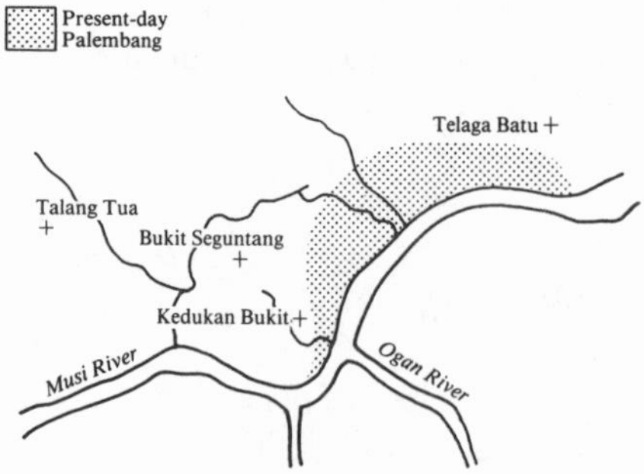

history the ruler was an important chief who was able to forge alliances with other Sumatra chiefs, which allowed him to expand his state. On the everyday level, as indicated in the Telaga Batu inscription, the Śrīvijaya monarch fulfilled certain functions expected of a chief: he was a judge, he collected revenues, and he received the services of those subject to his authority. The traditional avenues to power and legitimacy were thus available to him.

In the seventh century, Buddhism was grafted onto traditional Sumatran terminology. Traditional values such as references to mountains, oaths, and a cult of dead chiefs were integrated with Buddhist religious symbols and thought. The adoption of Buddhism was useful in international relations, but Buddhism also allowed the Śrīvijaya monarch to establish and enhance his legitimacy within his own system. Syncretic royal ideology was diffused to the various levels of society as the king's subjects were given a new blend of magical beliefs and rites.

The inscriptions testify to the ability of the Śrīvijayan kings to synthesize indigenous cultural symbols with new systems of legitimacy derived from Indian and Buddhist sources. An example of Buddhist piety is reflected in the seventh-century Talang Tua inscription recording the dedication of a public park. In this inscription the sovereign expressed his desire that the merit gained by the deed and all his other good works should be shared with all creatures and should bring them closer to enlightenment. The Ligor Plate inscription of 775, with its record of the dedication of a monastery near Nakhọn Si Thammarat to the Buddha and to the Bodhisattvas Padmapāni and Vajrapāni, refers to the Śrīvijaya king as "the patron of the *nāga*s, their heads halved by the streaks of the lustre of gems."[16] A similar association can be seen in the Telaga Batu inscription, which is carved on a large Buddhist ceremonial stone, the upper edge of which is canopied by the heads of seven serpents (*nāga*s). Since the seven-headed *nāga* is a well-known symbol in Indian iconography it could well be argued that in this instance a wholesale borrowing of an Indic image had taken place and that it had become an important part of the Śrīvijaya system of statecraft. But surviving local oral tradition indicates that the seven-headed *nāga* of Indic tradition fit with indigenous patterns of belief.[17] It can thus be taken as evidence that the Śrīvijaya king was syncretizing local and foreign patterns in creating his own royal style.

In the Kedukan Bukit inscription we see the Śrīvijaya ruler consolidating his state and at the same time fulfilling the traditional Sumatran role of war chief. In the Śrīvijaya expedition against the rival riverine center of Malāyu, for which he had allied himself with surrounding chiefs to form a military force with a potential of twenty thousand soldiers, the king led at least two thousand into battle, establishing hegemony over the manpower of the Batang Hari River network and forcing it into submission.[18] Having proven his worth by ordeal by seeking *siddhayātrā*—a military quest for the mythical supernatural prowess of the enlightened Buddhist ruler that is also mentioned in the Kedukan Bukit inscription—the Śrīvijaya monarch was able to assume legitimately the traditional role of a Sumatra war chief. This also allowed him to exercise considerable influence over peacetime politics. The Malāyu expedition may thus be seen as a quest for symbolic legitimacy as well as a campaign undertaken out of the necessity to impose control over a rival port.

A consistent theme of the Śrīvijaya inscriptions is that the monarch was responsible for the common prosperity, or lack of it, for all his subjects. The ruler was not only royal but also rich. Continuing prosperity protected his right to rule. This theme is projected in the Telaga Batu inscription as the notion of ripening fruit. Acts against the king were *tālu (tālu muah),* "subject to punishment."[19] The sense implied is that if the proper code of conduct were not observed the empire would "not reach its perfect state."[20] In the Kotakapur version the king warns: "to them [who plan revolts] the fruits of the sins contained in their wicked deeds will be turned."[21] To those who followed the king were promised prosperity for the future: *vṛddhi* ("growth, prosperity"), *subhikṣa* ("prosperity"), *siddha* ("arriving at a perfect state"), and *sānti* ("eternal quietude of Nirvāṇa").[22] The Telaga Batu inscription also promised the secret Buddhist formula of final liberation from the cycle of rebirths, *tantrāmala,* to faithful subjects.[23]

Another Palembang inscription announces a curse against all those guilty of the Buddhist prohibitions against love of self, anger, and greed —*kāma, krodha,* and *lobha*.[24] Those who disturbed the system by indulging in these vices would be swallowed by a big river that was controlled by the Śrīvijaya king. The inscription also speaks of a battle in which the blood of the people ran red in the waters or soil near this river. The implication is that in the Śrīvijaya heartland the king held a magical control over the waters of the Musi River or some other principal river. A folktale from the Palembang region records that the origin of local civilization occurred when the water of the various rivers was weighed and a settlement was established where the water was the heaviest.[25] The legend represents the practical notion that the people searched for fertile lands where the silt content of the water was right for wet-rice cultivation. It is interesting that the legend's emphasis is on the sanctity of water; such sanctity is consistent with the use of a water oath in the Telaga Batu inscription to pledge the loyalty of the king's subordinates.

The Kotakapur version of the Telaga Batu inscription in Bangka invoked two gods: *Ulu,* Old Malay for "high" and "mountain," conveying the traditional Southeast Asian perception of the holiness of mountains; and *Tandru n Luah,* "the God of the Waters of the Sea," to guarantee the loyalty of Bangka's population.[26] The Śrīvijaya king's association with these two indigenous gods may well be the basis of references to the titles "Lord of the Mountain" and "*Mahārāja* of the Isles" in Arab accounts of Śrīvijaya. The connection of the Śrīvijaya monarch with the magical properties of water was also mentioned by Arab observers. They particularly noted that the Śrīvijaya *mahārāja* had bewitched the crocodiles of his river to allow safe navigation to his estuary.[27] The Arab geographers' tale of the daily propitiation of the estuary with gold bricks is part of this same association of magical power over the water with the king. A similar tradition was preserved into the nineteenth century among the people of Lampong in southern Sumatra. As reported in an early nineteenth-century ethnography, "The Island people of that country are said to pay a kind of adoration to the sea, and make it offerings . . . deprecating its power of doing them mischief."[28]

The Śrīvijaya king's prowess was also considered responsible for the agricultural prosperity of his domain. Abū Zaid remarked in the tenth century that the "Mahārāja's island is extremely fertile . . . things always grow there."[29] Chao Ju-kua, an early thirteenth-century south China port official, related that the Śrīvijaya king could not eat grain on a specific day of the year. If he did, the year would be dry and the grain dear. It is also reported that the king could bathe only in rose-water; were he to bathe in ordinary water a great flood would engulf the fields of his subjects.[30] In the Talang Tua inscription (684), the king expressed his concern "that all the clearances and gardens made by them [his subjects] should be full [of crops]. That the cattle of all species raised by them and the slaves they possess should prosper . . . that all their servants shall be faithful and devoted to them . . . that, wherever they may find themselves, there be in that place no thieves, no ruffians, no assassins and no adulterers . . . that there arise among them the thought of Bodhi and the love of the Three Jewels."[31] Another Śrīvijaya inscription associates the king with the sun.[32] This inscription indicates that the rays of the sun, so vital to crop growth, were obscured when the king was away.[33]

Śrīvijaya was clearly a center of economic redistribution. One key to the successful operation of its economic network was the king's ability to acquire a share of customs duties and trade profits collected at his subordinate ports.[34] A Cōḷa inscription from Tañjāvūr in south India dated 1030–1031 describes thirteen Southeast Asian ports conquered by the eleventh-century naval expedition of Rājēndra Cōḷa I, all of which are considered by historians to have been subordinate to Śrīvijayan authority.[35] Of those thirteen, eight were mentioned for their military strength, while only Śrīvijaya-Palembang was noted for its "golden gates" and royal treasury filled with gold. The Telaga Batu inscription makes specific reference to "a treasury of gold and property" that was situated at the center of the Śrīvijaya royal court *(kraton).*[36] The practical role of the king as dispenser of material wealth as well as his role as the source of moral and spiritual benefit was reinforced by the mystical legend surrounding this central treasury, which was closely guarded from outsiders. The inscription mentions the efforts of the king's enemies to secure information on the location of the gold and jewels kept in the treasury. If the treasury were robbed, the inscription warns, a curse would fall upon the district governors *(dātu).* The implication is that if the treasure were stolen the entire state would crumble; the stolen treasure might be spent by the king's enemies to recruit mercenaries and to destroy the *kraton.*[37]

According to the account of Abū Zaid, the treasury's wealth was normally shared by all the citizens of the king. Arab sources identify the *mahārāja* as being responsible, through the prosperity of trade, for the welfare of his subjects. Commercial revenues converged at the capital and were redistributed to the loyal following, including local land-based chiefs as well as Malay seamen allied with the king. Alliances with local chiefs formalized by charters guaranteed the safe passage of goods in different segments of the trade network. In return the local chiefs received a guaranteed income. The "privilege" of protecting trade was granted to a favored chief. The system depended on a strong central ruler to enforce personal loyalties as well as to prevent jealousy on the part of those chiefs not favored. As the central government had a vested interest in local markets, loyal subordinate chiefs had a vested interest in preserving the central entrepôt as the source of their common prosperity. The Śrīvijaya chief was their common banker. His wealth was shared with his "family" of subjects.[38]

As the holder of his subjects' prosperity the Śrīvijaya chief was the focus of a cult of veneration. Śrīvijaya statuary and remains have been found bearing the sculpted images of the faces of kings. The statues also bore inscriptions warning future generations not to deface them.[39] The Telaga Batu inscription indicates that such a personality cult was an important part of the king's legitimacy and an attempt by the Śrīvijaya rulers to establish a sense of ancestral continuity, possibly utilizing the existing custom of venerating dead chiefs. Reference is made to *rūpinaṅku,* "my picture," meaning the material image of the king or something attributable to the king that was used for magical purposes. The same type of exclusive reference is made earlier in the inscription when it is suggested that rebels placed special emphasis on destroying the per-

Sanskrit rock inscription, Sumatra.

The Telaga Batu inscribed stone with seven-headed *nāga* canopy, Sumatra.

Avalokiteśvara, the Bodhisattva of Compassion. Early Śrīvijaya era, Palembang, Sumatra.

sonal orders of the king, thereby symbolically destroying the king's magical powers and replacing them with their own. "Making people crazy" was part of this plot.

Despite his positive attributes—although the Śrīvijaya king was a military hero, a traditional chief, and the upholder of common prosperity—he still faced the problem of political fragmentation, which appears to have been prevalent in the area. Chao Ju-kua's thirteenth-century account provides a hint of the divisive tendencies that plagued Śrīvijaya:

> When they (the people of Śrīvijaya) are about to make war on another state they assemble and send a force as the occasion demands. They then appoint chiefs and leaders, and all provide their own military equipment and the necessary provisions.[40]

In Sumatra the elements of discord and division were contained in the concept of chieftainship. There was traditional reliance on alliances for political union, which caused an inherent instability since alliances could and would be broken and depended so much on a ruler's personal prowess. If indeed political union, as Chao Ju-kua reports, normally took place only in times of emergency, how then did the Śrīvijaya monarch maintain control over his broad domain?

One means the Śrīvijaya monarch ritually employed was the act of "oath taking." The Telaga Batu inscription, as noted earlier, is carved on a Buddhist ceremonial stone with a canopy of seven *nāga* heads; the water oath is recorded on this stone (page 87). A funnel below the text drained off the water that was poured over the stone during ceremonies. One is told of the sacred function of the oath in the first line of the inscription; a traditional Malay magic formula and the magical Buddhist invocation *"Om"* are given, followed by the oath itself.[41] The same oath is given in the Kotakapur, Karangbrahi, and Palas Pasemah inscriptions.

Taking the oath symbolized one's allegiance to the Śrīvijaya monarch. "If you embellish this curse on this stone, whether you are of low, middle or high descent," warned the text, you would be struck down with calamity for being disloyal to the ruler. It is implied that the water the oath-taker drank had magical properties that could visit some unnamed horror on the disloyal, such as the rotting out of the insides of the offender or eternal damnation in hell. While to the unfaithful was promised more than death alone, the curse promised rewards, such as the secret formula for final liberation *(tantrā-mala),* to faithful subjects:

> If you [execute these disloyal] actions, you will be killed by this curse which is drunk by you. However, if you are submissive, faithful (and)

> straight to me and do not commit these crimes, an immaculate *tantrā* will be my recompense. You will not be swallowed with your children and wives.[42]

This reference to being swallowed may refer to the *nāga*s sculpted on the head of the stone, which might devour those who betrayed the oath. That this was one possible consequence of disloyalty is indicated by the Arab geographer Ibn Khurdādhbih, who commented that in the mountains of the *mahārāja* of Zābaj (Śrīvijaya) there were snakes that devoured men.[43] Being "swallowed by the water" in a Palembang inscription also represented the threat of the death one could expect for being unfaithful.[44] One scholar believes that the first two lines of the Telaga Batu inscription that are written in a so-far unidentified Austronesian language seem to include an appeal to the "spirit of the waters," who was the guardian of the oath and whose support was the ultimate source of the Śrīvijaya monarch's legitimacy.[45]

The Telaga Batu oath is not alone in its use of magical imprecations as a means of protection. Key words in the localized Buddhist tantric lexicon are revealed in the Talang Tua inscription (684). In the view of O. W. Wolters, the tantric tradition provided Śrīvijaya with "an armory of magical formulae" that blended well with local tutelary spirits.[46] Wolters especially notes numerous Chinese records reporting the importance in Śrīvijaya of a tantric text known as the "Peacock" *sūtra*. This Indian text honors a powerful spiritual force that is represented as a peacock and offers its devotees numerous formulas for protection against dangers. Interestingly in light of the Telaga Batu inscription's curse, the "Peacock" *sūtra* was commonly invoked in India at oath-taking ceremonies and in courts of law to make witnesses tell the truth. I-ching, the Chinese monk who visited Śrīvijaya in the second half of the seventh century and recommended that all Buddhist pilgrims from China ought to spend time studying there prior to their departure for India, translated from Sanskrit into Chinese a "Peacock" *sūtra* text that he had acquired in Śrīvijaya.[47]

Thus, the ultimate response to the divisive tendencies to be found in the local concept of chieftainship was the appeal to the Śrīvijaya blend of indigenous and Indic supernatural powers, which culminated in the symbolic act of oath taking. This water oath was taken by the state elite and other individuals who were likely to have had personal contact with the monarch and who are enumerated in the Telaga Batu inscription (and will be discussed below): the king's personal bondsmen, members of the royal household, and those state personnel who administered the realm and voluntarily took the oath prior to assuming their posts to secure their obedience to the ruler; and various subordinate chiefs of the hinterland, other coastal centers, and former rivals conquered by force who were required to render homage.[48]

Śrīvijaya in its patronage of Buddhism imposed a new religious system that was primarily intended to impress upon the hinterland populations that the royal ideology was superior to traditional systems of belief. Buddhism, then, became a useful means to awe the hinterland population into submission. Indigenous symbols such as water, snakes, and mountains were incorporated into the oath-taking ceremony, which ended with the sharing of a Buddhist *tantrā-mala,* guaranteeing prosperity and security as long as the participant adhered to the terms of the oath. In effect this was an act of subjugation: by taking the water oath a local elite accommodated its functional roles and structural organization to the demands of the state. Threats of dire magical consequences, when backed by the real threat of military power, were sufficient to convince a local elite that the new system was beneficial.

As such the military campaign against Malāyu, the strongest of Śrīvijaya's riverine system opponents, was the single most important factor giving Śrīvijaya the authority to administer the water oath. Victory over Malāyu made good the Śrīvijaya king's claim to *siddhayātrā* and thereby focused attention on him as the stabilizer of both the cosmic and mundane worlds. As he had done previously in developing alliances with Malay seamen and upriver tribes who formed the core of his military strength, the Śrīvijaya ruler extended assurances of the great wealth and glory to be had under his rule to the established elites of other coastal centers in the Strait of Malacca region, offering them a continuing although subordinate role in the developing maritime state.[49]

Srīvijaya's State Structure

Early Śrīvijaya statecraft reflected the Malay riverine culture from which it arose, although it was not until the mid-seventh century, when inscriptions record the rise of Śrīvijaya, that this culture generated a classical Southeast Asian state. The major reason was the tendency toward political fragmentation. The divisive nature of Malay society was recognized in ancient Malay myth. One myth records, for example, that when a boatload of Malays reached land they would almost immediately split into factions.[50] Malays based in the Strait of Malacca region were members of small socioeconomic units and needed some new principle of organization to generate an entity as politically sophisticated as a state.

The Telaga Batu inscription suggests how this came to be in the case of the earliest Malay riverine state.

At the center of the Śrīvijaya state was the king, who personally addressed the Telaga Batu inscription to all those under his command. It is significant that the text of this inscription is directed in the first person to the king's servants, as opposed to the Kotakapur, Karangbrahi, and Palas Pasemah inscriptions, which instead implore a divine force to carry out the necessary punishments on those subordinates of the king who revolt against the state. The differences in the texts of these inscriptions indicate that near the center of the Śrīvijaya king's domain his power was unquestioned, while in the state's upriver and coastal hinterland the king was forced to emphasize the more theoretical and mythical aspects of his kingship because his power was less direct.

The Telaga Batu inscription first outlines the structure of authority in the core of the Śrīvijayan state. Here the king was surrounded by his kinsmen and his close associates. Immediately below the king in importance was the crown prince, the *yuvarāja;* the prince next in the line of succession was the *pratiyuvarāja;* then came the other princes of the royal family, the *rājakumāra*. These three princely ranks were distinct from that of the *rājaputra,* "sons of kings born of lower queens."[51] In establishing a state hierarchy, as this inscription seems to be doing, the fact that the *rājaputra* were regarded as being of inferior status in relation both to the king's other sons and to the royal family is very important. The stipulated hierarchy of the inscription would have permitted succession to the throne by the king's legitimate sons but not by the *rājaputra*.

Surrounding the royal family and at the heart of the central administration were the various royal officials named in the text. Highest in status among this group were the *dandanāyaka,* royal judges who exercised the king's power of adjudication. Next were the *nāyaka* and *pratyaya,* considered to have been two categories of administrators.[52] *Nāyaka* were revenue collectors, while *pratyaya* managed the landed property of the royal family. It is interesting that *pratyaya* appears in compound with *hāji,* "the king," as *hājipratyaya*. This term distinguished a confidant of the king, meaning that the *pratyaya* were in personal contact with the king and were very important members of the king's administrative staff.[53] If this assignment of their function is correct, then the Śrīvijaya monarch derived a notable amount of his revenue from some landed base.

At the time of this inscription, when Śrīvijaya was consolidating its power, it is unlikely that revenues derived from the state's control over the China trade could have sustained the monarchy. The titles of administrative office listed in the Telaga Batu inscription indicate that the Śrīvijaya king was initially able to formulate his legitimacy by drawing upon the indigenous resource base under his control, and then he added to this material and symbolic resource pool as Śrīvijaya expanded its hegemony over the rival centers of power on the Sumatra coast and in the strait region. The Śrīvijaya ruler's local economic base was populated by the *hulun hāji,* personal bondsmen of the king as defined by the inscription, who were controlled by their own local chiefs, *mūrdhaka.*[54]

The Telaga Batu inscription divided the king's subjects into two categories: nonelite were "slaves" *(hulun)* and the elite were "lords" *(tuhan).* As chief of a regional unit, the Śrīvijaya monarch would have expected the multiple services a Sumatran subject was customarily obliged to give his local chief. Consistent with traditional practice, in addition to providing labor and revenues to their chief the chief's followers also served as the nucleus of his army. Reference to the core of the Śrīvijaya monarch's nonelite supporters as *hulun*—slaves—implies that there was a greater than normal expectation of commitment than would have been the case in a more typical chief-subject relationship. "Slavery" in this instance is better thought of as a bondage of personal service owed to one's lord, in this case the Śrīvijaya monarch. In early Southeast Asia such bondage normally resulted from debt foreclosure, purchase, alliance, or capture in war.[55] That the expectations of loyalty from these royal bondsmen was greater than that of nonbondsmen is reflected by the focus of the Telaga Batu inscription's curse on the king's nonbondsmen elite, who needed to have a more abstract threat held over them. While in times of peace these personal bondsmen of the king would have provided labor services and shared their production with their "chief," in times of war *hulun hāji* troops would have fought beside various professional and mercenary troops, all contributing to the success of the Śrīvijaya monarch.

Other officials of the center included: *kumārāmatya,* "ministers not of royal blood"; *kāyasatha,* "clerks"; and *sthāpaka,* the "priests" or technical supervisors for the erection of divine images and the construction of buildings who directed rather than actually worked on these projects. In contemporary Javanese epigraphy *sthāpaka* assumed important roles in royal inauguration ceremonies. One may therefore assume that these were "Brahman" advisors, religious specialists who advised the king in the Indian method of construction and in the proper routine for performing religious ceremony—particularly that of installation.

Indian ritual was important in the Śrīvijaya monarch's attempts to consolidate his rule; the systematic incorporation of Indian cosmology promoted his legitimacy. By assigning Sanskritic titles to all those who were subordinates to the king, the Telaga Batu inscription documents the Sanskritization process taking place as the Indic culture provided a certain unity and prestige to the new system of statecraft that was emerging in Śrīvijaya. The educational backgrounds and training of the "Brahman" religious specialists allowed them to assume useful roles as clerks or technical advisors to the Śrīvijaya ruler, and they helped to legitimize the rule of this superior "chief" in his quest to distinguish himself from other traditional Sumatran chiefs.[56]

The ascent of Śrīvijaya in the seventh century was in part the consequence of a challenge by Malāyu (the Batang Hari River system) to the earlier southeast Sumatra-based entrepôt of Kan-t'o-li, which had been the dominant port in this part of the strait region.[57] In order to reestablish the paramountcy of the southeastern Sumatra coast vis-à-vis Malāyu the Śrīvijaya ruler undertook to forge alliances with Malay seamen and various hinterland chiefs until he had surrounded Malāyu with Śrīvijaya allies. As we have already seen, the Kedukan Bukit inscription makes a direct reference to such alliances when it speaks of a potential force of twenty thousand troops under the personal command of the ruler of Śrīvijaya. Only two thousand troops were actually called upon for the battle against Malāyu, however, and it is likely that only two thousand could have been put in the field under the direct command of Śrīvijaya at this time. The remainder of this Śrīvijayan "army" were the tribesmen of subordinate chiefs who fulfilled their part of the alliance with Śrīvijaya by remaining neutral or by terminating their relations with Malāyu. This was the traditional Sumatran way of conducting war.

Alliances that helped to establish the rule of the Śrīvijaya monarch were thus an integral and important part of the state's development. While Kan-t'o-li had been a relatively isolated port state that had encountered few challenges to its position due to the traditional character of the remainder of the island (i.e., ports in the area had not yet begun to vie for the international trade), circumstances had changed by the seventh century. The consolidation of T'ang rule in China in the late sixth and early seventh centuries presented new opportunities for trade to ports on the coast of Sumatra.[58] Śrīvijaya took advantage of the Chinese preference for recognizing a single power within the region and thereby cut off these ports' aspirations to be granted "preferred" status in the trade by the Chinese court. By threat of force, Śrīvijaya brought rival ports under the dominance of its capital. The Śrīvijaya system expanded from a limited core domain to include assorted "vassal" relationships with a wide range of subordinates who were allowed to retain varying degrees of autonomy in relation to the capital.

In its quest to dominate, the burgeoning Śrīvijaya state relied on military alliances with subordinates who were willing—or were forced—to accept the superiority of the Śrīvijaya monarch. Those who did not take this view were stripped of official status and recognition. This is shown in a Śrīvijaya inscription fragment where the phrase *bharu nirbhāra* appears, which may be translated "lords without a charge or function," indicating that those unfaithful to the king would be isolated by having their functions and thus their power taken away.[59] Only those faithful to the king were rewarded. In the Telaga Batu inscription there also occurs the phrase *samaryyādamāmu,* "your realms [or] your newly acquired regions," a reference to parcels of land or districts granted to loyal civil and military servants.[60]

As noted earlier, Malay seamen are believed to have initially formed the nucleus of Śrīvijaya's military might. In a traditional island-based Malay chiefdom, the role of the chief was to provide a land base and munitions of war to a group of followers in return for a share of any booty returning from a war campaign.[61] Prestige was defined in terms of service to one's ruler. In turn, the Malay sea peoples viewed a king as powerful and to be feared.[62] The tenth-century geography of Ibn Rusta provides an example of such a body of Malay mercenaries in a traditional pattern of service to a local chief who had pledged his followers to the Śrīvijaya king. It mentions an official known as a *harladj* who had an island named for him and was "head of the *Mahārāja*'s army."[63] This island, situated in the Riau or Lingga Archipelago, was famous for its camphor. From a cliff on the island inhabitants gave protection to or harrassed ships passing through the strait.

Relationships between the Malay sea peoples and the *mahārāja* of Śrīvijaya were similar to those established between the Śrīvijaya ruler and the military leaders and chiefs of the Sumatra hinterland. The *mahārāja* was capable of investing power, for example, naming the island Ibn Rusta referred to in honor of his vassal. What attracted people to Śrīvijaya was its prestige. The king was royal, rich, and known to promote the general well-being of his people. For a group that sold its services as mercenaries, participation in the division of the royal treasury meant a regularization of income. That military leaders shared in this wealth is clear from the Arab geographers' account of the redistribution ceremony at the death of a *mahārāja,* when gold from Palembang harbor was divided first among the royal family and then among the military commanders.

In the list of people linked to the Śrīvijaya king there were two major classes of military commanders at the top of the hierarchy, well ahead of the priests (whose contributions to Śrīvijaya's statecraft were more theoretical; i.e., they were a source of ideas and plans) and also above those who were regarded as members of the king's administrative staff. First in importance was the *parvvāṇḍa,* "a rather high official, in command of troops or of a small district. . . ."[64] The fact that *parvvāṇḍa* appears in association with the term *nisaṃvarddhiku (nisaṃvarddhiku parvvāṇḍa)* is of particular interest. *Nisaṃvarddhiku* stands forth in the Telaga Batu inscriptions when the responsibilities of royal princes are described. Those charged with *nisaṃvarddhiku* were directly accountable to the king. A Palembang inscription fragment, for instance, shows what these commanders did: one *nisaṃvarddhiku parvvāṇḍa* was personally entrusted by the king to bring a rebellious area under control.[65] Thus the word *nisaṃvarddhiku* designated personal responsibilities to the Śrīvijaya monarch.

The Telaga Batu inscription also identifies the *senāpati* as a second category of important military commanders. While *parvvāṇḍa* commanded royal troops, *senāpati* were commanders in the private armies of the Śrīvijaya king's subordinate chiefs. This association is reflected in the inscription's text, where *senāpati* appears with *bhūpati* ("vassal chiefs"). *Senāpati* were thus military commanders of "vassal troops."

Another category of military commander appearing in the state's hierarchy was the *pratisāra,* whose position in the inscription indicates their subordination to the two higher ranks of military commanders. Since *pratisāra* is followed immediately in the inscription by the term *hulun hāji,* "the king's personal bondsmen," the two would appear to be connected. As noted, *hulun hāji* would have participated in Śrīvijaya's army, and it is reasonable to expect that *pratisāra* were their commanders. As coordinators of troops of royal bondsmen the *pratisāra* would have been under the command of *parvvāṇḍa* rather than *senāpati* (see fig. 3).

Despite the seemingly foreign hierarchical order imposed in the Śrīvijaya state by the assignment of Sanskritic titles in the Telaga Batu inscription, implying that the indigenous elite might not have been able to maintain their own power bases except through some quality associated with these Indian titles, it appears that indigenous elites continued to maintain their own alliance networks. In coming to terms with local chiefs—and to integrate them into his system of statecraft—the Śrīvijaya monarch synthesized his new policy from the existing system of political organization. The Telaga Batu inscription lists "vassal chiefs" *(bhūpati),* to whom were assigned a high district-level office in a ranking immediately following that of the "sons of kings born of lesser queens" *(rājaputra).*[66] The vassal chief's district-level office was that of *dātu,* the traditional Malay title for an important chief. A *dātu,* according to the inscription, held a *dātu* province *(parddātuan),* which was distinguished from land belonging to the king personally (called *kādātuan*). Royal princes were usually ap-

Figure 3
Śrīvijaya's State Hierarchy based on the Telaga Batu Inscription
(Arrows indicate flow of authority in addition to that implicit in the hierarchical arrangement.)

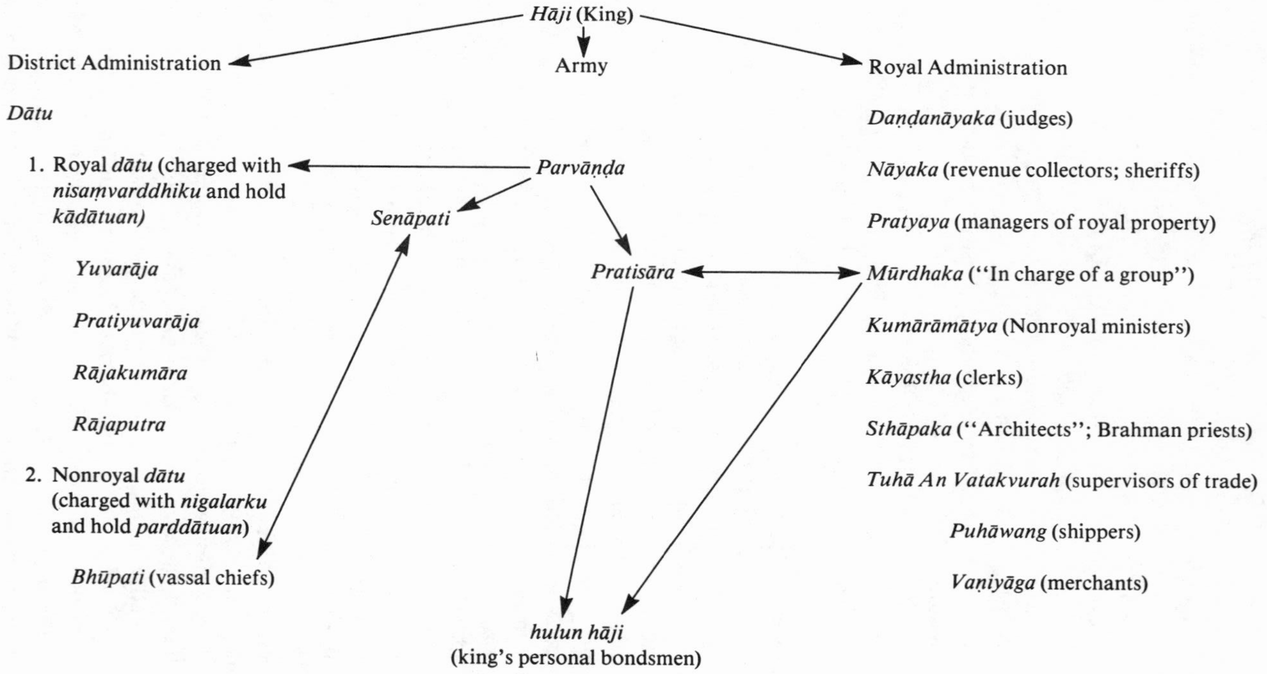

pointed to *dātu* positions as well, probably governing *kādātuan,* and were charged with *nisaṃvarddhiku,* "personal responsibility to the monarch." Those of nonroyal status who filled *dātu* positions were charged with *nigalarku,* "loyalty to the monarch."[67] The distinction between the terms *nisaṃvarddhiku* and *nigalarku* related to the danger to the king posed by members of the royal family. Royal *dātu* were believed to be potentially more dangerous than nonroyal *dātu.* Since he was of royal blood a royal *dātu* was a threat to the king's rule because he was a legitimate heir to the throne. Those *dātu* charged with *nisaṃvarddhiku* were subject to far more severe punishment for failure to carry out their responsibilities than those charged with *nigalarku.*

The Telaga Batu inscription gives the impression that as soon as the king received information about suspect actions by one of the royal *dātu* "he would immediately take measures. He would organize an expedition in order to have the culprit brought to the capital, where he would be liable to punishments: but, it is added, the expedition would hardly be necessary; the culprits would already have been killed by the effect of the imprecation," the curse associated with this inscription.[68] Not only was the threat of a curse imposed upon royal *dātu,* but the king also promised to order the immediate execution of anyone in such a position who challenged the throne. To the *dātu* charged with *nigalarku* there was no such threat of physical retribution; only the threat of the curse was held against them. Thus, in the Kotakapur, Karangbrahi, and Palas Pasemah versions of the Telaga Batu inscription, the Śrīvijaya monarch could merely invoke the curse and could not or would not undertake other measures to protect his position.

If we were able to map the geographical distribution of those appointed and charged with one or the other of the *dātu* positions, it would be extremely enlightening. For instance, the Kotakapur inscription (line 4) states that the rulers of Bangka were charged with *nigalarku.* As nonroyal elite, their position as *dātu* in the Śrīvijaya system did not demand total subservience to the capital but allowed them considerable autonomy. The king did not hold out the threat of direct force against them, submitting the threat of the curse as a warning against disloyalty. The potential for disorder inherent within alliances with subordinate local chiefs was fully recognized by Śrīvijaya's ruler. The Telaga Batu inscription expressed the king's fear of rebellion in the frontier regions of his state, where loyalties to the capital were likely weakest. Here, too, emphasis was placed on the curse exacting vengeance rather than on a specific military response: "[If] you plot against me in the frontier regions of my state, [then] you are not submissive and will be killed by the curse."

The proper function of a *dātu* was apparently to serve as the king's "eyes" (line 6) in the areas outside the capital. After a warning that actions taken independently of the capital in an attempt to build a base of power would be punished, the inscription then promises that if those persons who have attempted actions against the king are punished by the *dātu,* then "I shall not take measures against you."[69] Allied areas were thus given a high degree of autonomy out of the necessity of formulating a political and economic base for the state.

When the Telaga Batu inscription speaks of nonroyal *dātu* there is reference to the clans and descendants of those *dātu* who would suffer under the curse if a revolt against Śrīvijaya were supported. It mattered who your antecedents were. One enjoyed status in accord with the position with which one's family had been endowed, as recognized in the inscription's elaboration of the royal family. Regional clans seem to have dominated the subordinate localities of the Śrīvijaya empire. Rather than remove a dominant group from power in an area and then attempt to subjugate the remaining population, it was important that Śrīvijaya incorporate this local elite. Emphasis on the family membership of subordinates is made several times in the inscription. Family ties are repeatedly mentioned. There is a warning issued to those who "charge members of your family to conspire" (line 6). The joint responsibility among family members for one's improper actions is stressed: "[you] will be killed . . . with your wives and children . . . your posterity will be punished by me . . . you will be killed by the curse. You will be punished with your children, your wives, your posterity, your clans, and your friends" (line 19). Finally, the inscription notifies servants of the state that if they had any knowledge of their relatives' participation in a revolt they too would be punished, even though they themselves did not participate (line 21).

Among the last groups recognized in the Telaga Batu inscription were those people associated with commerce. First encountered are the royal officials known as *tuhā an vatakvurah,* "supervisors of trade and crafts." Next appear the *puhāwang,* "shippers," and *vaṇiyāga,* "merchants." The former term is given in the Malay form rather than in the formal Sanskrit employed for the other titles in the list in order to distinguish the *puhāwang* as indigenous traders and shippers who used the Śrīvijaya capital as their home port and who were supervised by royal officials with a specific jurisdiction over their activities—officials such as the *tuhā an vatakvurah.*[70]

This use of indigenous vocabulary to distinguish these seamen as being Malay demonstrates that in the Śrīvijaya era Malay seamen were still providing the ships and passage for international merchants traveling between Southeast Asia and China. An early Palembang inscription refers to merchants in general as "migratory men," comparing them with birds that traveled over long distances.[71] In the Telaga Batu inscription the shippers and merchants were included in the list of those who were considered potentially dangerous to the king—probably due to their contact with foreign powers. Merchants were regarded as likely spies for the king's enemies. Thus the movement of foreigners and their goods was undoubtedly regulated in conformity with the requirements of the state.[72] In particular, foreign merchants would not have been allowed to establish a direct commercial relationship with interior sources of supply. A policy of suppressing the foreigner was impossible, however. The advantages to be derived from trade revenues, which were a vital asset to the expanding Śrīvijaya state, required that hospitality be extended.

Trade was conducted under royal control, taking place in specific marketplaces under the supervision of royal officials, as may be seen in the Telaga Batu inscription's reference to *tuhā an vatakvurah,* the "supervisors of trade and crafts." Chao Ju-kua provides a clue to the role of such royal officials in his description of trade in Śrīvijaya's ports:

> They calculate first the value of their articles according to their equivalents in gold or silver, and then engage in (the) barter of these articles at fixed rates. As for example, one *tong* of *samshu* is equal to one *tael* of silver or two *mace* of gold, two *tong* of rice are equal to one *tael* of silver, ten *tong* being equal to one *tael* of gold. . . .[73]

The key to trade in Chao Ju-kua's account is the establishment of fixed rates of value for various commodities in gold and silver equivalents prior to any exchange within Śrīvijaya's marketplaces. This indicates an administered market (as opposed to a modern "price-making" market):[74] Śrīvijaya's supervisors of trade were likely involved in setting standards and "fair prices" for commodities, thereby maintaining the social and economic harmony of the port of trade. Arab sources, for instance, report that it was common knowledge that merchants based in the ports of the western Malay Peninsula coast they knew as "Kalāh" devalued pure tin by adding substances to it, a factor important in establishing a fair rate of exchange, calling into question the integrity of commercial transactions in Kalāh's ports.[75] Śrīvijaya ports, on the other hand, were considered "fair." In the fifteenth century Malacca merchants used weights on hand-held scales that bore the Malacca ruler's stamp certifying that they were of proper weight standard. The indented stamp was so placed that peeling off small layers of weight was impossible—just as a modern coin has rims on its edges to prevent the shaving of its metal. It has been suggested that this practice predated Malacca and originated in the Śrīvijaya age.[76] Śrīvijaya's "supervisors of trade" would have taken responsibility for such standards.

The nature of trade in Śrīvijaya is further documented in the 1118–1119 account of Chu Yü, son of the chief administrator of the Canton port from 1099 to 1102.

> Every country in the southern ocean has its chief. San-fo-ch'i [Śrīvijaya] is invariably described as a great country. . . . The land has a great deal of sandalwood [a product of Java and the eastern archipelago] and frankincense, and these products are [Chinese] trade goods. San-fo-ch'i ships send frankincense to China, and the [Chinese] Trade Office treats the product as a [government] monopoly and reserves a percentage to sell on its own account. In recent years San-fo-ch'i has established [its own] monopoly in sandalwood. The ruler orders merchants to sell it to him. The cost of the product [therefore] increases several times. Foreign merchants do not dare to purchase it privately. This is a clever system. . . .[77]

This description documents a thriving and peaceful trade center, but implies that in earlier times Śrīvijaya promoted "free trade" within its ports instead of imposing monopolies on certain products.

In economic terms the Śrīvijaya king utilized his hinterland political relationships to collect goods at designated river-mouth centers of exchange where goods met and flowed outward. This entire process was dependent on the network of political control developed by Śrīvijaya kings in the mid-seventh century, a system that was an extension of the structure, or "code" of the indigenous society of the Strait of Malacca region—that is, even though the hierarchical structure described above employed Indic titles, the structure was in essential ways still indigenous.

The Śrīvijaya Legacy

Śrīvijaya came into existence because of its ability to organize the commercial exchange of Southeast Asian products—products from the Java Sea realm as well as those goods produced in its own hinterland—for those of China and the West. Successfully facilitating this exchange provided the Śrīvijaya monarch with income beyond that which he would normally have derived from his own immediate economic base: the Musi River Delta between Palembang and the coast and Palembang's upriver hinterland.[78] Because he redistributed revenues derived from this trade, the Śrīvijaya "chief" rose above his fellow Sumatra and Malay chiefs *(dātu)* in status, and the ensuing prosperity of his burgeoning state attracted more followers.

As an indigenous chief the Śrīvijaya monarch could draw upon local beliefs that chiefs possessed magical qualities. Traditionally a chief's use of magic influenced his followers' prosperity in this lifetime as well as in the next. The Telaga Batu inscription stresses this locally defined power but also associates the Śrīvijaya monarch with a higher level of magic—that derived from Buddhism—to further reinforce his stature. Not only did Buddhism provide new magic, it also gave the king international prestige. The royal capital of Śrīvijaya became a major pilgrimage center and the Śrīvijaya ruler and his representatives became participants in Buddhism's international intellectual dialogue of the seventh- through tenth-century era.[79] His prowess was well publicized (e.g., in the Śrīvijaya inscriptions discussed above) and was intended to impress his followers—to awe them into submission. The emphasis on magically derived legitimacy was critical to insure that the king could maintain his authority during periods marked by drops in port activity due to regular fluctuations in the volume of international trade, often the consequence of disorders at either end of the trade route.

The concern for legitimacy in the early Śrīvijaya inscriptions reflects the inherent weakness of the Śrīvijaya state system. Nonpersonal allies—that is, local chiefs *(dātu)*—and their client networks were willing to enter into a confederation with the Śrīvijaya ruler in order to share in the state's wealth as well as to draw upon the *mahārāja*'s special magic. Upriver land-based allies, in exchange for their subordination and delivery of local production to downriver ports, received a portion of the income and goods from the trade routes. For Malay seamen, being party to the redistribution of Śrīvijaya's wealth was an alternative to piracy; in return they became the Śrīvijaya navy, safeguarding the maritime passage through the Strait of Malacca. If deprived of a part of this wealth, however, none of these allies had reason to facilitate the flow of goods to and from Palembang or to maintain a political alliance with Śrīvijaya.

The leaders of subordinate groups could have attempted to replace the Palembang-based rulers, repeating the cycle of state consolidation: assuming authority over Palembang or another of the potential coastal entrepôts at the mouths of the Strait of Malacca riverine networks, constructing a viable system of polity, attracting and conducting international exchange at their principal port, and mobilizing the subsequent wealth to extend their authority over rival coastal centers and their upriver hinterlands.[80] While internally defined legitimacy and networks of alliance were critical to the construction of this system, the key variable was access to the external income that provided the foundation for an otherwise unstable hegemony.

Kinship in Śrīvijaya was defined in traditional terms: the monarch was a Sumatran chief, and he dealt with his subordinates within traditional structures of relationship. In the Śrīvijaya state external trade was integrated with the internal economic and political networks using systems of alliance: the Śrīvijaya chief brought the various internal networks together and connected them to the international trade network. Śrīvijaya was able to define its relationship with foreign merchants in much the same terms: the king was the "chief" of one people dealing with the "chiefs" of others. The Śrīvijaya state developed continuing "treaty" relationships with different groups of people who would normally have owed each other nothing. Trade transactions became social and political strategy; reciprocity among representative chiefs of the various peoples became the basis of a redistribution network, organized by Śrīvijaya's rulers, that guaranteed the network's continuing prosperity. Maintaining the harmony of the economic and social relationships was the ultimate function of the Śrīvijaya state and its ruler.

If Śrīvijaya defined its authority in traditional Sumatran terms, as is being argued, then the "destruction of the center" would have had a tremendous psychological impact. One can thus postulate the effect of a raid on Śrīvijaya's capital in 1025 by seamen based in the south Indian domain of the Cōḻa monarchs. The Tañjāvūr inscription of Rājēndra Cōḻa (1030/31) referred to the conquest of the Śrīvijaya capital and its treasury as if it symbolized the desecration of the source of Śrīvijaya's legitimacy and power.[81] Śrīvijaya never regained its old prosperity and control after the Cōḻa raid. By 1079–1082, its capital had moved from Palembang to the central Sumatra port of Jambi.[82] Java had become a "dominant entrepôt" area and the ports of northern Sumatra and the Malay Peninsula were beginning to function independently as alternative "centers."[83] Yet the seventeenth-century *Sejarah Melayu,* the court chronicle of Malacca's history, in its description of the rise of Malacca in the fourteenth and fifteenth centuries purposely connected Malacca genealogies to Śrīvijaya-Palembang and not to Śrīvijaya-Jambi.[84] This substantiates the legacy of Śrīvijaya in Malay history—and the success of the Palembang monarch in establishing a political network within the context of Malay-Sumatran culture. The Śrīvijaya state had achieved "kingdom" status, in that it had sufficiently integrated its riverine and coastal centers with its upriver hinterland. Despite its political demise, Śrīvijaya-Palembang remained a viable symbol of Malay unity and common prosperity and was the standard for all Malay riverine states that followed.

5

The Śailendra Era in Javanese History

From earliest times the coasts of southeastern Sumatra and northeastern Java have formed a single commercial and cultural unit. While historians have had considerable interest in the southeastern Sumatra-based Śrīvijaya state, early Javanese history is perhaps the least understood and most controversial among that of Southeast Asia's classical civilizations, despite epigraphic and archaeological records surpassed only in Cambodia and Burma.[1] Yet most of Java's written records are of post-eleventh-century origin, and as a consequence there is little agreement on Java's pre-eleventh-century history. It is this pre-eleventh-century age, however, that produced Java's most impressive monumental remains, notably the Borobudur and Prambanan temple complexes of central Java. Historians currently debate whether these historical treasures were products of a civilization governed by indigenous Javanese monarchs or by rulers (a) culturally influenced by Śrīvijaya, (b) politically allied and subordinate to Śrīvijaya, (c) intermarried with the Śrīvijaya royal line, (d) based in Java but directly ruling both Java and Śrīvijaya, or (e) based in Sumatra and directly ruling both Śrīvijaya and Java. Further, there is heated discussion of whether the civilization that produced the major central Javanese temple complexes previous to A.D. 1000 was governed by strong, unifying central governments or is better understood as being subject to a number of semiautonomous regional zones governed by regional chiefs.

This chapter examines the evolution of a "Javanese state" from the fifth through the eleventh centuries—an era corresponding to the existence of the Śrīvijayan maritime state discussed in chapter 4. It especially considers the role of maritime trade in this development process and whether or not the particular patterns of early Javanese wet-rice civilization came to emerge because of opportunities afforded by maritime trade. To make this analysis it is necessary to examine the Śailendra line of rulers who at various times throughout this pre-eleventh-century era claimed authority as both Javanese and Śrīvijayan monarchs.

The Emergence of Early Riverine States in Western Java

The earliest written reference to Java is found in Ptolemy (A.D. 100–170), who provides separate references to Yāvadvīpa (Iabadiou) and Jawadvīpa (Sadadibai) (see chap. 2). Recent historiography has associated Ptolemy's Yāvadvīpa with the Jelai River system of southwestern Borneo, an area known by the Chinese as Yeh-p'o-t'i that was said to be located next to She-p'o (Java).[2] By the fifth century, however, Yeh-p'o-t'i's commerce had been absorbed by emerging coastal centers on Java's northern coast; Chinese sources began to omit references to Yeh-p'o-t'i and referred thereafter to the She-p'o (Java) realm alone. There were two fifth-century Javanese centers with which the Chinese interacted: Ho-ling in central Java and Ho-lo-tan/t'o on the northwestern Java coast.[3]

The story of the north Indian Buddhist pilgrim Guṇavarman records the emergence of Ho-ling as a political entity from what was previously a tribal society. In 422, Guṇavarman stopped at Ho-ling on his way to China. There he stayed for several years, patronized by the queen mother and preaching Buddhist theology with great success; the king of Ho-ling asked Guṇavarman's advice on whether to attack his enemies.[4] The emergence of Ho-ling involved competition among several groups and the assistance of an Indian advisor, which denotes the use of Indic culture as the basis for the establishment of the local "ruler's" supremacy over other chiefs. Ho-ling sent envoys to China in 430 and 440 but is not mentioned in sixth-century Chinese records, suggesting that international contact with central Java was limited until two centuries later when in the 640s and 660s Ho-ling again sent embassies and was visited around 640 by a Chinese monk who remained to study under a Javanese Buddhist master.[5]

Meanwhile Ho-lo-tan (or Ho-lo-t'o) sent seven missions to the Chinese court between 430–452. Chinese records of Ho-lo-tan also reflect the instability of that age. In the report of a 436 mission the king of Ho-lo-tan, who held the Indic royal title Viśāṃvarman, was said to live in fear of his enemies both inside and outside his realm and thus requested diplomatic assistance and weapons from the Chinese. Ho-lo-tan was once a peaceful and prosperous land but at that time was being attacked from all sides; its people (the king's supporters) were fleeing the country. When the king's son usurped the throne Viśāṃvarman was forced into exile.[6]

Historians have connected the references to Ho-lo-tan with four undated mid-to-late fifth-century inscriptions of the king Pūrṇavarman who ruled the Tarum River basin just east of present-day Jakarta, a land known as Tārumānāgara in the inscriptions.[7] These inscriptions are similar in style—that is, they have Sanskrit verses in an early south Indian script—to the *yūpa* inscriptions of Kutei on the southwestern Borneo coast, epigraphy associated with the Yeh-p'o-t'i coastal center. One of Pūrṇavarman's inscriptions discovered near the shore of Jakarta Bay notes that in the twenty-second year of his reign Pūrṇavarman gave his attention to the drainage problems of the coastal area, altering the course of the river to provide a new outlet.[8] The other three inscriptions were found on a hillside near Bogor, south of Jakarta, and are associated with footprints carved in stone symbolizing "the three conquering and victorious footprints of Viṣṇu." These footprints denote a great victory by Pūrṇavarman, who is described as being "ever efficient in destroying hostile *kraton* [courts/states] and salutory to princes who are devoted subjects."[9] These inscriptions of Pūrṇavarman demonstrate several aspects of the emergence of political systems in early western Java.

Recent studies of the historical ecology of western Java reveal that the region did not develop a wet-rice *(sawah)* agricultural system until the seventeenth century, although dry-rice *(ladang)* cultivation was practiced earlier.[10] While a wet-rice society was by necessity more deeply committed and bound to a specific agricultural area, as for instance was true of the populations inhabiting the river plains of central and eastern Java in a later age, western Java's dry-rice agricultural population was more mobile and was capable of escaping the grasp of an oppressive court elite or an unsettled political environment—situations similar to those reported in Chinese references to Ho-lo-tan in Viśāṃvarman's time when Viśāṃvarman's subjects fled the country because of constant disorder. The possibilities for the successful development of an agrarian-based court *(kraton)* in western Java were thus limited; the alternative was to build a maritime-focused court/state requiring the establishment of a coastal port and the recruitment of Malay sea populations.

This was Pūrṇavarman's intent in the mid-fifth century as he supervised the construction of a new river outlet—possibly because of the silting up of the mouth of the Tarum River—to make his port more accessible for trading vessels.[11] A further benefit from this project was the alleviation of the potential for upstream flooding, which increased the capacity for dry-rice production in Pūrṇavarman's upstream hinterland. Significantly, Pūrṇavarman's fifth-century coastal development project corresponds to the southern shift of the international maritime route from the Isthmus of Kra and Funan realm to the Strait of Malacca region (see chap. 3). Development of the Tarum River estuary as an economic

Map 5
JAVA IN THE CLASSICAL ERA

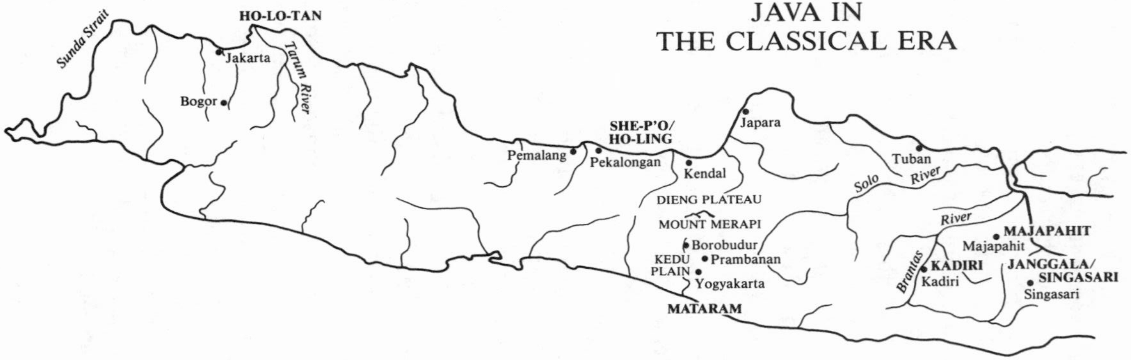

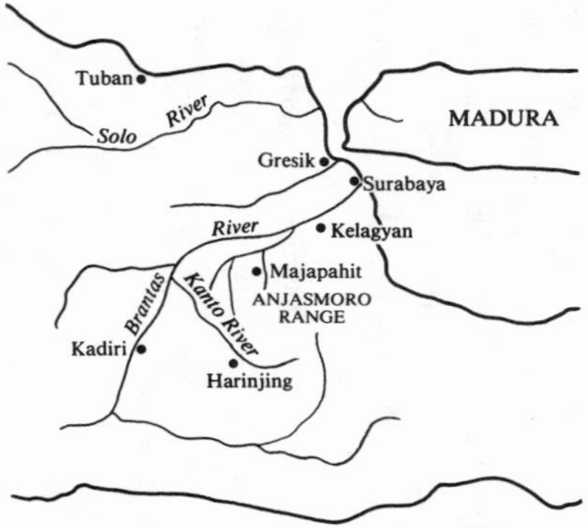

EARLY BRANTAS RIVER SYSTEM
HYDRAULIC NETWORKS

PRAMBANAN AREA
TEMPLE COMPLEXES

center, with a coastal port supported by upriver dry-rice cultivators, facilitated the Tārumānāgara ruler's rise and allowed him to claim kingly status. The developed river system provided surplus rice to feed foreign merchants utilizing the port facilities. Pūrṇavarman's Bogor inscriptions show that his initial political consolidations were brought about via wars "destroying hostile *kraton,*" the bases of rival chiefs within the Tarum River system, and constructing alliance networks by being "salutory to princes [i.e., subordinate chiefs] who are devoted subjects." Such victories and alliances guaranteed the security of the international traders visiting the new port but also encouraged the flow of local production (rice) from upriver population centers ruled by local chiefs to Pūrṇavarman's would-be coastal entrepôt.

One further dimension of the Pūrṇavarman inscriptions should be emphasized. An important aspect of Pūrṇavarman's quest for power—as documented by his inscriptions—was an association with Indic religion. Consistent with other emerging Southeast Asian centers, Pūrṇavarman relied on Indian religious tradition to reinforce his legitimacy and to elevate his magical status above that of his fellow chiefs. Pūrṇavarman's victories were glorified in his inscriptions by the symbolic integration of Indic and Javanese traditions; for example, Viṣṇu's three footprints, taken from early South Asian tradition, corresponded to Javanese conceptions of feet as the locus of power.[12] The economic development of the Tarum River estuary was sanctified by the bestowal of a thousand cows upon "Brahmans," a priestly elite employing the "sacred language" of the inscriptions to record the glory of Pūrṇavarman. The three Bogor inscriptions stipulate that Pūrṇavarman was "tantamount to . . . Viṣṇu," a semidivine being worthy of being followed. The personal focus of this quest for legitimacy is clear but does not appear to have been transferred to the western Java-based rulers who followed him. It remained for the central Javanese ruler Sañjaya to provide further definition of Javanese sovereignty in the early eighth century, drawing from these earlier developments in western Java.

Pūrṇavarman's efforts are thus comparable to those of the early Śrīvijaya monarchs. Ports in the strategic coastal zone at the end of the Strait of Malacca and at the western edge of the Java Sea first emerged as important commercial centers because of their roles as intermediaries for the exchange of eastern Indonesia's spices, contrary to Funan, which began as a way station. These spices were transported to southern Sumatra and northwest Java coast ports by Malay seamen, and in these commercial centers the spices were traded to merchants traveling the East-West maritime route from India to China. But these fifth-century Java and Sumatra coastal centers never achieved "kingdom" status. Their power was localized, concentrated in the coastal centers at the mouths of riverine systems rather than integrated with their upriver hinterlands. There was, as noted in the discussion of riverine exchange networks in early Southeast Asia in chapter 1, an inherent potential for conflict as one or another would-be coastal entrepôt attempted to establish its dominance over the international trade, monopolizing contact with the international traders and access to Indonesia's spices and other desired products.

The western Java coastal centers failed to satisfactorily recruit the Malay sea populations they needed to become successful entrepôts, nor were they able to develop a rice culture producing sufficient surplus rice to sustain the sovereignty of their elites. In the end the western Java coastal realm fell subject to Śrīvijaya's authority in the seventh century. Unlike them, Śrīvijaya's port-based elite had constructed the crucial alliances with the strait region's Malay sea peoples, who became the basis for Śrīvijaya's evolution as the dominant entrepôt in the region. The Palembang-based Śrīvijaya ruler consolidated his state by first establishing his authority over the competing entrepôts of Malāyu/Jambi in Sumatra and then, according to the 686 Kotakapur inscription found on Bangka Island, prepared to launch a naval expedition against rival ports on the western Java coast.[13]

The Sunda Strait region and western Java coast are considered by historians to have been commercially if not politically subordinate to Śrīvijaya's authority for most of the period from the late seventh to the mid-tenth centuries.[14] There is a void in the epigraphic evidence concerning western Java until an inscription dated A.D. 932, which makes reference to a "King of the Sunda Straits" who was reinstalled to royal status.[15] This inscription appears to be related to three Javanese inscriptions of similar date recovered on the southwest Sumatra coast side of the Sunda Strait.[16] Together these four inscriptions point to the reemergence of Javanese authority over the Sunda Strait realm.

Sources and Interpretations of the Śailendra Era's History

A Nakhọn Si Thammarat inscription ("Side A") from the Malay Peninsula dated A.D. 775 makes reference to the Śrīvijayan empire; on the reverse of the same stone is an undated inscription that speaks of the Śailendra family that is known to have ruled in Java in that same eighth-century era.[17] Using the Nakhọn Si Thammarat inscriptions as evidence that Śrīvijaya was the dominant political entity in the Southeast Asian archipelago in that age, some historians have proposed a "Sumatran period" in Javanese history: the ruler of Śrīvijaya is seen dominating central Java's statecraft and culture in the eighth and ninth centuries A.D. in an age characterized by Śrīvijaya's Mahāyāna Buddhist influence and Java's most impressive temple architecture. But a mid-ninth-century Nālānda inscription (860) from the Mahāyāna Buddhist monastery in the Bihar region of northeastern India honoring a Southeast Asian *mahārāja* who sponsored a religious foundation, notes that this *mahārāja* was descended from the Śailendra family of "Yavabhūmi" (Java) and ruled "Suvarṇadvīpa" (Śrīvijaya).[18] The Nālandā inscription suggests a quite different interpretation of the Nakhọn Si Thammarat inscription: that Java-based rulers of the Śailendra family held authority over the Śrīvijaya realm and that during the eighth and ninth centuries it was Java, not southeastern Sumatra, that dominated the Southeast Asian archipelago.[19]

The Śailendras came to power around the mid-eighth century. They introduced the Indic title *mahārāja* to distinguish themselves from other regional chiefs and established their base in central Java. Patrons of Buddhism, the Śailendras during the height of their power in central Java constructed impressive monuments and temple complexes, the best known of which is the Borobudur on the Kedu Plain. Their court attracted Buddhist scholars from afar and was acclaimed internationally as a center of Buddhist learning. They were the precursors of a new concept of statecraft in Java—the concentration of political power in a single authority—which by the tenth century was clearly being realized.

The most widely accepted reconstruction of Śailendra history was done by J. G. de Casparis, who stressed the linear succession of Javanese and Śrīvijaya rulers, intermarriage between the Java-based Śailendra and Sumatra-based Śrīvijaya royal houses, and the consequent assumption of rule over Śrīvijaya by Śailendra-related monarchs after rival Javanese elites had superseded the authority of Śailendra monarchs in Java; that is, Śailendra kings lost their seat in Java and ended up ruling Sumatra.[20]

Casparis' reconstruction is based on his view that the two Nakhọn Si Thammarat inscriptions are related. While the "Side A" inscription dated 775 clearly refers to Śrīvijaya monarchs, Casparis dated "Side B" in the early 780s, noting the reference in "Side B" to a Śailendra monarch who was the "killer of his enemies." This Śailendra monarch, he argued, was not ruling Śrīvijaya but was related to the Śrīvijaya monarchs through an alliance. The "killer of his enemies" in the Nakhọn Si Thammarat inscription was the same individual described as the "heroic king Dharaṇīndra" in the 782 Kĕlurak inscription recorded near Kalasan in central Java, the Śailendra ruler of Java "whose valour was established by the conquest of rulers in all directions . . . who was given to attacking great warriors hostile to him."[21] The Nakhọn Si Thammarat and Kĕlurak inscriptions thus honored the establishment of Śailendra polity in Java following an era of upheaval.

Casparis theorized that between 732, when Sañjaya, a patron of the Hindu god Śiva, issued a major inscription at Caṅggal in central Java, and 778, when a regional chief constructed a temple at Kalasan in honor of the tantric Buddhist goddess Tārā and his Śailendra monarch, a major political transition took place in Java.[22] The Kĕlurak inscription supports this theory. This inscription employed a new script, a north Indian Nāgarī script also utilized by contemporary Pāla rulers in northeastern India, the chief supporters of the Buddhist complex at Nālandā, and especially stressed the patronage of Buddhism by the Śailendra monarch.[23] This patronage of Buddhism is best evinced in the sophisticated Śailendra monumental art and architecture, with the Borobudur representing the cosmological center of Śailendra power and the spiritual center of the Śailendra realm in the Javanese world. It was Buddhist patronage that the Śailendra monarchs had in common with the rulers of Śrīvijaya, as well as with the Pāla monarchs of India.

After the inscription of the 780s, there is a gap of information until 824, when an Old Javanese and Sanskrit inscription reports the reign of the Śailendra monarch Samaratuṅga, who Casparis argued was allied to the Sumatra-based Śrīvijaya rulers via his marriage to a Śrīvijaya princess (see fig. 4).[24] But an Old Malay inscription dated 832 from Gandasuli in central Java recorded the "restoration of order" by a new line of kings, led by the regional chief Patapān and symbolized by the construction of four monasteries *(aśrama)* dedicated to the Hindu god Brahma. Casparis postulated that when Samaratuṅga died the sovereignty of the Śailendra line in Java was challenged by this regional chief, who had a legitimate claim to the throne because of his marriage to a Śailendra princess, Samaratuṅga's daughter. The new line of kings united the Hindu and Buddhist traditions as the basis of its legitimacy.[25] An 842 inscription reports that Śailendra temples were maintained by a Śailendra princess, wife of Pikatan, Patapān's son.[26] This act seemed designed to justify Pikatan's right to assume the Śailendra *mahārāja* title as Javanese sovereign. Thereafter the Patapān line began the development of a Hindu temple complex at Prambanan around 863, perhaps related to the cult of the Hindu sage Agastya, and continued as well to maintain the Śailendra Buddhist temples.[27]

Casparis speculated that, in trying to assume authority over Java, Pikatan came into conflict with Samaratuṅga's Śailendra heirs, specifically the "brother-in-law" Bālaputra, named in the Nālandā inscription

Figure 4
Early Javanese Rulers

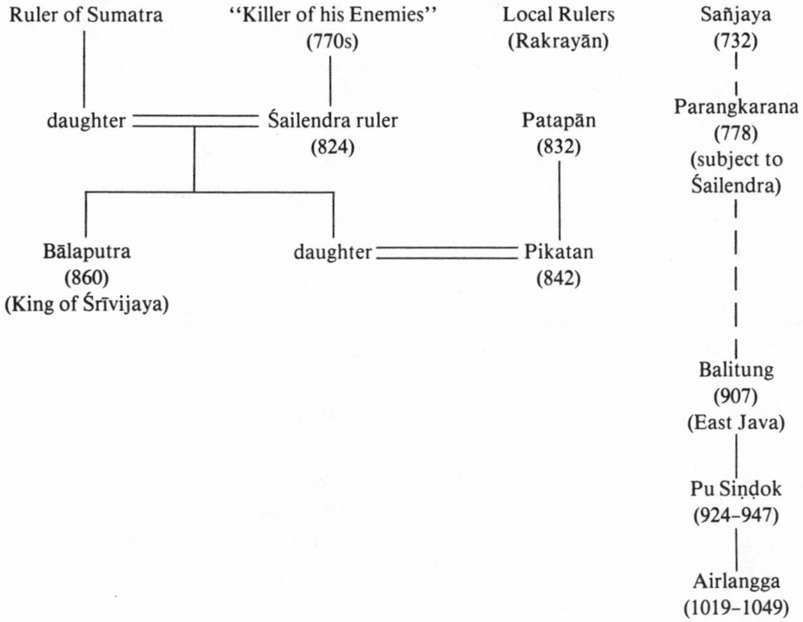

of 860 as the *mahārāja* of Śrīvijaya (Suvarṇadvīpa). The Nālandā inscription traces Bālaputra's ancestry, reporting that he was the younger son of the *mahārāja* Samaratuṅga, who was in turn the son of the Śailendra *mahārāja* of Java (Yavabhūmi), who bore the title "killer of his enemies," that is, the Śailendra ruler of the Kĕlurak and the Nakhọn Si Thammarat inscriptions.[28] Noting the Nālandā inscription's reference to conflict within the Śailendra realm, Casparis proposed that in 856 Bālaputra was defeated by Pikatan, whereupon Bālaputra retreated to Śrīvijaya, the country of his mother, to become the first Śailendra ruler of Śrīvijaya. Thus in the late ninth century Śrīvijaya was ruled by a Buddhist Śailendra ruler, while Java was ruled by Pikatan and his successors, who patronized Śiva.[29] While Casparis' chronological reconstruction has been criticized, no historian has yet substantially refuted his view of Śailendra rule of Java and Śrīvijaya as being distinct from each other, and that Śailendra sovereignty in Sumatra did not begin until the latter half of the ninth century.[30]

Of related interest are Arab and Chinese references to the Javanese and Śrīvijaya realms during the Śailendra era.[31] Zābaj was at first an

Arab toponym for Java as a whole and may be roughly equated to Chinese references to She-p'o (Java) and Indian references to Jāvaka or Yāvadvīpa. As Arab perceptions of the Indonesian archipelago became more precise by the late ninth century, being for the first time based upon personal experience, Zābaj came to be attached to the *mahārāja*s who ruled Java in the toponym "*Mahārāja* [of] Zābaj." The end of the Śailendra line in Java and the transfer of Śailendra rule to southeastern Sumatra may well be reflected in tenth-century geographies, which referred to the *mahārāja*'s base in Sribuza (Palembang) rather than in the Zābaj of earlier works. These references could be seen as documenting a transition in Java's political fortunes and thus giving credence to Casparis' theory that Śailendra rule over Java and Śrīvijaya did not overlap but was instead separate. Sribuza's capital in post-tenth-century references was clearly a maritime center, "a city built on wooden piles at the edge of a large tidal river/bay," said by Ibn Sā'īd (1274) to be the largest of the Zābaj domain.[32] Here the ruler levied taxes on ships sailing to China according to the *'Ajā'ib al-Hind* (ca. 1000).[33] Similarly, Chinese references to Śrīvijaya (Shih-li-fo-shih) changed to San-fo-ch'i around A.D. 900.[34] Śrīvijaya (Sribuza, San-fo-ch'i) from the mid-tenth century onward was thus the realm of the king of Zābaj, the *mahārāja,* the Śailendra ruler of Śrīvijaya, whose authority encompassed the Strait of Malacca region, but not Java.

Although the southeastern Sumatra and northeastern Javanese coasts formed a single commercial and cultural unit, histories of the Śrīvijaya and Javanese cultures have often ignored the intense interactions between the Bangka Island and Sunda Strait areas.[35] The early Arab geographers quite correctly referred to Zābaj as a single commercial unit—centered in southeastern Sumatra and encompasing Sumatra, Java, and the lower Malay Peninsula—until the mid-tenth century, when political transitions finally divided the old Zābaj realm into separate Śrīvijaya and Javanese commercial sectors. This transition was marked not only by a new Arab focus on the Sumatra-based Sribuza maritime state but also by new Chinese references—dating from 960 when the Sung dynasty assumed power—to San-fo-ch'i, the "three Vijayas" ("victories/cities of victory") of Palembang, Jambi, and Malāyu, none of which was in Java. The toponym used earlier by the T'ang dynasty was Shih-li-fo-shih (Śrīvijaya), which is less precise.[36]

The Sung court records after 960 mention as well an era of warfare between Śrīvijaya and the new rulers of the Javanese state, by then based in eastern Java, which ended when the south Indian Cōḷas raided Śrīvijaya's ports in 1024–1025, and with the political consolidation of central and eastern Java under the authority of the eastern Javanese monarch

Airlangga shortly thereafter.[37] In the ninth century eastern Javanese merchants had begun to actively secure spices in the eastern Indonesian archipelago, exchanging Javanese rice for spices and sandalwood that were then transported to Śrīvijaya's ports for sale to foreign merchants.[38] By the tenth century, after the demise of Śailendra authority in Java, eastern Java ports were capable of acting independently of Śrīvijaya as commercial centers and competently attracting international traders. Śrīvijaya, envious and fearing that rulers in eastern Java would establish a monopoly over the spice trade and that consequently merchants would begin to bypass Śrīvijaya's ports, launched an attack on eastern Java's new commercial centers around 925. A Javanese inscription provides evidence of an attack by the Malāyu-based army of Śrīvijaya in 928–929. This force landed in eastern Java and advanced to the area near Ngañjuk, where it was defeated by Pu Siṇḍok, the current Javanese *mahārāja*.[39] The inscription depicted Pu Siṇḍok saving the Javanese realm and laying the political foundation for future east Java-based rulers. There then followed a century of conflict between Java and Śrīvijaya, reported in Chinese sources, until the Cōḷas eliminated Śrīvijaya's economic competition.[40]

The points of controversy within Casparis' reconstruction of Śailendra history are questions concerning his linear reconstruction of Javanese history, whereby an unbroken succession of monarchs ruled a singular and centralized Javanese state from Sañjaya's 732 inscription onward. In a summary critique of Casparis' view of early Javanese history, one historian provided the following insight:

> I remain unconvinced that, in early Hindu Java, there was only one sovereign at a time. The historical sources at our disposal enable us to conclude that there were several independent rulers, some of them enjoying the title of *mahārāja* and others without that title. It does not necessarily follow, however, that the former were supreme rulers because they were known as *mahārājas*. To ascribe supreme authority to a ruler merely because the inscriptions mention him as a *mahārāja* and at the same time to deny authority to others who may possibly also have had sovereignty would be inconsistent with what is known of the social structure of the Hindu-Javanese period at this early state of its history.[41]

In support of this view, many historians now believe that early Javanese history was marked by dynastic transitions and various upheavals that promoted regional autonomy. In an attempt to elevate their status above that of other regional chiefs the Śailendra rulers introduced the *mahārāja* title to Java, a foreign-sounding title to awe their subjects and one they hoped could be transformed into power. Sacred ritual and especially the encouragement of temple construction by Śailendra monarchs were also intended to maintain and enhance Śailendra prestige and "reinforce the aura of divine majesty."[42] Yet the Śailendra and other Javanese monarchs were incapable of consolidating their authority over a significant portion of the Javanese political realm or transforming this realm into a widespread state system dependent upon the political and economic leadership of a monarch until at least the eleventh century, when the center of Javanese authority was concentrated in eastern Java. Rather, central Java-based monarchs of the Śailendra era held hegemony over a limited area.[43]

Javanese Statecraft in the Śailendra Era

Early Javanese society was a self-sustaining socioeconomic order characterized initially by village clusters called *wanua,* which in reality were comprised of several hamlets that shared a common market *(pkĕn).* Village clusters were inhabited by "children of the *wanua*" *(anak wanua)* and ruled by a village council of "elders" *(tuha)* or "fathers" *(rāma)* who were the greatest among equals. Significantly, central Javanese epigraphy suggests that the most important village cluster official was the head of the local water board *(hulair),* denoting the importance of wet-rice agriculture to the village economy. The development of Javanese wet-rice agriculture in the central Java plain required the cooperation of several communities that were all dependent on the equitable sharing of water from the same river or its tributaries. As a consequence supravillage units of economic and social cooperation emerged, known as *watĕk.* These were initially water management networks for the construction, maintenance, and distribution of water within the regional *watĕk* irrigation systems.[44]

These regional irrigation networks serving several village clusters were supervised by a regional chief *(rakrayān).* A *watĕk* was thus a limited ecological region ruled by a chief who held the power to dispose of the material *(dĕrwaya haji)* and labor *(bwat haji)* resources of the *watĕk* in various types of redistributions to his followers. The *rakrayān* ruled from the village cluster from which he originated and normally emerged from among the village cluster elders, initially functioning as an "elder brother" among the regional *(watĕk)* population.[45] The *rakrayān*'s potential for power, like that among other early Southeast Asia political elites, depended on his personal initiative and his ability to generate prosperity from his regional resource base and to gain the cooperation of his subordinate village populations and their elders. A successful *rakrayān* ruling a prosperous *watĕk* region might in turn bring other *rakrayān* and their subordinate village cluster networks into a confederation under his authority, which had the effect of elevating such a *rakrayān*'s status to that of a "king" *(rāja)*. His own village cluster thereby became a royal court *(kraton)* from which he ruled.

The central Java rice plain thus came to be composed of village clusters and their peasant producers, who were governed by village elders, who themselves came under the authority of *rakrayān,* who ruled *watĕk,* initially units of supravillage water management. *Rāja*s were regional chiefs who consolidated prosperous *watĕk* regional networks under their rule and were essentially equal in status to other *rakrayān* who were successfully constructing alliance networks in the Śailendra era and who may or may not have claimed *"mahārāja"* status. What seems to have distinguished the *rāja* from his fellow *rakrayān* was the *rāja*'s ability to establish his elite status via his and his subordinates' patronage of religion. Court-based officiants who functioned as both record-keepers and priests sanctified and legitimized a *rāja*'s rule by conducting elaborate rituals.[46] Through their efforts ritual leadership became critical to the *rāja*'s high status. However, it was intertwined with a successful economic and administrative policy that generated the surplus production from a *rāja*'s ricelands necessary to finance the maintenance of his staff of priests/clerks, the construction of royal temples, the performance of elaborate and impressive ritual on the *rāja*'s behalf, and to perpetuate the flow of traditional economic redistributions to the *rāja*'s alliance network.

Pre-eleventh-century epigraphy reflects the concentration of political power at the regional level. Although a Javanese ruler claimed *mahārāja* status and may have had other regional chiefs in various ways recognizing his overlordship, his powers were still ultimately derived from his possession of *watĕk* regional rights over a network of *wanua* village clusters. Thus a central Java-based *mahārāja* is best understood simply as an important *rakrayān* regional chief. A ruler claiming *mahārāja* status, along with other important regional chiefs who did not claim this lofty title, exercised the rights and obligations of a *rakrayān* and little more.

The inscription currently considered definitive on early Javanese statecraft is the charter of Balitung, dated 907 and discovered at Kedu in central Java, which enumerates the eight ancestors of the monarch Śri Mahārāja Rakai Watukura dyaḥ Balitung. All eight ancestors bear the *rakrayān* title, and all except the first, Sañjaya, are also designated *"mahārāja,"* an assigned status confirmed in all but two cases in inscriptions individually issued.[47] But in a 732 inscription Sañjaya claims to be the *rakrayān* of the Mataram region who also holds the title of *ratu,* a Javanese equivalent of the Indic *mahārāja* title introduced by the Śailendras.[48]

Six inscriptions, dated 872–880, inscribed on twelve plates found at

Polengan near present-day Yogyakarta, which were issued by the Mahārāja Rakrayān of Kayuwangi or by a *rakrayān* subordinate to him, document the regionalized nature of central Javanese statecraft.[49] The six inscriptions deal with the construction and maintenance of the sanctuary of Gunung Hyang ("The Mountain of the Gods"), a local or regional temple complex reflecting the same religious ideology as the Hindu temple complex Sañjaya founded on the Diëng Plateau in north central Java. In these inscriptions the Rakrayān of Sirikan, Pu Rakap, was rewarded by the Mahārāja Rakrayān of Kayuwangi in 872 with a land grant. Pu Rakap reciprocated by building a temple *(prasada)* and assigning to it tribute rights due from a part of lands "under his jurisdiction" *(watĕk)* made tax free *(sīma)* by act of the Mahārāja in 875.[50] In 876 another *rakrayān,* Pagar Wĕsi, also assigned income from lands "subject to his jurisdiction" *(watĕk)* to this temple. The Rakrayān of Sirikan in turn presented gifts to Pagar Wĕsi and his family in 877—seemingly Pagar Wĕsi and Pu Rakap were allies, confirming their relationship via periodic gift exchanges. Pu Rakap at the same time assigned to the temple part of the income from the land granted to him in 872 by the Mahārāja, but only did so after first asking the permission of the elders of the village clusters involved.

The fact that Pu Rakap did not have to similarly consult the elders of the lands in the 875 *sīma* grant whose income he initially assigned elucidates the rights of a *rakrayān* regional chief. Rights to lands held as a *watĕk* region could be assigned at the will of the *rakrayān* regional chief holding those rights. For lands that were not *watĕk* lands, that is, lands not yet subject to a regional chief or uncultivated or "free" lands, the regional chief held only those rights assigned to him by agreement of the local village cluster's elders. As a further example of the Rakrayān of Sirikan's authority vis-à-vis the village cluster elders, in 878 Pu Rakap again endowed income to his temple after first purchasing the right to this income from the village cluster elders; in 880 he assigned more land rights after purchasing them and obtaining the approval of the village cluster inhabitants as a whole.[51] It would thus appear that an individual claiming *mahārāja* status could assign the privilege to negotiate rights with unattached *wanua* village clusters not previously incorporated into a *watĕk* region to favored *rakrayān* regional chiefs, but in such instances, as is well illustrated by these ninth-century inscriptions, the authority of the *mahārāja,* who was not viewed as the representative of the affected local population, was limited. In effect the Rakrayān of Sirikan's right to extend his authority over lands adjacent to his *watĕk* lands was being recognized by the Mahārāja of Kayuwangi, who termed this recognition of what would probably have transpired anyway a "land grant." The right of Pu Rakap to assume authority over these "free" lands was subject to the approval of the local residents, represented by their elders, who in this instance held the absolute administrative right to the land, but who were offered the opportunity to become subject to the Rakrayān of Sirikan for whatever benefits this new arrangement might provide.

These inscriptions as well as others demonstrate three important facts about early central Javanese statecraft. First, the relationships among *rakrayān* regional chiefs, including those between those claiming *mahārāja* status and those who did not, was marked by a limited confederation based upon periodocally renewed reciprocal interactions. Thus the Rakrayān of Kayuwangi was seemingly politically superior to the Rakrayān of Sirikan, and the Rakrayān Pagar Wĕsi was the Rakrayān of Sirikan's ally; each of these relationships was maintained via reciprocal gift exchanges. Second, these ninth-century inscriptions reflect the consolidation of landholding at the regional level under a *rakrayān,* a member of an indigenous landed elite who was expanding his authority through the confederation of previously autonomous *wanua* village clusters with his *watĕk* territorial base. Third, a critical role in this confederation process was played by the pretext of a donation to a temple. Under the authority and patronage of this *rakrayān* a regional temple became a center providing unity beyond the *wanua* level of socioeconomic integration. The transfer of land rights to this temple were negotiated by the *rakrayān*—the inhabitants of the local village clusters and their elders did not initiate transfers of rights to local production to the Rakrayān's regional temple in the 878 and 880 inscriptions. In return for their promise to pay tribute directly to the *rakrayān*'s temple the village cluster elders and inhabitants received gifts. In these instances transfers of gold, silver, and clothing were made to the affected village cluster's population as payment for the land rights bestowed upon the temple by the Rakrayān of Sirikan.[52]

This gift exchange involving the Rakrayān of Sirikan's temple reinforced the image of Pu Rakap, his temple, or ideally both, as the symbolic source of local prosperity; it served notice that he had good connections with the gods of ritual. The temple, emphasizing Indic religious symbols and integrating preexistent local beliefs *(adat)* with Indian cosmology to ideologically support the interests of the *rakrayān,* might also have become the center for the *rakrayān*'s management of the lands under his authority.[53] *Rakrayān* in general who already enjoyed economic power derived from their *watĕk* rights—demonstrated by their lavish gifts as recorded in Javanese inscriptions—were beginning to concentrate some of their capital in temples.[54] Gifts bestowed upon temples, such as those of the Rakrayān of Sirikan, generated merit for the regional chief and raised his status as well as others', including his *mahārāja* superior and his allied *rakrayān,* who participated in his endowments; gifts to a *rakrayān*'s temple offered the opportunity for the *rakrayān*'s network of allies to demonstrate their generosity as well as their continuing loyalty. The economic return from such endowments was perhaps secondary to the "symbolic capital"—the religious, social, and political status—derived from the gifts to the temple patronized by the *rakrayān.*[55]

Interestingly, from the eighth century on central Javanese *mahārāja*s who emerged from among the *rakrayān* ranks do not appear to have had economic capital superior to that of the *rakrayān* who assumed subordinate status to the *mahārāja.* Rather, the *mahārāja*'s elite status depended on the symbolic capital bestowed by his ritual leadership and successful development of temple networks. The temples of subordinate *rakrayān* claimed legitimacy by serving as local representatives of the *mahārāja*'s central temples—as for instance the Rakrayān of Sirikan's temple looked to the "royal" temple complex on the Diëng Plateau as the source of its sanctity. Thereby early Javanese *mahārāja*s more than political or economic authority exercised a "ritual sovereignty,"[56] sanctifying their *mahārāja* status by constructing impressive temple complexes and by patronizing "Brahman" priests who performed elaborate rituals that endowed them with sacred powers and reinforced their "aura of divine majesty."[57]

A *mahārāja,* as a *rakrayān* regional chief competing with other regional chiefs, needed to constantly confirm his role as the ultimate source of his subjects' prosperity. The sacred ritual at the *mahārāja*'s *kraton* helped to create this impression as the court became the ceremonial center of the realm, the source of religion, ritual art, and ritual literature.[58] These cultural promotions were paid for through "the lord's [monarch's] due" *(děrwaya haji)*: in return for capable rule a *rakrayān*/ monarch received a percentage of local production and labor services by the region's inhabitants to which the monarch was entitled *(gawai haji)* or "work done for the lord" *(bwat haji).* The monarch held the further right to "favor" *(anugraha)* or assign his right to a share of local production or labor to another individual or to a temple; in the latter instance these rights of the monarch became the "possession of the god" *(dewa děrwaya)* or "work done for the god" *(bwat hyang).* Such rights could also be temporarily assigned to accomplish the construction of public works such as dams and bridges.[59] Effective assignment of the monarch's rights to local production and labor service could stimulate production and the distribution of goods, while also maintaining the interdependent relationship between the royal *kraton* and the autochthonous *wanua* village clusters via the emphasis of the "gift" or "favor" implicit in the *anugraha* assignment that was the consequence of the monarch's actions. Monarchs thus benefited from converting tribute to the lord *(bwat haji)* into tribute to the god *(bwat hyang),* whether receiving in return direct or indirect economic benefit or symbolic capital as the initiator of the gift and chief patron of the deity.[60]

The sanctity of Hindu rulers in central Java was initially concentrated in the temple complex on the Diëng Plateau, which was originally a sacred "mountain of the gods," a center for the worship of indigenous deities that by the sixth century had become the locus of a Javanese Śaivite cult.[61] The reign of the *rakrayān* Sañjaya in the early eighth century was critical in the development of the central Javanese statecraft described above. Sañjaya's 732 Caṅggal inscription provides information about the royal Śaivite cult on the Diëng Plateau.[62]

In this 732 inscription, Sañjaya erected a *liṅga* that he associated with a mountain, praising Śiva, Brahma, and Viṣṇu and invoking the immortals residing in the cosmic universe "who used to inhabit an island *(dvīpa)* [*bhūmi,* a land] of great prosperity known as Yava [i.e., Ptolemy's Yāvadvīpa]." But according to the inscription the Yāvadvīpa land had disappeared; Sañjaya was invoking the spirits of this former Yāvadvīpa realm. Sañjaya claimed to be the current and intimate representative of the ancestors of Yāvadvīpa, as well as the patron of the sacred "field of Śiva," the Diëng Plateau temple complex.[63] Sañjaya thus established his legitimacy on the sacred ground of the Diëng Plateau by bringing together several earlier cults into a new, syncretic Śaivite cult.[64] The 732 inscription notes that after Sañjaya had subdued neighboring *rāja,* elevating his feet above their heads and symbolizing his sovereignty in a traditional Javanese way, all goodness prevailed, there was peace and prosperity, and there was no fear among men:

> Then there came forth (one) who was rich in good qualities . . . who had his feet high above other kings of good family who were standing on the ground. This king was named Śri Sañjaya, son of the [rulers of Yavadvīpa]; he was glorious, honored by learned men as a scholar in the subtleties of the *śastras* [Indian legal texts that focus on the maintenance of harmony among the social order], a ruler who had courage . . . and had . . . subdued many neighboring monarchs *(rājas),* and his fame like the splendor of the sun spread in all quarters. When he ruled the Earth [Java] who has the waves of the ocean for her girdle and mountains for her breasts, . . . ["all goodness prevailed, there was peace and prosperity, and there was no fear among men"].[65]

Chinese references to Java also indicate a transition in Javanese statecraft corresponding to Sañjaya's early eighth-century rule, eighth-century records showing a very different state from that which existed in Java during the seventh century. The *Revised Annals of the T'ang* described the Javanese state the Chinese knew as Ho-ling, which corresponds to Sañjaya's realm in time and place, as "exceedingly rich":

> The ruler lives in the [capital] city of She-p'o [Java]. . . . His ancestor Chi-yen moved eastward to the city of P'o-lu-chia-ssu. . . . On the borders [of Ho-ling] are twenty-eight small countries, all of which owe allegiance to Ho-ling. . . . On top of the mountain there is the province of Lang-pi-ya. The ruler frequently ascends this mountain to gaze at the sea.[66]

This was a Ho-ling state superior to the modest political entity in central Java depicted in earlier Chinese accounts.[67] A new state had been created, a state with an inland base, a mountain, and "twenty-eight small countries" (i.e., *wanua* or *watĕk*) allied to it.

The Śailendra era, like that of Sañjaya immediately prior, was characterized by multiple regionally based power centers—at least three are documented as being contemporary with Śailendra rule and more may have existed but have not left inscriptions—as revealed in the various inscriptions issued between the eighth and tenth centuries by those who claimed *mahārāja* status. Balitung's 907 inscription, for instance, reconstructed a line of non-Śailendra rulers who were descended from Sañjaya.[68] While in the so-called Śailendra era in the eighth and ninth centuries central political authority was tentative and the structure of rule was in a constant state of flux, from the tenth-century inscription of Balitung on a different Javanese state began to appear that demonstrated a higher degree of unity than had been achieved previously, with power clearly concentrated in a single *kraton*. In this new era *mahārāja* status was consolidated and elevated as three *kraton* at Janggala/Singasari, Kaḍiri, and Majapahit emerged consecutively as the loci of economic as well as symbolic capital.

The Tenth Century: Post-Śailendra Era Transitions

Balitung, Rakrayān of Watukura, issued at least three copies of his version of the royal genealogy of Java in 907: two in central Java were inscribed on bronze plates, while a third, in eastern Java, was inscribed on stone. Thereafter the center of authority in Java moved to eastern Java. However, evidence of a high order Indic civilization in eastern Java predates this shift. A Sanskrit inscription dated 760 records the dedication of a temple to the sanctified Indian sage Agastya by Gajayāna, son of King *(narapati)* Devasingha, who ruled from the *pura (kraton)* of Kañjuruhan, a realm in the upper reaches of the Brantas River, a fertile mountain plateau surrounded by four volcanoes.[69] Historians have argued that Gajayāna, a Śaivite patron of Agastya, was descended from Sañjaya and had fled to eastern Java sometime after 732 to escape from the Buddhist Śailendra dynasty.[70] This argument is based on references in the *Revised Annals of the T'ang,* as quoted above, that the ancestor of Chi-yen, the new ruler of Ho-ling in the eighth century, had moved eastward to the city of P'o-lu-chia-ssu in a previous age. Historians believe that this relative of the earlier Ho-ling rulers returned to the She-p'o (Java) *kraton* to replace the previous Śailendra rulers, restoring Śaivite worship as the basis of royal legitimacy.[71]

Other historians stress the indigenous development of a *kraton* on the upper Brantas Plateau, an area well suited for wet-rice cultivation. The favorable topography made irrigation uncomplicated; the Hariñjing canal system in this area dates to 804. The village elders *(bhagawānta)* themselves—and not a ruler *(raka* or *rāja)* claiming rights over their villages—claim to have initiated the construction of the local irrigation network.[72] In 891, a locally based and independent Rakrayān of Kañjuruhan ruled from a regional base at Singhasari in the midst of the plateau.[73] Historians believe that Balitung conquered this *rakrayān* and the remainder of eastern Java at the beginning of the tenth century, but the fact that most of Balitung's inscriptions were issued in central Java demonstrates that central Java was his base.[74] It remained for Pu Siṇḍok, who reigned around 928, to establish a royal *kraton* in eastern Java and begin in earnest the integration of central and eastern Java into a single polity.

Pu Siṇḍok, in an inscription dated 937, had reported hostilities between Śrīvijaya and the Javanese realm.[75] The inscription eulogized Pu Siṇḍok for saving the eastern Java realm from a 928–929 Śrīvijaya attack. In Casparis' reconstruction of Śailendra history, *kraton* based in eastern Java had by this time become active and direct participants in international trade, which unsettled the Śailendra rulers who by then occupied the Śrīvijaya throne. They were concerned that eastern Java would increasingly come to control the eastern archipelago spice trade, with the result that the trade would bypass Śrīvijaya's ports. Thus the Malāyu-based Śrīvijaya army mounted an expedition against eastern Java. After making some progress toward the hinterland, they were defeated by Pu Siṇḍok. Central Java had been ignored, according to this reconstruction, because of the new importance of the Brantas River Delta as a source of Javanese royal power and as the base for interinsular trade.[76]

Caṇḍi Kidal, pre-Majapahit era, eastern Java.

Upper terrace, Borobudur.

Borobudur, central Java.

Śiva temple, Caṇḍi Loro Jonggrang, Prambanan, central Java.

Caṇḍi Plaosan, Prambanan, with Ratubaka Plateau in background.

Sanggariti mountain "bathing" temple, eastern Java.

There is evidence, however, that central Java was not removed from the Javanese commercial developments of the tenth century. Archaeological surveys in the late 1970s and early 1980s have turned up an abundance of Chinese ceramics that date from the tenth century widely distributed from the north coast of Java to the Ratubaka Plateau to the south.[77] The presence of these foreign goods is evidence that international trade was taking place. The coastal centers Pemalang, Kendal, and Japara participated in this trade but were not linked to their hinterlands via river networks like other areas of the Southeast Asian island realm, including eastern Java.[78] Rather, a major road network connected the Kedu Plain to the north coast commercial centers via Parakan, and a branch road ran via Wonosobo to the Diëng Plateau, then northwest to the neighborhood of Pekalongan (see map 5).[79] This means that a central Java-based ruler could have become involved in the international trade despite the seeming isolation of his *kraton* in the interior rice plain. Furthermore, a central Java base was less vulnerable to an attack from outside Java than was the Brantas River system in eastern Java. Thus the 928 Malāyu attack against east Java shows that the interior of the Brantas region could be easily reached by an army from overseas, not that central Java was any less important as a participant in the international maritime trade.[80]

In another reconstruction, the transfer of the Javanese state's base from central to eastern Java is seen as the result of the drain on the central Javanese economy resulting from the burst of temple construction that took place from the early eighth through the early tenth centuries, as Javanese monarchs used all the resources at their disposal to build temples.[81] However, most of this temple construction was done by regional chiefs *(rakrayān)* rather than by those claiming *mahārāja* status. Aside from the Diëng Plateau complex there were only four major state-level temple complexes constructed in the name of a central Javanese *mahārāja:* Caṇḍi Sewu, Caṇḍi Plaosan, and Caṇḍi Loro Jonggrang at Prambanan, and the Borobudur. While the Borobudur was constructed under Śailendra patronage for the worship of the deified ancestors of the Śailendra dynasty, Loro Jonggrang and Sewu were built with the cooperation of various members of the realm, notably subordinate *rakrayān,* and Plaosan was built by the *mahārāja* and his state administrators with the cooperation of local *rakrayān,* each of whom contributed one or more buildings.[82] The labor *(bwat hyang)* necessary for this temple construction does not appear to have been a burden, and indeed agriculturalists were not actively needed for the temple construction. Royal bondsmen and professional artisan groups provided the continuous labor for this construction—Brahmans or other religious specialists laid out temples, sculptors carved the statues and reliefs, bondsmen carried stones and performed the preparatory shaping and chipping of stone, while local *rakrayān* provided the labor force for the construction of specific buildings by temporarily assigning their normal rights to labor *(bwat haji)*.[83] Work in central Java's paddy fields could, as now, be done largely by women, freeing men to work on the temples.[84] Furthermore, temple construction could have been of a seasonal nature, corresponding to the slack periods of the growing cycle, as work schedules were arranged so that they would not diminish local agricultural productivity.[85] One historian finds that this "picture of a despotic ruler, forcing his subjects to build splendid edifices to his own glory, resulting in economic collapse [is] rather improbable."[86]

The Java historical tradition treats the transfer of power to eastern Java as one among numerous cyclical shifts of Javanese *kraton* due to various crises, such as invasion by an enemy who desecrated the *kraton,* necessitating the abandonment of the old royal compound in favor of another, the new *kraton* becoming the ruler's source of a new and more powerful prowess. In Javanese literature a Javanese *kraton* was normally shifted on the average of every fourth generation prior to the fourteenth century.[87] The events responsible for these transfers were either the fabrications of ancient historians with the cycle concept in mind or the consequence of belief in a cycle of kingship based on the actual history as it was passed on by oral historians. In the eyes of Java's own historians, Java's early history was a product of the cycle concept: it was believed that a catastrophe would take place if every fourth monarch did not establish a new *kraton,* which resulted in the periodic movement of a *mahārāja*'s palace compound, even within the immediate area. Such moves were elaborate, requiring the ritual creation of a new world order *(maṇḍala)* in which the center of the cosmos was transferred to the new royal center and there was a corresponding establishment of a new cosmic mountain via the construction of a new state temple as the replica of Mount Meru, the center of the universe (see chap. 1).

Internal as well as external evidence suggest that a major crisis did occur in the first quarter of the tenth century and this crisis, viewed by early Javanese historians as an omen that the current order had come to an end, was the major reason for the transfer of the Javanese royal *kraton* to eastern Java. The early tenth century was marked by incessant wars among various *rakrayān,* as documented in the contemporary epigraphy. This disorder could well have been viewed as provoking the wrath of the gods, who responded with the major earthquake or volcanic eruption that one historian argues took place around 925, when the royal *kraton* moved from central to eastern Java. This historian postulated, based on his study of Javanese and foreign literature, that a cataclysmic explosion of Mount Merapi produced ash rains and landslides not unlike those produced by the eruption of Mount St. Helens in the United States in 1980. This made the fertile Kedu and Mataram rice plains temporarily uninhabitable, and thus central Java was abandoned in favor of eastern Java.[88] The Śrīvijaya raids of the early tenth century were therefore directed at the new Javanese population center and locus of royal power in eastern Java's Brantas River basin.

The economic consequences of the transfer of royal authority to eastern Java had an impact on the evolution of Javanese statecraft. We have already seen that the resource bases of Javanese rulers, whether they were of *mahārāja* or *rakrayān* status, were essentially equal in central Java. Differences in status were the results of political alliances, reinforced by the construction of temple networks and the establishment of a superior spiritual prowess. In the late ninth century, however, there was a new concern among central Javanese monarchs for their economic base. The reign of the Mahārāja Rakrayān of Kayuwangi was especially critical to the development of the *kraton*'s economic leadership, although there was still significant regional political autonomy during his reign.[89] The promotion of agricultural development was apparently central to the Rakrayān of Kayuwangi's attempt to extend his royal resource base—bringing new lands into production by converting woodlands to wet-rice fields (882) and requiring in inscriptions dated 879 and 881 that unirrigated farmlands *(tĕgal)* should be converted to wet-rice fields.[90]

The movement of the royal *kraton* to eastern Java provided the opportunity for Javanese rulers to follow up on the Rakrayān of Kayuwangi's earlier initiatives and to secure a more ample economic base in the east than was possible in central Java. First, eastern Java's agricultural development potential was greater, partially due to the fact that the area was less populated and free of previously existing claims to *watĕk* authority by *rakrayān* and other elites. In the post-tenth-century epigraphy of eastern Java the authority of a *mahārāja* over land is more direct, and *mahārāja*s held *rakrayān* rights over a more extensive personal economic base. Second, there was greater access to the sea from the eastern Java hinterland. Eastern Java had a wide coastal plain that could be developed as a center of wet-rice production and the Brantas and Solo rivers that drain this plain were both navigable, allowing good internal communication among regions and especially the flow of local production from the highlands of the Brantas Plateau to the coast and, vice-versa, goods from the coast to the hinterland. A base in the coastal plain or even in the upper Brantas region made it possible for Javanese monarchs to participate in and supervise international trade more directly than central Java monarchs, who had been more isolated in the interior. Eastern Java monarchs thus had new opportunities for the acquisition of wealth, which in turn meant more economic redistributions and temple constructions to reinforce the ruler's power and prestige. Unlike central Java monarchs who had to share the financing of such activities—often undertaken primarily by the *mahārāja*'s allied *rakrayān*—eastern Java monarchs had greater economic resources at their personal disposal for such enterprises.

By the time Airlangga came to power early in the eleventh century, not only had the status of the *mahārāja* been elevated but the possibilities for economic achievement implicit in the new eastern Java order had been consolidated as well. This is clear from a 1037 inscription of Airlangga reporting that the Brantas River had burst its dikes, flooding many local villages and making it difficult for trading vessels to reach the Javanese monarch's port.[91] The *mahārāja*'s income was greatly diminished. Although previous efforts by individual communities to control the Brantas had proven fruitless, the *mahārāja* intervened and had two dams constructed. Through this effort and his continuing leadership, prosperity returned.[92]

Airlangga's reign was critical to the evolution of a Javanese state system. A 1041 stone inscription reported that a "great catastrophe" took place in 1016, when Airlangga's father-in-law and predecessor to the throne Dharmawangśa Teguḥ was killed along with his *kraton* elite by an enemy (Śrīvijaya), who destroyed the *kraton*. The Cōḷa raid of 1024–1025 eliminated Śrīvijaya's hold over central and western Java—Śrīvijaya's authority in central Java at that time was supported by alliances with regionally based *rakrayān,* who relied on Śrīvijaya's assistance to maintain their autonomy from eastern Java-based *mahārāja*s. Thereafter Airlangga began to "reestablish order," consolidating his authority over all of Java and Bali. He proceeded to modify the style of Javanese statecraft by placing emphasis upon a localized Javanese culture rather than patronizing unadulterated Indian cultural forms as had been the case during the era of central Java sovereignty.[93] Airlangga ascended the throne as the victorious Śrī Mahārāja Rakrayān Halu, establishing a *kraton* at the unidentified capital Kahuripan in the northeastern corner of east Java.

While Airlangga's maritime interests are confirmed in his 1035 inscription, the same inscription also demonstrates the evolution of royal authority in eastern Java. More complex techniques of water management were necessary to develop *sawah* cultivation in the lower Solo and Brantas river plains than were required in central Java or even in the upper Brantas Plateau. In the coastal river plain the flow of water had to be regulated; otherwise the land was subject to periodic flooding. This had to be accomplished by a complex regionwide water management network if these lands were to be regularly productive, a degree of management significantly greater than that required for the functioning of the less technically sophisticated irrigation networks of earlier Javanese civilization. In eastern Java's epigraphic records Airlangga and other eastern Java monarchs provided the expertise and management necessary to facilitate this development and were rewarded with the opportunity to assume reciprocal rights over this land. Their personal powers vis-à-vis those of previous *rakrayān* who served as managers of *watĕk* regional irrigation networks in earlier times were considerably enhanced.

Except for the fifth-century western Java inscription that records Pūrṇavarman's diversion of a river near present-day Jakarta—and although wet-rice cultivation was extensively practiced in central Java well before the shift of Java's royal authority to eastern Java in the tenth century—the remaining epigraphic records of the building of early Java's hydraulic systems were issued in eastern Java.[94] These inscriptions are related to the construction of major water management systems that would bring the Brantas River and its tributaries under control. The Brantas was a turbulent river with a propensity to cause major destruction of wet-rice fields when it periodically overflowed its banks, explaining why local efforts to protect the fields from regular inundation appear to have been insufficient. Indeed, in each of the early centers of wet-rice cultivation in the Brantas River system there is a corresponding post-ninth-century inscription that records not only the building of a major component (e.g., dam or canal) of a regional hydraulic system but also an eastern Java monarch's involvement in this construction or in the continuing direction of local elders or regional political authorities to guarantee that the hydraulic system would be properly maintained or managed.[95]

Inscriptions from the Hariñjing River system provide a unique five-century history of a hydraulic system in a region northwest of Kaḍiri in the upper Brantas basin. In 804 a dam was built and a canal excavated under the direction of the village elders—not a ruler claiming rights over their village cluster—to connect the Hariñjing River to the larger Kanto River, which flows from the Kelud volcanic mountain into the Brantas at present-day Kertosono. In 921 the descendents of the "elders" who had constructed the water management network had their authority over the region's hydraulic system confirmed by the *mahārāja* Tuloḍong (919–921).[96] Then in 1350 a stone inscription recorded the restoration of the 804 dam under the Majapahit monarchs, and, suggesting that the original dam had been inadequate to control seasonal floodwaters, states that the dam "was now so solidly reinforced that it would last forever, for all the inhabitants of the valley east of Daha [Kaḍiri]."[97] The Hariñjing inscriptions also record "canal ceremonies" that were held every third day of the realmwide festival celebrating the annual harvest.[98] As well, there appears to have been a temple constructed at the origin of the Hariñjing River's waters on Mount Kelud to commemorate the completion of the Hariñjing hydraulic system.[99] This temple and the "canal rituals" may be compared to those at assorted "bathing places" that are distributed throughout central and eastern Java. At such places water flowed from the top of a sacred mountain through a temple to a system of channels and basins that carried water to the land below. While historians have generally stressed that such mountain bathing places were centers for the worship of ancestors and of mountain spirits, these likely also assumed roles as centers for irrigation network worship rites.[100] Through ritual such as this the ruler established a symbolic communication with his realm's rivers, one that was important to the general prosperity of the state's economy.[101]

The Śailendra Era in Overview

The thesis that the transfer of the Javanese royal court to eastern Java provided increased opportunities for the development of the ruler's economic base—and consequently enhanced the state's political powers—offers a new insight into the history of the Śailendra era. The Śailendras first emerged as rulers of one among several important socioeconomic regional units *(watĕk)* in central Java during the early seventh century. The initial Śailendras were *rakrayān,* rulers of *watĕk* that integrated village clusters *(wanua)* participating in a regional irrigation network. As *rakrayān,* these earliest Śailendra rulers provided the administrative expertise necessary to maintain the local irrigation system and, through their patronage of Indic religion, constructed sacred cults to legitimize their regional integration of *wanua* into *watĕk*. By the early seventh century central Javanese *rakrayān* began to construct supra-*watĕk* networks, drawing together several *rakrayān* into alliance networks. The alliance leader, the economic equal of his subordinate *rakrayān,* came to his leadership role principally through his own initiative and patronage of a superior cult of legitimacy. He enjoyed a superior magical prowess and thus could symbolically guarantee the prosperity of those who subordinated themselves to his leadership. Subordinate *rakrayān* built local temples that mirrored the cult ritual of the leading *rakrayān*'s central temple complex. Eighth-century Javanese monarchs were thus important as the source of a cultural integration of the central Javanese realm.

Their power was, however, limited. As economic equals to their subordinate *rakrayān,* and because the central Javanese wet-rice economy functioned best at the local and regional levels and required minimal centralized economic leadership by a higher authority, leading *rakrayān* had few opportunities to politically dominate central Java's wet-rice economy except through their "sacred sovereignty."

Around 732 Sañjaya, claiming status as the Rakrayān of Mataram as well as *ratu,* a Javanese equivalent of the *mahārāja* title, installed the leading central Java Hindu cult at the Diëng temple complex, drawing legitimacy from indigenous cults previously associated with the Diëng Plateau and integrating them with a localized Śiva cult in which Sañjaya was Śiva's semidivine worldly patron. By the mid-eighth century the Śailendra *rakrayān* had replaced Sañjaya's line as the dominant *rakrayān* among central Java's rulers of *watĕk* regions. The Śailendras called themselves *mahārāja*s and introduced a Buddhist cult that was concentrated in a new sacred center located at the Śailendra *watĕk* base in the Kedu Plain. Their central temple, the Borobudur, symbolized the Śailendra world order; other newly constructed Buddhist temples in the Śailendra realm were in various ways preparatory to the higher order Buddhist theology depicted on the terraces of the Borobudur cosmic mountain. The Borobudur sanctified Śailendra rule; association with this "cosmic mountain" brought prosperity to their realm.[102]

Central Java became an internationally recognized pilgrimage center and an acclaimed center for Buddhist scholarship. The visits of Chinese and Indian pilgrims were no doubt used by Śailendra monarchs and their clerical staffs to validate the Śailendra *mahārāja*s' special patronage of Buddhism and their claims to subsequent magical prowess. The patronage of Buddhism was also the Śailendras' link with the Śrīvijaya maritime state, which in the eighth century held sovereignty over the previously autonomous river outlets on the western Java coast. The importance of this patronage of Buddhism by both Śrīvijaya and the Śailendras as the symbolic source of each realm's sovereignty made possible a peaceful intellectual and cultural exchange between the two states. International pilgrims and no doubt Śrīvijaya- and Java-based scholars as well moved between Śrīvijaya and Javanese Buddhist centers with ease. The ninth century was the high point of this religious and cultural exchange and can be depicted as an "era of good feeling." The cultural dialogue between these two states is reflected in the inspired Buddhist art of the period distributed among the sites of Śrīvijaya's authority in Sumatra and the Malay Peninsula, as well as in central Java. This art was neither of Śrīvijayan nor Javanese origin alone but was a product of the interaction of both. This eighth and ninth century "good feeling" between the

Śailendra and Śrīvijaya realms explains the reference to the Śailendras in the Nakhọn Si Thammarat inscription and adds credence to Casparis' thesis that a marriage alliance took place between the Śailendra and Śrīvijaya *mahārājas*, formalizing a political relationship that went beyond the cultural relationship.

One reason that this peaceful interaction was possible was the essentially complementary nature of the pre-tenth-century economies of Śrīvijaya and central Java. While the Śailendra realm in central Java was a productive, regionally integrated wet-rice economy with limited supralocal economic linkages or ambitions, Śrīvijaya's economy and sovereignty depended primarily on international trade and strong state interest in stimulating the flow of local production from upriver hinterlands to coastal entrepôts. Central Java inscriptions do not show great concern on the part of Javanese *mahārājas* for economic integration or development of their *watĕk* until the tenth century. Except for Pūrṇavarman in the fifth century, who did not create a lasting state, only in the eleventh century do Java-based rulers assume a conspicuous role as facilitators of international commerce.

Pre-eleventh-century Javanese monarchs appear to have been quite willing to recognize Śrīvijaya's supremacy in the international commercial arena. Their lack of interest in international trade is partially explained by the fact that they derived sufficient income and assistance as traditional *rakrayān* regional chiefs ruling *watĕk* regions to accomplish their desired ends, which were chiefly concerned with the construction of temples that enhanced their ritual sovereignty. Royal ambition in Java thus dictated a preference for symbolic rather than material ends.

As we have seen, however, archaeological evidence does not support the conclusion that the central Java heartland was ever economically isolated during the Śailendra era. Central Java epigraphy records a developing hierarchical marketing network that began with local periodic markets known as *pkĕn*. In chapter 1 it was argued that the *pkĕn* marketing network corresponded to the *wanua* village cluster, and thus supported the integration of local peasant populations. Since *pkĕn* marketing units were imbedded within a *watĕk* region, *watĕk* have thus been understood to have been self-contained irrigation and marketing units supporting the social, economic, and political cohesion of the unit as well as its autonomy vis-à-vis the centralizing ambitions of *mahārājas*. Yet at the same time the *pkĕn* markets provided the forum for the *watĕk*'s external commercial contacts, the place where "foreign" merchants were allowed to trade, and thus facilitated the flow of local production upward to supralocal market centers as well as receiving in return the downward flow of foreign goods for local consumption from the supralocal markets. These goods were then redistributed within the *pkĕn* to participating *wanua* producers.

Such supralocal marketing links provided the basis for other types of integration beyond the *watĕk* level, interaction that was not inherent within the autonomous *watĕk* irrigation systems of central Java, and to some extent must have facilitated the attempts of *rakrayān* to develop the supra-*watĕk* focused religious networks that were so critical to their claim of sovereignty as Javanese *mahārājas*. It may therefore be proposed that previously established ties beyond the *watĕk* and *pkĕn* markets to supralocal market centers became the basis for *watĕk* participation in hierarchical political and religious networks that concentrated ultimately in a *mahārāja*'s *kraton* and his central temple complex.[103] The religious centers (temples) and political centers *(kraton)* built by those who claimed *mahārāja* status would thereby have integrated *watĕk* with major urban centers and centers of consumption, connected by the road networks of central Java. These urban centers not only drew the production of the *watĕk,* via the *pkĕn* markets, but also created a demand for foreign goods that was supplied by itinerant merchants who connected these hinterland centers and their indigenous exchange networks to ports on Java's northern coast. While in the Śailendra era in central Java there is no definitive evidence that *mahārāja*s or other land-based elites significantly directed the development of this marketing system, international merchants were present in royal centers of power and patronized royal temples.[104] Airlangga's 1037 inscription as well as later inscriptions of eastern Java-based monarchs reflect far greater and more regular interaction between rulers and merchants at various levels of the state system than was true in central Java and reveal that there was an explosion in the potentials for meaningful economic cooperation.

The tenth and eleventh centuries brought demands for monarchs in eastern Java to take a larger role as economic leaders. The development of the lower Brantas River basin wet-rice agricultural system required their involvement and also gave them more direct access to the northern coast. This meant extending their economic and political sovereignty, and in the process they became more than "ritual sovereigns" ruling from semiautonomous regional irrigation networks. Airlangga provides an example of this transformation. After consolidating his economic base in the Brantas basin, he instigated the construction of an effective irrigation system in the coastal plain, at the same time using the flood control system to develop an anchorage capable of accommodating foreign ships. As a result, the entire realm prospered. The emphasis on shared prosperity reflected in Airlangga's 1037 inscription resulting from the inspired economic leadership of a *mahārāja* is quite different from the emphasis on the *mahārāja*'s spiritual sovereignty as the source of prosperity that is stressed in earlier central Javanese inscriptions. It denotes different concerns as well as different expectations of a *mahārāja*. The commercial leadership that eastern Java ports began to exercise from the time of Airlangga's reign lasted until the Dutch effectively assumed authority over the Javanese coast in the seventeenth century (see chap. 9).

By the early tenth century, then, Javanese statecraft had taken on a different character. It was the Śailendra era, however, that provided the foundations for the flowering of the Javanese economy and statecraft. The Śailendra legacy to Java included the concept of the *mahārāja* and a further definition of Indic-style rule. The Śailendras demonstrated the effectiveness of patronage to temples as the source of legitimacy and symbolic capital and through the establishment of temple networks began the process of political integration by drawing subordinate *rakrayān* and their temples into confederations. This stimulated the development of an integrated economic infrastructure whereby local products began to make their way, through supralocal markets, to Java's coastal ports.

While the political order that the eastern Java rulers established clearly did not achieve the centralized status they often claimed, there was significantly more power concentrated in the royal court from the tenth century on than there had been previously. Of most significance for this study, the increased interest in the world outside Java and the capacity for action among eastern Javanese monarchs dictated that Java in the future would have a more positive relationship with the sea. While the introspective central Javanese "states" were limited in their potential for economic development—as too for political centralization—once the royal court was firmly entrenched in eastern Java, *mahārāja*s began the integration of wet-rice plain and riverine economic systems that led to a higher level of political integration.

6

Temples as Economic Centers in Early Cambodia

In chapter 3 it was proposed that Southeast Asia's early history can be understood as being characterized by a series of economic and social transformations. In tribal societies, a reciprocal sharing of economic resources among family, community, and religious groups maintained the social unit. The development of entrepreneurial activities brought social imbalances, resulting in the transformation of the indigenous economy and the emergence of political entities based on redistributive exchange. Several early Southeast Asian societies went beyond these primary levels of integration, developing organizational mechanisms for the acquisition, control, and disposal of resources in pursuit of collective goals, most of which were political.[1]

The Khmer state that came to be based in Angkor—at its height from the ninth through the thirteenth centuries—demonstrates this transformation thesis. Especially noteworthy is the development of Khmer temples as centers of redistribution and the "continuous and massive movement of products" from villages toward temples.[2] Khmer temples collected and ultimately returned to the countryside a portion of the local output, goods that represented a significant share of the society's total economic production. These goods were redistributed according to the wealth, power, or prestige of the recipients. With the temple network as its base, Khmer society went beyond primary redistributive integration and reached a higher level of centralized economic control. The massive public works projects directed by Khmer monarchs—highlighted by the construction of Angkor Wat by Sūryavarman II in the early twelfth century and the even more impressive Angkor Thom by Jayavarman VII at the end of the same century—required a degree of economic and social integration high enough to provide the economic resources necessary to fund and carry out these projects. They could not be supplied by a simple redistributive economy. To achieve these ends, goods and services from the Khmer agrarian system had to be channelled into the hands of those representatives of the state who were responsible for the achievement of broadly political goals. They created an integrated state political system.

Although separate mechanisms of administration were developed in each temple, Khmer temples were never autonomous from Khmer society and its stratified political order. At the primary level, Khmer temples were subject to the authority of a landed elite and were an instrument by which this elite reinforced its economic and political control. Temple staffs were often members of elite families, and the staff of a local temple was frequently supervised by members of the local landholding elite who had entered the clergy or by priests who owed their positions and their prosperity to continued patronage by that elite. Normally, the consolidation into an estate of an elite's land rights in regional agrarian communities was legitimized by the construction of a temple, with income from specified estate lands designated to support the temple's activities. Collections, gifts, and offerings flowed to the temple as part of a cycle of economic redistribution. They flowed outward in the form of support for the performances of rituals and construction and in so doing reinforced the prowess of the elite as patrons of the temple deity and as the source of prosperity in the eyes of the local inhabitants.

By the height of the Angkor era, local temples and their cults had been integrated into a statewide network of temples that was ultimately tied to the king's central temple at the royal capital. The priests from local temples participated in rituals at major royal temples that were constructed at strategic points throughout the state. They as well as their aristocratic patrons derived legitimacy from this participation. In return local temples helped to finance the activities of the central temples by assigning to them a portion of the annual collections. Under the guise of religion, Khmer monarchs, who dominated the central temples and their staffs, could draw part of the wealth of their realm to the royal capital without creating an elaborate secular bureaucracy to collect revenues in the state's name.

This chapter summarizes research on early Cambodian history and through Khmer temple inscriptions examines the political and economic transformation of the Khmer state. From these inscriptions we know that temples consistently served as centers for the collection of economic resources and that the development of the temple network paralleled the development of the Khmer state.[3] Yet temples were not centers for the redistribution of economic capital alone; they were equally important as centers for the redistribution of "symbolic capital." The temple network came to integrate the Khmer realm in two ways. On the one hand, temples linked disparate agricultural regions horizontally into an ever-expanding economic network whose wealth fueled the Khmer state. On the other hand, temples were the locus for the manipulation of cultural symbols to vertically integrate the higher and lower levels of the Khmer socioeconomy. As institutions imbedded within the traditional socioeconomy, temples assumed the leading role of "limiting and disguising the play of economic interests and calculations."[4]

Khmer Religion

In early Cambodia Hindu forms of religion were introduced in temples and temple ceremony to provide the basis for legitimizing political (and by implication economic) integration. As noted in chapter 1, local elites used the Śaivite religion to reinforce indigenous symbols of authority relationships. Since Śiva was referred to in Indian philosophy as the "Lord of the Mountain," proprietors of early Khmer temples were able to connect the worship of Śiva to indigenous beliefs in the sanctity of mountains, which were believed to be the abode of ancestor spirits responsible for the prosperity of the living. Equally responsible for the success or failure of the living were various local spirits who bestowed fertility on the land. Such fertility spirits were represented in early Cambodia by a *liṅga,* a stone or metal phallus usually inserted upright in a circular "vulva" *(yoni).* Since Indian tradition associated the *liṅga* with Śiva, the god of fertility, it was possible to link Śiva with these traditional spirits as well. Thus worship of Śiva "fit" with indigenous traditions in which worship of mountains and phallic symbols was necessary for the society's success.

Worship of Śiva in Cambodia became formalized in the *devarāja* ("god-king") cult of Jayavarman II (770–834), which was based on a mountaintop that became the site of his realm's principal temple at the center of the royal capital.[5] In the Brahmanical concept of the universe, a circular central continent, Jambudvīpa, was surrounded by seven oceans and continents. In the center of this continent was Mount Meru, around which the sun, the moon, and the stars revolved. On its summit was the city of the gods, where Indra, the "Lord of Heaven," reigned.[6] On the slopes of Mount Meru was the lowest of paradises (Lokapāla) where the "Guardians of the World" resided. Jayavarman II accordingly centered the cult of the *devarāja* at his capital city of Hariharālaya, south of Angkor on the edge of the Great Lake (Tonle Sap) in central Cambodia, on the summit of "Mount Mahendra," the Khmer equivalent of Mount Meru.

While building a Khmer state through a combination of conquest and the formation of a network of personal alliances, Jayavarman II also consolidated the worship of regional deities in his royal *devarāja* cult.[7] He incorporated the veneration for mountains, subordinated local ancestor spirits to the worship of Śiva, and then proclaimed himself Śiva's representative on earth. By associating himself with Śiva and the royal mountain, Mount Mahendra, he symbolized his ability to guarantee the flow of life-power from the spirit realm to his subjects. The establishment of the *devarāja* cult tied Jayavarman spiritually to his supporters, and the cult became an emblem of the unification of the Khmer realm. Henceforth, although there were struggles for power within the royal domain, struggles for local independence were denied religious sanction.[8] The Khmer monarch from Jayavarman II's time on could monopolize temporal power within the realm, power that was justified by a royal cult in which he alone could represent Śiva or any other Indian deity.

The royal capital and its realm were thus under the protection of the "Lord of the Heavens," and the king, his representative on earth, was the "Lord of the Mountains," the guardian of law and order, the protector of religion, the defender of his land against external foes, and the sum of all authority on earth. From the summit of Mount Mahendra (Mount Meru, the center of the universe), the *devarāja* entered into a relationship with the divine world. The royal temple was dedicated to the living monarch—the god-king—and it became his mausoleum when he died.

The blending of the indigenous cult of ancestor worship with the Indic religious forms gave the monarch magic properties that conferred immortality upon him. Statues and *liṅga*s of gods placed in the central and subordinate temples of the Khmer realm were portraits and symbols of kings, their names a fusion of monarchs' personal titles with the names of the gods. Jayavarman's successor, Indravarman I (877–889), constructed a stone temple to shelter the royal Śiva-*liṅga* Indreśvara in which the *devarāja* resided, and he thus became associated with Indreśvara.[9] Although early Khmer kings such as Jayavarman II and Indravarman I were identified with Śiva, in the early twelfth century Sūryavarman II assumed an intimate relationship with Viṣṇu and built Angkor Wat to honor this union. He became the *Viṣṇurāja* rather than the *devarāja*. At the end of the same century, Jayavarman VII was the Bodhisattva Lokeśvara who decorated the faces of Angkor Thom's Bayon temple complex (see page 144) and was honored in a new *Buddharāja* royal cult. Whether the *devarāja, Viṣṇurāja,* or *Buddharāja,* the Khmer king was the intermediary between man and the divine powers, the upholder of the established order *(dharma)* handed down by his ancestors, the intercessor with the spirit world for the fertility and prosperity of his realm. His capital city, with his royal temple at its center, was constructed in the image of the universe interpreted in terms of the Indic Mount Meru.[10]

The key religious elite of the Khmer realm was not composed of legalistic Brahmans but devotional *(bhakti)* ascetics—"wayward Brahmans" who were not interested in Vedic ritual sacrifices and preferred to stress Śiva's grace rather than the laws of orthodox Hinduism.[11] Gifts to Śiva or to any other "Hindu" or local deity linked to him brought one merit and thus hope of a superior death status.[12] A political overlord—a landed aristocrat—not a Brahman priest as in Vedic India, was viewed as having the foremost spiritual influence on his followers' lives and their hopes for salvation. The secular landed elites performed customary ritual roles, including providing those of lesser spiritual prowess *(śakti)* opportunities for enhancing their prospects after death. Political allegiance, expressed by personal loyalty, was based on indigenous attitudes about death and spiritual prowess. As acts of homage, and in theory to secure the favor of their overlord, subordinates offered presents to temples or erected statues or *liṅga*s in honor of the god-king.[13] Landed elites saw subordination to an overlord as providing further means of earning merit and satisfying their death wishes.[14] Gifts to ritual priests (Brahmans) were rare. Merit was earned by personal achievement rather than by honoring "Brahmans." Temple priests were not honored because of the rituals they performed; they benefited instead through their superintending of temples.

Jayavarman II's *Devarāja* Cult

Jayavarman's *devarāja* cult was a watershed in the history of Khmer religion. Even though Khmer kings after Jayavarman II began to formulate their own royal cults, they continued to venerate his *devarāja* cult. Although his *devarāja* cult was like other personal *liṅga* cults that promoted a chief's prowess, Jayavarman's spectacular achievements guaranteed his status as an ancestor of note among his Khmer "kin" who followed him. Early Khmer epigraphy glorified rulers in terms of their personal achievements and spiritual prowess, which rewarded their subjects with prosperity in this life and the next. Jayavarman's reign established new criteria for accomplishment; his military victories were so impressive that simply honoring his spiritual capabilities was insufficient to praise his powers as king. Jayavarman's religious rites not only consolidated Khmer ritual in a statewide cult, they also used a new sacred vocabulary to proclaim the king's glory and abilities.[15] After Jayavarman's reign, succession disputes ended with the victor reaffirming the ancestral claim to lead the Khmer people in his generation in return for the loyalty of his subjects.[16]

The most important aspect of Jayavarman's *devarāja* cult was his incorporation of local deities—and in particular the indigenous ancestor worship—into the state's religious ceremony. While earlier Khmer monarchs had to some extent brought together the local and "Hindu" gods, they had always been worshiped separately, and indigenous deities were never placed in "Hindu" temples. In the indigenous belief system of Cambodia, death was held to represent the passage of the spirit into the realm of the ancestors. Death rites ushered the spirit into this world of the dead. In return for faithful worship of the dead, the ancestors granted a certain life-power to the living. Additionally, indigenous deities were traditionally important as "protectors" of the local realm; a chief was the repository of their prowess and could activate their powers on his subjects' behalf. To proclaim their legitimacy, Jayavarman II and subsequent Khmer monarchs merged the worship of Indic deities such as Śiva, Viṣṇu, and the Buddha with the indigenous deities and ancestor spirits, and even installed the local deities in the king's "Hindu" temples to represent his control over the traditional protective forces of his realm. True to this tradition, Angkor Thom's Bayon focused on the central shrine, which was dedicated to the Buddhist Bodhisattva Lokeśvara, but the Bodhisattva (i.e., Jayavarman VII) was surrounded by images or Śiva and Viṣṇu, as well as those of important indigenous protector deities. Beginning with the reign of Jayavarman II, Khmer monarchs did not build temples or invoke the cults of past monarchs to honor their ancestors but to install the traditional protectors of their ancestors and past kings in their central temple compound.[17] The *devarāja* cult and the Khmer royal cults that were initiated in its image exalted but did not deify the reigning monarch. At their deaths, however, Khmer monarchs were elevated to divine status so that their superhuman powers might be drawn upon by the living. Jayavarman II is the first example of the deification of a Khmer monarch at his death.[18] He was known posthumously as Parameśvara.

The significance of this synthesis is also shown in the oath of loyalty that was sworn to Sūryavarman I in 1011 by his administrative corps *(tamrvāc).*[19] In this instance these subordinates of the state requested that, in return for their faithful service, the king first maintain their family ancestral cults and then, secondly, that he perpetuate their families. Through proper observance of the rites calling forth the protective forces of the ancestors, their kin would be guaranteed the resources necessary for a prosperious life.[20] The oath ends: "May we obtain the recompense of people devoted to our masters in this and the other world." The emphasis of this oath was not on Sūryavarman's genealogical legitimacy, nor his divinity, but on the concerns of the present: that the monarch

Central tower, Angkor Wat. Photo by Charles Mark.

Angkor Wat, Cambodia. Photo by Charles Mark.

Ornamental *apsara,* divine dancers who lavish the joys of paradise upon the elect. Angkor Wat; photo by Charles Mark.

Angkor Thom, the Bayon. Photo by Charles Mark.

Relief of naval battle, Angkor Wat. Photo by Charles Mark.

The Bayon, face of Lokeśvara. Photo by Charles Mark.

guarantee the prosperity of the Khmer people and secure for them a superior death status.

This emphasis on the prosperity of the present is also the theme of the bas relief of Angkor Wat, which shows the departure from the "present" and deteriorating age—the *kali yuga* in Indian cosmology—and a return to the first or golden age *(kṛta yuga)* that was represented by Sūryavarman II's reign (1113–1150).[21] According to this depiction, the new age began when Sūryavarman II seized the throne from two "kings" (one of whom was an elderly uncle), put down a civil war, and went on to regenerate a *maṇḍala* (i.e., he restored order in the world). True to the literary battle scenes of the *Kurukṣetra,* the episode of the Indian *Mahābhārata* epic on which the Angkor Wat relief is based, the king's dead enemies and their supporters descended into the underworld to be judged by Sūryavarman, who assumed the role of Yama (Viṣṇu), the judge of the dead.[22] After the dust of the battle had settled, Viṣṇu churned the creative ambrosia of the universe to sustain the golden age.

Indian symbols were used in this bas relief to make a Khmer statement; the use of the "Hindu" conventions of Viṣṇu and the "golden age" drew attention to Khmer tradition. Sūryavarman's identification with Yama, the judge of the dead, was consistent with Khmer views of a sovereign's powers, where obedience or disobedience to one's overlord had consequences in the afterlife. While in Indian tradition the *Kurukṣetra* battle initiated the last age of the world (the *kali yuga* age of the present), at Angkor Wat the battle episode was used instead to introduce the first, or golden age (the *kṛta yuga*), which was still said to exist. The message of the Angkor Wat bas relief was that it was a privilege to live in Sūryavarman's generation when internal peace was restored and the Khmer military marched to the edge of the Southeast Asian mainland.[23] As in the oath of loyalty to Sūryavarman I, the emphasis of Angkor Wat's bas relief was not on royal genealogy but on the present golden age that had been initiated by Sūryavarman II's personal accomplishments, which had fulfilled the Khmer people's expectations of one who claimed to be their monarch.

The depiction of Viṣṇu churning the creative ambrosia also supported the traditional conviction that the Khmer monarch was the source of his subjects' economic welfare. In the Angkor era the king was the creator and director of public works that were designed to ensure prosperity—in particular the Khmer hydraulic system, a network of waterworks that irrigated some twelve and a half million acres, constructed around the Khmer capital at Angkor and in a number of regional domains under Khmer authority. Without this hydraulic system, the water supply was irregular and thus limited agricultural productivity. The *nāga,* the water spirit, was widely portrayed in Khmer art, and was a central figure of popular religion.[24] Chou Ta-kuan, Mongol envoy to Angkor in 1296, reported that the Khmer people believed that their ruler slept with a *nāga* princess, and that the result of their union was the country's prosperity.[25] This report implies that the Khmer monarch enjoyed a ritual relationship with the spirit of the soil that released the fertility that guaranteed the earth's productivity. In this same tradition Yaśovarman I constructed an artificial lake *(baray),* Yaśodharataṭāka, northeast of his new capital city of Yaśodharapura (Angkor) at the end of the ninth century. According to the inscription reporting this event, the king wished to "facilitate an outlet for his abundant glory in the direction of the underworld."[26] This underworld, also depicted as the place from which Khmer monarchs judged the dead, was the abode of the *nāga*s, the source of fertility. Another inscription notes that Yaśovarman, "resplendent with glory," made the lake "beautiful as the moon to refresh human beings."[27] Yet another inscription equates Yaśovarman's lake with the moon, which in Indian tradition provided life-sustaining ambrosia.[28]

A 1980 examination of the Angkor era water management system demonstrates that Yaśovarman's lake was not a critical source of water for the Angkor region's agricultural production in a technical sense, though as the focus of Khmer religion it was important symbolically in the Khmer system of "theocratic hydraulics."[29] Archaeologists have assumed that water seeped through the dike base of Yaśovarman's lake (which measured four miles long by one mile wide) into collector channels outside the dike, which subsequently carried the water to surrounding fields.[30] But studies conducted in the late 1970s found that Angkor-era agriculture was based instead on bunded-field transplanted wet-rice cultivation that allowed the planting of approximately fifty million fields.[31] In the Angkor region floodwaters would slowly rise from the lake to its tributaries, but would rapidly recede after the rainy season. A network of dams and bunds diverted and retained the receding floodwaters of the Great Lake, the Tonle Sap, after the rainy season. The Khmer lacked the technology to build large-scale dams that could have allowed an integrated regionwide hydraulic system; instead they depended on a network of small, simple earthworks on minor streams to retard and spread floodwaters into clay-based ponds, which stored the water for later use.[32] Archaeological evidence demonstrates that Angkor itself was not a major center of this water management network but rather the hill Phnom Kulen, which was located upriver from Yaśovarman's lake some fifty kilometers northwest of Angkor. Phnom Kulen was near the headwaters of the Siem Reap (river), which flowed from that area through Angkor to the Tonle Sap. A network of small earth dams regulated the flow of water downstream from Phnom Kulen to Angkor.

One striking feature of the water management network at Phnom

Kulen is that its dams, in addition to their effectiveness in managing water, all were constructed running east-west and north-south. Similarly, throughout the Angkor region Khmer temples were constructed at the intersection of east-west and north-south oriented moats and roads, which was done purposely to project the image of the heaven on earth *(maṇḍala)* that had been initiated by Khmer monarchs.[33] In addition to being consistent with Indian and Khmer cosmological focus on east-west and north-south, the water management network was consecrated by the traditional symbols of fertility. A number of *liṅga*s were carved in the rocky riverbed between Phnom Kulen and Angkor, suggesting the sanctity of the water that flowed from this mountain region to Angkor.[34] It is significant that Jayavarman II consecrated his *devarāja* cult at Phnom Kulen, which became the original "Mount Mahendra," prior to the establishment of his new capital downriver at Hariharālaya and the consecration of a new Mount Mahendra there.[35] The original Mount Mahendra at Phnom Kulen was thus not only a source of legitimacy for later monarchs who drew upon the protective powers of Jayavarman's *devarāja* cult but it was also seen quite correctly as the source of the Angkor region's water supply, a fact that enhanced the possibilities for success for the monarch's subjects.

In these examples and others, Khmer inscriptions and archaeological evidence well reflect the growing religious sophistication of Khmer society in the Angkor era. The sacred language and symbols of "Hindu" religious philosophy proclaimed the king's glory and abilities. The king was filled with life-sustaining energy derived from "Hindu" and indigenous deities, as divinity flowed from the heavens or from the earth and permeated him, endowing him with the power to dispense "purifying ambrosia" or other less abstract forms of prosperity upon his subjects.[36] While local deities and spirits protected the monarch and his subjects, "Hindu" gods suffused Khmer monarchs with their superior creative and purifying energy, enhancing further the prospects for prosperity in this and other worlds. Having now an overview of the Khmer religious system, let us step back and examine the economic and political implications of this system's evolution from pre-Angkorian to Angkorian times.

Temples and Khmer Statecraft in Pre-Angkorian Khmer Society

The principal concern of the leaders of early Khmer society, as reflected in their epigraphy, was the establishment and endowment of local temples, for which they accrued religious merit and economic return. Key figures in the foundation of these early temples were the consentual leaders of local populations, rather than persons claiming royal authority. Inscriptions recording such activities emphasize the religious prowess rather than the physical might of the local elites who were establishing the temples. Regional leaders held official titles; the power of the landed elites was seemingly recognized by those claiming the authority to rule over the Khmer people by the bestowal of titles on these preexisting leaders, giving them "new" authority as district officers in the state administration. In such a way the landholders, the regional economic, social, and political leadership, were integrated into an emerging state system.

The actions taken by landed elites reported in nonroyal inscriptions involved the worship of local and "state" divinities to "acquire merit" and to "exhibit devotion."[37] Inscriptions celebrated the presentation of gifts made to the temple by local leaders as part of their worship, and the wealth of those making the gifts was stressed and donations were carefully calculated. The landed elites who were responsible for this epigraphy emphasized the giving of gifts to temples as the foremost means to ensure the prosperity of society. The literacy of the temples' patrons was also acclaimed in the inscriptions recording gifts, as if this literacy, in addition to the merit they acquired as temple benefactors, legitimized the donors' status as the leaders of society. Gifts were normally provided not by single "officials" but by several "officials," members of the landed elites, who made endowments as a group rather than as individuals, denoting the existence of kinship-type bonds among the Khmer aristocracy who may or may not have been blood relatives. The landed elites' patronage of temples as a group, thus, may be seen as in some way formalizing their political alliances. Maybe one man could not afford to make a gift by himself and took up a collection from those who would benefit by the gift.

The Khmer aristocracy concentrated economic resources under a temple's administration, whether to acquire the merit associated with such donations, to allow for a more efficient management of an elite's resources, or to avoid the revenue demands of those political elites claiming rights to a share of the local landed elite's possessions. The foremost method of accomplishing this goal was to donate land to temples. Boundaries of donated lands were clearly defined in the inscriptions, usually associated with place names—perhaps a village, an estate, a pond, or the riceland of another landholder. Past and present holders of the assigned lands were enumerated, along with the mode of the property's acquisition and its price if acquired by purchase;[38] the land's productivity (rice yield) was even estimated. Inscriptions reporting assignments of populated land gave the parcel's current occupants and spelled out what portion of the occupants' production was assigned to the temple. If the land was unpopulated a labor force was assigned the task of working the newly donated lands. These laborers were counted—males, females, females with children—and their ethnic identity (e.g., Mon or Khmer) was recorded.[39]

It is not uncommon to discover that the relatives of the donors of such land endowments were members of the priesthood servicing the local temple, and who became managers of the assigned property.[40] In many instances the donor family rather than the temple staff managed family land assigned to a temple, the temple receiving only a designated share of the income. What was transferred by donors was not "ownership" of land but the right to income from land. As explained in chapter 1, control over manpower and production rather than ownership of land was critical for early Southeast Asian state development. To Khmer elites "landholding" meant rights to the production and labor service of the inhabitants of a parcel of land rather than absolute possession of it. In land donations to temples, only certain rights over the land were transferred; while inhabitants of the assigned land normally continued to farm the land, the recipient temple collected much or all of their production. Donated property was usually subject to a combination of claims, those of the temple receiving the donation as well as those of the donor's family, who retained certain personal rights to the property—for example, the right to a share of the land's production as well as administrative or political rights over the inhabitants.

The economic diversity of local temples is reflected in the variety of donations "for the service of the property" assigned: domesticated animals, goats, buffaloes, cattle, coconut palms, fruit trees, areca nuts, betel leaves, clothing, a threshing floor, plus numerous individual objects are examples.[41] The type and size of gifts to temples not only indicate economic specialization within early Khmer society in order to create such wealth but also the developing institutional capacity to utilize and administer this production. An economic system was emerging centered in the temple. The assignments of land and its production by Khmer aristocrats turned temples into local storage centers; goods deposited in temple storehouses were a source of social and economic power, reinforcing the prestige of the temples' primary benefactors, the local landed elites, who influenced the redistribution of the temples' stores in support of their followers (including those working for the temple). Income from the temple was utilized by a local elite to maintain a variety of subordinates and was redistributed to expand the family's social and political power.

The concentration in temples of the authority to manage local resources had a significant impact on the process of local political integration. The implication of such centralization for the economic control system is reflected in epigraphic references to the "joining together for the enjoyment of the gods," whereby a single or several landholders shifted a share of the income (goods and services) destined to one god or temple to that of another or amalgamated the administration of one temple's lands with that of another.[42] This joining together or joint usufruct is termed *saṃparibhoga* or *miśrabhoga.*[43] Through these actions a pattern of subordination of one local deity to another as well as one local temple to another began to emerge in Khmer society. Regional temple networks came to be sustained and controlled by a secular, landed elite who transferred income from their lands or donated material goods and services to temples in the network.

During the Angkor era *miśrabhoga* arrangements were normally not undertaken without the approval of the king himself, but in pre-Angkor society private landholders and not a royal authority dominated the concentration of economic resources and the amalgamation of temple administration. Prior to the ninth century Khmer monarchs were concerned only with recruiting as their allies the local landed elites who had initiated such transfers and consolidations, confirming the transactions rather than challenging them. This is illustrated in the records of the reign of Jayavarman I (657–681) who was based in northern Cambodia and northeastern Thailand (a region the Chinese knew as "Chen-la"). Jayavarman actively extended his authority over local communities and an important aspect of this process was his attempt to bestow legitimacy upon local temples.[44] His recognition of land income transfers is the topic of seven of his eight surviving royal edicts.[45] Five involve coparticipation and the consolidation of land management under the authority of regional temples.[46] However, during the reign of Jayavarman's predecessor Īśānavarman I (616–ca. 635), such shifts of income rights and land management consolidations had been undertaken with neither the monarch's involvement or his favor; Īśānavarman was merely mentioned as having reigned at the time they took place.[47] Īśānavarman and other early Khmer monarchs seem not to have had sufficient authority to manipulate the temples controlled by dominant regional political elites, which were growing into centers of regional religious and economic power. On the other hand, Jayavarman I's inscriptions show an attempt by the monarch to dominate lands and temples, even though he clearly did not have authority in land transactions. His royal edicts, although expressing his concern for land, never claim that the monarchy's authority over land superseded that of the local landed elites.

An inscription of the Angkor-era ruler Jayavarman IV (928–941) also speaks of a Khmer monarch's concern for land, forbidding the careless grazing of buffaloes that might destroy good riceland.[48] But in expressing this concern Jayavarman IV still had to take an indirect approach and respect the landholding rights of the local elites. In this instance Jayavarman ordered a royal official to notify the region's political leader (a *khloñ viṣaya*—a district chief) of his wishes; the local leader in turn decided to acknowledge the edict by permitting it to be published in his district. Clearly it was the regional chief's option to acknowledge Jayavarman IV's concern for the local lands; it would appear that the chief equally had the option of ignoring this expression of royal interest. Thus while Angkor-era kings had a greater involvement in land transfers and assignments, early Khmer rulers could only express interest in the transfers of income and management rights of lands that were part of a regional elite's domain. Even in later times the nonroyal private sector, dominated by landed regional elites, was still quite strong and functional.

Jayavarman II, whose reign (770–834) marked the transition from pre-Angkorian kingship, was particularly adept at forging alliances with powerful regional families and their networks of supporters.[49] The "commander of the royal army," Mratāñ Śrī Pṛthivīnarendra, was a regional chief from the eastern Khmer realm who was allied to Jayavarman by marriage.[50] This kinship linkage was critical to Jayavarman's establishment of a territorial base along the Mekong and drew to Jayavarman's cause two brothers, members of the Mratāñ's personal alliance network, whose ancestral home was Angkor Borei near the old Funan capital of Vyādhapura at the edge of the Mekong Delta.[51] At the insistence of the Mratāñ these brothers and their family were rewarded for their service; Jayavarman assigned the family significant land grants in territories in an area west of the Tonle Sap following its conquest by Mratāñ Śrī Pṛthivīnarendra, the two brothers, and their allies for Jayavarman.[52] Not only did Jayavarman bestow income rights to this land, but seemingly to perpetuate his alliance with this family Jayavarman married one of the brothers' sisters.[53] Mratāñ Śrī Pṛthivīnarendra made requests of Jayavarman for redistributions to other of his followers and their families, who were given land assignments, titles of honor, and posts at court.[54] It was Mratāñ Śrī Pṛthivīnarendra, a commander of troops and the leader of an extensive regionally based alliance network, rather than a temple priest who performed the critical Mount Mahendra ceremony consecrating Jayavarman's rule and initiating the royal *devarāja* cult.[55]

Within the Khmer realm religious foundations (i.e., temples) of powerful local families, who also held official titles in the Khmer state's administration, became a means of integrating the land and its production into the structure of the state.[56] Family temples and their properties were subordinated to central temples placed strategically throughout the realm. A portion of the production collected by private temples was channelled to the state temples. In return the priests of local family temples received validation through periodic participation in the rituals of the central temples. Local family cults also became legitimized via their worship by Khmer monarchs and their subordination to royal cults. In these times temples were not just religious centers but were important links in the state's economic and political network. Religion supplied an ideology and a structure that could organize the populace to produce, tap this production, and secure a region's political subordination, without the aid of separate, secular economic or political institutions.

Temples and Temple Networks in the Angkor Era

A regular order of royal priorities becomes discernable in the activities of four great Angkor kings: Indravarman I (877–889), Yaśovarman I (889–900), Rājendravarman II (944–968), and Jayavarman VII (1181–1220). They first built public works, usually large water reservoirs, or rehabilitated the capital, including the hydraulic works. They also built ancestral temples honoring their immediate predecessors. However, similar patterns were not followed in the period between the reigns of Rājendravarman II and Jayavarman VII (968–1181), leading historians to describe the reigns that occurred during this time as a "zone of imprecision."[57] Yet within this zone of imprecision the reigns of Jayavarman V (968–1001) and Sūryavarman I (1002–1050) left a great abundance of inscriptions and along with the reigns of Udayādityavarman II (1050–1066) and Sūryavarman II (1113–1150) were eras of great royal construction. During these four reigns the seeming "imprecision" may well reflect the rapid growth of population in the Angkor area and the resulting tensions in property relations as powerful families at the court competed for economic resources—especially land and labor—turmoil that ultimately benefited the kings.[58]

In the reign of Sūryavarman I, who is viewed in Khmer history as a usurper, a process can be observed by which royal favor enabled some elite families to prosper at the expense of others.[59] Those families who especially prospered were those who had willingly subordinated their own interests to the king's and were incorporated into the royal "bureaucratic" order. At least sixteen major inscriptions recording the histories of "bureaucratic" families were issued between 1002, the beginning of

Sūryavarman's reign, and 1080. In two inscriptions from Sdok Kak Thom, for example, Sūryavarman I is assigning land to officials of high rank for the purpose of increasing production that could be shared by the officials and the state.[60] Royal inspectors were sent to the site of the land to be transferred to validate the transaction, especially to determine if the land for development was "unowned." This did not mean that the land was unoccupied but that another aristocratic family did not hold rights over the land. Indeed one of the inscriptions notes that villagers were already occupying the land and that the king turned over rights to the production and labor of these well-established agriculturalists to the family receiving official recognition. One noticeable feature of this transaction was the role of the local temple in the proposed development scheme, for the villagers came under the administration *(cāt camnāt)* of a family temple.

From this evidence we can see that Khmer monarchs in the pre-Angkor era were clearly incapable of projecting this degree of royal interest. Pre-Angkor monarchs could only recognize the possession of land rights, rather than having wide powers of land assignment. In tenth-century Cambodian epigraphy, on the other hand, although the extent of the king's authority over religious establishments (temples) is unclear, the king became more actively involved when the resources of two or more temples were merged. The religious network forged by Angkor's kings insured that the landholding rights of Khmer elites would remain fragmented; only those in royal favor could consolidate or extend their property rights. This was done by forbidding *miśrabhoga,* the joining of the rights to lands of more than one local estate's temple, without the approval of the king himself.[61] As noted earlier, *miśrabhoga* consolidations, initiated by regional elites, were common in pre-Angkorian society as a means by which a regional elite established its power base. Seemingly in the Angkor era *miśrabhoga* consolidations were closely supervised in order to limit the growth of a regional elite's resources. Land-right transfers to temples not involving the king still took place, but Angkor-era monarchs were as a matter of course asked to sanction the transactions. The Khmer monarch became the spiritual overlord of private property rights, acting as a judge in disputes, but in most instances only interfering when his participation (or that of his officials) was first solicited.

The apparent key to the Khmer capital's control over manpower was its ability to form "lord-subordinate" alliances with local leaders. Kings, acting from a center of authority, fragmented the power of potential enemies by formulating agreements in which these prospective opponents became subordinates of the state. Eleventh-century Khmer inscriptions show that Sūryavarman I, whose rule marked a high point in Khmer administrative development, was particularly adept at incorporating the chiefs of peoples on the outer edges of his personal domain. After "conquering" a territory with his armies, he recruited the local chiefs (elite) of the "defeated" peoples as district chiefs *(khloñ viṣaya)* and their power status changed little.[62]

It was during Sūryavarman I's reign in 1011 that the king's administrative corps *(tamrvāc)* pledged an oath of allegiance, swearing to become the local "eyes" of the king and pledging to feed the capital with information about local activities.[63] *Tamrvāc* who pledged their loyalty to Sūryavarman were most active in the districts of those appointed *khloñ viṣaya* and were likely intended to serve as a reminder of the king's authority in the *khloñ viṣaya*s' regions and as a source of information in regard to their loyalty. However, in later inscriptions *tamrvāc* are specifically listed as being among those royal officials whose rights in a temple domain were voided. This suggests either a royal response to local pressure to remove royal officials, or it may also suggest that *tamrvāc* became too closely allied to the local *khloñ viṣaya.* The elimination of the *tamrvāc*'s local authority—which in such instances could have been utilized to reinforce the local elite's authority at royal expense—would thus have had a negative impact on the power of the *khloñ viṣaya.*

Early historiography on classical Southeast Asia depicted the Khmer state as a social pyramid with the king and his elite sitting on top and little contact between them and the people below.[64] In Sūryavarman I's state, however, there seems to have been a more intense relationship between the royal capital and the local populations. The Khmer state protected regional interests by incorporating the local status quo into its formal structure instead of replacing the local landed elites with officials sent out from the capital. It further benefited local communities by making its army available to guard the entire state, maintaining order in the regions under state control and protecting the domain from invasion. Unlike pre-Angkorian inscriptions, which denote that the presence of court officials at the local level was small, Sūryavarman's inscriptions indicate the physical presence of royal officials to administer the transfer of land and to directly collect revenues due to the king, as well as local visits made by the royal retinue *(kaṃsteṅ).* The *kaṃsteṅ* was a mobile body of state administrators who traveled from place to place within the realm, acting on disputes that could not be solved locally or on affairs that were considered to be within the state's area of interest.[65] The *kaṃsteṅ* was thus a periodic visible symbol of the king's administration, while the *tamrvāc* represented royal interest locally in the king's absence.

Sūryavarman's reign thus represents a critical phase in the development of an integrated Khmer economic and political order, with the

Khmer temple network assuming a major role in the developmental process. The prosperity of families in the Khmer realm—a prosperity based upon control over the production of land and manpower—came to depend more and more upon royal favor. Interestingly, in the period immediately prior to Sūryavarman's initiatives, as the Khmer realm moved into the theoretical "era of imprecision," the percentage of royal inscriptions actually decreased during Rājendravarman's and Jayavarman V's reigns. The most impressive new temple construction of that period was being attributed to named officials and not viewed as being due to the king's direct initiative. Although the number of royal inscriptions relative to those of his subordinates increased during Sūryavarman's reign, temple construction inaugurated by families subordinate to the king continued to greatly outnumber that of the Khmer monarch. Only in Jayavarman VII's reign did the old pattern of royal institution of temple construction again overshadow the efforts of Khmer "aristocrats."[66] This new pattern does not demonstrate weakness at the center; instead it came about through the intensified integration of the regional aristocracy into the Khmer state as "bureaucrats." They were given official bureaucratic titles; their authority over land and manpower was recognized; and they were charged with responsibility for the expansion of the Khmer state's economic base. Along with this recognition, however, went the responsibility of sharing their land's production with the state. Land transferred to aristocratic families was assigned specifically for the benefit of family temples, whose staffs assumed responsibility for supervising its development. Because they were subordinated to royal temples, these family temples had to share the local production received with the central temples and thus with the Khmer kings who had made the original assignment.

What developed through this pattern of land assignment and development was a network of private and temple landholding rights that was subject to the supervision of the monarchy. Angkor's society was elite-dominated. The king held the power to maintain elites with patronage and at the same time needed to prevent or neutralize the emergence of rival power centers. Elites were linked to the royal court through the Khmer temple network, if not through the bestowal of royal favor. Angkor's rulers were capable of reducing local power centers to subordinate provinces of their government, but in the process of awarding territorial grants or property right transfers they were not able to dispense landholding rights at will. The landed elites subject to the Khmer state did have independent rights and were not subject to the constant demands of the state. In the Angkor era, although local autonomy was assaulted—sometimes with a good deal of energy—the landed aristocracy retained power. The Khmer state system was not highly centralized or "bureaucratic," nor was it a "feudal" order in which the king assigned bureaucratic duties to a landed elite who derived their landholding rights and status as a consequence of the king's favor. Records of land assignments to families and their temples during the Angkor era reflect constant friction between the center and its periphery and provide evidence about the nature of the relationship between the Khmer monarch and his regional elites.[67]

"Ownership" of land in the Khmer realm, as noted above, was embedded in a system of rights held by related people. Exclusive property rights imply the exclusion of various official claims that would otherwise have force. The king in theory held the final authority to validate landholding rights, although this authority was not normally exercised—Sūryavarman I's initiatives were unusual; the Khmer monarch thus assumed the role of patron placing land under the "exclusive" control of favored families and their temples. The aristocracy, drawing their livelihood from the land, theoretically owed their continued prosperity directly or indirectly to royal favor.

Exercising the Khmer monarch's theoretical land rights, Sūryavarman I thus dealt directly with the lineage of Pas Khmau, which he viewed as being constantly violent to his interest, by dictating that henceforth their land was to be controlled by the Khmer kings and the lineage's resources merged with those of the king's temples.[68] However, this was not a total seizure of land as aristocratic "rights" over the land were not reassigned to another family. In the Sdok Kak Thom inscription cited above, a family of officials claimed land and rights over land that was administered by a family temple. Rights over this land had been granted by a series of kings—new settlements *(sruk),* provisions, and manpower had been endowed to equip the temple and to guarantee the growth of the community around it. In the turmoil associated with Sūryavarman I's rise to the throne the landholding family had apparently sided against Sūryavarman. Sūryavarman gained authority over areas where the family held land but did not reassign all this family's land rights to his direct supporters. Instead, Sūryavarman forced a temple priest related to the family—who was responsible for the property's assessment—to leave the temple staff and to marry a younger sister of Sūryavarman's first queen. Some of the original family's land rights were reassigned, and the family was provided new rights over land in an area beyond the royal core where it would seemingly be less a threat to royal interests. The temple's livelihood and as well the family's prosperity were said to have been devastated in the disturbances of the era. Thus Udayādityavarman II renewed Sūryavarman's endowment, allowing the new family of officials to clear land overgrown by forest, consecrate temple statues, and build its economic well-being.[69]

In other instances Khmer monarchs imposed their authority locally by forbidding temple staffs to employ people living on and cultivating assigned land to also work temple lands, withdrawing certain rights of local officials over land assigned to temples, or favoring families loyal to the capital by exempting their temple lands from the demand of the king's officials.[70] In these inscriptions Khmer monarchs reveal two purposes in their dealings with the land endowments of local temples: on the one hand they intervened where possible to limit the power of potential rivals, and on the other hand they desired to enhance the economic strength of their supporters. Avoiding possible conflict, Khmer kings rarely intervened in local temple affairs unless there was a direct threat to royal interests but adeptly employed their right to assign their supporters' income rights to unsettled lands; rights to previously settled land left vacant could be solicited from the king by a family, the land rights of extinct lineages could be reassigned, and landholding rights to unpopulated and overgrown land could be assigned.[71] Families with existing estates were sometimes encouraged to resettle in new territories.[72]

Several Khmer monarchs expressed concern that too much of a family's resources was committed to the financing of temple affairs. In such cases they intervened to maintain the family's economic well-being. A family in one such instance had transferred so many of their income rights to support temple activities that the king, upon finding their resources insufficient to maintain the family's everyday requirements, ordered a halving of royal assessments on the unassigned land they had remaining.[73] In another instance the rights on land transferred to a temple were excluded from the revenue claims of various officials but income rights not subject to revenue claims were explicitly distinguished from other landholding rights of the donor's family, which provided the family's subsistence and allowed them to carry out government requirements.[74] Yet the substantial transfers of land rights to family temples by Khmer aristocrats and kings continued to be made, where family members who were members of the temple staffs were assigned the exclusive right of administering this land for the temples' (and their families') benefit.[75]

If land assigned to a temple was not to be administered by the temple staff, the heads of the family or other members of the lineage might act as property managers on the temple's behalf, utilizing income from the land to erect buildings, construct hydraulic projects, secure additional manpower to work the land, or in general ensure that the land's productivity would increase. The dominant landholding families thus also benefited from the development of temple land and the accumulation of wealth by the family temple. This income was tapped for redistribution by the family to its supporters in various forms. Family-temple relationships were rarely questioned by Khmer monarchs, who instead attempted to obtain a share of the wealth accumulated locally by the right their central temples had to a percentage of the local temples' income. However, as will be discussed below, income from local temples covered only a small percentage of the royal temples' expenses and this revenue sharing was more symbolic than critical to the financial well-being of the state temples. In this light the revenue demands of central temples upon local family temples would appear to have had more political and social than economic importance. Royal interest in local temples, aside from guaranteeing the financial well-being of allies and limiting the economic resources of potential rivals, was more concerned about a local temple's ritual being in harmony with that of royal temples than about making a local temple economically subordinate to a royal temple.

The existence of a hierarchical religious network gave the monarchy control over ritual. Moreover, the elaborate royal cults developed by Khmer monarchs helped to integrate subordinates with the center.[76] The king's powers were generated by ceremony. The royal court, its activities, and its style recreated a world of the gods—in theory a heaven on earth, in which all greatness and glory were concentrated. By successfully fulfilling his role as the hypothetical focus of all sanctity and power, the king maintained the orderliness of the world. Subordinate centers of power in the Khmer realm sought to imitate the ritual of the royal court.[77] This ritual unity was more important than administrative control in maintaining the state's dominance over areas outside its core. Territorial unification was not sufficient to sustain the realm. This came about through the integration of indigenous folk traditions, symbols, and religious beliefs into a cult that was visibly concentrated in the center.

The participation in the state's rituals by those who worshiped local spirits emphasized the subordination of local deities and their temples to those of the state, thus enhancing the king's image as the holder of supreme spiritual power and divine prowess among the living. There were thus political implications to the institution of a centralized Khmer religious network system. As temple collections flowed from local to central temples and the integration of local and central cults became concentrated in central temples, the Khmer temple network facilitated the Khmer monarchy's manipulation of the regional landed aristocracy—themselves integrated into the royal "bureaucratic" order by having official religious and secular titles bestowed upon them—via the subordination of these aristocrats' local temples and cults to the monarchy's temples and cults.

Endowments to temples represented the mobilization, organization, and pooling of economic resources (capital, land, labor, and so forth) to support portions of the overall ritual process of the temple—for example, financing a single event in the temple's religious calendar of ritual, the construction of a building in the temple compound, clothing for a temple image, or a subsidy for a temple priest. While this redistribution of economic capital was central to a temple's existence, the mobilization of "symbolic capital" was also critical, as temple endowments generated one or more ritual contexts in which honors rather than material returns were distributed to and received by donors. In this way economic capital was converted to culturally symbolic capital, honors that enhanced the stature of the donor in the minds of his kin and clients.[78]

An endowment permitted the entry and incorporation of Khmer corporate units (e.g., families and kings) into a temple as temple servants (priests, assistants, and so on) or as donors. The donor represented a social, economic, or political unit; the gift was a means by which the group or its leader could formally and publicly receive recognition. While an endowment supported the deity, and often returned some material advantage to the donor, perhaps more important were the symbolic returns of the "donation."[79] Rulers—regional elites or Khmer monarchs—were patrons and protectors of temples, ensuring the continuance of a temple's services, resources, and rules. They were not "rulers" of temples, however, but were servants of the temple's deity, human agents of the lord of the temple—a stone image that could not arbitrate in the real world on its own behalf—who protected and served the deity.

In the Indian tradition a ruler's relationship with a temple represented a symbolic division of sovereignty, whereby the ruler became the greatest servant of the temple's lord, his patronage of the temple's deity sustaining and displaying his rule over men.[80] Yet kings and others who claimed political authority were subject to challenges by those who perceived their shares and rights—a consequence of other individual or group endowments to a temple—to be independently derived from the sovereign deity. An example of the competition to claim the shared sovereignty of the secular (the ruler) and the sacred (the temple) is provided in the Khmer realm, where local elites and kings each patronized temple deities. The issue of who was the ultimate servant of the temple's lord had political significance and explains the attempts by Angkor's monarchs to subordinate the deities of local temples to those of royal temples or to integrate these local deities into royal cults.[81]

The returns from temple donations thus had both economic as well as political implications and explain the significant flow of economic resources from rulers at various levels to Khmer temples. If an identification with a deity was as essential to legitimize rule as seems to have been the case in the Khmer realm, then instead of material returns upon one's investment symbolic returns must have been equally desirable, especially to Khmer kings who never reaped substantial material benefit from their assignment of local income rights to local temples. The temple's redistributive role was thus critical to issues of sovereignty in both the secular and sacred Khmer world order and raises questions of how to equate economic and symbolic capital, if it is really possible to quantify this conversion process, and whether there was any attempt to achieve "equity"—topics beyond the scope of the available historical records.[82]

Family and Central Temples as Economic Centers

The extension of agriculture into previously uncultivated lands and the construction of hydraulic networks to facilitate the production of rice surpluses were central to the development schemes of Khmer kings and their subordinates.[83] Khmer temples at the state and regional levels fulfilled three economic functions in the agricultural development process. First, they were centers of investment ("banks"), the source of investment capital and management; donors' gifts were redistributed to individuals or groups of peasant and bondsman cultivators as capital investments (e.g., seeds, livestock, and land to be cultivated), which stimulated the agrarian sector. Second, temples were repositories of technological information and knowledge, directly or indirectly supporting scholars, astrologers, and artisans whose expertise and literacy could be drawn upon by cultivators. Third, Khmer temples were supervisory agencies that involved agricultural laborers in the development process, offering sufficient returns to encourage them to remain on the land. As noted earlier, lands assigned to temples for development were often unpopulated, requiring the assignment of a labor force with no previous claim to the land's production. This work force might be acquired by moving a population, possibly war captives, from an area peripheral to the state's core domain to the lands to be developed.[84] Laborers assigned to develop new lands were incorporated into the local economic and social system by temples. Lone peasant cultivators could not likely have borne the economic burdens of shortfalls in production as they brought new land into production or implemented agricultural technology associated with the construction of irrigation projects.[85] Temples, however, could mobilize their storage and redistributive mechanisms to meet the subsistence needs of the laborers in such an event, drawing from material resources assigned for this purpose by kings or regional elites. Temples were also in charge of agricultural development, engaging diggers, scribes, managers, and other specialists, combining the technical expertise and human resources necessary for the extension of agriculture.[86] Furthermore, temples offered laborers emotional security; workers sought not only personal economic profit but also worked for the spiritual gain derived from service to a temple's deity.[87]

A twelfth-century inscription from Trapaeng Don On illustrates the economic function of a "personal" or family temple. This inscription is especially valuable because it contains parallel Old Khmer and Sanskrit texts that are identical in context and permit full translation of both texts.[88] The founder of this temple was an individual claiming to be a Brahman, who had been the head herdsman for several kings. He had saved the treasures paid to him for his distinguished service and purchased lands, adding these lands to those he had acquired in other ways, and then had built a temple to complete the foundation of his estate:

> (These kings) have favored me by placing various kinds of duties upon me. On the riches that they deigned to present to me, and for the treasures that have been amassed by the labor of my people, I have built a temple, I have purchased "slaves," I have bought lands, I have purchased pawned lands, established boundaries, built fences, built walls, dug ditches and reservoirs.

Certain lands from this estate were assigned to support the temple's activities (see fig. 5). This assigned land was divided into (1) a "common field of the cult" from which the harvest went into the common granaries of the temple, (2) "the field of the servants of the cult," (3) "the field of the chief priest" *(purohita),* and (4) the "sustenance fields" of the temple *kñuṁ* ("bondsmen"),[89] agricultural laborers bound to serve the temple. There were nineteen adult *kñuṁ,* nine men and ten women, who worked the "common field of the cult" and the "field of sustenance"; other *kñuṁ* are likely to have farmed the additional fields that provided income for individual members of the temple's staff.[90] The nineteen *kñuṁ* were divided into two groups; each labor team worked on the "field of the cult" half of a lunar month. This division of the lunar month was a feature of the Indian dating system adopted into the Khmer system.[91] Inscriptions recording the assignment of *kñuṁ* to temples usually gave two lists, equal or approximately equal in length, for the bright and dark fortnights respectively. Temple treasuries, repositories for food

Figure 5

Temple of Trapaeng Don On: Redistribution of Temple Land Production

(X = *redistributed shares of land's production*)

Temple staff and temple residents fed from temple lands	*Lands held by temple* "common fields of the cult"	"fields of the servants of the cult"	"fields of the chief priests"	"fields of sustenance"
Temple priests	X	X	X	
Temple officiants	X	X		
Temple assistants	X	X		
Hermits (residents of *aśrama*)	X			
Temple laborers				X

produced by the *kñuṁ* on the temple's behalf, were normally constructed in pairs, one for the deposit of each fortnight's collected production.[92] Temple *kñuṁ* worked for their own subsistence or for other masters with coexisting claims on the land (e.g., the donor's family) during periods free of temple duties.[93]

The persons in charge of the temple were relatives of the founder:

> All these rice fields, land, means of subsistence, and the slaves of the gods belong to that one of my relatives who is a *pandit* and possesses *dharma*. This relative will be the *purohita* of these gods and let the slaves of these gods and the others be subjected to him.

The property, however, was not free of limitations, for the inscription continues: "Let him [i.e., the *purohita*] not sell or give away the slaves and the lands of these slaves. . . ." Thus the land assigned to support the temple and its staff was at the personal disposal of the relatives of the temple's founder, the Khmer aristocrat and "bureaucrat," but with certain restrictions.

Lands assigned to family temples were in some cases divided among the temple personnel or in other instances were considered together as "fields of the cult"; the temple personnel received shares of the "sacrificial rice" from the "fields of the cult." The temple *kñuṁ* "bondsmen" who worked the land had "fields of sustenance" apportioned to them by the temple staff for cultivation. They were allowed to retain a portion of their production from their assigned land or were given a share of the harvest from the produce collections belonging to the entire temple. Family temple lands also had specific obligations to the state, except when there was a royal decree relieving the temple of these responsibilities.[94] Land assigned to temples was free of direct revenue obligations to the state; especially forbidden were collections by royal officials who normally derived a portion of their income from making assessments for revenue demands.[95]

In an inscription from Sūryavarman I's reign (1028) a military leader bearing a royal title received the land rights and property of a royal enemy.[96] In developing his estate this individual consecrated a Śiva-*liṅga* and built a temple around it. Thereupon the king required the payment of *miśrabhoga* duties to a royal temple, although the inscription does not state the amount and type of duty that was imposed. Thus the "family" temple of this state "bureaucrat" was linked, as a criterion of its establishment, to a central temple. The duties paid to the royal temples in *miśrabhoga* linkages of smaller local temples to larger royal temples were relatively small and were more symbolic than economically critical to the central temple's existence. For instance, a typical local temple in Sūryavarman I's reign received an income of 25,000 kilograms of hulled rice annually but shared only 90 kilograms of it with a designated central temple.[97]

That only limited demands were placed on local family temples is further conveyed in the accounts of the Khmer royal temples. The Ta Prohm temple's rice needs during the reign of Jayavarman VII were said to be 6,589 kilograms daily for cooking and 2,512,406 kilograms annually.[98] This rice fed the temple's personnel, who included 18 high priests, 2,740 officiants, and 2,632 assistants—among whom were 615 female dancers, 439 learned hermits who lived in the temple monastery *(aśrama),* and 970 students. A total of 12,640 people lived within the walls of the temple compound. The sum of rice consumed annually was thus 2,512,406 kilograms, of which only 366,800 kilograms were delivered by villages assigned to the temple and 42,157 kilograms from royal storehouses, together covering less than one-fifth of the temple's rice consumption.[99] Villages assigned to the central temple supplied rice through their local family temples, but in comparison to the total amount of production annually drawn by local temples from their assigned lands the annual payment of roughly 90 kilograms of rice that these family temples were obliged to pay to a central temple was insignificant. The central temple's primary source of income was the temple's own assigned lands worked by *kñuṁ* "bondsmen" at the behest of Khmer monarchs and state elites. State-level central temples thus functioned economically in a fashion similar to the local family temples, but on a much larger scale.

Following the twelfth-century inscription of Jayavarman VII in his Prah Khan temple complex describing the Khmer realm as being composed of 306,372 subjects inhabiting 13,500 villages, one historian calculated that Khmer subjects were producing roughly 38,000,000 kilograms of hulled rice annually for 20,000 gold, silver, bronze, and stone gods.[100] Each worker supplied an average of 120 kilograms of hulled rice, or 60 percent of his productivity.[101] The potential of the flow of production to and the concentration of economic resources in Khmer temples is demonstrated in the Ta Prohm inscription's enumeration of the temple's stores, which contained a set of golden dishes weighing more than 500 kilograms; a silver service of equal size; 35 diamonds; 40,620 pearls; 4,540 gems; 523 parasols; 512 sets of silk bedding; 876 Chinese veils; a huge quantity of rice, molasses, oil, seeds, wax, sandalwood, and camphor; and 2,387 changes of clothing for the adornment of temple statues.

The Khmer Temple Network in Southeast Asian Perspective

The Burmese state of Pagan, at its height from the eleventh to the fourteenth centuries, also drew economic support from a temple network. The economic basis of both the Khmer and Pagan states was irrigated rice agriculture, and the ensuing wealth from this production was concentrated in temples. In the Khmer state, the temples were integrated into the state structure—temple officiants were state functionaries subordinate to secular powers, and conflict between the state and religious institutions did not arise. In Pagan, however, rights to produce from the land shifted to the Buddhist monastic order *(saṅgha)* and away from secular political authority. Socioeconomic power shifted from the Pagan monarchy to a rival, hierarchical order dominated by monks. With an increasingly diminished control over the economic resources in their domain, Burmese kings were forced to redefine the structure of the Pagan state; a new state system was organized around a new Theravāda Buddhist elite.[102]

In contemporary Java, there was a pattern of royal temples and local temples—the latter built under the patronage of local rulers—similar to that in the Khmer realm. Although hundreds of small, local temples existed, during the eighth through the tenth centuries only four major temples—Caṇḍi Sewu, Caṇḍi Plaosan, Caṇḍi Loro Jonggrang, and Caṇḍi Borobudur—as well as the burial temples of kings were built.[103] The central temples were built under the authority of Javanese rulers claiming *mahārāja* status but with the cooperation and support of their state authorities and regional chiefs. The temples helped integrate the state; three levels of state offices and corresponding temple networks emerged at the state, regional, and village levels.

Javanese temples operated within a royal ritual policy that was intended to consolidate and extend the state's political authority.[104] The primary level of competition for political power, which was based on how much economic power one or the other could control, with economic power being linked to temples, was at the regional and state levels. The regional elites *(rakrayān)* controlled regions *(watĕk)* and subordinate village clusters *(wanua),* while *mahārāja*s attempted to draw the *rakrayān* and *wanua* under royal authority. One strategy employed by the kings was to urge *rakrayān*s to stage great festivals. For example a ruler would encourage the establishment of a local family temple, usually assigning the land to the temple as *sīma,* land free of royal revenue demands for taxes and services, but would require the temple's benefactor (a *rakrayān*) to stage a great public festival in honor of the temple's foundation.[105] Such ceremonies and festivals were a means of redistributing wealth that might otherwise have been used in ways disruptive to society —and to the king's sovereignty.

In the Singhasari-Majapahit era (eleventh through fifteenth centuries) eastern Javanese monarchs generously donated land to religious institutions throughout the countryside, freed temples from numerous royal taxes and dues *(dĕrwaya haji),* and also prohibited royal administrators and soldiers from entering religious domains to make demands on their own behalf.[106] The latter prohibition prevented collections by royal tax collectors and officials who were also working for local magnates and village authorities. Transfer of *dĕrwaya haji* thus often was of more consequence in a negative sense to local officials, especially *rakrayān* regional chiefs, than the king.[107] The transfer of the rights and property of local leaders to religious institutions subtracted a portion of the wealth directly available to a local magnate. A temple's establishment under royal patronage also provided an institutional foothold from which Javanese rulers could attempt to extend their political and economic power in the hinterland beyond the centers of royal power.

The redistributive functions of Khmer and Javanese temples are summarized in figure 6. In this diagram the state's resources flow as donations or dues (gold, land, livestock, food, and manpower) from villages and local and regional temples to the state's central temples. Returns may have been in kind, utilizing the temple as a "bank." In such instances the donor received a material (i.e., "economic capital") return upon his "investment," either directly via a prescribed rate of return or indirectly through the greater productivity achieved regionally as a consequence of the temple's efficient management of land. Returns might also have been "symbolic capital," which contributed to the legitimacy of various regional and state aristocrats through the performance of temple ceremo-

Figure 6
Temple Hierarchy in Angkor and Java (Classical Era)

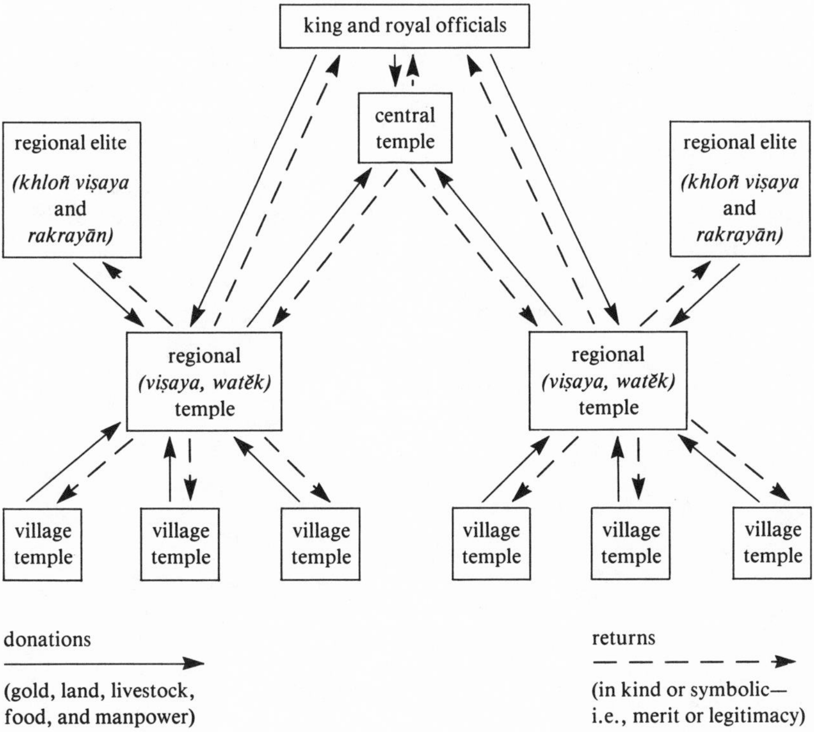

nies that emphasized the donor's superior spiritual prowess or through the act of recording the gift in an inscription that perpetually honored the donor's piety.

Thus in Java, as in the Khmer realm, temples never became independent of those in political authority, whether at the local or state level. Rivalries and tensions developed, rather, among local and state authorities whose power was based on their control over manpower, landholdings, and temple administration. There was never a shift of socioeconomic power away from the secular authorities to a religious order. However, both the Javanese and Khmer monarchs were limited by the very nature of their policy of utilizing temples and temple networks as a means of integrating their domains economically and politically. Neither developed a centralized bureaucratic order, depending instead upon assignments of land rights and impressive titles to those in royal favor to elicit the loyalty of semiautonomous regionally based landed elites. Yet neither appears to have been lacking in the ability to finance major royal projects. In both realms, in the absence of a bureaucratic system for collecting large amounts of income for the state's treasury, temples were viewed as important centers of economic accumulation that could be tapped to finance the king's patronage of religion. Most conspicuous were temple construction and elaborate temple ceremonies and festivals, which provided a pretext under which the state's economic and social resources could be mobilized to achieve the state's political goals. These goals mainly focused on the construction of a state-dominated political system replacing the previous system, which had been built on a series of personal alliances. In both systems temples assumed major roles in the process of political integration.

7

Eleventh-Century Commercial Developments in Angkor and Champa

The foregoing discussions of early Javanese and Cambodian history showed that the state elites in these river plain states shared control of land and authority with a number of other regional elites and institutions and developed a style of statecraft based on the interdependence of political, economic, and religious institutions. Since income derived from the land was the major source of a ruler's ability to function as a sovereign, providing him with economic as well as symbolic capital with which to construct alliance networks, a successful sovereign in these states had to have either immense personal charisma or greater economic resources at his personal disposal than did would-be rulers from competing elites within his realm.

A state system depending upon income from its agrarian sector alone was limited in its development potential, however. In a river plain state it was only when those claiming sovereignty became actively involved in external economic affairs that the supreme powers of the state vis-à-vis competing elites and institutions became secure. Economic leadership in the commercial sphere provided a new source of income for Javanese and Khmer monarchs in the tenth and eleventh centuries and enhanced each state's political accomplishments. However, during this same era the Angkor-based realm's neighbor, the Cham state on the lower Vietnamese coast, experienced the negative aspects of state participation in the international trade and the dangers posed when a state elite could not control their coastal commercial centers. This chapter compares the commercial activities of the Khmer and Cham states to discern the impact of international trade upon each state's rulers and systems of statecraft.

Sūryavarman I and Khmer Commercial Expansion

As noted in chapter 6, the water supply in the area surrounding Angkor was irregular, such that natural conditions did not allow for the expansion of its economic base and thus limited the state's potential for extending its political authority. An elaborate system of irrigation networks was constructed around the Khmer capital at Angkor during the ninth through the eleventh centuries. This network controlled the monsoon season flooding of the Tonle Sap, stored monsoon rainwater for later use, and allowed three and possibly even four rice harvests per year. To encourage the expansion of wet-rice cultivation royal assignments (grants) of landed estates were made to favored elite families as well as to the various temples of the realm. In some cases, an agricultural work force was also supplied. These new estates were then integrated both symbolically and physically into the state's economic system via the state's ritual network. To acquire and maintain their legitimacy, local temples, founded on the new landed estates by elites subordinate to the state, were required to relinquish a small percentage of their annual harvest to the state's central temples. The ritual of these central temples, so critical to the authority of monarchs, was chiefly financed by the production of lands assigned and developed under the supervision of the central temples' administrators.

The Khmer state's centralized temple complex thus related land and population to the king's capital. Temples controlled land, the manpower on the land, and the land's productive output. Religious development was viewed as an aid to the state's economic development. The extension of cultivated land in the tenth and eleventh centuries was thereby connected to the endowment of religious establishments. Rich temples formed economic bases that were tapped for construction projects, the development of irrigation, rice production, and so on—projects that were healthy for the economy as a whole and that the central government could not always cover financially.[1] The Khmer realm's general economic prosperity is reflected in an urban development that took place in the tenth and eleventh centuries. In the epigraphy of this period urbanization becomes noticeable in the reign of Rājendravarman II (944–968) and continued under Jayavarman V (968–1001), but reached its fullness under Sūryavarman I (1002–1050). For example, the epigraphy mentions only *twelve* place names ending in *-pura,* a Sanskrit term used to identify urban areas, during the reign of Jayavarman IV (928–942), *twenty-four* in the period of Rājendravarman II, *twenty* under Jayavarman V, but *forty-seven*—more than double those of his immediate precessors—in the reign of Sūryavarman I.[2]

Expansion of the state's agricultural base allowed the dramatic political expansion of the Khmer state during the tenth and eleventh centuries. By the first half of the eleventh century Khmer monarchs had pushed their control to the west into the Chao Phraya Valley of present-day Thailand and toward the Isthmus of Kra of the Malay Peninsula. While tenth-century Khmer political interests had been directed toward the eastern portion of the realm, Sūryavarman I reversed this pattern with his activities in the west. Sūryavarman's extension of Khmer authority into the Lopburi region had strong economic implications, for control of the lower Chao Phraya provided access to international commerce at Tāmbraliṅga, the Chaiya-Suratthani area of southern Thailand, giving the Khmers a more direct contact with the international trade routes than had previously been the case.

Merchants active in the Khmer domain shared in this prosperity and these accomplishments. There are over twenty specific references to merchant activity in the Khmer realm during the period from the reign of Harṣavarman I (922) to that of Harṣavarman III (1071). Most of these are concentrated in Sūryavarman's reign, as the new commercial opportunities available from the extension of Khmer administrative control into the region north of the Dangrek mountain range and into the former Dvāravatī area of central Thailand in the west resulted in the development of new commercial networks. Although the Khmer state was an inland wet-rice state, anything useful to the economic strength of the realm was encouraged.[3] Thus Sūryavarman himself took an active role in furthering Khmer commercial aspirations.

Merchants are identified in Khmer epigraphy as *khloñ jnvāl* and *khloñ jnvāl vanik. Khloñ jnvāl vanik* were itinerant, or traveling merchants, while *khloñ jnvāl* were resident vendors.[4] In an inscription from Vāt Prāh Ēinkosei (968), a permanent merchant quarter *(travāṅ vanik)* is even identified.[5] Most Khmer epigraphic records provide examples of merchants who personally served the state. For example, local merchants *(khloñ jnvāl)* are shown serving in the retinue of a district chief *(khloñ viṣaya)* during the reign of Udayādityavarman II (1050–1066).[6] The nature of their services can be seen in an inscription from Bān Thāt Thong (922). When the district chief of the area called Dharmapura was required to collect gold, silver, and "precious objects of all sorts" to be offered to members of the royal family, he obtained them from four or five merchants who were residents of his district.[7] Similarly, the inscription of Tuol Pei (992) is addressed to a noble *(mratān)* requesting that he procure certain specified goods for the royal family from the merchant Vāp China.[8] There are also two inscriptions from Bantāy Prāv that refer to traveling merchants *(khloñ jnvāl vanik)* who were members of the king's retinue *(kaṃsteṅ).* In the reign of Sūryavarman I (1012), a *khloñ jnvāl vanik,* identified as a member of the *kaṃsteṅ,* made a gift of a "slave" and an "infant" to the local temple, as did other members of the retinue.[9] In 1071, Harṣavarman III's retinue included a *vanik* of Gaāṅ Laṃpoh, who was *"khloñ vanik"* to the *kaṃsteṅ.*[10] Many royal endowments to temples were transacted using merchants as intermediaries. For example, in a late tenth-century inscription from Prāsāt Cār, several *khloñ jnvāl* directed the sale of land rights for the royal retinue *(kaṃsteṅ),* for which the buyer paid a quantity of money (silver and other precious objects) and clothing.[11]

Although the inscriptions record surveys of commercial activity by royal agents, there is no evidence of merchants being heavily taxed.[12] A strong king such as Sūryavarman benefited merchants' activity by establishing standards of weights and measures.[13] In return, Khmer kings expected certain services, in reality a form of taxation, such as those performed by the merchants who are named in the epigraphy. "Donations" to temples by royal subordinates were encouraged by the Khmer government.[14] Worship services at "central temples," in which the state took a particular interest, required that scented woods, spices, gold and silver, and cloth goods be presented to the deity. As indicated in the epigraphy, these were acquired from merchants; in return the merchants were reimbursed with land, buffaloes, rice, jewelry, and "slaves."[15] This service relationship between merchants and kings is clarified in the late tenth-century Prasat Cār inscription mentioned above, in which the local population, in receiving their payment of silver, cloth goods, and salt in exchange for land that they had been asked to sell, declared to the royal judge who sanctioned the transactions that "all these goods that we receive allow us to perform our royal service. The rest serves for our sustenance."[16] The emphasis here is on *service* and not on pious "gift giving."

The Khmer state under Sūryavarman developed administrative mechanisms for the extraction of revenues.[17] The epigraphic evidence examined reflects the incorporation of merchants into this revenue collection process. Most notably, merchants became official members of the state's administration, which bestowed upon them official status as members of a district chief's retinue or that of the king himself. The inscriptions focus upon the role of such merchants in facilitating the flow of goods to the chief's or king's center of authority, or as intermediaries in endowments to temples and the source of items used in the temple ceremonies so critical to royal legitimacy. Further, merchants were essential as the suppliers of goods to the king's *kaṃsteṅ* when it made its periodic trek among the subordinate centers of power within the Khmer domain. As inscriptions note, merchants were specifically designated as the "official merchants to the *kaṃsteṅ,*" elevating their status and paying them recognition for their service to their king.[18]

Khmer kings utilized merchants' special ability to mobilize the distribution of various goods, acquired through the indigenous marketing networks that the merchants controlled. The king was careful not to heavily tax merchants, although he did conduct surveys of commercial activity within his domain. Khmer kings thus came to recognize the benefits to be derived from commerce—directly via the flow of goods to their court and indirectly from the prosperity generated by the developing marketing system that encouraged local production and in the end, owing to the king's right to receive set percentages of local production, brought additional revenues to the treasury.

Sūryavarman appears to have been especially perceptive of the contributions that commerce and the activities of merchants made to the economic well-being of his state. The growth of the Khmer commercial economy during Sūryavarman's reign can be examined by mapping the distribution of Khmer inscriptions that refer to marketing activity. The center of Khmer administration during the tenth and eleventh centuries is indicated by using Battambang, Sisophon, Prāḥ Vihār, Sambor, and Kompong Cham as the points for the construction of a pentagon, within which was the Khmer heartland.[19] Sūryavarman's reign brought the extension of Khmer administration west of this "core" to the region of Lopburi, north of present-day Bangkok in the Chao Phraya River basin, with the area between under constant Khmer occupation.[20] Both archaeological and epigraphical evidence indicates that the initial western penetration of the Khmers into the Lopburi region actually occurred in the reign of Rājendravarman II (944–968).[21] While information on a continuing relationship between the Khmer core and Lopburi is lacking, Sūryavarman I consolidated these earlier contacts by incorporating this western territory into the administrative structure of the Khmer empire.[22] Inscriptions from Sūryavarman's reign reflect the development of commercial communication between the Khmer core and the Lopburi area following this integration.

Mapping shows that commercial communication generally followed the river systems of the Khmer domain (see map 6).[23] The main routes radiate out from the Khmer core around the Tonle Sap. In the eastern part of the empire a major commercial route followed the Sen River north to Prāḥ Vihār.[24] From this point goods were carried across the Dangrek range to commercial centers in the area of the Bān Thāt Thong inscription.[25] This zone also had contacts with the Mekong communication network. In an inscription from Bān Thāt dating to the reign of Jayavarman VI (1080–1107), reference is made to "barges" that used the Mekong.[26] Vietnamese traders such as the Yvan of Kaṃvaṅ Tadiṅ mentioned in a Phum Mīen inscription (987) likely used a Mekong River route to enter Cambodia, coming from Nghê-an through the Ha-trai pass and down the Mekong.[27] Nghê-an in turn had contact with commercial developments of the Red River Delta and the Vietnamese capital at

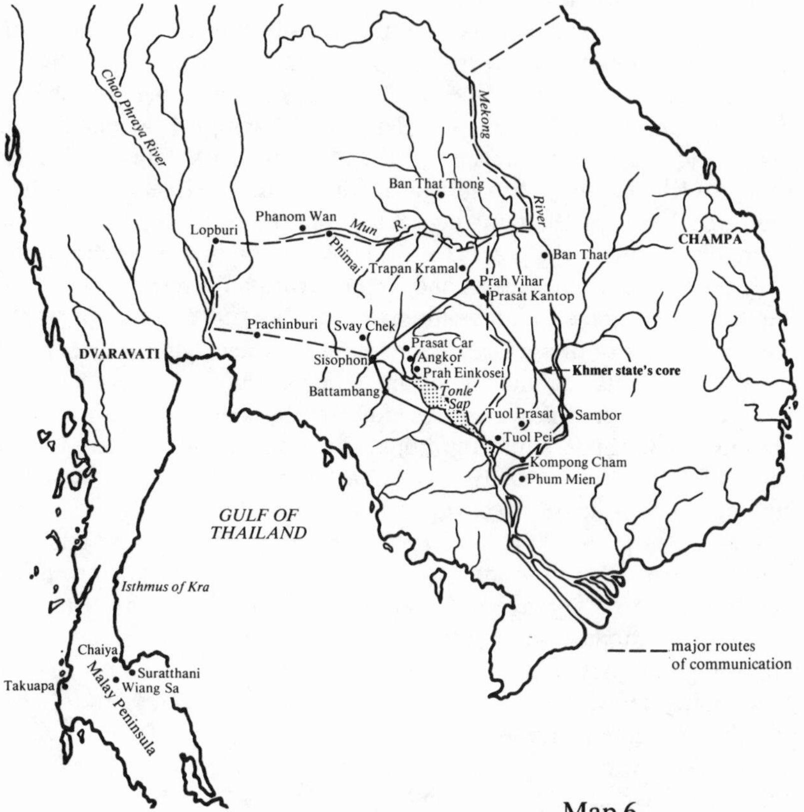

Map 6
DISTRIBUTION OF
COMMERCIAL ACTIVITY IN
THE KHMER DOMAIN

Thang-long. An overland route then connected Bān Thāt to Prāsāt Kantop, avoiding the Khong rapids south of Bān Thāt and allowing a more direct access to the Khmer core. Sambor (Sambupura), located below the Khong rapids, was connected more to an eastern route than to a western route, serving as a center for Khmer contact with hill peoples to the east who provided "slaves," deer skins, and forest products to the Khmers.[28]

An east-west route north of the Dangrek mountain range and following the Mun River system also developed in the time of Sūryavarman. Inscriptions from the Phanom Wan and Phimai areas that date to the last ten years of Sūryavarman's reign (1040–1050) indicate that "goods from China" as well as many other commercial items were available in local markets.[29] Phimai, which ranks with Lopburi in its importance to the Khmer, was the center for regional government in the northwest.[30] The integration of both areas into the Khmer empire was initiated by Sūryavarman and communication between the two western centers, made by overland transport, was desirable for its economic as well as for its political potential.[31] The development of such communication and exchange networks aided Sūryavarman's efforts to integrate these outlying territories into his domain.[32]

Epigraphy from the Battambang (Wāt Bāset) and Svay Chek (Bantāy Pṛāv) areas shows commerce passing through this region to Lopburi and the west. These two areas developed into major commercial centers in the reign of Sūryavarman I, indicating that this was the main route to the west from the Khmer heartland.[33] Six of seven inscriptions of a commercial nature from these two temples date to Sūryavarman's reign. The Wāt Bāset inscriptions record the bestowal of honors upon the "chief of royal artisans," who was responsible for the construction of that temple under Sūryavarman.[34] At least eighteen merchants are identified in two inscriptions dated 1042; there is also reference to government supervision of weights and measures and recognition of royal agents who were surveying local commercial activity.[35] Cloth goods, including silk, and spices were among the goods being traded there. An inscription from Bantāy Pṛāv indicates the presence of a *vanik* from Wāt Bāset (Gaāṅ Lampoh), reflecting regular commercial intercourse between these two centers.[36] *Khloñ jnvāl vanik* ("itinerant merchants") are very evident in Bantāy Pṛāv inscriptions, as opposed to *khloñ jnvāl,* indicating that Svay Chek was most important in these times as a center of communication and exchange between the Khmer core and its western provinces.[37] In the Wāt Bāset inscriptions *khloñ jnvāl* ("local merchants") dominate, reflecting Battambang's importance as a local economic center in an emerging hierarchical marketing network (discussed below).

Such epigraphic evidence implies that during the reign of Sūryavarman I western trade routes developed and assumed an important economic position in the Khmer state. Although inscriptions report the incorporation of Lopburi into the administrative structure of the state during Sūryavarman's reign, they provide little information on the economic interchange between Lopburi and the Khmer core.[38] However, control of Lopburi gave the Khmers direct access to the trade routes of the Isthmus of Kra. The Chaiya-Suratthani area, which was known as "Tāmbraliṅga" *(Tan-liu-mei)* to the Chinese,[39] was an important commercial center. Mahāyāna Buddhist votive tablets of similar style and dating to the tenth and eleventh centuries have been found between Chaiya and Lopburi, indicating if not a cultural contact between the two areas, then at least communication.[40]

Archaeological remains from the area between the Isthmus of Kra and Lopburi do not give much information on a commercial relationship either. A Sūrya image found at Chaiya has been associated with the eleventh-century style of the south Indian Cōḷa dynasty.[41] Other Cōḷa-style remains from the Wiang Sa area on the isthmus date to the same tenth- and eleventh-century period, and denote a transpeninsular route between the west coast Malay Peninsula port of Takuapa and the Bay of Bandon.[42] Archaeological research on the Malay Peninsula demonstrates that Takuapa was the terminus of the Arab-Persian trade until the mid-eleventh century, when it was shifted to the Kedah coast.[43] "Kalāh," as Middle Eastern seamen called the Isthmus of Kra region of the western Malay Peninsula coast, was the center of this Arab-Persian trade, while Śrīvijaya-Palembang was the center of China trade. Kalāh's ability to handle the trade of two worlds was the source of its importance. The Arabs knew it as a place where a large amount of profit could be made, a fact reflected in the quantity and quality of artifacts found there. A Khmer presence in the Suratthani area would have thus given the mainland commercial networks further access to the international China market as well as this Western market of Persian and Indian goods.

The presence of "goods from China" at Phanom Wan west of Phimai in the Mun River system during Sūryavarman's reign indicates the commercial importance of these new "western contacts."[44] As the epigraphy shows, tenth-century "goods from China" had entered the Khmer core from the eastern part of the domain. In the Tuol Pei inscription, the royal family requested that the district chief of an eastern commercial center acquire goods from a China trader.[45] The activities of Vietnamese and Cham merchants in the Khmer core are recorded in the eastern Phum Mīen inscription of 987.[46] Other tenth-century inscriptions of a commercial nature are concentrated in this eastern direction, but those of Sūryavarman's reign reverse this with a western concentration. While this proliferation is a reflection of Sūryavarman's interest in extending Khmer administration into the western provinces, there are strong commercial implications as well. With Khmer control over Lopburi, "goods from China" could now reach Phanom Wan via Tāmbraliṅga and Lopburi using the Chao Phraya River system, rather than from the east. Such a direct interaction with the international routes no doubt was viewed as an asset to the internal development of the Khmer economy in Sūryavarman's time.

Thus Sūryavarman attempted to establish regular commercial intercourse with the south Indian Cōḷa state and the Lý state that was based in the Red River Delta of Vietnam.[47] Sūryavarman appears to have been especially intent upon establishing a flow of trade from south Indian ports to the Southeast Asian mainland via the Isthmus of Kra and Suratthani area. Goods could then have been transported north from the isthmus to Lopburi, where they would have followed the two exchange networks that evolved in Sūryavarman's reign. The first entered the royal heartland in the Sisophon area; the second encompassed the region north of the Dangrek mountain range, with a link to the core at Prāḥ Vihār and a possible connection to the Mekong River in the east (see map 7). Under Sūryavarman's rule the commercial economy of the Khmer state achieved such importance that the upper Malay Peninsula receded from the patterns of power and trade in the island world and was drawn into those of the mainland. The contacts of this area came to lie not with the international trade route but with a more local route that went across the Bay of Bengal to south India and Sri Lanka.[48]

While the Khmers initially took an interest in extending their commercial influence into the Malay Peninsula during Sūryavarman's reign, by the end of the eleventh century Khmer rulers were occupied with internal political strife as well as external pressures on their eastern borders. Around 1050, Angkor's relationship with the Isthmus of Kra was challenged by the Burmese as they expanded into the Malay Peninsula; the Khmer state offered little resistance.[49] About this same year Cham raids sacked Sambupura on the Mekong and Sūryavarman died. Shortly thereafter the center of political authority shifted north into the Mun River Valley beyond the Dangrek mountain range. Little interest in further commercial developments is reflected in Khmer epigraphy from then until the late twelfth century.

Although the evidence discussed above indicates more than casual involvement, the Khmer state's participation in the international commercial routes must be regarded as a secondary concern of Sūryavarman and other monarchs. Khmer rulers were committed to developing their agrarian base around Angkor as well as to overcoming Cambodia's peripheral position, geographically speaking, to the major East-West maritime routes. Thus Sūryavarman expanded his economic base by encouraging his subordinates to bring unused land under cultivation, extending his political hegemony from his core domain, and then making diplomatic overtures to the Cōḷas and the Lý state in Vietnam. With Sūryavarman's death his successors chose to internalize the Khmer polity rather than to promote a stronger interaction in the supraregional trade routes. However, the Khmer state's neighbor to the southeast, the Cham state that controlled the southern portion of present-day Vietnam, had a more compelling desire to penetrate these international commercial channels.

Champa and International Commerce: Eighth-Century Contacts

The earliest Chinese references to the Cham state of Lin-yi date to A.D. 190–193.[50] Caught between the domain of Funan to the south and the Chinese province on the northern Vietnamese coast, the Cham realm's early history was characterized by shifting alliances among regional centers that were concentrated at the river mouths of the Cham coast, not unlike that of the Śrīvijaya realm that was examined in chapter 4.[51] During the early third century the great Funan ruler Fan Shih-man brought the Chams under Funan's authority; the earliest Sanskrit inscription attributed to the Funan state was discovered in Cham territories and records that Lin-yi was a vassal territory under Funan hegemony.[52] The Chinese envoys K'ang T'ai and Chu Ying, who visited Funan in the 240s, reported that Funan's ruler at that time, whom they call Fan Hsun, had established an alliance with the Chams around 220, and that together the Chams and Funanese were making naval raids and land attacks against the Red River Delta region.[53] During the mid-fourth century the semiautonomous Cham ruler known to the Chinese as Fan Fo, taking the Sanskrit title Bhadravarman, began to develop a Sanskritic administrative core, erecting the first temples in the Cham holy city of Mi-so'n on the fictitious Mount Vugvan, the Cham equivalent of Mount Meru, the abode of the ancestors, and consecrated the Śiva-*liṅga* Bhadreśvara, beginning the Cham tradition of assigning to the state's central deity the reigning king's Sanskrit name.[54]

In the fifth century Lin-yi emerged from under Funan's suzerainty, responding in part to the new circumstances afforded when Chin dynasty rulers began to encourage the expansion of maritime trade in the Southern Seas. Cham ports became intermediate stops for merchant ships navigating the South China Sea; ships put into Cham ports prior to their entry into Chinese harbors.[55] During the mid-fifth century a dynastic crisis in Funan resulted in the flight of a Funan prince to Lin-yi, where he is said to have become king of the Chams.[56] This king, Fan Tang, was officially recognized by the Chinese throne in 491 when he was granted the title of "General Pacifier of the South, Commander-in-Chief of the Military Affairs of the Seashore, and King of Lin-yi."[57] Chapter 3 related this recognition to China's perception of Funan's demise as the dominant commercial center in the Southeast Asian realm and the Lin-yi coast's ascendency as the major commercial and political power on the lower Vietnam coast by the end of the fifth century.

In 605, however, a Chinese general undertook the task of forcibly opening the region for trade.[58] The Cham state of Champa (from which is derived the name of the Chams) as it was then known in its epigraphy, its capital at Tra-kieu near present-day Đa Nang, reacted favorably and soon became a secondary entrepôt on the main international route, servicing shipping and sailors traveling between the Malay world and Canton. By 758 the Chinese reported that the Cham state had developed commercial centers at Kauṭhāra (present-day Nha-trang) and Pāṇḍuranga (present-day Phan-rang) and began to call the state Huan-wang.[59]

In general, early Cham epigraphy reflects an internally oriented wet-rice state.[60] The Cham state had a system of classical Southeast Asian statecraft, drawing its legitimacy from a Hindu-Buddhist cult that emphasized the Cham king's association with Śiva and his consort Bhādradhpatīśvara. By the seventh and eighth centuries the Cham state had evolved a loose balance between its wet-rice economy and its participation in the external realm of international trade. An important factor necessitating this balance was the fact that the Cham coast was strategically located on the principal maritime route between the Śrīvijaya empire and China, a position that allowed the Chams the opportunity to take advantage of the economic benefits offered by participation in the trade along this route.[61]

Contrary to their usual lack of information on commerce, merchants, and the sea trade in general, Cham inscriptions dating to the eighth century report two sea raids that threatened the state's very existence. A Sanskrit inscription from Nha-trang informs us that in 774 "ferocious, pitiless, dark-skinned men born in other countries, whose food was more horrible than corpses, and who were vicious and furious, came in ships . . . took away the [temple *liṅga*], and set fire to the temple . . . ," thus desecrating the Po Nagar temple near Nha-trang.[62] This was followed by a second raid by a similar group in 787, when a Pāṇḍuranga temple was burned.[63] Historians have traditionally identified these dark-skinned and demonic seafarers with Javanese or Malay sailors—a group similar to the Malay sea nomads who were the strength behind the Malay state of Śrīvijaya's hegemony (see chap. 4)—seamen who could be used to control shipping, but who in times of political turmoil might turn to piracy as the source of their livelihood.[64]

To understand these eighth-century inscriptions, the Cham state's relationship to the trade routes in that period must be examined. Since both raids were directed not at the Cham capital near Đa Nang, but at the two port areas recognized by the Chinese as being of commercial importance, the Malay raids reflect two possible conditions. If the Śrīvijaya state were still the dominant power in the strait region, then the rise to prominence of the Cham ports located in the southern areas of the Cham coast might well have posed a threat to Śrīvijaya's economic hegemony over the southern maritime route.[65] In this instance the raids are explained as having been initiated by Śrīvijaya to prevent the rival development of the Cham ports.[66] Alternatively, if Śrīvijaya were no longer a viable political force during the eighth century, as some historians have proposed, then the raids on the Cham ports were undertaken by sea pirates—groups who had formerly supported Śrīvijaya's control over the Southern Seas, but who in the eighth century had become pirates.[67] Cham ports, recognized in that period as prosperous centers of commerce, no doubt presented attractive sources of plunder.

Chinese records help to explain the circumstances surrounding these events. The eighth century was a period of political turmoil in southern China following the rebellion of An Lu Shan in 756. When Canton, the major Chinese port of that period, was sacked by a rebel Chinese army in 758, Canton's foreign merchant community, especially the Persians, Arabs, and other merchants who participated in the southern maritime route, began to shift their commercial operations to the Vietnam coast. Chinese sources lamented that thereafter "only four or five vessels of the barbarians of the south and west (or southwest) come each year."[68]

The Hanoi area of the Cham's Vietnamese rivals benefited most from this relocation of the foreign merchant community's base of operations. A late eighth-century (792) Chinese account reported an appeal to the Chinese emperor:

> Lately, the precious and strange (goods) brought by ocean-junks have mostly been taken to An-nan (the port of Hanoi) [probably Long-bien, north of present-day Hanoi] to be traded there. I wish to send an officer

> to go to An-nan and close the market, and request that your imperial majesty send one central (government) official to accompany him.[69]

Cham ports prospered from this shifting trade focus as well. As a result, Cham rulers were forced to come to terms with the new commercial presence. Immediately prior to the Canton turmoil of the late 750s, the Chams initiated a diplomatic relationship with China. The Cham ruler's increasing interest in trade is revealed by the official Cham mission sent to China in 749, which presented the Chinese emperor with one hundred strings of pearls, gharuwood, cotton, and twenty tame elephants, all goods that T'ang dynasty sources considered to be specialties of the Cham ports.[70] These ports, the Chinese records note, became transitory points between the Malay world and An-nan and Canton; normally Cham traders used An-nan to acquire fine commodities such as Chinese silks and manufactured items.

After these eighth-century records, there is little evidence of the realm's commercial stance until the eleventh century, when several inscriptions, as well as external information from China, allow further speculation on Cham attitudes toward commerce.

Champa and International Commerce in the Tenth and Eleventh Centuries

Tenth- and eleventh-century Cham history reflects an ongoing hostility between the Chams and the Vietnamese Lý state to the north, which had newly won its independence from Chinese authority (see map 7). An increasingly important element of these hostilities was the use of naval warfare. Two major Cham naval campaigns, one in 979 and the second in 1042, had a significant impact upon the integrity of Cham hegemony.

In 979, a naval expedition attributed to the Chams was launched against the Vietnamese capital of Hoa-lu' in the Red River Delta.[71] In reply, the Vietnamese destroyed the Cham capital of Indrapura in 982, eventually forcing the Chams to move their capital farther south to Vijaya (Binh-đinh). Cham raids against the northern Vietnam coast in 1042 again brought retaliatory action. In 1044, Lý Thái-tông led a seaborne expedition that was said to have routed the Chams and killed their king Jaya Siṃhavarman II.[72] Shortly thereafter, in 1050, a Cham inscription recorded a royal expedition against the Cham port of Pāṇḍuranga. The people of this port were described as "vicious, threatening, and always in revolt against their sovereign," and they refused to recog-

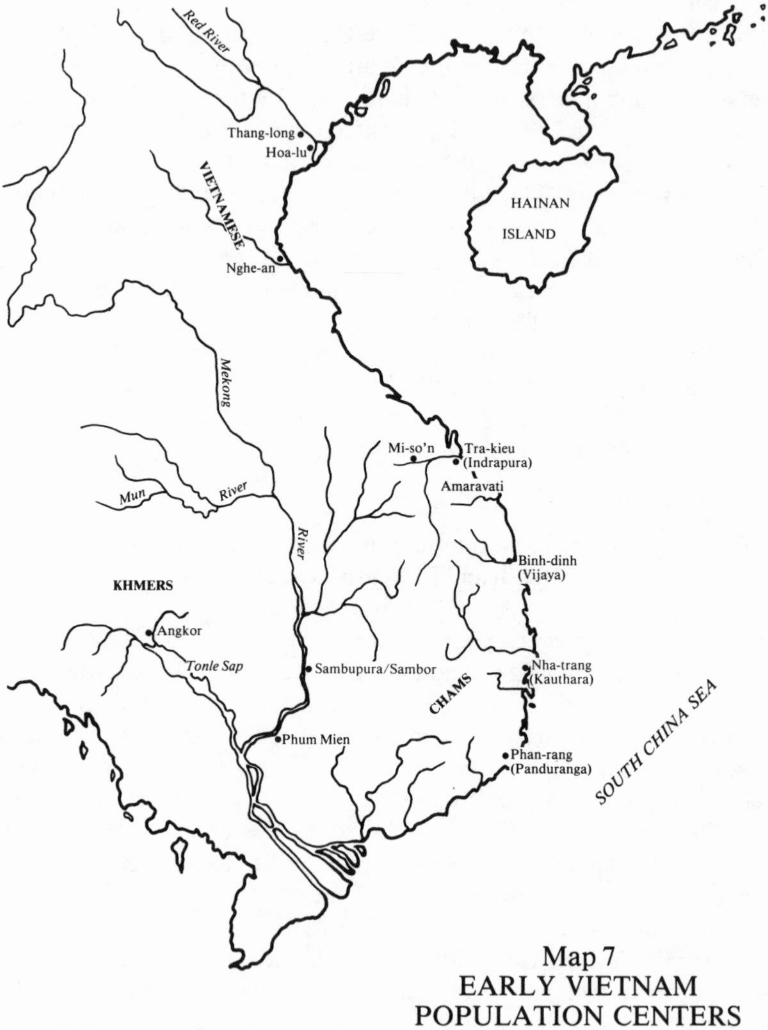

Map 7
EARLY VIETNAM
POPULATION CENTERS

nize the Cham ruler's authority.[73] The available records of this period indicate that this final event was related to the two previous naval expeditions and was the culmination of a commercial problem that the Cham rulers were facing during this time.

Two Arabic script (Kufic) inscriptions, dating between 1029 and 1035, from Pāṇḍuranga (Phan-rang) evince the existence of a sizable commercial group (possibly some three hundred strong) resident in Pāṇḍuranga and indicate that Pāṇḍuranga was a major port on the Cham coast in the mid-tenth century.[74] One inscription records the selection by this community of one of its members—a Muslim—as "agent of the bazaar," whose duty it was to represent local merchants and to protect their interests when dealing with Cham authorities. That earlier commercial groups had a regular interaction with the Cham monarchy is evident from a tenth-century Chinese reference to a 958 visit to China. On this visit the ambassador of the Cham king Indravarman III presented the Chinese emperor rose water, flasks of "Greek fire," and precious stones.[75] Significantly, this official envoy of the Cham king was a Muslim named Abū Hasan (P'u Ho-san). In 961, Abū Hasan returned to China bearing a letter from the new Cham king Jaya Indravarman I and presented fragrant wood, ivory, camphor, peacocks, and twenty Arab vases—all supposedly commercial products available in Cham ports—to the Chinese monarch.[76]

Thus we see that Cham monarchs were responsive enough to commercial activities during the mid-tenth century to be able to and willing to take advantage of the opportunities afforded when Canton was fully reopened to foreign commerce under the later Chou (951–959) and then the Sung (960–1279) dynasties. They utilized a member of Pāṇḍuranga's merchant community, Abū Hasan, to further the commercial relationships between this major Cham port (its merchant community dominated by Muslims) and the reopened Chinese harbors.

The reason for such a positive response by the Cham ruler is reflected in Chinese references from the Sung era to Champa's harbors, where ship cargoes were inspected by a king's agent upon a ship's arrival in port. After registering all commodities carried by a ship and noting how many goods were unloaded, the king's agents collected one-fifth of each kind of commodity in the name of their monarch before authorizing the sale of the rest. Concealed freight was seized.[77] This income financed various royal activities, not the least of which were Cham ambitions for military conquest—especially against the north. Not only was the emerging Lý state a political threat, but, from an economic perspective, the Lý ports were the Cham state's chief commercial rivals. The harbors of the Vietnam coastal region, as noted above, served as major centers for the

China trade, while those of the Cham domain were of only secondary importance. In this light it is possible to see the Cham-Vietnamese hostilities of the tenth and eleventh centuries not only as attempts at political expansion but as having commercial implications as well.[78]

There are two likely points of competition during these times: the port of Vằn-đồn in the northeast corner of the Red River Delta at the Bạch-đằng River mouth was emerging as a prominent port and an interior trade route connecting Vietnam and Angkor was also becoming important. This latter diversion was a serious threat to Cham trading, especially with Angkor. An eleventh-century overland trade route from the Vietnamese port of Nghệ-an west through the Ha-trai pass and turning south along the Mekong River into the Khmer heartland was noted earlier.[79] Traders using this route are specifically mentioned as being of Vietnamese origin in Khmer inscriptions as for example in a 987 inscription from Phum Mīen on the lower Mekong.[80] The presence of a Vietnamese trader in this lower Mekong area allows speculation on Pāṇḍuranga's strategic position vis-à-vis the Angkor domain. Pāṇḍuranga was located just north of the Mekong Delta, where it likely controlled much of the commercial traffic moving into the interior. The Vietnamese trader would have normally traveled to Phum Mīen after first stopping at Pāṇḍuranga. The development of an alternative northern route overland from Vietnam would have significantly diverted trade from Cham ports and threatened their prosperity. It was therefore in the interest of the Cham commercial community to cooperate with the Cham rulers in their expeditions against the Vietnamese.

It is significant that the Cham coast had been consistently regarded as a center of piracy in earlier centuries.[81] The source of tenth- and eleventh-century Cham maritime strength came from peoples similar to those who in the eighth century had pillaged the Cham coast; that is, the "Malay" seafarers. A ninth-century Khmer inscription is of interest because it refers to a victory over "thousands of barks with white sails," which historians attribute to the Chams.[82] A Cham-Malay relationship can also be seen in the Javanese influence upon Cham culture. This influence is most visible in Cham temple architecture of the ninth century, notably at Mi-so'n, the leading temple complex and religious center of the Cham monarchs.[83] A two-part Cham inscription dated 908–911 from Nhan-biêu reports two official diplomatic missions to Java (Yāvadvīpa) by a favorite of the Cham monarch Jaya Siṃhavarman.[84] A Javanese inscription from this period makes specific reference to the activities of both Khmer and Cham merchants in Java.[85] This Javanese contact no doubt equally attracted Malay traders and seafarers to Cham ports, particularly Pāṇḍuranga. Cham monarchs directed the piratical energies of these seafarers against the prosperous Vietnamese domain in 979 in an expedition that not only benefited the Cham state but improved the economic status of the Cham commercial community as well.

Continuing hostilities between the Chams and the Vietnamese during the remainder of the century diminished the powers of the Cham monarchy, however.[86] The Cham capital at Indrapura was destroyed in the 982 raid and political control was fragmented. Between 982 and 1050, as a result, the southern Cham domain, including the port of Pāṇḍuranga and its seafaring groups, became virtually autonomous. The two Arabic script inscriptions dating to this period, for instance, show the considerable autonomy of Pāṇḍuranga's merchant community.

It is likely that the final Cham naval expedition against the Vietnamese in 1042 utilized seafarers from Pāṇḍuranga. In fact, based upon Chinese records that clearly regard the Cham coast as a pirate lair in the eleventh century, it is quite possible that a number of the naval raids attributed to the Chams during this period were actually initiated by semiautonomous sea nomads who used Cham ports as their base of operation.[87] Finally, in 1044 the Lý seem to have had enough of this harassment and vented their wrath upon the Chams, killing the king. The new Cham monarch appears to have himself had enough of Pāṇḍuranga's autonomy and in 1050, as part of his recentralizing activities, he restored Cham royal authority over the port by force of arms.[88]

Another Po Nagar inscription, which records the Cham king's expedition against Pāṇḍuranga, noted that the king symbolized the restoration of his authority over this southern port by rebuilding the Po Nagar temple complex and assigning "slaves"—Khmers, Chinese, men of Pukam (Pagan), and Thais (Syam)—to the temple.[89] These "slaves" were most probably war captives who had formerly been residents of Pāṇḍuranga—former seafarers who had been captured by the Cham monarch in his expedition against their "pirate lair." It was normal Southeast Asian practice to make dependents of one's enemies. For example, after the Lý raid upon the Cham capital cited above, five thousand war captives were transported back to the Lý capital and resettled. In the classical era war captives were placed on the conquering state's lands as laborers. Generally, they became the bondsmen of the state's monarch, although their services might be reassigned to a temple or to a royal favorite. This resettlement pattern was consistent with the agricultural focus of classical Southeast Asian wet-rice states. The resettlement of war captives was of great importance to the expansion of the Khmer state's agricultural base in the tenth and eleventh centuries, for example. Since Champa's ports were recognized internationally as slave trade centers, it is likely that such war captives would normally have been marketed in Cham coast ports and these "slaves" were present in Pāṇḍuranga's maritime community.[90]

The Cham monarch sent three embassies to China between 1050 and 1056 and five to the Lý capital between 1047 and 1060.[91] This sudden flurry of diplomacy is best characterized as the Cham ruler's assurance to the Chinese and the Vietnamese that he now had his domain, including Pāṇḍuranga and its marauding seafarers, firmly under control.

It is of interest in this perspective that the Chams launched a land attack against the Lý in 1068, and when Vietnam responded with a naval attack against Vijaya the Vietnamese found it remarkable that they met resistance only from a Cham army and not from a Cham fleet.[92] The reason for the absence of naval resistance, based on the above historical reconstruction, was that the Cham king had temporarily diffused the old source of Cham naval support by his conquest of Pāṇḍuranga in 1050 and could not or would not draw upon this community for his country's naval defense at that time.

Khmer and Cham Commercial Contacts in Perspective

The central political authorities in both the Khmer and Cham states during the tenth and eleventh centuries desired external commercial involvement. Khmer and Cham rulers hoped to acquire a share of the profits to be derived from commerce and attempted to expand their commercial contacts through diplomatic means. They sent official embassies and gifts to the monarchs of the Cōḷa, Chinese, and Vietnamese states, all participants in international trade. But while in the tenth and eleventh centuries the Khmer kings of Angkor benefited from their positive economic stance, the interaction of the Cham domain with the commercial channels proved disastrous.

The different experiences of the two states were related to each state's internal strength. During the tenth century and the first half of the eleventh century the Khmer state was successfully expanding both politically and economically. Increasing urbanization, the extension of the Khmer irrigation network and the corresponding extension of agriculture, widespread temple construction, as well as the ability of the Angkor-based state to make even the most remote areas of its domain subject to Khmer administration, show the state's significant capabilities. Champa's tenth- and eleventh-century history, on the other hand, is marked by critical fluctuations. Its geographic position on the coast, as opposed to Angkor's more protected position in the interior, contributed to Champa's vulnerability. Cham rulers not only solicited the aid of foreign merchants and seafarers to expand their economic opportunities but also utilized the merchants' navies for their coastal defenses and expeditions of conquest. This relationship demanded strong leadership to keep these potentially disruptive forces in check. On the positive side, the relationship helped to generate the expansion of Cham trade with China, bringing commercial prosperity. The threat that these merchant groups and seafarers posed to the integrity of the state when they established their autonomy from central Cham authority was a decidedly negative aspect, however.

The Cham relationship with the sea became a problem as early as the eighth century when the Cham coast was subjected to at least two naval attacks. The geographic position of Pāṇḍuranga in the south, far removed from the center of Cham political authority in Indrapura and later Vijaya, was no doubt ideal from the Cham monarch's point of view. In the south, potentially dangerous commercial groups and foreigners could be kept isolated, away from the Cham state's capital in the north. There the foreigners were less likely to harm either the Cham treasury or the state's central cult of legitimacy.

A generally negative attitude toward merchants is well conveyed in Cham epigraphy by its general failure to mention them. There is but one direct reference in Cham inscriptions to a merchant. In this inscription, dated 875, merchants were among those enumerated in a list—which included kings, warriors, priests, and state ministers—who were likely to abscond with a temple's wealth.[93] People who came from the sea, who would have included merchants, are described in Cham epigraphy as "dark-skinned," "demonic," "vicious," and "stupid" and were considered a threat to Cham civilization. The Chams were overly conscious of status distinctions. The Cham social hierarchy was clearly defined: aristocrats were Hindu, commoners became Mahāyāna Buddhists, and merchants were Muslims.[94] It is thus to be expected that merchants, being both Muslim and bad, would have received no positive mention in the temples of the Cham aristocrats.[95] In the Khmer domain, likewise, there were few references to merchants except during Sūryavarman I's reign, a period when the Khmer state was interested in encouraging commercial relationships.

These attitudes are consistent with the center-oriented forms of Southeast Asian statecraft seen in wet-rice states, particularly Java. Because the Khmer realm of Angkor was among the foremost wet-rice economies of classical Southeast Asia, it would seem appropriate that the hierarchical, integrated exchange network model outlined in chapter 1 would apply. Unfortunately, the Khmer epigraphy discussed above does not provide sufficient documentation for a definitive view of a hierarchical

Pagan remains, Burma.

Cham temple relief, Saigon National Museum. Photo courtesy Truong Buu Lam.

Cham temple architecture in Mi-so'n region of Vietnam. Photo by Stella Snead.

Khmer marketing network. Yet there are clues. There is, for instance, a distinction drawn between itinerant merchants *(khloñ jnvāl vanik)* and resident vendors *(khloñ jnvāl)* who are shown inhabiting permanent merchant quarters in Khmer urban centers.[96] While there is no further elaboration of those engaged in commercial activities such as one finds in the extensive lists of merchants in Javanese epigraphy, the simple distinction between itinerant and locally based merchants in Khmer epigraphy, as well as inscriptions that imply the important commercial role of major urban centers in the expanding tenth- and eleventh-century Khmer economy, when related to the other parallels between Javanese and Cambodian statecraft indicate that such a marketing network may have also existed in the Khmer state.[97] Such similarities suggest that the proposed model of an integrated, hierarchical exchange network in a classical Southeast Asian wet-rice civilization based on patterns of exchange in early Java well applies to the Angkor-era state and provides further insight into the nature of economic, social, and political interdependency within the Khmer realm.[98]

On the other hand, evidence of commercial activity within the Cham realm does not show a similar level of integration. The Cham state has often been considered a wet-rice civilization that favorably compares to that of the Angkor-based Khmer state.[99] Champa's use of the Indic vocabulary and religious style associated with the wet-rice state tradition begun by Funan has contributed to this image. Champa had an impressive central temple complex at Mi-so'n, and Cham inscriptions speak of Cham administrative capacity in a vocabulary similar to that of the Khmer. Although it speaks of a centralized administration and presents the image of an integrated wet-rice socioeconomy, however, Cham epigraphy as well as external sources reflect an incomplete synthesis of the classical wet-rice state traditions on the part of Champa. Cham political and economic networks are more appropriately understood in relation to the riverine networks common to the island world of Southeast Asia and may be discussed using the model of riverine system exchange introduced in chapter 1 (see fig. 1).[100]

Because of the geography of the southern Vietnam region with its narrow coastal plain, highland interior, and multiple river systems flowing from the highlands to the coast, Cham political authority was concentrated in coastal and riverine centers near the coast. The Cham royal center ("capital") was shifted among several of these river-mouth urban centers over time, which has been explained by historians as representing corresponding shifts from one dynasty's rule to that of another.[101] In reality they reflect the transfer of authority from the elite of one Cham riverine system to that of another, comparable to the establishment of the supremacy of a point *A* in the riverine system model over various A_1s and their subordinate riverine networks. Despite the transitions from "dynasty" to "dynasty" and various transfers of the Cham "capital" from river-mouth urban center to river-mouth urban center, the Cham sacred center of Mi-so'n, located on the edge of the highlands and upriver from the urban center of Tra-kieu on the coast, continued to serve as the locus for Cham royal ceremony and to provide unity to the Cham realm.[102] Similar to other island world riverine political systems, the Cham realm did not have the extensive hinterland agrarian development that is found in the wet-rice states of Southeast Asia's classical age—Java, Pagan, the Khmer state to the west, and the Vietnamese state to the north.[103] Indeed, in the region north of the Mekong Delta where Cham authority was concentrated there was no expansive plain that could have served as an economic core for Champa's monarchs.[104] As a consequence, there was a good deal of Cham interest in the sea, which was seen as an alternative source of income.[105]

We have seen that a successful Southeast Asian ruler was one who emerged from a group of competing chiefs or land-based elites, each with their own network of allies. He rose above his competitors through his ability to guarantee prosperity for his followers, whether through the redistribution of the spoils of war, by developing the agrarian base of his realm, by simply bringing peace to a domain previously torn by competition for power among various factions, or by negotiating and facilitating external trade contacts between his realm's ports and foreign merchants.

A chief thus emerged as a monarch because of his personal prowess and especially as a consequence of his initiative in generating income for his subjects. The opportunity to share in this prosperity encouraged other chiefs and their allies to honor the monarch's sovereignty, although they retained a considerable degree of autonomy within their regions beyond the royal core. There the monarch's authority depended on his manipulation of symbols, magical spells, and oaths of allegiance rather than physical might. Once a ruler was no longer able to guarantee his followers' economic prosperity or to redistribute income to regionally based subordinates, these allies had no reason to participate in the monarch's system apart from the symbolic status bestowed on them through the ruler's religious cults. With the loss of economic prosperity, however, serious questions were soon raised regarding the magical qualities of these cults, and the autonomy of the regional units began to reemerge.[106] In each of the classical Southeast Asian states there is ample evidence of this periodic regional autonomy and resistance to the centralizing ambitions of monarchs, even in the great Khmer wet-rice state that was centered at Angkor. Khmer monarchs as well as other classical rulers depended upon their own economic resource base—the production of laborers on royal lands in the wet-rice states or in the case of Śrīvijaya, the revenues derived from trade—as the main source of their income. Classical rulers could not rely upon the regular flow of revenues from regional subordinates to finance the state, nor were they able to completely transcend the local socioeconomic hold of regionally based landed elites to create an interdependent state system.

Unfortunately for Cham monarchs the revenues collected in the Cham coast ports subject to royal authority were insufficient to maintain the alliance networks. As a secondary rather than primary center of international commercial exchange Cham ports had a limited trade volume to tax—especially during eras when the international maritime route was in a state of flux due to disorders on either of its ends. In such times Cham rulers would have had difficulty making redistributions sufficient to maintain the loyalty of the state's maritime allies, whereupon these seamen became pirates. The Chinese tried in vain to make Cham rulers responsible for the behavior of their coastal populations; in fact the Cham rulers were often unable to control the actions of this maritime population. Cham coast piracy, which was well known among the international maritime community, further weakened the appeal of Champa's ports to international traders and increased the likelihood of Cham political instability.

Unable to amply tap the surplus production from their land base and incapable of securing sufficient return from port cesses to maintain the loyalty of the seamen based in their ports, Cham monarchs were forced to seek alternative sources of income to maintain the alliance networks critical to their sovereignty. Thus the state's rulers found it necessary to direct their supporters to venture outside the Cham realm on a regular basis for plundering expeditions against Champa's neighbors, the Vietnamese to the north and the Khmer to the west. This plunder dynamic explains why Cham history is dominated by one military expedition after another. Cham expeditions were undertaken to acquire both material wealth and manpower—in the form of slaves. Champa was known widely as a major source of slaves (e.g., war captives) who were traded at Cham ports to various buyers from the Asian world.[107] This wealth was then redistributed among the participants of the expedition, the warriors and seamen who in return acknowledged the Cham rulers' sovereignty. Successful plundering expeditions were thereby a means of reinforcing the Cham monarch's image as the source of his allies' prosperity in the absence of a sufficient internal resource base.[108]

The Cham state has been characterized in this chapter as a loose and marginally interdependent alliance network among a series of river-mouth urban centers and their upriver hinterlands on the southern Vietnam coast. The redistribution of plunder directly or indirectly—as for instances in local temple endowments—from successful military expeditions was the means by which the loyalty of the inhabitants of the Cham riverine networks was maintained. An incomplete synthesis of the Funan wet-rice state tradition, the Cham state may thus be viewed best as a Southeast Asian riverine state of the Śrīvijaya sort that depended on an alliance network among the leaders of coastal and upriver population centers for its existence, and by its very nature was politically and economically unstable.

The limited Cham epigraphic references to commerce, unlike those of Cambodia and Java that are distributed beyond the coastal ports in the Khmer and Javanese hinterland, are concentrated in the river-mouth centers on the Cham coast and report the activities of itinerant, maritime-oriented, and externally focused commercial communities. There is no indication of a hierarcy of locally based and itinerant merchants comparable to those documented in Cambodia and Java's epigraphy. Unlike Śrīvijaya's rulers, who derived their initial success from the redistribution of wealth accumulated from the state's role as a major facilitator of East-West trade, and Khmer rulers, who received income from the wet-rice core surrounding Angkor, Champa's rulers were forced to maintain the loyalty of their subordinates, including Malay seamen, by keeping these supporters "in the field," active on various expeditions against their neighbors. The inherent institutional weakness in the Cham state ultimately sealed its fate. Vietnamese retaliatory expeditions finally drained the Cham realm of its manpower during the fifteenth century.[109]

8

Transitions in the Southeast Asian Commercial and Political Realms, A.D. 1000–1400

Through the ninth and tenth centuries, when the T'ang state was slowly collapsing and China was splintering into numerous regional political entities, the international trade did not fall off to any great degree because of the efforts of the Southern Han and Min regimes based respectively at Canton and Fu-chou.[1] Yet new pressures were building up along the sea routes in South and Southeast Asia. Where previously the political development of these regions was such that there had been little conflict among major regional powers, the tenth century saw the beginnings of such conflict, particularly with the rise of maritime power in eastern Java and on the Tamil section of the east coast of India. Added to this interregional competition was the major upsurge in trade that followed the reunification of China under the Sung dynasty (960–1279) and its efforts to reopen the communications of the Southern Seas (Nanyang) over the final third of the tenth century.

The hundred years following the upsurge along the trade route saw a serious weakening of the position of Śrīvijaya as the dominant entrepôt in the Strait of Malacca region, as political and economic strains proved too great for it. The Śrīvijayan rulers first sought to consolidate their position with diplomatic maneuvers in the direction of India and Sri Lanka and then followed with a war against Java.[2] The Javanese counterattacked in 992 but in 1016 suffered a devastating raid from their enemies, allowing the Śrīvijayan ruler to refer to himself as "king of the ocean lands" when he sent a richly laden mission to China the following year.[3] Yet, within a decade, the Cōḷa navy of India's Coromandel Coast had sacked the legendary riches of the Śrīvijayan capital and for the next fifty years was to play a role in the politics of the strait area.[4] The attack of 1025 disrupted the concentration of the international route through the Śrīvijayan ports along the strait, and by the last quarter of the eleventh century the trading pattern had become more diffuse. No longer was the chief focus of the route on the southeastern Sumatra coast and its control of the Strait of Malacca. In 1178, Chinese sources stated:

> Of all the wealthy foreign lands which have great store of precious and varied goods, none surpasses the realm of Ta-shih (the Arabs). Next to them comes the She-p'o (Java), while San-fo-chi (Srivijaya) is third; many others come in the next rank.[5]

Indeed the main thrust of international commerce moved toward the produce of Sumatra and the riches of the developing ports of east Java and the imported spices they offered. The 1025 Cōḷa expedition was critical to the Southeast Asian mainland as well. By removing Śrīvijaya's presence from the ports of the upper Malay Peninsula, the Cōḷas cleared the way for the expanding mainland states to fill the resulting power vacuum.[6]

The location and type of commodities involved in the Sung maritime trade demonstrate what areas the Chinese were familiar with as well as those they did not know.[7] Chao Ju-kua, superintendent of maritime trade at the China coast port of Ch'uan-chou, reconstructed the world he knew in a 1225 work on maritime trading patterns that derived much of its information directly from the seamen and traders themselves.[8] He divided Southeast Asia into an Upper Shore (Shang An), including the mainland and the Malay Peninsula, a region with which the Chinese had had contact in prior centuries, and a Lower Shore (Hsia An), covering Sumatra and the Java Sea, whose trading network had been in former times controlled by the Śrīvijaya state. On the former were Champa, the Khmer state, and the east coast of the peninsula; the latter included the old favored coast of southern Sumatra, the ports of Java, and the south coast of Borneo. Two areas are conspicuously missing from this Chinese view in any geographical detail—the hinterland of the isthmus and the eastern islands beyond the Java Sea. Yet where the latter, merely referred to en masse as the Ocean Islands (Hai Tao), were concerned, the Chinese still had an idea of the types of goods that the area produced and that it took in exchange.[9]

With the weakening of the old international trade system greater numbers and different types of foreign traders pursued Southeast Asian goods more directly into Southeast Asia itself. With the rise of new ports on the southeastern coast of China, Fu-chou and Ch'uan-chou supplementing the older port of Canton, and increasing commercial strength in southern India, the foreign traders not only continued to transport the goods of East and West but wished to acquire Southeast Asian commodities more directly themselves.[10] While they initiated trade on the coasts of the Philippines, northern Borneo, and north and west Sumatra, they dealt still with intermediaries, notably the Javanese, in obtaining the increased flow of spices from the eastern archipelago. These traders also began to penetrate core areas of the lowland empires on the mainland, though they appear to have gone no farther inland.

Because of their more technologically sophisticated ships and organization, Arab traders in the early tenth century were gaining prominence in Southeast Asia. Arab seamen supplemented Malay sailors as carriers of international cargoes between India and China; the greater trade volume of that age (as opposed to the limited volume of the earlier luxury trade) went beyond the ability of the Malay sailors to provide transport. But between the twelfth and thirteenth centuries the Arab role in Southeast Asian trade diminished.[11] This decreasing Arab role in Southeast Asian trade was in part due to the entry of Chinese traders into Southeast Asian markets during this era, as well as to the continuing instability of the Persian Gulf political realm after the demise of the 'Abbāsid dynasty in the mid-tenth century. While Middle Eastern trade continued, especially following the rise of Fatimid rulers in Egypt in the late tenth century, the Red Sea became the western terminus for the Asian maritime route. Red Sea ports focused their commercial contacts upon the Indian and Sri Lankan coasts, as Red Sea-based merchants rarely ventured beyond South Asia into Southeast Asian waters.[12] Instead Western traders depended upon contacts with a multiethnic group of traders who worked the India-to-Southeast Asia leg of the international maritime route to acquire Southeast Asian and Chinese merchandise.

During Sung times southern Chinese interest was once again exclusively directed to the sea after the fall of K'ai-feng in 1127 and the subsequent closing of the overland caravan routes across the Central Asian steppes. All tribute with trade that came to the Chinese capital at Hang-chou after that date came by sea, while before that date approximately 35 percent of the tribute missions were coming by land.[13] The Sung government looked to the sea not only as a valued source of revenue but also for the first time began to integrate the sea into China's defense strategy. A Chinese navy was built that became the foundation for later Mongol and Ming naval expeditions. Although the entry of Chinese private merchants into Southeast Asia had begun before this time—during the ninth and early tenth centuries—in the Sung era such contacts expanded overseas. Chinese merchants boarded Malay ships and traded in the Southern Seas before the appearance of Chinese junks in the Nan-yang. Initially working out of the North China Sea, junks from the Chinese commercial fleet were seasoning as far to the west as Lamuri on the northern coast of Sumatra before the end of the twelfth century, and by the mid-thirteenth century Chinese junks and traders were active in the Indian Ocean.[14] The Arab traveler Ibn Battuta described with amazement the size of Chinese junks he found in India during the early fourteenth century; he boarded one of them and voyaged to the northern Sumatra coast and said of the Sea of China (which probably meant the Indian Ocean eastward from India to the Chinese coast) that "travelling is done in Chinese ships only."[15]

By the thirteenth century this commercial pattern had set the framework for the trade developments of the following years. From the thirteenth to the seventeenth centuries, though political upheavals led to a different configuration of states, Java with its control of the spice trade was the dominant commercial power, and its dominance influenced much that was going on around it. Javanese power continued over southern Sumatra and surrounding island ports in the Strait of Malacca through the fourteenth century, resisting even the intrusions of the newly formed Ming dynasty (1368–1644) in China. The predominance of Chinese shipping in the western Indian Ocean disappeared in the early fifteenth century, giving way to expanding shipping based out of Indian ports, largely due to a changing stance vis-à-vis commerce by Ming rulers and the substantial growth in Western demand for Asian goods that resulted in more Western ships covering this portion of the route. No longer was it necessary for Chinese ships to provide transport in this commercial sector. Chinese junks withdrew to the South China Sea and concentrated their activities in the fifteenth and sixteenth centuries on ports in the Gulf of Thailand and Java. They also lost in competition with the Javanese in the Moluccas in the fourteenth century and finally were satisfied to buy spices secondhand from Javanese ports.[16]

The Eleventh-Century Struggle for the Malay Isthmus

By the first half of the eleventh century, the Khmers of Cambodia had pushed their control to the west into the Chao Phraya Valley of present-day Thailand and toward the Isthmus of Kra. Where tenth-century Cambodia's commercial interest had been directed toward the eastern portions of its land, Sūryavarman I (1002–1050) reversed this pattern with his activities in the west (see chap. 7). Sūryavarman's extension of Khmer administration into the Lopburi region had strong economic implications. Control of the lower Chao Phraya River provided access to international commerce at Tāmbraliṅga on the Chaiya-Suratthani coast of southern Thailand, giving the Khmers a more direct contact with the international trade routes than had previously been the case (see map 8).

After the Cōḷas eliminated Śrīvijaya's power over the isthmus, the Khmers established their own influence over Tāmbraliṅga.[17]

Stronger Khmer commercial relationships with the Isthmus of Kra are indicated by Sūryavarman's diplomatic initiatives with south India. In 1020, before Rājēndra Cōḷa's Southeast Asian raid, Sūryavarman sent presents to the Cōḷa king; in chapter 7 it is argued that this act was the culmination of eleventh-century Khmer commercial expansion. A Sūrya image found at Chaiya has been traced to the eleventh-century style of the Cōḷa dynasty.[18] Other Cōḷa-style remains from the Wiang Sa area on the isthmus date to the same tenth- and eleventh-century period, indicating the existence of a transpeninsular route between the west coast port of Takuapa, the terminus of the Persian-Arab trade until the mid-eleventh century, and the Bay of Bandon.[19]

As the Khmers were developing commercial contacts with the West, the Burmese were pushing south into the delta of the Irrawaddy and were also moving toward the Isthmus of Kra. After establishing a base at Pagan in the tenth century, the Burmese in an eleventh-century expansion annexed the Mon kingdoms of Pegu and Thaton in lower Burma. Here the Burmese established control over the Mon commercial centers, one of which was "Papphala," the Burma coast port the Cōḷas claim they sacked in 1024–1025. Around 1050 the Burmese were expanding into the Malay Peninsula, where they encountered little resistance from the Khmers.[20] It would appear that after 1050 internal disorder prevented a Khmer presence in the Malay Peninsula, leaving the isthmus to the Burmese. The Chams were applying pressure on the eastern Khmer border, Sūryavarman died, and the center of Khmer political power temporarily shifted north into the Mun River Valley beyond the Dangrek mountain range.[21] Cambodian epigraphy reflects a corresponding lack of interest in commercial affairs until the late twelfth century.

Tenth-century disorder in the region the Chinese knew as the Nan-chao region north of the Burmese and Khmer realms appears to have blocked the overland commercial networks connecting the Irrawaddy plains and China and thus generated Burmese interest in opening commercial channels to the south.[22] Prior to the closing of the northern route Burma had served as a center of exchange between northern India and China; overland trade to Bengal via Arakan had been of major economic importance to the Burmese heartland. Commercial centers on the Malay Peninsula provided an alternative source of foreign commodities for this India trade after the route to China had been closed. The isthmus port of Takuapa was located well within the range of Mon coastal shipping. The Mon port identified as Papphala in the Tañjāvūr inscription, located somewhere on the Pegu coast of lower Burma, could thus have connected the overland route to northwest India with this maritime route. Papphala's channel of communication with the isthmus was disrupted by the Cōḷa raid.

Under Anirruddha (1044–1077), there was new interest in restoring commercial intercourse with the isthmus. Around 1057, Anirruddha followed his conquest of Thaton by moving his armies south to Mergui. From Mergui, one historian believed, the Burmese forces crossed the isthmus.[23] Burmese military success in this direction is reflected in a request by King Vijayabāhu I (1055–1110) of Sri Lanka for aid against the Cōḷas, to which the Burmese king ("the king of Rāmañña") responded with "peninsular products," which were used to pay Vijayabāhu's soldiers.[24] The Cōḷas did not look favorably upon this show of support. In 1067, they launched an expedition against "Kaḍāram" (Takuapa), in "aid of its ruler," who had been forced to flee his country and had sought Cōḷa assistance: "Having conquered (the country of) Kaḍāram, (he) was pleased to give it (back) to (its) king who worshipped (his) feet (which bore) ankle rings."[25] Cōḷa administrative problems in Sri Lanka made this intervention short, however; by 1069–1070, south Indian control over Sri Lanka had been eliminated. The *Cūlavaṃsa,* the Sri Lankan Buddhist chronicle, records that in 1070, after Vijayabāhu I gained control, many costly treasures were sent to the Pagan king; then in 1075, Buddhist priests from Burma were invited to Sri Lanka to purify the order.[26]

Takuapa's position as the dominant port on the peninsula was dealt a death blow by this second Cōḷa raid; the archaeological evidence from the Takuapa area terminates in the second half of the eleventh century, the period corresponding to the raid.[27] It is significant that the Cōḷa inscription recording the 1067 raid states that "Kaḍāram" was the object of this attack. South Indian inscriptions from the early eleventh century were consistent in their reference to the king of Śrīvijaya as the ruler of Kaḍāram, calling him the *Kiḍārattaraiyaṇ.*[28] Thus in one historian's interpretation the eleventh-century south Indian Perumbur inscription has a reference to a revolt by Kaḍāram against Śrīvijaya's control in which the Cōḷa ruler was called upon to put down this revolt and restore Śrīvijaya's sovereignty.[29] However, such an interpretation ignores the possibility of a Burmese presence on the Isthmus of Kra.

As noted above, the 1025 Cōḷa raid resulted in a loosening of commerce in the strait region, with new ports developing as alternative entrepôts to Śrīvijaya-Palembang. By the late eleventh century the northern Sumatra coast was becoming an important commercial center. The Kedah coast was more strategically located to be a part of this new pattern of Malacca Strait commerce; there are even architectural similarities between Kedah and northern Sumatra temples constructed in this period, reflecting direct contact between the two coasts.[30] A Burmese military presence at Takuapa, followed by the second Cōḷa raid, sealed Takuapa's fate and reinforced Kedah's attractiveness—Takuapa was no longer a port that could offer security to foreign merchants. Archaeological remains at Takuapa and Kedah suggest that such a shift occurred, with evidence at Takuapa ceasing and that of Kedah showing a dramatic increase during the second half of the eleventh century. As a consequence of early eleventh-century disorders the port elites of Takuapa transferred their operations to the new "preferred port" at Kedah, which explains the Arab geographers' continued use of "Kalāh" to identify their preferred Malay coastal entrepôt—that is, the Arabs used Kalāh to identify their preferred port wherever it was in the Isthmus of Kra region on the western Malay Peninsula coast. Similarly, even after Palembang had been replaced by Jambi as the capital of the Śrīvijaya maritime state, the name "Śrīvijaya" still identified the ports of the southeastern Sumatra coast.[31] It is significant that in 1070 the eastern Isthmus of Kra port of Tāmbraliṅga presented its first tribute to the Chinese court since 1016.[32] This mission may be seen as a response to the events of 1067: while the Cōḷa raid against Takuapa and the shift of Kalāh to the Kedah coast established a new pattern on the west coast, Tāmbraliṅga's mission was sent to reassure the Chinese that its east coast status was unchanged.[33]

After the 1067 Cōḷa raid the Burmese moved to ensure their external trade connections. The importance of communication networks linking Burma with northern India was recognized by Kyanzittha (1077–1112) in his restoration of the Bodhgāyā shrine in Bengal.[34] An inscription from Bodhgāyā (1105–1106) recorded that ships laden with large quantities of jewels had been sent by the Burmese ruler to finance the restoration and the endowment of the Buddhist monument.[35] The fact that this mission was sent by sea is indicative of Pagan's new status as a participant in the regional trade of the Bay of Bengal. An inscription from Pagan records another mission that Kyanzittha sent to either south India or Sri Lanka:

> Then the king wrote of the grace of the Buddharatna, Dhammaratna, and Sangharatna (upon a leaf of gold with vermilion ink). The king sent it to the Chōli prince. The Chōli prince with all his array, hearing of the grace of the Buddha, the Law and the Church, from King Srī Tribhuwanādityadhammarāja's mission . . . he cast off his adherence to fake doctrines, and he adhered straight away to the true doctrine. . . .[36]

Although stated in religious terms, there are strong economic implications in this account. Campaigns that were clearly military in character, and probably economic in purpose, were recorded as religious missions; military campaigns became "quests for relics." By triumphantly bringing back relics and sacred treasures the king could justify the expenses of campaigns whose "benefits might remain obscure to the people of the kingdom."[37]

A network of Buddhist religious diplomacy had actually preceded Kyanzittha's efforts. Śrīvijaya's rulers had endowed temples (*vihāras*) at Nālandā in Bengal during the tenth century and at Nāgapaṭṭinam on the Coromandel Coast in the early eleventh century.[38] In 1090, the Cōḻa king Kulōttuṅga I (1070–1122) renewed an endowment of village revenues to the Nāgapaṭṭinam *vihāra*.[39] According to the inscription recording this action certain people who were occupying the previously granted lands were evicted, indicating that the earlier grant (1006) had been ignored for some time. It is apparent that in 1090, Kulōttuṅga saw some benefit in restoring the original grant. By the early twelfth century the Nāgapaṭṭinam *vihāra* had come under the control of the Theravāda school of Buddhism, which was soon to become dominant in Burma.[40] Since Kyanzittha's inscription indicates that Pagan was actively seeking a trade alliance with either south India or Sri Lanka in this same period, it is conceivable that the "Chōli prince" who received his mission was Kulōttuṅga himself. In this case the restoration of the earlier grant, the conversion of the *vihāra* to Theravāda Buddhism, and Kyanzittha's claim to have converted the Chōli prince all were connected.

The last line of the Shwesandaw inscription quoted above includes the statement that the Chōli prince showed his gratitude by presenting to Kyanzittha "a virgin daughter of his, full of beauty," together with other presents.[41] Kulōttuṅga's pattern of beneficent diplomacy is also recorded in Chinese sources. A stone tablet inscription dated 1079, which was discovered in a Taoist monastery temple in Canton, states that the Cōḻa king ("Ti Hua Ka Lo"), also known as the "lord of the land of San Fo Tsi" (i.e., Śrīvijaya), was the temple's benefactor. Kulōttuṅga's gift totaled 600,000 gold cash (a standard of measure used by the Chinese)—a sizeable sum—which drew the praise of the Chinese court and bestowal of the title "Great General Who Supports Obedience and Cherishes Renovations."[42] It is difficult to resist the conclusion that the diplomatic efforts of both Kulōttuṅga Cōḻa and Kyanzittha were economic in motive, even though they were clothed in religious garb. Closer economic ties by sea to south India and Sri Lanka would have provided new economic potential for Pagan, and, as Kyanzittha's inscription indicates, royal patronage was granted to efforts to open these new channels of communication.

Evidence of such commercial contact is provided in a thirteenth-century Pagan inscription noting that a native of India's Malabar Coast made a donation to a *nānādēśī* temple at Pagan.[43] The *nānādēśī* was one among several organizations of south Indian itinerant merchants in existence during the Cōḷa period whose activities also took them to the northern Sumatra coast in the late eleventh century.[44] A similar group is associated with the Takuapa Viṣṇu temple, which has been dated to the ninth century.[45] The thirteenth-century Pagan inscription indicates that the merchants' temple had been present there for some time; the recorded gift provided for the construction of a new shrine *(maṇḍapa)* for the temple compound, which was also dedicated to Viṣṇu. Further evidence of a continuing economic relationship between Pagan and south India is reflected in an 1178 Chinese note on the Cōḷas: "Some say that one can go there by way of the kingdom of P'u-kan [Pagan]."[46]

By using these records to reconstruct the history of the late eleventh century, it appears that as Burma came to dominate the Takuapa region and as "Kalāh" shifted to the Kedah coast, the Burmese empire became a focal point of regional commerce. South Indian merchants who were formerly active at Takuapa moved their activities either south to Kedah or north to the regional commercial centers of the Burma coast. In the process the old dominance over international trade enjoyed by Śrīvijaya along the Strait of Malacca was shattered even more. Java and the northern Sumatra ports drew the major international route south and west, the Burmese drew the regional route of the Bay of Bengal north, and the Isthmus of Kra came to exist essentially as a transition area to the mainland states.

The Upper Malay Peninsula in the Twelfth Century

In the following decades, the upper Malay Peninsula became the center of a multipartite interaction among the Singhalese of Sri Lanka, the Burmese, and the Khmers as the regional trade route developed. Based on his study of Buddhist votive tablets and other evidence, historian G. H. Luce believed that Pagan controlled the isthmus from 1060 until roughly 1200.[47] Examining the chronicles of Nakhọn Si Thammarat together with additional evidence, David Wyatt has revised Luce's dating, suggesting that from 1130 to 1176 Tāmbraliṅga was under Singhalese hegemony.[48] To support his position, Wyatt cites Pali literature from Sri Lanka that regarded Tāmbraliṅga ("Tamalingāmu") as an important twelfth-century center of Buddhist scholarship. Indeed, a Polonnaruva inscription from the reign of the Singhalese king Vikkamabāhu I (1111–1132) may even record the "conversion" of Tāmbraliṅga to the Mahāvihāra Theravāda school.[49] This inscription honors a great scholar *(thera)* of the Sri Lanka *saṅgha* named Ānanda who was instrumental in purifying the order in that land.[50] In the chronicle the prince and princess of Tāmbraliṅga fled to Sri Lanka after an invasion of their land. After a period of exile the king of Sri Lanka assisted them in their return home—an event that Wyatt believes took place around 1130—imposing his sovereignty on the new rulers in the process. About 1176, King Narapati (Narapatisithu of Pagan, 1174–1211) of Pegu (Hansavati) made an expedition into the isthmus and established Pagan's control over the Tāmbraliṅga area "with the permission of the King of Sri Lanka."[51]

Although the farthest extent of archaeological evidence documenting Pagan's control over the peninsula has been found only at Mergui, the Pagan king Cañsū II (Narapatisithu) claimed control over peninsula ports at Tavoy (a town near Mergui), Tenasserim, Takuapa, and Phuket—all on the west coast.[52] Burma's twelfth-century influence on the upper peninsula is substantiated by the *Cūlavaṃsa.*[53] When in the 1160s the Burmese refused (or monopolized) the trade in elephants and blocked the way across the peninsula to Angkor, the Singhalese responded with a retaliatory raid. In this account five ships from Sri Lanka arrived at the port of "Kusumīya" (Bassein) in Rāmañña (lower Burma) led by a certain Kitti Nagaragiri. Furthermore, a ship commanded by a government treasurer reached Papphala, the Mon port mentioned in the Tañjāvūr inscription, where Singhalese troops fought their way into the country's interior to the city of Ukkama and killed the monarch of Rāmañña. This brought the kingdom under Sri Lanka's influence. The people of Rāmañña granted concessions to the Singhalese and envoys were sent to the community of monks on the island with the result that the Theravāda monks interceded with the Sri Lankan king on behalf of the Burmese.[54]

Since only six ships reached Burma, this could not have been the record of a large-scale war but rather of a successful naval raid against lower Burma. Such a plunder expedition was similar to those undertaken by the Cōḷas in the eleventh century, with additional emphasis given to gaining trade concessions. It is unlikely that the raid penetrated to Pagan and killed the Burmese king. There has been an attempt by historians to show that the death of King Alaungsitthu (1113–1165?) coincided with this raid and that the 1160s was a period of general disorder in Burmese history. However, translations of inscriptions that have been made in the 1970s indicate that Alaungsitthu ruled until 1169, four years after the date of the Singhalese raid.[55] Rather than a period of disorder, this was a time of great prosperity according to Pagan epigraphy of the 1160s, with normal state affairs continuing vigorously. Burmese chronicles, however, record that during Alaungsitthu's reign the lower Burma provinces were in a state of "anarchy" and "rebellion," suggesting that a local governor had become quite powerful and attempted to assert his independence from Pagan. "Ukkama," the residence of the "king" killed by the Singhalese has been identified as a commercial and administrative center of lower Burma—possibly Martaban, a later capital of the area—where a local governor could well have been put to death by the raiders.[56] Governors in lower Burma derived considerable income from trade revenues generated by the regional commercial networks. Such an obstruction of commerce may actually have represented an attempt to establish independent control over this lucrative trade. It is notable that one of the attack ships was led by a Singhalese treasurer, an individual who would have had a great interest in increasing trade revenues. Herein the raid of the Singhalese on lower Burma can be seen as the high point of the twelfth-century competition for control of the isthmus and is best explained in terms of an interruption and difficulties concerning the patterns of trade and communication in this area.

Epigraphic evidence from Sri Lanka supports such an economic interpretation of the raid. An inscription from the twelfth year of the Singhalese king Parākramabāhu I (1165) records a land grant to a certain Kit Nuvaragal (Kitti Nagaragiri) as a reward for carrying out a successful expedition against "Aramaṇa" (Rāmañña).[57] The expedition had been sent against "Kusumīya" (Bassein), which had been sacked. When the people of Aramaṇa sent envoys to conclude a treaty, Parākramabāhu granted favors to Kitti Nagaragiri—for forcing envoys to be sent and *not* for a great military achievement. At the death of Parākramabāhu in 1186, his successor Vijayabāhu II concluded a final treaty of peace with Burma, and through the remainder of the twelfth century the way to Cambodia remained open.[58]

While the twelfth-century relationship of Sri Lanka and Burma is relatively clear, that between Sri Lanka and the Khmer state is not. As indicated in the *Cūlavaṃsa,* the major reason for the 1160s conflict between Sri Lanka and Burma was Sri Lanka's concern that Burma was preventing free access to the communication channels between Sri Lanka and Angkor. This explanation is indicative of the peninsula's relationship to the Khmer core domain as well. The upper peninsula was significant as the intermediary between Sri Lanka and Angkor, so that it was more important as a source of economic and cultural contact than as an area to be dominated politically. As a result Sri Lanka was willing to risk a war with Burma to preserve the peninsula's neutrality.

Further evidence of contact between Sri Lanka and Angkor is provided in two twelfth-century inscriptions from Sri Lanka. One from late in the century specifically states that friendly relations with Cambodia were maintained.[59] In the second inscription, one of the city gates at Polonnaruva was called "Kambojavāsala," reflecting a possible Cambodian settlement in the city.[60] Of particular interest is the *Cūlavaṃsa*'s reference to the interception by the Burmese of a betrothed Singhalese princess en route to "Kamboja," a story that is presented as one of the events leading to the 1160s war.[61] A marriage alliance between the Singhalese and the Khmers suggests that such alliances were a common tool of the Singhalese royal house. The cross-cousin marriage patterns of the Singhalese royalty favored continuing relationships, and to form such an alliance with Cambodia would have provided long-range benefits.[62]

Thus, as in the eleventh century, the northern Malay Peninsula played an important role in communication between Cambodia and the West. From the other direction, Chinese authors of the Sung period saw the upper east coast of the peninsula as being within the Cambodian sphere of influence, and one of them believed that its markets produced some of the best incense available:

> Beyond the seas the Teng-liu-mei gharuwood ranks next to that of Hainan [where the price of incense had become too high]. It is first rate. Its trees are a thousand years old. . . . It is something belonging to the immortals. Light one stick and the whole house is filled with a fragrant mist which is still there after three days. It is priceless and rarely to be seen in this world. Many of the families of the officials in Kuangtung and Kuangsi and families of the great ones use it.[63]

Cambodian interaction with the peninsula is evinced in the relationship between the Khmer realm and Tāmbraliṅga on the east coast of the Isthmus of Kra. The last recorded embassy of the latter to the Chinese court was that of 1070, while Cambodia sent embassies in 1116, 1120, 1128–1129, and 1131.[64] Either of two conclusions can be drawn: (a) that the Khmers came to dominate the upper coast between 1070 and 1130, such that they sent embassies and Tāmbraliṅga did not; or (b) that with Cambodia's internal political problems in the late eleventh and early twelfth centuries Tāmbraliṅga became a neutral port. In the twelfth century Chinese merchants were dealing directly with the sources of supply on the peninsula, Sumatra, and Java, eliminating their earlier need for a dominant port of the Śrīvijaya type. Tāmbraliṅga, as a recognized source of forest products, would not have needed to advertise these products by sending embassies to the Chinese court. This differed from the case of the western Chen-la (used consistently by the Chinese to designate the Khmer realm) state of Lo-hu (Lavo), which sent a present of elephants to the Chinese court in 1155 in search of recognition.[65] This mission indicates that the Chao Phraya Valley (Lo-hu) was then free from Khmer control. If, as noted previously, Southeast Asian states sent embassies to China primarily in times of stress, then the Khmer, who were more concerned with pressuring Vietnam and Champa in the east during the first half of the twelfth century, needed to undertake missions to reassure the Chinese that the disorders—and the consequent expressions of political independence by population centers like Lo-hu that had formerly been subject to Khmer authority in Chen-la's western territories—would not interrupt the flow of southern commerce.

The independence of the formerly subordinate western regions of the Khmer realm corresponds in time to the increasing number of military expeditions that the Khmer monarchs waged against their eastern Vietnamese and Cham neighbors. These expeditions assume an important role in Khmer history from the late eleventh century on, and Khmer inscriptions imply that Khmer monarchs, like their Cham neighbors, began to depend more and more on war booty to finance the activities of their court. Khmer inscriptions eulogize successful expeditions of royal "conquest" and consequent redistributions of booty to Khmer temples. The increasing importance of these plunder expeditions as a source of state revenue demonstrates the inability and/or unwillingness of or lack of necessity for Khmer monarchs to increase the state's direct revenue collections from its agrarian base.

As explained in chapter 6, the Khmer state's "ritual sovereignty" statecraft depended on endowing temple networks with revenue assignments rather than on creating an elaborate bureaucracy that could tap its realm's agricultural production. The success of this system is reflected in Khmer inscriptions that report the widespread prosperity, general stability, and continuous expansion of the state's agrarian base despite periodic wars of succession and invasions by the Vietnamese and Chams, which also dominate Khmer history from the eleventh century on and must have placed additional financial burdens on the state. In contrast, chapter 7 noted that the Cham realm had inadequate revenue potential of its own to fund the affairs of the Cham state, and Cham rulers therefore pursued the wealth of their neighbors to finance their statecraft instead. It is puzzling, then, that although the Khmers developed a wet-rice agrarian system that was more than capable of supplying the state's needs (see chap. 6), Khmer monarchs pursued plunder anyway. Their obsession with war may have been a necessary response to the periodic Cham incursions; that is, the best defense was a good offense. A second possibility is that these wars represented a quest for the prowess and personal honor that were bestowed upon a Khmer king who led a successful expedition against the Vietnamese and Chams, and thereby fulfilled the Khmer subjects' expectations of their monarchs. If this were the case, the Khmer military, which appears to have been perpetually active, could have lived off its plunder. It is also conceivable, thirdly, that, like the Burmese state of Pagan, Khmer monarchs had so lavishly endowed state temples to promote ritual sovereignty that they had to explore alternative sources of income to provide for their personal activities—for example, to initiate new temple construction and ritual and to pay the various troops that participated in Khmer military campaigns—instead of increasing the assessments of their agricultural producers. A fourth possibility is that, even more than revenue, the Khmer monarchs needed manpower to staff the state's ever-active military and administration and as well to meet the labor needs of the expanding agrarian system and their ambitious construction projects. As noted in chapter 7, Sūryavarman I, facing such ballooning expenses, encouraged the development of urban and international commerce, which he tapped through the formalization of service relationships with merchants. But his economic initiatives were not adequately carried through by his successors, who lost control over the commercially important western sector of Sūryavarman's realm and seem to have depended more on war booty as a prime source of additional state funding and manpower.

Both Khmers and Chinese participated in a twelfth-century China/Cambodia exchange network. Sūryavarman II (1113–1150) was personally involved in trade relations with China and possessed his own fleet.[66] During his reign Chinese trading vessels visited Cambodia with cargoes of silk goods and porcelain.[67] In 1147, "specific favors" were conferred upon the Khmer state by the Chinese.[68] Sung porcelain has been excavated at Angkor, but there is a noticeable gap in the epigraphic evidence of any commercial relationship until the reign of Jayavarman VII (1181–1218) when the inscriptions of Ta Prohm (1186) and Prāḥ Khan (1191) make reference to Chinese articles.[69] In addition, an inscription from the Phimānākas palace temple at Angkor Thom mentions a flag made of colored Chinese silk.[70] The Prah Khan inscription also includes a reference to localities in the northern access zone to the peninsula, including Ratburi and Petburi, but there is no record of any specific relationship between Angkor and the Isthmus of Kra.[71] A Cham inscription makes reference to a campaign by Jayavarman VII on the peninsula in 1195, which would indicate an attempt to restore a formal relationship.[72]

On the other hand, archaeological remains reflect a cultural and economic tie between the isthmus and Cambodia rather than direct Khmer political presence. Earlier historians used the Khmer inscription of the Grahi Buddha near Chaiya, which they dated to 1185, as proof of Khmer administrative control over the upper peninsula, but when the inscription was revealed to be a product of the last decades of the thirteenth century, many dropped this conclusion. However, the eleventh-century inscription from Phimai (1041) discussed in chapter 7, recorded the local use of an animal dating cycle typical of later Thai rather than Khmer practice.[73] This inscription provides early evidence of Thai-speaking peoples who were administratively incorporated into the Khmer government of Sūryavarman I.[74] Significantly, this same animal cycle was used in the Grahi Buddha inscription. Historians have argued that this reference to the Thai animal cycle necessitates the assignment of a date to the Grahi Buddha later than 1185. However, based on the Phimai inscription's earlier use of this animal cycle and on evidence of a communication network connecting Phimai and Lopburi in the eleventh century, it is indeed possible that Thai-speaking peoples had reached the lower Chao Phraya Valley and the peninsula by the late twelfth century and had taken their place within the mixed cultural configuration of that area with its international commercial routes and communications.[75] This would reestablish a late twelfth-century date for this inscription and show a definite Khmer cultural presence in this key area at that time.

Clay Buddhist votive tablets scattered between the Bay of Bandon and Nakhọn Si Thammarat provide further evidence of communication between the isthmus and Angkor. These twelfth-century tablets have been linked to the multiple figures of Angkor Thom, and represent a departure from earlier Mahāyāna style tablets of the eleventh century; they have more affinity to Theravāda Buddhism.[76] Thus, a common Theravāda Buddhist religious interest, as with Mahāyāna in the earlier centuries, encouraged regular communication among Pagan, Sri Lanka, and Cambodia. The *Cūlavaṃsa* records twelfth-century religious interaction between Pagan and Sri Lanka. By the mid-twelfth century, Tāmbraliṅga had also become a center of the Theravāda Buddhist school. Legend records that Pagan was converted to the Singhalese Theravāda school at the end of the twelfth century when five monks returned to Burma from a pilgrimage to Sri Lanka and built the Chapata temple under the patronage of King Narapatisithu. One of these monks was said to have been the son of a Khmer king, probably Jayavarman VII.[77] Indeed, art historians believe that the Preah Palilay temple at the Angkor Thom Bayon, constructed during Jayavarman VII's reign, exhibits a Theravāda Buddhist style that was introduced from Burma via the Chao Phraya Valley.[78]

As noted, Burma and the upper Malay Peninsula lay on a regional route of communication across the Bay of Bengal that connected Sri Lanka to Pagan and Angkor. While historians have in the past postulated that the Isthmus of Kra was politically dominated by one or another of these powers at various times in the century, the evidence cited above indicates that Burma, Cambodia, and Sri Lanka each had a real interest in the peninsula but that this interest was more of a commercial nature, making attempts to dominate the peninsula politically both unnecessary and perhaps undesirable. That explains why the raid of the Singhalese on lower Burma in the 1160s can best be understood in terms of an interruption and difficulties concerning the pattern of trade and communication in the area. The Burmese had come to dominate this trade and had blocked the way across the peninsula to Angkor, thereby bringing the retaliatory raid from Sri Lanka. Through the end of the twelfth century the way was reopened and rapidly became a path for the spread of Theravāda Buddhism to the western and central sections of the Southeast Asian mainland, establishing a cultural relationship of great significance for later centuries.

Thus, the upper Malay Peninsula receded from the patterns of power and trade in the island world and was drawn into those of the mainland. In addition, where previously it had been the locus for outside contact with the islands and the international routes for the Mons of Rāmaññadesa and Dvāravatī in Burma and Thailand, now the isthmus provided a more regional contact for the wet-rice states of Pagan and Angkor and through them to the northern mountain areas where the stirrings of the Thai-speaking peoples were becoming ever more important.

The Decay of Southeastern Sumatra Entrepôts

In the twelfth century Southeast Asia's spices were becoming popular in Europe; the cure for all sorts of ailments was sought in mixtures of pepper, ginger, cinnamon, sugar, cloves, and especially nutmeg. Furthermore, Southeast Asian spices were useful as flavoring for meats that were increasingly a part of the European diet.[79] By the thirteenth century this Western demand had greatly enhanced the commercial importance of Southeast Asia as a source of trade goods in Western eyes and as the source of valuable spices in particular. The name Java became synonymous in the West with spices; to Javanese ports came Western traders whose bases were spread throughout southern India, Sri Lanka, and Southeast Asia.[80]

During this time merchants based on the Java coast carried on two kinds of external trade, a trade with East and West (primarily with India and China) in spices and other luxury goods, and an export-import trade in rice to the Moluccas and to other parts of the eastern and western archipelago in exchange for spices and cloth.[81] The spices were marketed to Eastern and Western merchants in Java's coastal ports.[82] Java's success as the intermediary of the international spice trade was based on a mutual dependency that came to exist between Java and the islands of the eastern archipelago. The great demand for their spices in international markets made it more economically expedient for the eastern archipelago's populations to concentrate their energies on spice production rather than on subsistence agriculture. Java on the other hand had the ability to produce a surplus of rice and enjoyed a strategic position geographically adjacent to the international maritime route. The goods Marco Polo observed in Java on his return to Europe by sea from China at the end of the thirteenth century were goods the Javanese received in exchange for their own products on the intrainsular trade route. His list of Java's trade goods included sapanwood (used in making red dye) and diamonds from western Borneo, white sandalwood incense from Timor, nutmeg from Banda and the Moluccas, and pepper from north and east coast Sumatra ports. He reported that

> Java . . . is of surpassing wealth, producing . . . all . . . kinds of spices, . . . frequented by a vast amount of shipping, and by merchants who buy and sell costly goods from which they reap great profit. Indeed, the treasure of this island is so great as to be past telling.[83]

The Chinese were already importing Southeast Asian spices in quantity from Java by the twelfth century. Pepper produced in northern Sumatra was also in demand, and Chinese consumption of Javanese-supplied pepper was quite substantial.[84] Southeast Asian pepper was regarded as of lower grade than that produced along India's Malabar Coast, but it was cheaper and more directly available to the Chinese. Eastern Javanese monarchs, who controlled the redistribution of spices from the eastern archipelago, fostered this trade.[85]

In the face of growing Javanese commercial stature ports in the Malacca Strait region diminished in importance as centers of international trade. The unsettled nature of the strait realm in the thirteenth century is demonstrated in local chronicles that report Thai incursions into the region during the latter part of the century. In the late thirteenth century a Thai political system was evolving in the lower Chao Phraya rice plain in the region between the declining Angkor realm to the east and the Burmese domain of Pagan to the west. While this emerging Thai state depended on the fertile wet-rice lands of central Thailand as its economic base, the records of this civilization indicate that Thai monarchs depended on their control over the trading of rice as a principal source of income rather than upon revenues directly assessed on landholders.[86] The

Thai state's economic interests are demonstrated by the late thirteenth-century efforts of a Thai monarch to develop a commercial link with the main international maritime route via direct confrontations along the Malay and Sumatra coasts.

Ramkamhaeng, who reigned over the Sukhothai state until 1317, informs us that his power extended to the sea in the south.[87] This claim is validated in a Chinese source relating that around 1295 the Thais were ordered by the Chinese not to again wage war with Malāyu/Jambi on the southeastern Sumatra coast.[88] Did the Thais indeed undertake a naval expedition against the southeastern Sumatra coast? Early nineteenth-century ethnographers recording local oral tradition in the Jambi region found several legends of wars with the Thais; one legend holds that Jambi was devastated by a Thai army led by a Jambi prince.[89] While Jambi legend admits the inability of Jambi to defend itself from the Thais, the *Hikayat Raja Pasai,* the court chronicle of the northern Sumatra Samudra-Pasai pepper entrepôt, proudly reports that ports along Sumatra's northern coast were able to repulse Thai attacks, adding credence to the theory that there was a Thai attempt to impose their interests in the strait region during the late thirteenth or early fourteenth century.[90]

Whether their motives were political or economic, the Thai incursion was a singular effort. The Chinese record a tribute mission from an independent Malāyu/Jambi in 1301, shortly after the Yuan court's warning to the Thais to refrain from future raids upon the Sumatra coast.[91] On the other hand, Chinese sources report that Singapore Island (Tumasek) in the strait region was subject to the Thais in the early fourteenth century, before this area came under Malacca's authority.[92] Arab navigational treatises, drawing information from twelfth- through fourteenth-century sources, also describe Singapore Island as the last point on the "Coast of Siam."[93]

One wonders who supported the Thais on this maritime expedition, since there is little historical record of a Thai "navy." Likely supporters were the independent communities of Malay seamen of the post-Śrīvijaya age, groups with no clear commitments to any major political authorities who had become pirates to support themselves. With memories of their past glory, such groups might have willingly thrown in their lot with the Thais in return for promises of booty from this expedition, although potentially more important was the possibility of regularizing their future income if the Thais could reestablish political order in the strait. These seamen, as in earlier days, had a double potential; they could further the political ambitions of the Thais by serving as the Thais' naval force, or, if political disorder in the region continued, they could go on preying upon the shipping channels and obstructing Thai commercial interests they might at one time have assisted.[94]

Any thoughts of restoring the Śrīvijayan maritime state the Thais may have had were, however, frustrated. The system of economics upon which the Śrīvijayan state was based had passed. In earlier centuries the southeastern Sumatra coast had become commercially prominent due to its strategic position relative to the Strait of Malacca and the Java Sea. At the edge of both, the Śrīvijayan realm had monopolized the flow of Southeast Asian commodities into the channels of international trade that were concentrated in Śrīvijaya's ports. By the thirteenth century the southeastern Sumatra coast was no longer the point of primary access to the goods from the Java Sea, having been replaced by Java ports. While the Javanese ports became primary in the thirteenth century, Sumatra coast centers assumed a secondary commercial role, and did not regain commercial stature again until demand for Sumatran pepper elevated commercial centers of the Sumatra northern coast to first-order status in the late fourteenth century.[95]

Java extended its authority over southeastern Sumatra's ports during the thirteenth-century reign of Kĕrtanagara (1268–1292), which was critical to Java's commercial expansion. The last mission from Palembang to China is reported in 1277, and by 1286 Javanese power had reached Jambi.[96] An inscription with this date is found on a Buddha recovered from the Batang Hari River near Palembang; the inscription proclaims the installation of the Buddha by four Javanese officials under the authority of Kĕrtanagara "for the joy of all the subjects of the country of Malāyu."[97] How far north the power of Kĕrtanagara extended is unknown. The Javanese were interested in neither reestablishing Śrīvijaya's old empire nor able to. Rather, they were intent upon destroying potential rivals in the lucrative trade and in serving notice to the strait region, which had by that time lapsed into a state of general disorder whereby widespread piracy was endangering shipping passing through the strait, that they would intervene, if necessary, to facilitate the passage of trade ships through to Java's ports.[98]

However, in imposing their authority over the strait the Javanese found that their interests ran counter to those of the Chinese, who were themselves assuming a new role in Southeast Asian commerce. The old T'ang and Sung tributary system had passed; both the Yuan and Ming were concerned with Southeast Asian affairs and were willing to take direct action in Southeast Asia if it was necessary to guarantee the flow of goods to Chinese ports.[99] This interest is reflected in Yuan warnings in the late thirteenth century that future Thai incursions into the strait would not be tolerated. When the Javanese challenged what the Yuan conceived to be China's authority to supervise commerce in the strait, the Yuan chose to mount a naval raid in 1292 against the Javanese, ostensibly to establish who was dominant over Southeast Asia's sea channels. Piracy in the strait was a major issue in bringing on this confrontation. Thus when the Yuan court called for tributary missions from the strait it was in essence an attempt to draw from would-be strait entrepôts guarantees of security for the maritime trade route, while also limiting Java's role in the region. In return for tributary exchanges of trade goods with the Chinese court, China was now willing to guarantee the independence of China's allies from Javanese or Thai control or to restore order in states beset with internal strife through direct intervention.

By the late thirteenth century it is doubtful whether the Jambi region held any commercial prominence. The memory of Śrīvijaya may have induced the Thai attack against the old Śrīvijaya heartland as well as the Chinese attempts to resurrect the old tributary order of Sung times; the Chinese still looked to Malāyu/Jambi as their designated authority over the strait commercial realm.[100] Yuan dynastic records report a tributary mission led by two Muslims from Malāyu/Jambi in 1281, a mission that was undertaken by the remnants of a maritime community resident in Jambi at that time. In 1293, the leader of the Yuan expedition against Java notified the Yuan court that Malāyu/Jambi had been issued imperial orders to show their submission to the throne by sending sons or brothers of the rulers to the Chinese capital. This was done in 1294.[101]

Chinese records of Palembang illustrate the transition taking place on the southeastern Sumatra coast. Palembang did not respond to late thirteenth-century Yuan initiatives to once again solicit tributary missions from Southeast Asia, which supports the conclusion that in that age Palembang was subject to Jambi's authority.[102] Not until the early Ming period in the fourteenth century did Palembang seem to regain some degree of independence. Ming histories viewed Palembang as a minor commercial center, attributing its poverty to Javanese conquest and the fact that thereafter "few trading vessels [went] there," and made reference to Palembang as the "Old Harbor."[103]

The commercial role of the southeastern Sumatra coast by the fourteenth century had become insignificant; its leadership over Sumatra's commerce was being assumed by developing pepper centers clustered along Sumatra's northern coast, beyond the Javanese commercial sphere.[104] There were only two ports on the northern Sumatra coast invited by the Yuan to send tribute missions to China in the late thirteenth century. One was La-mu-li (Lamuri/Ramni), a port on the northern tip of the island frequented by Arab traders since at least the tenth century A.D.[105] The second was Su-mu-tu-la (Samudra), which during the thirteenth through the fifteenth centuries came to dominate north coast trade.

Samudra-Pasai as a Riverine System Center of Trade

The name Samudra first appears in Yuan records when a Chinese mission returning from the Coromandel Coast of India in 1282 stopped at Su-mu-tu-la. The ruler of Su-mu-tu-la sent two ministers, both Muslims, to accompany the Yuan envoys on their return voyage.[106] Marco Polo claimed to have visited Su-mu-tu-la on his return voyage from China shortly thereafter in 1292 but had little to say about the port except that its population had not yet converted to Islam and that it was settled by primitive fishermen and farmers.[107] The conversion to Islam took place soon after, sometime around 1296, the date on a gravestone attributed to a local chief who is named in local literary records as the state's founder and first sultan. This conversion must in some way have related to Samudra's participation in the international trade that was dominated in that period by Muslim seamen. By the thirteenth century Samudra was a regular stop for voyages between India and China. While it would appear that Samudra was initially less significant to the Indian Ocean traders than was Ramni to the north, by the fourteenth century Samudra had emerged as the preeminent port on the northern Sumatra coast.[108]

Early references to Samudra as an entrepôt among external sources place it on the Pasangan River, the longest river in that area of the Sumatran coast. However, all the gravestones of Samudra's rulers have been found in a small village called Pasai, located upriver on the more southern Pasai River. It appears that the center of royal authority was shifted there in a later period, possibly for protection against piracy and other raids from the sea.[109] Ibn Battuta's mid-fourteenth century account of his visit to the urban center of Samudra noted that it was located a little inland from the coast. He traveled four miles by land from a coastal port he called Sarha to the city of Samudra, which he reported was "large and beautiful."[110] The Samudra ruler, according to Ibn Battuta, assigned an "admiral" *(laksamana)* who supervised the affairs of the Sarha port as the Samudra ruler's agent.[111] Local tradition holds that Pasai was established as the seat of power for a son of the first Samudra ruler—Pasai was founded by the sultan on a spot where his hunting dog was attacked by a mousedeer "full of fight," which was considered auspicious—but two or three generations later Pasai subjugated Samudra. The transfer of royal power to Pasai is explained as the consequence of a war between the two urban centers that was blamed on the sultan of Samudra, who brought on the war when he eloped with one of Pasai's women against the advice of a wise old court official. The first reference to Pasai in the Yuan court histories dates to 1309, when three embassies from Southeast Asian states are recorded: one from Champa, another from Palembang, and the third from Pah-sih (Pasai).[112]

The legend of the founding of Pasai is one among many preserved in the *Hikayat Raja Pasai.* This court chronicle is a semihistorical romance in which the events described were, to those who compiled the text, subjectively rather than objectively true.[113] The *Hikayat* was the first among the histories *(sejarah)* composed by archipelago Muslim states; its earliest sections (those considered to have the most historical accuracy) must have been composed by the late fifteenth century.[114] While in later archipelago chronicles indigenous traditions dominate, the *Hikayat Raja Pasai* more consciously adapted Indian folktales to the local Malay folk tradition; the use of Indian, Islamic, and local symbols are all important to the *Hikayat*'s narration. The image of the Samudra-Pasai court projected by the *Hikayat* is that of a cosmopolitan urban center on the edge of jungle. The cosmopolitan atmosphere of the royal palace, the pageantry and colorful activities of its court, and its lavish display of wealth, which was continually shared with the subjects of the Samudra-Pasai rulers, were all necessary to "awe" the upriver populations. These hinterland people, who largely turned their backs to the Islamic civilization of the coast and retreated upriver, might otherwise have had little desire to participate in the state's activities. In gaining the participation of their hinterland populations, Samudra-Pasai rulers instituted tributary or reciprocal gift-giving exchanges that provisioned the coast with the forest products (especially pepper) that were necessary for the coastal population's international trade.

It is tempting to cite the conversion to Islam by Samudra's late thirteenth-century elite as an explanation for this port's fourteenth-century success. The *Hikayat Raja Pasai* as well as the various chronicles of later Malay states preserve the legend that the first conversion of a state within the entire island realm took place in Samudra-Pasai and view the subsequent prosperity of Samudra-Pasai, Malacca, and other Muslim states of the archipelago as a direct consequence of this event.[115] According to the *Hikayat Raja Pasai,* Samudra was founded one generation before its ruler converted. The *Hikayat* relates a symbolic tale of the migration of the founder of the Samudra-Pasai state from a place in the north—possibly Ramni—to Samudra, and shortly thereafter Samudra became prominent as a commercial center. The story stresses an alliance between this adventurer and the native population of the hinterland as the source of his future success.[116]

Early Ming histories note that "merchants from all sides collect at this place (Samudra-Pasai), and as the country is distant and the prices high, the Chinese who go there make more profit than elsewhere."[117] But in the early fifteenth century a report of internal strife in Samudra-Pasai was given by the Chinese Muslim scribe and translator Ma Huan, who had accompanied one of the voyages of the Muslim eunuch Cheng Ho.[118] Cheng Ho made a series of early fifteenth-century expeditions into the south, one of the reasons being to put down piracy in the area and to thus stimulate the flow of commerce to south China. Such internal strife is a common feature of the *Hikayat* story, especially after the shift of the center of royal power to Pasai.

The history of the Samudra-Pasai realm as it is projected in the *Hikayat Raja Pasai* and in Chinese and Western sources can be understood in terms of the diagram of decentralized Southeast Asian riverine political systems that was introduced in chapter 1. Samudra and its successor Pasai were both strategically located downriver urban centers in adjacent river systems that flowed from the Sumatra interior, which allowed the Samudra-Pasai rulers to dominate commerce flowing upriver to the interior and downriver to the coast from their center of royal power. In Ibn Battuta's account the coastal port he calls Sarha was equivalent to a point *A* in the riverine system model. Located some four miles inland was the urban center of Samudra, the locus of royal power, which may be seen as functioning as a point *B*. Consistent with the riverine system model, Samudra-Pasai's growth depended on its elite's success in forging political and economic links with its upriver hinterland. This hinterland was the critical source of commodities that provisioned the international traders who began to utilize the local port.

That an exchange relationship was achieved is documented in external accounts that describe the diverse commodities available to international traders at Samudra-Pasai. These accounts indicate that Samudra-Pasai's initial fourteenth-century emergence as a commercial power was related to its provision of goods to Indian and other Western markets. Unfortunately there are only two surviving reports on this early trade, one belonging to Friar Odoric, a Western cleric who never traveled to Southeast Asia himself but acquired a knowledge of Southeast Asia in India during the early fourteenth century, and the other to Ibn Battuta, who provides occasional descriptions of Indian Ocean trade in his account of his travels in the mid-fourteenth century.

Odoric indicates that Samudra's reputation as a prosperous port of trade was high in India and reports that the entrepôt had a "great abundance of produce," naming among the foodstuffs available there pigs, fowls, butter, and rice, and also noting the local availability of gold and tin.[119] His emphasis on foodstuffs shows that there was a local trade in bulk commodities for immediate consumption rather than a trade in the luxury goods that are normally stressed in Western and Chinese accounts of Southeast Asia's early maritime trade. It would seem that the view of Samudra in early fourteenth-century Indian ports, as reported by Odoric, was that Samudra was a source of provisions for travelers passing through the Strait of Malacca region rather than a source of trade goods —the spices and Chinese goods most desired by India-based traders who traveled to Southeast Asia in that era. Odoric refers to a trade in metals —he noted that gold and tin were utilized as local mediums of exchange —indicating that exchanges in precious metals as well as exchanges in kind were a part of the normal course of this port's trade. Since there is no report by Odoric of the export of bulk commodities of food from Samudra to India it would appear that Samudra was developing two levels of exchange, one a local network that dealt in consumable foods, the other an international trade that depended on the exchange of precious metals for local products.

Ibn Battuta acknowledged Samudra's emergence as a major international commercial center in his account. Exports from Samudra listed in his journal include coco-palms, areca-palms, aloes, various varieties of fruit, camphor, bamboo, tree incense, cloves, nutmeg, and mace.[120] Since most of these were not local products, Samudra must have had considerable contact with other commerical centers not only along the Sumatra coast but also, and especially, with Java. Camphor, for instance, is known as the major export of the western Sumatra coast prior to the fifteenth century, notably from the Barus region. Cloves, nutmeg, and mace were all products of the eastern Indonesian archipelago that would have reached Samudra-Pasai via Java's ports. It would seem that the availability of these spices was critical to the initial emergence of Samudra-Pasai as a major international entrepôt. The marketing of Javanese spices attracted Western merchants to Samudra-Pasai by eliminating the necessity of their traveling to Java. But what was unique about Samudra-Pasai among Sumatra coast ports that drew both Western and Javanese traders?

Exploring the second part of this question in turn answers the first. Java's developing commercial contact with China in the fourteenth century made the northern Sumatra coast important to Javanese commercial interests. Northern Sumatra was the source of pepper that was much in demand among Chinese merchants. The Chinese, as previously noted, desired Sumatran pepper, which was less expensive than that of India's Malabar Coast though inferior in quality.[121] Nicolo Conti, an adventurer who traveled to Southeast Asia in 1435, describes Samudra-Pasai as "a very noble emporium of the island [i.e., Sumatra]," and his is the first Western account to stress Samudra-Pasai's role as a point of collection for pepper.[122] Ma Huan's account of Cheng Ho's early fifteenth-century expeditions also reports that Samudra-Pasai was the northern Sumatra collection center for pepper. He describes Samudra-Pasai as a commercial center where "there are foreign ships going and coming in large numbers, hence all kinds of foreign goods are sold in great quantities in this country."[123] Ma Huan knew Samudra-Pasai during the time when Chinese influence in the Strait of Malacca area was at its height, yet remarkably he acknowledged no Chinese trade at Samudra-Pasai, as opposed to other "foreign" trade. Implicit in Ma Huan's omission of reference to Chinese merchants in the northern Sumatra commercial realm is the fact that an active maritime trade existed between the northern Sumatra coast and Java in the late fourteenth and early fifteenth centuries such that Java's ports supplied China markets with Sumatran pepper.[124]

Thus the key to Samudra-Pasai's commercial success was the Samudra-Pasai coastal elite's ability to concentrate the marketing of northern Sumatran pepper production at their entrepôt by mobilizing the flow of pepper and other goods from their upriver and subordinate river system hinterlands to their port. Ma Huan's report on Samudra-Pasai describes the "people who reside over against the mountains" as the source of Samudra-Pasai's pepper.[125] Indeed, as already noted, the legend of Samudra-Pasai's founding attributes the state's success to an alliance between the coastal and upriver populations. A "prince" from another northern Sumatra riverine system sought a new home after his exile by the rulers of his old homeland. Arriving on the Samudra-Pasai coast, this prince traveled upriver to the hinterland where he negotiated an alliance with the chiefs of the interior populations. He is said to have been recognized as being royal and rich (the two essentials for legitimate and successful rule in the eyes of the local population) and as a source of future prosperity.[126] Having secured the backing of the interior leadership, the prince then led a force that was composed of these chiefs and their warriors back downriver, where they assisted him in establishing hegemony over the coastal realm. Thereafter the hinterland chiefs retreated to their upriver homeland leaving the coastal domain for the prince, who thence became the first ruler of Samudra-Pasai.

Applying the riverine system model to this legend and the other accounts of the Samudra-Pasai entrepôt (see fig. 1), the new ruler may be seen establishing his authority over a point *A* or *B* (Samudra and its port of Sarha in Ibn Battuta's account), but depending on alliances with chiefs at upriver points *C* and *D* in the interior. Although these chiefs had contributed to the ruler's rise to power, they had withdrawn to the hinterland where they continued to maintain their old patterns of chieftainship. Ibn Battuta distinguishes between the coastal population and that of the interior as being a Muslim coast and a "heathen" hinterland, a view confirmed by Odoric.[127] Ibn Battuta comments that the relationship between the two was not peaceful, as there was constant warfare that he views as resulting from the attempts of the Muslim coast to convert the heathens of the interior. But Ibn Battuta also states that Samudra-Pasai depended on the export of "aromatic plants" (pepper?) that were to be found "in districts occupied by the infidels; in the Muslim districts they are less plentiful."[128] It would seem that the wars with the interior that were considered by Ibn Battuta to have been due to the religious fervor of the coastal regime were in reality economic in motive, as the coastal rulers attempted to secure the "aromatic plants" from the hinterland's population to market in their port. Ibn Battuta adds credence to such a conclusion by his statement that the "infidels pay the Muslim lords a poll-tax to secure peace."[129] This reflects a "tributary" relationship whereby the residents of the interior were expected to provide commodities that the residents of the coast could export; if deliveries were not made it would seem that the population of the interior was subject to a military expedition by the coast's rulers to extract these commodities by force. Ibn Battuta's reference to frequent raids against the "heathen of the hinterland" indicates that Samudra's rulers faced continual difficulty drawing goods from their upriver realm. That this relationship was a perpetual problem in the history of the Samudra-Pasai state is reflected in the *Hikayat Raja Pasai,* which interprets the numerous hostilities between the coast and its interior as political rather than economic conflict.

Samudra-Pasai's subordinate commercial realm must have included much of the northern Sumatra coast, including Barus on the west coast as well as Ramni on the northern tip of the island. Ibn Battuta sailed along the eastern coast of Sumatra for twenty-one days on his way to China from Samudra in the mid-fourteenth century and regarded all the countries along the coast as being part of the sultan of Samudra's domain.[130] A Pasai inscription dated 1389 claims Pasai's authority over the ruling family of the Malay Peninsula's Kedah coast, although there is no known evidence on the Malay Peninsula to substantiate this claim.[131] Ma Huan's account of the expeditions of Cheng Ho reports chasing a usurper into the northern Ramni (La-mu-li) realm in 1412, implying that Samudra-Pasai and Ramni were related; thereafter Ramni began to send envoys to China, whereas previously only Samudra-Pasai had been sending "diplomatic" missions.[132] Implicit in Ma Huan's account is the belief that Samudra-Pasai's dominance over other coastal commercial centers such as Ramni was economic rather than political in nature, since the Chinese in their written records were always extremely sensitive to issues of political supremacy. Ramni's response to Chinese initiatives, that is, the sending of envoys to the Chinese court, indicates its political autonomy. Ma Huan reports other conflict between Samudra and its neighboring riverine systems. There was an attempt by a "tattooed-faced king of Nagur," a rival northern Sumatra port later known as a pepper center, to usurp the Samudra-Pasai throne;[133] Ma Huan also notes friction between Samudra-Pasai and the Menangkabau realm to the south.[134]

Consistent with this evidence, in the riverine system model Samudra-Pasai's riverine network *(A)* can be seen establishing its commercial dominance at the expense of other Sumatra coast entrepôts and their river systems (rival A_1s) in its dealings with foreign markets (*X*s). Was this due to conquest over rival A_1s, or is it possible, since the available records do not reflect Samudra-Pasai's political supremacy over rival entrepôts, to view Samudra-Pasai's emergence as a dominant commercial entrepôt as being due to the importance of Pasai's pepper exports? In the latter instance the riverine system model would have had to be modified to accommodate a port system that attracted foreign traders because it controlled a single commodity or because of its superior marketing of a commodity that was the most important regional product sought by foreign merchants. Such a port would not only have attracted international traders who sought the primary commodity, but it would also have drawn local traders who transported the products of other areas to this first-order commercial center in the hope of marketing their secondary goods to the international traders. In this way the preferred port became a collection center; rather than traveling to numerous ports to acquire goods it was far more expedient for international traders to frequent one strategically located port. Thus Southeast Asia based traders initially carried Java's spices and China's goods to Samudra-Pasai not only to acquire northern Sumatran pepper but also to make contact with Western traders who because of the presence of Javanese and Chinese goods at Samudra-Pasai did not have to sail farther into the archipelago.[135]

The nature of trade at Samudra-Pasai, although insufficiently documented in the *Hikayat Raja Pasai,* is described by others. An international community of merchants was in residence there.[136] Ibn Battuta notes the role of the Samudra-Pasai ruler's representative as the supervisor of port trade and its various participants. It would appear that while the ruler or his representatives were directly involved in trade through the collection of port cesses paid in kind, the ruler did not hold a monopoly over the exchange of local pepper and other goods, although he derived an important portion of his state's revenues from trade that was conducted at his port. A colleague of Ma Huan reports that such duties in this and other Sumatra ports were not normally collected in gold but were paid with pepper.[137] This collection in kind is significant when one considers the possibilities of such an arrangement. The export duties collected in kind would have allowed the ruler to participate (through his representatives) in the marketplace as a seller of pepper. A prosperous pepper trade would thus have doubly benefited Samudra-Pasai rulers: a high rate of exports increased the amount of export duty collected—paid in pepper—which pepper was then marketed by the rulers' representatives. A substantial demand for pepper thus brought prosperity and increased profits not only to Samudra-Pasai's traders but also to its rulers.[138]

An anchorage fee was also levied by Samudra-Pasai's rulers on all ships entering the harbor—the rate was determined according to the size of the ship. Imports were subject to a standard duty of 6 percent, except for foodstuffs that were exempted.[139] It is likely that these import duties were also levied in kind. Goods in demand at Samudra-Pasai, as noted in a 1436 Chinese report—Chinese celadon and colored silks, Java-cloth (batik?), copper and iron, and numerous consumable goods—would have been appropriate for royal consumption as well as for redistribution to supporters of the Samudra-Pasai royal lineage. Although there is no definite evidence documenting the extent to which the ruler directly participated in trade, he must have at least made symbolic profit from the redistribution of foreign goods to points upriver from the coast.[140]

It is also significant that in almost all records of Samudra-Pasai's imports and exports there is reference to metals—notably gold, tin, and silver—as important commodities of exchange. Friar Odoric's early fourteenth-century account is the first, listing gold and tin as commodities available at Samudra-Pasai.[141] Ibn Battuta's mid-fourteenth century record states that the inhabitants of Samudra-Pasai conducted their trade using "pieces of tin and native Chinese gold, unsmelted."[142] What was the source of these metals? Did the tin come from Sumatran or Malay Peninsula mines—thus providing an early record of trade in Malay tin—and the gold from China or from local mines, or does reference to the exchange of metals at Samudra-Pasai indicate that its inhabitants conducted their trade not in kind, as is widely believed to have been the norm in pre-European Southeast Asia, but in some instances utilized precious metals as a medium of exchange?[143] Is it possible that the exchange of metals took place only in Samudra-Pasai's international commercial community in the acquisition of goods for export, while market exchanges for local consumption, such as foodstuffs, were transacted in kind? The latter theory is supported by records that Samudra-Pasai officials valued exported goods (notably pepper) in gold, suggesting that metallic values were commonly used in pricing goods for export. But the fact that cesses were collected in kind, while there is nothing to indicate that anchorage fees and import duties were collected after first establishing metallic values, leads to the conclusion that there were two types of exchanges taking place within the Samudra-Pasai port.[144]

The nature of Samudra-Pasai's continuing evolution as a center of trade is evinced in fifteenth-century reports that Pasai had to import food to feed its commercial community, evidence that is quite contrary to the early fourteenth-century view of Friar Odoric that Samudra-Pasai had an abundance of locally produced consumable food. That Pasai was importing food in the late fifteenth century is indicated by the Portuguese scribe, Tomé Pires, writing in the early sixteenth century. He specifies that Pasai exempted all foodstuffs from import duties—other imported goods being subject to a 6 percent duty—and that annually sixteen junks loaded with rice from Pegu in lower Burma and thirty from Ayudhya in Thailand supplied Malacca and Pasai before 1511.[145] The first plausible implication of this report is that Samudra-Pasai's interior population was becoming specialized such that their production of pepper and other commodities for the international trade did not allow them time to tend to the production of foodstuffs or did not necessitate their cultivation of food for their own consumption. If this was the case the interior population would have exchanged their "cash crops" for imported food, an exchange facilitated and encouraged by the omission of import duties. A second possibility is that the volatile relationship between Samudra-Pasai's coast and interior populations noted above prevented the flow of bulk consumables from the hinterland to the coast and thus necessitated the import of food—encouraged by the omission of import duties on foods—to feed Samudra-Pasai's commercial population.[146] While increased commercial specialization among the hinterland population may be plausible in explaining Samudra-Pasai's import of foodstuffs, the hostilities between the coast and hinterland must also have been a significant factor. Pires' early sixteenth-century report of the late fifteenth century supports this view, noting that Samudra-Pasai was a significant port despite frequent hostilities between the port administrators of the coast and the inland populations.[147]

Maritime Trade and State Development Circa A.D. 1300

The establishment in 1250 of the Mameluke dynasty in Egypt brought stability to the Red Sea passage from the Indian Ocean to the Mediterranean, and in 1368 the founders of the Ming dynasty overthrew the Mongolian Yuan dynasty and established their capital at Nanking, a city on the Yangtze River in China's commercial heartland. With the collapse of the overland caravan route across the central Asian steppes that the Yuan had organized, the maritime route between East and West that passed through Southeast Asia once again boomed. On the western end the Mameluke dynasty contracted with Venetian merchants to facilitate the flow of Asian goods into the growing European markets of the postcrusade era; on the eastern end the Ming began to solicit trade by sending maritime expeditions into Southeast Asia. Southeast Asians responded by expanding their marketing of pepper, tin, and spices, and new entrepôts emerged as well. The archipelago's trade was no longer dominated by entrepôts on the southeastern Sumatra and Java coasts; now regions on the northern end of Sumatra and in the Spice Islands of the eastern Indonesian archipelago that were the sources of these commodities became more direct participants in the trade route. During the fourteenth century, Southeast Asian states dependent on commercial revenues rose in the island realm at Samudra-Pasai, Malacca, Brunei, and Makassar and on the mainland at the Thai center of Ayudhya (1351) up the Chao Phraya River from the coast, at Pegu, the Mon center in lower Burma, and at a new Khmer center at the intersection of the Bassac and Tonle Sap rivers near present-day Phnom Penh—a location with more direct access via the Mekong River to the sea, which replaced Angkor in the early fifteenth century.

During the fourteenth to early sixteenth centuries a new pattern of world trade emerged linking the continents of Asia and Europe in an even more direct exchange of goods; the Southeast Asian trade regions described below were integrated into this world trade network. The new pattern left no single part of the world as the dominant "center" of the trading network. Each zone, along with the interconnected sea route from China to western Europe, was important to the whole system. Long voyages transporting goods intended for faraway markets were largely abandoned. The full participation in shipping of Chinese, Javanese, Indian, Burmese-Peguan, Persian-Arab, Italian, and Jewish traders from the Middle East and India broke down the long voyage into several consecutive small voyages. The exchange of goods in regional ports was intensive; each region in turn overlapped another. There were in fact many zones of trade dominated by a few seafaring people who sought profit from the transport of goods in each zone. The dominant ports in each trade zone became the chief distributors of foreign goods in their region as well as the source of local products for traders from another zone. The people of the Southeast Asian hinterlands were brought into contact with the outside world via such dominant ports, and they entered into the mainstream of regional history in this period after being left on the periphery through most of the premodern age.

There were at least six zones of trade through which goods from China had to pass before they reached northeastern Europe during this time. The first zone had its center in southern China, where traders carried goods in junks from one port to another. This zone included ports along

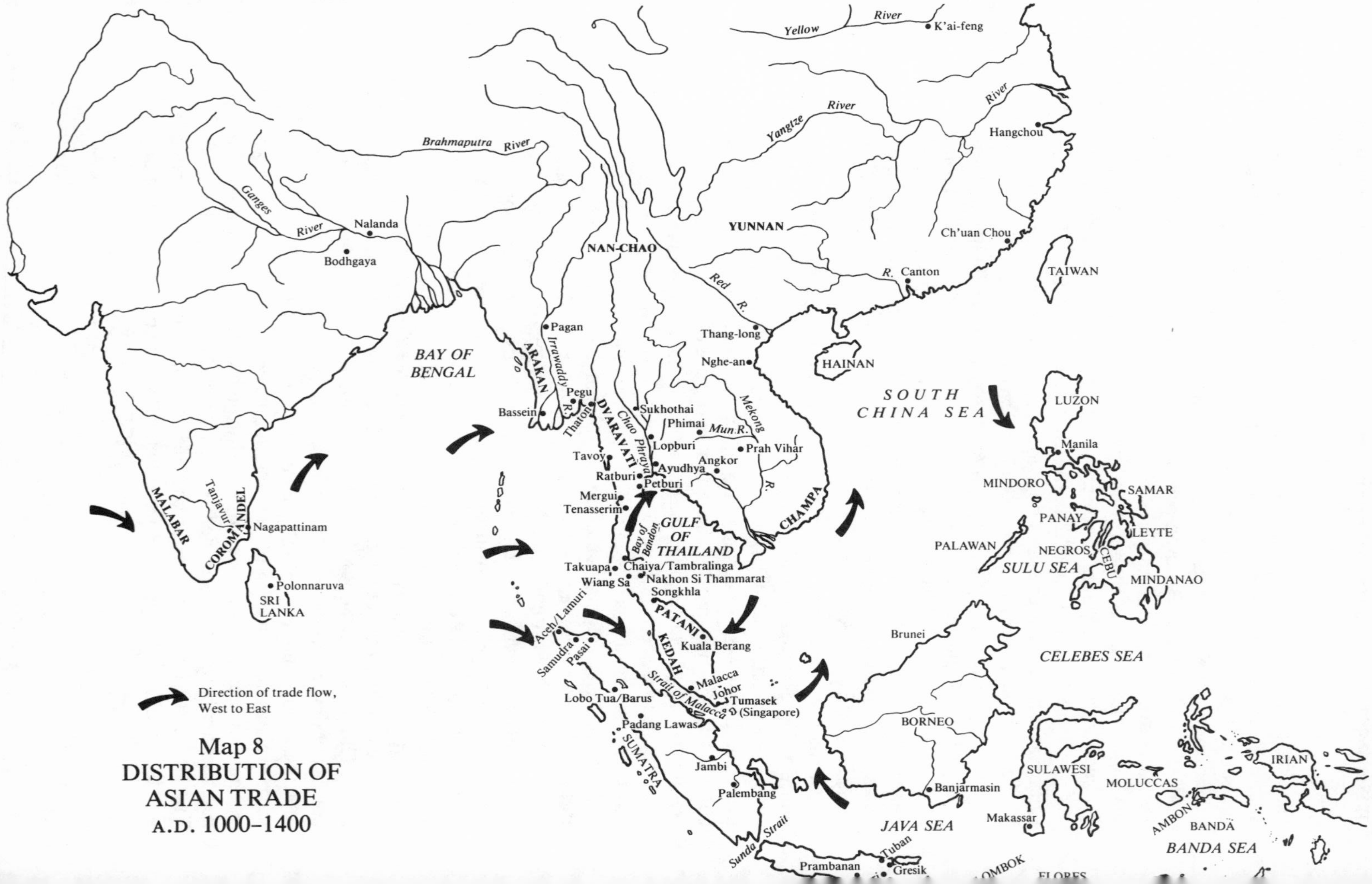

Map 8
DISTRIBUTION OF ASIAN TRADE
A.D. 1000–1400

the Vietnam coast, the Gulf of Thailand down the east coast of the Malay Peninsula, the Philippines, and made contact with another zone in the ports of Tuban, Gresik, Japara, and Demak in Java. The second zone was controlled largely by commercial groups based in Java and extended eastward to the Spice Islands and the southwestern ports of Sulawesi, northward along the coast of Borneo to the island of Mindanao, and westward to the ports of the east coast of Sumatra, merging with another zone at Malacca and the northeastern ports of Sumatra.

The third zone encompassed ports along the two coasts of India, especially in southern India and Sri Lanka, Gujarat, and Bengal. It connected with the second zone in the western Indonesian archipelago in the east, and the Red Sea in the west. The fourth zone focused upon Alexandria and included other ports of the eastern Mediterranean and Middle Eastern realm. Italian merchants dominated the fifth zone, and distributed Asian goods to the sixth zone, which extended from the Iberian Peninsula at the western end of the Mediterranean, where goods were redistributed to northwestern Europe and from there to the Hanseatic traders of the northern seas. The Hanse commercial network carried goods further to the east and northeast.[148]

By the beginning of the fourteenth century five commercial zones of maritime trade had emerged in Southeast Asia. Each of the five was a prosperous and independent regional picture of prosperity. Going from west to east, the first zone was comprised of a Bay of Bengal regional trade network that began on the Coromandel Coast of southern India and Sri Lanka and included Burma, the upper Malay Peninsula, and the northern end and western coast of Sumatra. The northern and western coasts of Sumatra became important in the post-1300 era due to increasing world demand for pepper. In particular, the Samudra-Pasai entrepôt became the principal supplier of pepper to Western and Eastern traders, supplementing the pepper exports of India's southwestern Malabar Coast that had met the more limited demand of earlier times. On the mainland Pegu in the Irrawaddy River Delta of lower Burma began to take part in the commerce involving northern Sumatra, the Strait of Malacca, and the Bay of Bengal, especially as a supplier of rice to provision the commercial populations from the East and the West who were frequenting the Malacca Strait's new pepper ports.[149]

The second commercial zone was the Strait of Malacca. This region, which would become the most important of the commercial zones by the fifteenth century—immediately prior to the European incursion—was in the fourteenth century still in a state of transition and was still a bone of contention between the Thais and the Javanese. Founded by a prince who claimed royal status as the successor to the rulers of the Śrīvijayan maritime empire of earlier times, Malacca's rise was due to the initiatives by the Ming dynasty at the end of the fourteenth century to fill what they perceived to be a political void in the area and to contain piracy, which was jeopardizing the steady flow of commerce into south China's ports.[150] By the 1430s, however, Malacca's prosperity would depend less on Chinese support and more on interaction with Javanese and other Southeast Asian merchants and networks. The Javanese continually dominated the flow of spices from the eastern Indonesian archipelago to Malacca, which was used as a trade intermediary through which to market Javanese rice and Java Sea spices as well.

The third trade zone included the upper Malay Peninsula's eastern coast, Thailand, and the lower coast of Vietnam, the regions bordering the Gulf of Thailand. The Thai state of Ayudhya developed in the first half of the fourteenth century in the lower Chao Phraya Valley and thrived as a result of new foreign contacts. Initially hostile to the rise of Malacca in the south, which was viewed as an intruder into the Thai political and economic sphere, Ayudhya began to export rice to Malacca in the fifteenth century and was as well a commercial center for trade with the Philippines and China.[151] Thai participation in this trade zone is well documented by deposits of their porcelains at the sites of numerous Southeast Asian ports active during the post-thirteenth-century era.[152] Meanwhile, following the demise of Angkor in the thirteenth and fourteenth centuries, the remnants of the Khmer civilization of Cambodia established a new base at the edge of the Mekong Delta, which provided them with a commercial link to the Malay populations on the northern fringe of the South China Sea.[153]

The Sulu Sea region comprised the fourth commercial zone and included the western coasts of Luzon, Mindoro, Cebu, and Mindanao in the Philippines, and the Brunei region of Borneo's north coast. All served to varying degrees as facilitators of trade between China and the Spice Islands to the southeast. These Spice Islands were the source of nutmeg, mace, cloves, sandalwood, and other more exotic commodities such as parrots and birds of paradise, all of which flowed through the Sulu Sea to China and Thailand in the north, as well as to Java and Malacca in the west. The Chinese presence was not new—Chinese traders had established these bases in the Philippines during the eleventh and twelfth centuries.[154] By the fourteenth century an intensive and extensive network of native trade had evolved to distribute imports and to gather the forest products desired by Chinese traders. This trade in both its internal and external dimensions stimulated major changes in Philippine society. It called for formal regulation of commercial contact between indigenous populations and the foreign traders and encouraged the formation of village clusters *(barangay)* that were controlled and protected by local chiefs *(dātu)*.[155] Archaeological research has revealed urban settlements of over five hundred households in the Manila area dating to the pre-Spanish period, as well as other urban sites on the Mindoro, Mindanao, and Cebu coasts. Each of these communities' trade links with China are demonstrated by their association with significant deposits of Sung and Ming porcelain dating to the thirteenth and fourteenth centuries. The archaeological remains of early Laguna, Mindoro, and Cebu society especially document the rapid growth of trade centers as people from the interior and other islands congregated around ports fortified with brass artillery—to protect against the piracy rampant in this region's sea channels—in response to the opportunities and demands afforded by foreign trade.[156] The Brunei coast of Borneo was important to the Chinese in its own right, for it was Borneo's jungles that provided camphor and other gums and resins used in China for pharmacological purposes.[157]

The Java Sea network was the fifth Southeast Asian trade zone, and included the Lesser Sunda Islands, the Moluccas, Banda, Timor, the western coast of Borneo, Java, and the southern coast of Sumatra. Eastern Java had emerged as the strongest among the archipelago's political systems by the thirteenth century and came to facilitate the Java Sea spice trade.[158] The new east Java-based state of Majapahit that came into existence at the end of the thirteenth century established a loose hegemony over the eastern and western archipelago. Because Java had limited control over the strait maritime realm there was a rise of piracy in the Strait of Malacca and along the southern Borneo coast in the fourteenth century. It was due to this piracy or the weakness of Java that Malay sea populations with Chinese support established Malacca at the end of the fourteenth century. Chinese traders then could avoid the Borneo coast route to Java and the Spice Islands and acquire the spices from the Javanese at Malacca or from Sulu Sea entrepôts.

Thus the foundation of Malacca at the beginning of the fifteenth century corresponded with these new commercial opportunities and undercut Samudra-Pasai's position as the most prosperous among western archipelago commercial centers. Malacca emerged as China's preferred trade intermediary shortly after its founding in 1402 by Prince Parameśvara, a fugutive prince-consort who was driven out of southeastern Sumatra or the Singapore Island region by Majapahit's forces in the previous century.[159] The state he founded became heir to the maritime influence and political and economic power that was previously enjoyed by the Śrīvijaya state. Initially Malacca specialized in facilitating Western trade with China, but with China's withdrawal from active participation in Southeast Asian affairs by the second quarter of the fifteenth century

Malacca was able to forge a new economic relationship with the Javanese, whereby Javanese traders began to shift their spice trade from Samudra-Pasai to Malacca. Samudra-Pasai consequently lost its reputation as a source of Javanese spices, and Indian Ocean merchants began to converge on Malacca to acquire them. A corresponding increase in demand for Sumatran pepper in Western markets softened the impact of this shift of the Javanese spice trade away from Samudra-Pasai, but by the early sixteenth century greater Western activity in the maritime routes and the enhanced economic opportunity in Malacca drew even Samudra-Pasai-based traders with their pepper to this new hub of Southeast Asian commerce.[160]

These new patterns of trade brought about a different type of state in maritime Southeast Asia. The increasing importance of local products, spices, pepper, and various forest products in the international trade, the intensity of Javanese-, Chinese-, and India-based shipping in the area that resulted in more competition among Southeast Asia's ports, encouraged a policy of territorial expansion that was actively pursued by important states in the Strait of Malacca region. The extension of control over territory that produced marketable products was essential to these states in order to prevent the flow of products to rival ports. Loose federations of port towns characteristic of earlier times disappeared as in the new states only one dominant port, usually also the seat of government, was tolerated. Power was extended from this port center over nearby ports as well as their upriver hinterlands. Samudra-Pasai, Malacca, and Pedir, the dominant ports of the Strait of Malacca region during the late fifteenth century, had varying control over their interiors and competed for commercial and political dominance over ports on the two coasts of the strait.[161] The extension of power by these maritime states was different in nature from that of the earlier Śrīvijaya age. A state's authority over another river system penetrated deeper into the hinterland. Śrīvijaya, as we have seen in chapter 4, was most interested in providing entrepôt facilities for foreign traders, utiiizing alliances with its supporters to assure the security of its ports.[162] Śrīvijaya rulers were less interested in mobilizing the flow of local products from their hinterland to their coastal ports, being content to provide a neutral commercial facility for the exchange of Western, Chinese, and Southeast Asian products. Port fees and foreign products acquired by the Śrīvijaya ruler in his ports were redistributed to the ruler's two groups of supporters, the leaders of the Malay seamen who facilitated the flow of trade through the Strait of Malacca to Śrīvijaya's ports and the chiefs of the upriver hinterland populations.

These redistributions reinforced the magical relationship between the ports' ruler and his allies, whereby the Śrīvijaya ruler shared his spiritual prowess with his loyal followers. Śrīvijaya was not engaged in administratively annexing the lands and people of the Sumatra hinterland and was concerned only with recognition of its authority by other ports. As described by O. W. Wolters, "the [Śrīvijaya] ruler was much more than a hoarder of material wealth . . . his influence promoted sensations of psychological well-being among his followers, for his person was the effective ceremonial centre."[163] New interest in more directly controlling the people, their production, and their access to foreign trade changed the administrative structure of early Southeast Asian riverine system states from one that was based on religio-mystical loyalty of the subordinate regions to the center to one that was characterized by military-administrative control by the center over smaller communities in its hinterland.[164]

Samudra-Pasai is best thought of as a transitional state, participating in the new patterns of trade but being incapable of subordinating the riverine systems of the Sumatra coast to the degree that Malacca and its successor Johor did on the Malay Peninsula, nor was it able to institute a monopoly on the export of pepper comparable to that accomplished by Aceh, which succeeded Samudra-Pasai as the dominant northern Sumatra political system in the early sixteenth century.[165] Samudra-Pasai's authority was confined to the Sumatra coast in a way similar to the pattern of Śrīvijaya's statecraft of the previous age. Although Samudra-Pasai's dominance over rival ports appears to have been more economic than political in nature, analysis of the state's history shows a higher degree of structured integration between the coast and its upriver hinterland than seems to have been the case in Śrīvijaya.[166] It is this movement toward a more integrated state system, explained in the *Hikayat Raja Pasai* and other sources as involving the subordination of the hinterland to the coastal populations, that is characteristic of the new Southeast Asian states that emerged at the dawn of the European maritime incursions. The history of Samudra-Pasai well illustrates the consequent frictions of this transition, as Samudra-Pasai's history is that of continuous hostility on the part of the hinterland populations to demands by the coast for their production.

Samudra-Pasai has been characterized here as illustrating a riverine state system that existed on the periphery of a hinterland civilization yet was dependent upon traditional relationships with its interior to mobilize the flow of hinterland products to its coast. As chapter 4 argues for Śrīvijaya, so too Samudra-Pasai's dominance over other ports and their Muslim elites had something to do with the redistribution of the spiritual prowess of the Samudra-Pasai ruler. This is best shown in the records of Samudra-Pasai's successors.

While Malacca assumed the leading position among commercial centers in the western Indonesian archipelago in the fifteenth century, Samudra-Pasai still retained importance as the source of Malacca's legitimacy. The Malacca court chronicle, the *Sejarah Melayu,* modeled the conversion of its ruler to Islam on that of the Samudra-Pasai monarch and cited these conversions as marking the turning point in Malacca's early history.[167] The *Sejarah Melayu* text, which was composed in the early sixteenth century, summarized the first half of the *Hikayat Raja Pasai* and noted that Malacca's sultans continued to draw upon Pasai-based Islamic scholars to legitimize this transfer of Malay commercial and political leadership from Samudra-Pasai to Malacca. In a later episode a Malacca sultan sent an envoy to Pasai to ask whether heaven and hell remain there forever. The envoy took with him seven *tahil*s of gold dust and two concubines to present to the Pasai theologians who were solicited to answer the question. The first answer given was based on the *Koran:* they remain there forever. But one of the Pasai scholars had second thoughts, realizing that the ruler of Malacca would not have sent so far afield for so obvious an answer. Thus an esoteric answer was given in private to the Malacca envoy to the latter's satisfaction, and the gold and concubines changed hands.[168] The light-hearted treatment of the "answer of Pasai" episode by the chronicler suggests that his audience was more interested in how the gold and concubines were to be won by the correct answer to the riddle than in Islamic theology. But it is important that Samudra-Pasai was regarded as the appropriate place to solicit such an opinion on Islamic theology. The records of the Aceh state, too, reflect the reverence held by the Acehnese toward Samudra-Pasai as the "cradle of Islam" and the source of legitimacy for Aceh's rulers. Pasai's Islamic scholars were patronized by Aceh's elite, and Aceh's sultans made regular pilgrimages to Pasai to renew their prowess.[169]

The Samudra-Pasai rulers' repeated difficulty with their hinterland populations must have related to the fact that the non-Muslim populations of this hinterland did not view the ruler as holding unusual spiritual prowess. Numerous sources honor Samudra-Pasai's ruler for his Islamic piety but record that despite the ruler's zealous patronage of Islam his hinterland populations had chosen not to convert. In this light the conversion of the Sumatra hinterland to Islam during the era of Aceh's hegemony must have been critical in better linking the interior populations to the Acehnese royal house, employing the "ritual sovereignty" characteristic of the classical age.[170]

The development of these more integrated state systems was encouraged by the fact that access to Chinese and Western markets could no longer be dominated by a single entrepôt. Furthermore, new marketing options were open to Southeast Asian traders within Southeast Asia itself. Southeast Asia's trade had become more than a "peddling trade" in luxury items. Beyond self-sufficiency, the commercially oriented states of Aceh, Malacca, and Johor among others depended upon rice and other food imports to feed their cosmopolitan populations. A bulk trade in rice, salt, dried fish, and pepper was thus established to provision these developing urban centers.[171] Revenue from trade and not agricultural tribute became the most vital source of a state's income, even in the case of the land-based rice states of Ayudhya and Java.[172] The old delivery mechanisms of the earlier age, often dependent upon personal alliances and oaths of allegiance between coastal rulers and hinterland chiefs, or relying totally on the natural flow of products from the interior to the coast, were insufficient to meet the demand for Southeast Asian products in the new commercial age. To increase the flow of hinterland products to the coast a greater degree of coast-hinterland economic and political unity was necessary.

9

Maritime Trade and State Development in Fourteenth-Century Java

The emergence in the thirteenth century of the Javanese court at Majapahit in eastern Java marked the beginning of new levels of both internal and external political and economic integration in Southeast Asia generally. Although central and eastern Java had been united by Airlangga after A.D. 1025, the division of the kingdom between his two sons in 1044 recreated two independent and often unfriendly rival states. The process of unification had to begin anew some two centuries later, when Rājasa (who was also known as Ken Angrok) founded the Singasari-based dynasty. By 1294, when Rājasa's descendent Kĕrtarājasa (1294–1309) came to the throne at Majapahit, rulers reigned over a far-flung maritime empire that included ports on Sumatra, the Malay Peninsula, Borneo, and the spice-producing islands of the eastern portion of the Indonesian archipelago.[1] This maritime empire was patrolled by a Javanese "navy" made up of a seafaring people resident in north Java coast ports whose loyalty to the empire was directly proportional to the Majapahit monarch's ability to deliver to them a substantial cut from the profits of the region's spice trade. No doubt, their economic domination of these overseas ports was more real than any true political control, but there is no question about Majapahit's economic and political control over eastern and central Java.

Throughout the fourteenth century the power of the Majapahit center continued to develop and ultimately led to a most significant transition, a change in the political structure that was to be a hallmark for the future of the entire region, for the developments that were clearly discernible in Majapahit Java from 1294 on would subsequently appear as features generally characteristic of Southeast Asian statecraft in the fourteenth through sixteenth centuries. Java was one of the first states to make the transition from the classical pattern of statecraft in which the wealth of the realm gravitated toward the center through a network of ceremonially defined tributary relationships to a state in which the royal house came to rely not so much on ceremonial relationships as on direct central collection of local specialties and local surpluses (which were sometimes initially justified as direct contributions to exclusively royal ceremonies). But it is not simply because Java was first that it can stand as a paradigm for an age. Equally important is the availability of material on the characteristics of pre-1300 Southeast Asian classical states and highly revealing sources that illuminate important features of the fourteenth-century change. As this chapter will demonstrate, external demand for Southeast Asian products, domestic integration in both the political and economic arenas, and regional control of the spice trade were all a part or a complex dynamic in which all three elements both acted upon and responded to the others.

Java in the Fourteenth Century

As noted in chapter 5, Java first began to blossom as a commercial power and center of international trade in the eleventh century. Increasing commercial interaction between the populations of the Javanese hinterland and port areas on Java's north coast was reflected in the inscriptions of eastern Java-based monarchs; indeed, the largest percentage of royal charters (metal plate inscriptions that record the monarch's official interaction with local communities and were intended to serve as legal records to document local rights or royal expectations of the community) issued during the tenth through the twelfth centuries concerned port or coastal settlements in the Brantas Delta region of eastern Java.[2] Both taxation and price-fixing were part of royal strategies intended to produce revenue for the royal treasury from the trade, but they also were utilized to control the trade and traders by mediating the foreigners' contact with the Javanese rice-producing hinterland and encouraging the development of commercial contacts beyond Java. Although inscriptions from this period provide the first references to foreigners attached to the royal court—and overseas trade was of increasing importance to the Javanese ruler as a source of revenue—this international linkage seems to have had little direct impact on village-level market trade.

Although a number of inland sites have produced a considerable quantity of tenth- and eleventh-century Chinese ceramic sherds and contemporary Chinese references to the volume of trade with this area imply a reasonable level of consumption of Chinese trade items outside Javanese court circles, there is no mention of imported luxury goods or of the presence of foreign merchants in local inscriptions.[3] Foreigners and foreign goods could well have been absent from the local market, for trade was not the only mechanism by which goods found their way into the countryside. Rather, it is believed that Javanese kings acquired prestigious foreign goods from overseas traders in Java's coastal ports and then redistributed these luxury items throughout the realm, including the hinterland, through alliance-making or the presentation of gifts. Such redistribution played a major role in shoring up the Javanese ruler's hegemony in this period, since such luxury goods were shared with those loyal to the monarch. On the other hand, nonprestige goods of foreign origin, specifically metals and dyes, do appear in local market lists and undoubtedly reached these markets via indigenous exchange networks. Such imported goods were funneled through eastern Java ports by Javanese traders who then took them into the hinterland, where they were traded for local products, especially rice. These traders could then market the rice in the coastal ports.[4] Once in the ports, this rice was exported to the eastern archipelago islands where it was exchanged for spices. These spices brought to Java on the return voyage were exchanged for foreign products brought by Eastern and Western merchants and the triangular trade pattern was completed.

Within Java, due to the demand for rice for export, marketing networks continued to evolve that united interior markets with Java's coastal ports. By the Majapahit era local produce moved via important hinterland market centers to north coast ports along a realmwide road system that served as a horizontal supplement to the vertical pattern of Java's river systems. In the fourteenth century all roads led to the Majapahit court and connected important regions that lacked a river route with the capital.[5] In the *Nagarakĕrtagama,* the Majapahit court's epic poem that was composed in the mid-fourteenth century, the crossroads near the royal court were cited as being: "south of the market place, that is the crossroads, sacred, imposing."[6] The road system and its intersection near the court were sanctified in the poem, reflecting the network's great importance to the livelihood of the Majapahit realm as a whole in the eyes of its monarchs. The ruler and his retinue periodically traveled along this road network, making what the *Nagarakĕrtagama* described as "royal progressions" to receive the personal homage of the various royal subordinates and to confirm royal authority over areas distant from the court that the king did not directly administer.[7]

In addition to their political importance, the roads were also a means for transporting rice and other trade goods. The *Nagarakĕrtagama* speaks of "caravans of carts" along Java's roads and of crowded royal highways.[8] Special reference is made to tradesmen who accompanied the royal progressions and who camped in open fields near the court's lodging at the conclusion of each day's journey.[9] These carts and tradesmen are well represented in the Majapahit era's temple reliefs. But use of the road network was seasonal because of the monsoons. Movement on the road network was concentrated in the dry season from March to September. The *Nagarakĕrtagama* describes road travel in the wet season:

> The road . . . over the whole length then was difficult, narrow. There followed rains. The incline being altogether slippery several carts were damaged there, colliding one with another.[10]

Because of the difficulty of transporting commodities along these roads, the bulk of Javanese rice was conveyed by river from the hinterland to the coast, and foreign goods moved upriver in return.

The "Canggu Ferry Charter of 1358" sheds some light on the movement of cartloads of goods and traders *(akalang)* to and from the royal court.[11] The context of the charter's comments indicates that traders traveled with cartloads of goods over Majapahit's roads and that ferryboats at critical river crossings in the road network were at least large enough to carry the traders' carts. Some seventy-nine ferry crossing "districts" are enumerated in the charter.[12]

Canggu was a commercial center on the Brantas River, and its importance in the Majapahit realm is reflected in the account of Ma Huan, writing about the early fifteenth-century maritime expeditions of Cheng Ho. Ma Huan wrote that one could reach the marketplace of "Changku" by sailing 70–80 *li* (twenty-five miles) upriver on the Brantas from Surabaya on the coast, and from there one could reach the Majapahit capital by walking for half a day.[13] The *Pararaton,* a Javanese account of the Majapahit era composed in the late fifteenth or early sixteenth century, confirms Ma Huan's report, describing Canggu as the point of collection for goods passing between the coast and the capital.[14]

The records of the Majapahit state provide a view of the interrelationship of trade and statecraft in the thirteenth and fourteenth centuries. Four Majapahit inscriptions dating to the second half of the fourteenth century are especially valuable since they register modifications in the way that the state collected taxes from three eastern Java commercial communities. In documenting these policy transitions, each inscription reported the traditional method of revenue collection that dated from the pre-1300 era, and in doing so demonstrated changes taking place in the Javanese socioeconomy that parallel developments in other Southeast Asian regions in the fourteenth and fifteenth centuries.

Javanese Trade and Statecraft in the Early Majapahit Era

The Ferry Charter of 1358 recorded a change in the status of ferrymen based in Canggu and Terung, located on opposite banks of the Brantas River. As noted above, the Canggu crossing was on a major road network that connected assorted hinterland population centers to the Majapahit court. Canggu was also an important trade center for Brantas River traffic; goods transported to the court from the coast passed through Canggu. The inscription's principal concern is the replacement of old state tax collections known as *dĕrwaya haji* with a new payment called *pamuja*. *Dĕrwaya haji* was collected by "tax farmers" known as *mangilala dĕrwaya haji* in inscriptions dating to the tenth century, when east Java-based monarchs had first begun to implement this revenue assessment process in their eastern and central Java realm. In these older inscriptions assorted individuals, among them merchants and other "foreigners" who seemingly had no local loyalties, were assigned the right to collect local revenues *(dĕrwaya haji)* on the state's behalf on their guarantee that the state would receive a share of the collection. The role of merchants and tradesmen as collectors may be seen, for instance, in the Pālebuhan (Gorang Gareng) eastern Java inscription dating 927, when the collectors of *dĕrwaya haji* included Singhalese, south Indians (*Paṇḍikira*s), Burmese (*Ramanyadesi*s), and port-based merchants *(bānyaga bantal).*[15] Although the specific *dĕrwaya haji* formerly collected at Canggu and Terung are not described in detail in the Ferry Charter, the inscription's proclamation of the new tax collection arrangement does provide clues about the nature of eastern Java's statecraft in the post-tenth-century era.

First, the charter freed the local ferrymen from their former responsibility to make payments of *dĕrwaya haji* to the local landed elite. Second, the inscription provided that the ferrymen could thereafter assume an independent status socially and politically from the local agricultural community and could, as a consequence, begin to interact directly with the royal court; they were no longer obliged to deal through the landed elite. Third, as a further symbol of their new social and political status the ferrymen were granted a place in the king's religious ceremonial. Their new status allowed them to participate as individuals or as a group in a new local festival honoring the Majapahit monarch. In support of this festival and as repayment for their recognition by the king, the ferrymen would provide specified amounts of flowers and cash as the new *pamuja* tax. Fourth, the ferrymen would be allowed to participate in the Caitra festival marking the renewal of the agricultural cycle that took place annually at the royal capital and in other locations near the capital.[16] At this festival the remainder of the ferrymen's yearly *pamuja* tax payments were due; among the *pamuja* payments due to the king at this festival were unspecified textiles.

The new social, political, and religious status of the ferrymen as revealed in this charter is of particular importance because it documents the emergence of a supralocal nonagrarian commercial community within the Java hinterland population. Moreover, the charter's emphasis on payment of taxes due to the state by direct assignment of these revenues to underwrite local and court ceremonies demonstrated consistency with the patterns of classical Southeast Asian statecraft whereby the ruler depended on sacred ceremonies and other religious donations to legitimize his rule. The conversion of revenue payments into the "symbolic capital" of the ceremonies bestowed merit on the ruler as a patron of religion, and his ritual emphasized the ruler's role as the source of his subjects' prosperity—as, for instance, in the Caitra festival.[17] Because of their contribution to local as well as state-level ceremonies that honored their monarch, the ferrymen—who previously had been grouped with the local agrarian population as commoners subject to the authority of the landed elite—were allowed the opportunity to assume a more direct relationship with the royal court. This revised the old pattern of polity whereby their contact with the state had been, at best, indirect and completely dependent upon the local agrarian community and its elite, who had represented them.

The fact that the ferry crossing between Canggu and Terung was critical in facilitating the flow to the court of hinterland goods as well as goods of foreign origin may partially explain the desire of the Majapahit monarch to establish a more direct relationship with this particular community. The new relationship no doubt allowed the ferrymen greater freedom to pursue their commercial affairs but also represented an attempt by the state to undercut the authority of the local landed aristocracy. Plates 9 and 10 of the Ferry Charter list among the privileges granted to the ferrymen exemption from legal rules that might have interfered with the efficient performance of their work. They were also allowed to organize cockfights and other gambling activities—activities that the *Nagarakĕrtagama* deemed appropriate to commercial centers—and to have the music of gong orchestras played at their worship services, as appropriate to their new religious status.[18]

One reason for the new royal relationship with people from this area may well have related to events of the previous year, when a naval expedition led by a west Java-based commercial rival of Majapahit had penetrated up the Brantas River to the Canggu area, demonstrating Canggu's strategic position on the riverine commercial route from the Majapahit court to the coast.[19] Of further interest in this regard is the ferrymen's partial payment of the *pamuja* tax in cash, flowers, and textiles. On the one hand, the cash payment documents the growing monetarization of the Javanese economy as a byproduct of Java's emergence as a major center of international trade, while the cess in textiles was consistent with earlier patterns of Javanese statecraft whereby Javanese monarchs exercised control over goods acquired from and dispensed to the international trade route. Java's monarchs traditionally shared luxury goods of foreign origin with those in royal favor in ceremonies of redistribution, thus reinforcing alliance relationships that were critical to the monarch's sovereignty.[20] Canggu's importance as a source of foreign or domestic textiles for redistribution is implied in the Ferry Charter's stipulation that the ferrymen supply textiles to the court as part of their *pamuja* tax payment, as well as the inscription's allusion to the maritime raid of the previous year.

The nature of the old *dĕrwaya haji* collections dating to pre-Majapahit times is further revealed in three letters addressed by the Majapahit court to the occupants of Biluluk and Tanggulunan, two neighboring communities located northwest of Majapahit and inland from the coast. These three letters were inscribed on metal plates that comprise the "Biluluk Charters."[21] The letters depict a prosperous area that depended on nonagrarian production for its income. Among the residents of the local community were:

1. salt dealers
2. palm-sugar dealers
3. butchers (meat packers of salt-cured and spiced meats; *dendeng,* salted water buffalo meat was a particular luxury in that era)
4. bleachers of textile
5. indigo dyers
6. millers of oil (*jarak,* a ricinus oil)
7. makers of vermicelli (*laksa,* a luxury), and
8. lime burners (lime was burned in the making of cloth)

The first letter, dated 1366, was addressed to the aristocratic families of the area and reminded them of the privileges held by visitors attending an annual festival staged locally. These visitors were exempt from the dues normally collected by members of the local elite from those who purchased or gathered salt in the saltlands; instead these visitors were to pay *pamuja*—the same royal festival tax imposed on the Canggu area in the Ferry Charter—as well as a second cess on salt collections *(pagagarem)* that was payable directly to the state rather than to the local elite (as had been the case previously). The noble families of Biluluk and Tanggulunan held income rights to a saline spring where people from other areas came to buy salt or to make salt themselves. Those who came to make salt in 1366 were first required to make a payment of 300 cash as *pamuja,* as well as a monthly salt duty *(pagagarem)* of 7 *ku* (one *kupang* was equal to 1/100 cash). At the time of the annual festival salt-makers and outsiders were allowed for a period of five days to scoop salt water from the spring without paying these duties. Those who still collected salt duties ("who acted as if they still held rights") at such times were compared to a person who took rice from a field not his own and according to the inscription would be fined accordingly.[22]

Subsequent letters dated 1393 and 1395 were addressed directly to local artisans *(parawangsa)* instead of the elite. Unlike the Ferry Charter's total withdrawal of the collection privileges held by the local elite over commercial affairs at Canggu, the Biluluk letters confirmed the revenue collection privileges of the elites of Biluluk and Tanggulunan. But these local elites, the 1393 letter noted, were the "chiefs of trade," who were entitled to *titiban* ("what drops in the lap"), compulsory payments and purchases by the local merchants and artisans who participated in the eight commercial trades. Like other merchants in commercial centers near the royal capital, local merchants and artisans were required to buy lots *(tiban)* at fixed prices set by the chiefs of trade.[23] Tradesmen in the Biluluk area were formerly obligated to buy four kinds of spices (these were likely used in the preparation of meats), ironware, earthenware dishes (Chinese ceramics), rattan, and cotton cloth—all trade goods acquired from other places in exchange for local products. *Titiban* was also a compulsory relinquishing to the chiefs of trade of part of their stocks by artisans who resided in or near the royal capital. The 1393 letter revealed that messengers from the royal court normally "came down" to collect for it a share of local *titiban* lots from the chiefs of trade, and these revenue collectors were paid for their efforts an additional fee *(tahil padugi)* that was collected from local tradesmen by the chiefs of trade.[24]

Finally, the 1393 letter stipulated that a new tax called *pamihos,* a fixed tax, was to replace former dues known as *arik purih* that were payable by local merchants and artisans to the chiefs of trade on thirteen different occasions. Five referred to family events, such as birth, marriage, and death, that were marked by special ceremonies; seven concerned household rights and duties, including the obligation of the households to entertain the elite's guests; the remaining one required that certain costs of travel and transport incurred by the chiefs of trade be assumed by the merchant and artisan community. The 1393 letter stipulated that these service dues payable to the chiefs of trade were no longer valid. The *pamihos* cess replacing the *arik purih* collections was a head tax that was to be shared by the chiefs of trade and the state.

The new arrangement, like the Ferry Charter, demonstrated a more direct royal authority locally. Both the Ferry Charter and the Biluluk Charters recognized the right of a local elite to rule the local population in pre-Majapahit times, although in the Biluluk Charters this was a commercial elite rather than a landed aristocracy. The implication of both records is that a closer relationship between the royal court and its nonelite subjects was developing. The court began to collect its revenue cesses more directly from its subjects—although the court still depended on the skills of the aristocracy in Canggu and the chiefs of trade in Biluluk to make these collections rather than receiving individual payments from each subject. The earlier practice of sending officials out from the court to receive royal shares of local revenue collections was also eliminated in the Biluluk Charters, with the local commercial elite now taking personal responsibility for these revenue transfers to the court. The use of commercial specialists to collect revenues was not new. As noted above, numerous records document the use of merchants and other nonagrarian "foreigners" to collect *dĕrwaya haji* revenues in earlier times.

Alliances with commercial elites were no doubt also intended to reduce the autonomy of the landed aristocracy, who had traditionally been well entrenched within their *watĕk* regions.[25] When the royal court shifted to eastern Java the monarch's ability to govern the Javanese hinterland was enhanced. This was because the monarch assumed the role as director of the development of the irrigation networks of the Brantas River basin. He also increased his income by facilitating international trade, as east Java ports emerged as major trade centers on the international maritime route.

In 1395 another letter from the Majapahit court was sent to the sugar-palm tappers of Biluluk, confirming the right of the holders of property rights (the "chiefs of trade") over local sugar-palm trees to receive one-half of the sugar collected by the tapper (apparently the tapper was allowed to retain the remaining half share). From this one-half share the chiefs of trade were required to make specified payments to the state. While this letter provides another example of greater state interaction locally, it also confirmed that the commercial elite of Biluluk was still permitted a share of the state's local tax collections. The unwillingness of the state to totally eliminate the revenue rights of this local elite—as opposed to the exclusion of the landed elite from a share in the *pamuja* cess that replaced earlier tax collections in Canggu—may reflect the state's desire to give the local elite a greater incentive to increase production. The 1366 letter to the Biluluk chiefs of trade also provides information about the state's relationship with the commercial populations of its hinterland, as this letter noted that the chiefs of trade were allied by marriage to the royal court, denoting a special relationship between the Majapahit sovereign and the leaders of this prosperous community of merchants and artisans.

Another record of the imposition of the *pamuja* tax on a commercial community is reported in the Charter of Karang Bogĕm dated 1384. Karang Bogĕm was on the north Java coast in the western part of the Majapahit state's territories. This inscription concerns a royal debt-bondsman *(kawula)*.[26] The bondsman had been a fisherman active in a nearby coastal center, but a royal court judge had fined him 120,000 cash as punishment for an alleged crime. Unable to pay the debt, he was made a debt-bondsman of the king and was assigned the task of developing a fishery on wasteland at Karang Bogĕm.[27] The royal court received one part of the fishery's production as repayment of the fine and another as payment of interest on the money invested by the court in the fishery. A further return on this economic initiative by the Majapahit court came in the form of a consignment of fish made to the state at the time of the court's Caitra festival.[28] The Charter of Karang Bogĕm imposed the *pamuja* festival tax—which was likely payable at the Caitra festival as well—on local traders, fishermen, and sugar-palm tappers, while exempting them from old *arik purih* dues that were paid to the landed elite (who held estates and bondsmen) of that area. To appease this elite, who were considered members of the royal family because of their alliance through marriage with the court, their *pamuja* tax cess was reduced by one-half. Herein, as in the Ferry Charter, the authority of a local elite —members of the extended family of the monarch no less—over commercial activity was being modified in favor of the court and the local commercial community, and the independence of the local commercial community vis-à-vis previously dominant local political institutions was established.

All three charters thus portray a growing standardization of the Javanese state's revenue collections. In widespread references the Majapahit court replaced tax assessments of earlier times—notably *dĕrwaya haji* and *arik purih*—with new state cesses, *pamuja* and *pamihos* respectively, that were payable more directly to the state. The three charters show the emergence of the state's revenue collection policy in the post-tenth-century era, wherein the state, with both an institutional inability to collect local cesses and a lack of sufficient physical prowess to impose direct authority over subject population centers, depended on alliances with subordinate elites. The state thus had initially turned to landed elites in agricultural communities (Canggu and Karang Bogĕm) and to chiefs of trade in a well-established commercial community (Biluluk). However, the Majapahit state's new *pamuja* and *pamihos* cesses were to be collected more directly than were the revenue collections of the pre-1300 era, seemingly to assure that the state would receive a larger share of such locally collected cesses. A new royal relationship with these three communities is most strikingly shown in the Canggu Ferry Charter's curtailment of the political rights of the landed elite; the emergence of Canggu as a commercial center was reinforced by the granting of independent political and social status to the ferrymen, who became the commerical elite of that community. In Biluluk and Karang Bogĕm, on the other hand, while the new revenue collection policy diminished the political rights of the local elite vis-à-vis the state, the state still recognized that the Biluluk chiefs of trade and the landed elite of Karang Bogĕm held local political authority that the state chose not to (or lacked the power to) challenge. It may not be a coincidence that both the Biluluk chiefs of trade and the landed elite of Karang Bogĕm had intermarried with the royal court, while the landed elite of Canggu had not—and were thus subject to the greatest revision of their political rights.[29]

The Javanese Economy Under the Majapahit State

Beyond the political implications of the new revenue settlements, the Majapahit government's new tax collection policies had positive implications for the Javanese economy. Replacement of the *dĕrwaya haji* and *arik purih* collection systems of the previous age with fixed yearly fees that were collected more directly from the producer himself would have theoretically allowed the producer more personal control over his surplus production. The previous settlements appear to have permitted those who held local revenue collection rights on the state's behalf (often recognizing rights that were already held by local landed elites) to assume control over the peasants' surplus. Guaranteeing a payment to the state, these "revenue collectors" undoubtedly kept for themselves any amount they could collect from peasant producers over and above the sum officially due from them to the state.[30] In earlier as well as Majapahit-era cesses the king's direct control and consumption of local revenue collections from the lands that were not considered subject to his personal and direct landholding rights does not seem to have been important to the state's existence. Rather than confront the local elites who dominated nonroyal lands with direct demands for a share of local production, which would have taken income away from them, the state depended on the flow of revenues from lands directly subject to the king to finance the court's activities.

This does not mean, however, that the state made no attempt to tap local production on nonroyal lands. Indeed, the new revenue settlements discussed above generally required that the royal revenues due from local producers meet the cost of local religious ceremonies that honored the monarch. The remainder of the revenues due to the state was assigned to finance ritual at the capital, in which representatives of the community were required to participate, or if the cess was collected in trade goods such as textiles, these luxuries were reassigned to royal allies. As noted above, such redistributions of royal revenue collections or of luxury goods of foreign origin at the state and local level were important to the Javanese monarch's sovereignty. Thus revenues due from nonroyal lands were indirectly collected in ways that allowed the local community to directly retain or to share in royal redistributions of their production.[31]

Royal policy that promoted reassignments as well as local retention of royal revenue assessments would have given the producer greater control of his produce, and thus would have stimulated production. A community that was able to keep a share of its production surplus and whose members could acquire profit from the sale of this surplus would have had an incentive to increase its rice output. The internal peace and security provided by the Majapahit state, which fostered the expansion of the marketing network; the development by that time of a realmwide road network; the growing concentration of nonagrarian populations (merchants, artisans, and government officials) in urban centers; and a general increase in foreign demand for eastern archipelago spices—all increased the demand for Javanese rice. Java's peasants accordingly increased their production in response to the new levels of demand emanating from hinterland and coastal market centers.

Improved marketing possibilities provided ample opportunity for an ambitious peasant to increase his family's income. The wide distribution and heavy concentration of Chinese ceramics in archaeological sites that date to the Majapahit era, literary and epigraphic references to local consumption of commercial products of nonlocal origin, and archaeological evidence that substantiates written records of monetarized exchange at all levels of the Javanese economy, suggest that the desire and the ability to consume imported or luxury goods was spreading beyond the elite during this era. The availability of these "foreign goods" would also have given peasant cultivators incentives to produce more rice.[32] However, given the importance of religious ritual in early Javanese society, Javanese peasants may not have been responding to new economic opportunity simply for the sake of their own personal or family consumption. Religious ceremonies and temples, too, might have provided incentives. New or expanded sources of income may have made it possible for many nonelite to become sponsors of religious ceremony for the first time. Indeed, in the three charters discussed above the king solicits the participation of the nonelite in state ritual. Investment of surplus income in state temple construction or religious ritual, especially that directly associated with the king, bestowed significant merit upon the donor and would have enhanced the status of the benefactor within the traditional system.[33]

The fact that the new *pamihos* cess collected in Biluluk as well as the *pamuja* tax due from the Canggu ferrymen were payable in cash rather than in kind shows the growing monetarization of the Javanese economy, a consequence of Java's commercial prosperity as a major international center of trade. Writing in 1225, Chao Ju-kua, the commissioner of foreign trade at the China coast port of Ch'uan-chou, was impressed by the use of precious metals in Java. He noted the use of alloyed coins minted with mixtures of silver, tin, lead, and copper; sixty small metal coins with holes in their centers were strung on a string; sixty of these were equal to one *tael* of gold and thirty-two equalled a half-*tael* of gold.[34] He also reported that the Chinese court prohibited trade with Java due to the flow of copper cash out of China to purchase pepper in Java.[35] Javanese traders circumvented this prohibition by referring to their country as Sukadana (Su-ki-tan). The early fifteenth-century survey by Ma Huan noted that countries located in eastern Java (Majapahit) and southern and northern Sumatra (Palembang and Lamuri/Ramni, respectively) used copper cash extensively. These accounts demonstrate that, whether following the example of China or utilizing the abundant supply of "copper cash" often available from China, the Southeast Asian countries along the main trade route in Java and the Strait of Malacca tended to use "copper" (generally an alloy of copper with tin, lead, and/or zinc) as the basis for their own monetary system.[36] Monetary flow in Java in the thirteenth and fourteenth centuries involved copper as much as it did gold and silver.

Gold and silver often assumed important roles not as currencies but as commodities and merchandise for the market; Java received considerable amounts of copper, gold, and silver in exchange for its pepper, cloves, and nutmeg. This exchange was a major component in the flow of copper cash out of China and the flow of species out of the West with the increased European demand for spices in the thirteenth century. A flow of Western gold and silver currency moved through the Middle East and India to Java.[37] Various travelers' accounts, substantiated by local sources, document the wealth of gold and silver accumulated in Java.

Western travelers thought of Java as the wealthiest place on earth. Marco Polo's comments at the end of the thirteenth century, quoted in chapter 8, are but one example.[38] While ninth- and tenth-century charters in Java make reference to payments in gold and silver by weight, there is rarely mention of gold in the thirteenth- and fourteenth-century charters, however, not due to scarcity but to the transition to the use of copper as the standard unit of exchange.[39]

Profits made on the exchange of Javanese rice for eastern archipelago spices and on the trade and transport of these spices for the goods and metals of the East and West that took place in Java's coastal ports were subject to royal taxes. It was from facilitating this international trade that eastern Javanese monarchs received significant income. The monarch's port fees and his right to a personal share of trade goods and profits provided the additional revenue necessary to finance the expanded domestic activities of the Majapahit court.[40] Various local and foreign sources speak of the Java monarch's administrative supremacy over north coast ports and their trade. Some of these sources considered Java-based merchants active in the international spice trade to be the monarch's "trade agents."[41]

To provision the key export-import sector with local products, especially rice, royal policy encouraged the participation of local productive units in the higher levels of the market economy. Recognition of the rights of Biluluk's artisan community vis-à-vis their chiefs of trade, for example, and of the independence of commercial communities at Canggu and Karang Bogĕm illustrate this aspect of the Majapahit state's economic policy. While the Majapahit state's new revenue settlements with these communities did not immediately add substantial income to the royal treasury, the new tax policies encouraged the production of local surpluses and the flow of these surpluses via the expanding marketing network to the coast, where their exchange for foreign goods was directly taxed by the state.

Because of the income potential of the commercial sector of the Javanese economy, Majapahit's monarchs did not have to enhance their collection and consumption of land taxes from lands subject to the authority of the state's landed elites. To increase its revenue demands on the agrarian sector the state would have had to encroach further upon the political rights and socioeconomic powers of these entrenched local elites. Majapahit's monarchs seemed reluctant to pose this challenge, and the inherent weakness of the Javanese political system was thereby revealed: the state depended on personal alliances forged with its local political elite to validate royal sovereignty. To avoid political confrontation that might immerse the state in widespread conflict, which would have benefited no group, the state instead encouraged the development of the Javanese nonagricultural economy and promoted the cause of merchants and artisans who could best assist in facilitating the flow of goods to and from Java's north coast ports.[42]

When in the fifteenth century Majapahit's authority was challenged by coastal commercial elites who broke away from the state's authority, Majapahit's rulers were deprived of their control over the international trade and its revenues, and the state ceased to exist. It was only when the emerging Mataram monarchy secured a share of the profits derived from the international trade that a stable state system again emerged in the late sixteenth and early seventeenth centuries.[43] In the *Nagarakĕrtagama,* the following passage connects the security and success of Majapahit with its economy:

> If destroyed be the peasants' cultivated lands (as a matter of course) will accompany them that (area) which has a shortage of means of subsistence; now that is the town [i.e., if rice wasn't produced, then towns, which consumed and marketed rice, would also suffer]. If there is not retinue [i.e., the king's retinue, his administrative corps and especially his military] in evidence there are the foreign islands coming to attack. Therefore equally they must be taken care of: stable will be both. That is the fruit of the speaking.[44]

The state thus provided the physical protection necessary to promote the realm's economic prosperity and to protect the realm from outsiders—note that the principal threat to Java's economy was seen as coming by sea from "foreign islands." With protection provided by the state military, the peasants could produce rice that the towns would in turn market, and the entire realm would prosper.[45]

The *Nagarakĕrtagama,* which speaks of the royal court in the time of Hayam Wuruk (Rājasanagara, 1350–1389), further illustrates the importance of trade to the early fourteenth-century Javanese socioeconomy. Although it is principally concerned with the idealized affairs of the court and its sanctified ritual activities, the *Nagarakĕrtagama* also indicates the importance of Bubat, a substantial commercial center located on the Brantas River in the hinterland. The poem makes it clear that Bubat was both frequented by foreign traders and the site of royal symbolism. Bubat was surrounded on three sides by large buildings (*bhawanas*), and its population resided in quarters *(mapanta)*—Indian and Chinese quarters receive special mention.[46] Here traders from India, Cambodia, China, Vietnam, Thailand, and other places gathered to pay homage to and to provision the Majapahit monarch.[47] Demonstrating the relationship between this trade and the state's authority, Bubat assumed special prominence in the *Nagarakĕrtagama* as the first center for the celebration of the Caitra festival. The Caitra festival celebrated both the Majapahit monarch's "divinity" and the beginning of a new year in the agricultural cycle. During the first seven days of the festival the Majapahit court "came down" to Bubat to participate in public amusements in a fair atmosphere.[48] Here games and gambling were permitted in a place more appropriate for such actions than in the sanctified court's urban capital. It was here in Bubat that the king received various collections in kind due to him from assorted commercial communities, for example the *pamuja* payments described in the charters mentioned above. Here, too, on the banks of the Brantas River the king celebrated the "passing over ceremony" that marked the coming of the new year. This act emphasized the life-bringing powers of the Brantas, which was the source of the eastern Java-based state's prosperity. The Brantas supplied the water necessary for eastern Java's wet-rice agriculture and also provided contact with the outside world from whence came luxury goods and revenues.

While the *Nagarakĕrtagama* refers to the state's commercial activities only occasionally and in the context of state ceremonies, the *Pararaton* offers much more. This court chronicle, composed in the late fifteenth or early sixteenth century, records the affairs of the Majapahit dynasty during the fourteenth century.[49] It provides a much longer list of centers of trade and commercial affairs than the *Nagarakĕrtagama*.[50] In one episode the *Pararaton* reports a maritime expedition that had been launched against Majapahit by the ruler of the Sunda Strait region in 1357 (one year previous to the Ferry Charter of Canggu). Even though the expedition sailed up the Brantas by way of Canggu to Bubat, it was defeated by the Majapahit ruler. According to the *Pararaton,* the Sundanese king had escorted his daughter to Majapahit with a large retinue of ships, in order to present her in marriage and thereby seal a formal alliance with the Majapahit king. When the Majapahit court refused to recognize her as a suitable queen of equal rank to the king, a battle resulted between Majapahit and Sunda forces in Bubat, a battle that the Sundanese lost.[51] This raid by the Sunda ruler is consistent with the patterns of riverine system competition common to the island realm in early Southeast Asian history.[52] In this instance the Sunda Strait ruler—who appears to have been in control of the riverine systems on both sides of the strait and who from this strategic location could have been a serious rival to Majapahit's commercial interests in the western Indonesian archipelago—sent a naval expedition up the Brantas River intent upon eliminating a rival and enhancing his commercial interests.

With Majapahit's victory, the Sunda Strait ruler's subordinates, the riverine systems of western Java and southern Sumatra, became vulnerable to the Majapahit state's ambitions. Although there is no evidence of an immediate Majapahit raid into that area in response to this possibility, twenty years later, in 1377, a punitive expedition was sent against Palembang, another competitor in this Malacca and Sunda Strait region.[53] Conflict among rivals for commercial hegemony in the archipelago trade network had been a common occurrence in the pre-Majapahit era. True to this tradition, Majapahit's rulers repulsed an invasion attempt for commercial dominance by a competitor, the Sunda Strait ruler, and this victory in turn confirmed Majapahit's success as the archipelago's leading maritime power. Whether this rivalry actually threatened Majapahit's authority or not, the potential symbolism of this event was not lost on the *Pararaton*'s author, who used it to confirm Majapahit's commercial leadership.[54] This tie with the riverine state tradition laid the foundation for Majapahit's legitimate succession as the facilitator of the archipelago's successful international trade. This story in the *Pararaton* thereby added to the ruler's legitimacy as the focus of Java's wet-rice tradition, the central theme of the *Nagarakĕrtagama*. While the *Nagarakĕrtagama,* like the Ferry Charter, consciously omitted reference to or trivialized the Sundanese raid because it was related to Majapahit's maritime affairs (the raid may well have been seen as reflecting the problems that Majapahit's participation in the international commercial sector posed to its wet-rice civilization), the *Pararaton* as well as later Javanese literature considered this event to have been of great importance. This was due to the *Pararaton*'s portrayal of Majapahit as both a wet-rice plain and maritime state; the realm's wet-rice core provided the essential commodity (rice) that made Java's dominance of the Southeast Asian spice trade possible. The interrelationship of the economic and political sectors was responsible for the state's success.

The evolution of royal power in Java thus culminated in the fourteenth century with the establishment of the Majapahit state. The time before was marked by expanding and contracting royal authority over the Javanese countryside.[55] Various inscriptions from the tenth to the fourteenth centuries reflect the initial inroads of royal administration into the state's regions. There was a growing political, economic, and social integration of the realm that produced a truly Javanese cultural form that is most conspicuous in the era's art and architecture.[56] Economically, the rice economy of eastern Java as well as the older region of central Java prospered.

Because of the increased external demand for Javanese rice, there emerged a hierarchical market network that united communities of local exchange with Java's coastal ports. Yet at the topmost levels of this mar-

Gaṇeśa, god of prudence and sagacity, standing on the heads of slain enemies. Eastern Java.

Caṇḍi Panataran, Majapahit era, eastern Java.

keting system there was a conscious separation of political and commercial function. Ports of trade were not political centers, and the state's political center was not a major commercial center. Majapahit's capital was located well in the interior up the Brantas River from the coast, where it was less likely to have been subject to direct contact with outsiders. The Majapahit court consciously located its marketplace on the periphery of the capital urban center to make sure that the commercial activities that took place there would not pollute the royal court.[57] According to the *Nagarakĕrtagama,* the court's major commercial affairs and contact with foreigners were transacted at Bubat, some distance downriver from the court. The commercial leadership of the Javanese state was thus downplayed in the *Nagarakĕrtagama,* and Majapahit's rulers fulfilled the Javanese tradition of wet-rice statecraft that traced its history to early central Java. Thus while the Majapahit monarch ruled both a wet-rice and maritime realm, it was his association with the Javanese wet-rice state tradition that was the most critical to his expression of legitimacy.

Majapahit's Fifteenth-Century "Demise"

A new order of Javanese statecraft evolved in the Brantas River basin under Majapahit's fourteenth century rulers. Majapahit monarchs assumed greater powers of economic and political leadership and enhanced their status as the source of cultural identity among their subordinate populations. Like earlier Javanese political centers, Majapahit was the focus of a chain of patron-client relationships, with the state-level center attempting to maintain itself economically and politically against the centrifugal forces of local-level alliance networks. Traditionally, when an old Javanese political center was lost regional units competed with each other to become the new center, building new networks of economic and political alliances and underscoring these relationships by establishing new sources of legitimacy.

To combat the divisive tendencies of the past, Majapahit's monarchs substantiated their legitimacy by fabricating links to eras of past glory, as in the case of the *Nagarakĕrtagama*'s emphasis that Majapahit's rulers were the legitimate successors to a line of monarchs who had ruled Java since the origin of a Javanese "state" in the sixth century A.D. They also patronized a tantric Śiva-Buddhist religion in which indigenous Javanese religious values dominated. The *Nagarakĕrtagama* is saturated with Buddhist and Hindu references. It begins with the Indian incantation "OM!" ("Prosperity!").[58] The royal family is described as being above mortals, and the king was an innately divine incarnation of a god.[59] The king was also the divinely ordained head of society, whose function was to give human life its appropriate place in the cosmic order.[60] Consistent with the patterns of Indianized statecraft practiced in earlier Javanese states, the Majapahit court and its kingdom were idealized as being created in the image of the universe as a whole. The Majapahit monarch provided for his subjects' well-being by maintaining order in his realm. His task was to enlarge his miniature cosmos as he created a heaven on earth *(maṇḍala)*.[61]

Rather than physically imposing his authority, the Majapahit monarch generally awed his subjects into submission to his glamorous court. The *Nagarakĕrtagama*'s story begins around A.D. 1250, when Kĕrtanagara (1268–1292) became king by destroying a "wicked man," "annihilating him altogether."[62] But it is observed that thereafter, "All of the bad people are giving up their evil minds, only fearing the manfulness of the honored king." Kĕrtanagara had been initiated in the secret tantric knowledge necessary to secure his realm's prosperity; it was his foremost duty to combat the demoniac powers that were rampant in the world. To accomplish this, Kĕrtanagara cultivated ecstasy through alcohol and sexual excesses, activities that shocked the compiler of the *Pararaton,* who characterized him as a drunkard who was brought to ruin by lust. In the *Nagarakĕrtagama,* on the other hand, which was composed in 1365 by Prapanca, the head of the Buddhist clergy at the Majapahit court, he was described as a saint and ascetic, free of all passion.

To combat the divisive tendences that had brought despair to his land, Kĕrtanagara erected a statue depicting himself as Aksubhya, the meditative Buddha, on the spot where Bharada, the ascetic who was believed to have carried out the partition of Airlangga's kingdom, had lived. The *Nagarakĕrtagama* viewed Kĕrtanagara's religious purification of Java as the cause of his descendants' glory as divine kings and reuniters of the realm.[63] Thus while Kĕrtanagara initially imposed his authority by force, his consequent success, as well as that of later Majapahit monarchs, was due to his innate divinity. Consistent with this pattern, Kĕrtanagara had sent a naval expedition against southeastern Sumatra (Malāyu) sometime around 1275, and commemorated the expedition eleven years later by having a statue of his father Viṣṇuvardhana (1248–1268), in the image of the Bodhisattva Amoghapāśa (the tantric "Bodhisattva of Compassion"), erected in the Batang Hari River system.[64] The statue's inscription records its dedication to the joy of all the subjects of the land of southeastern Sumatra and may be seen as an attempt to draw the area into a tributary relationship with Kĕrtanagara's court rather than to impose Javanese authority.

While the Majapahit state's efforts to extend its authority had varying results, the accomplishments of Majapahit's fourteenth-century monarchs provided a standard of achievement for their successors not only in Java but also among the Malay populations of the Indonesian archipelago.[65] The *Nagarakĕrtagama* and Majapahit's inscriptions report a state that impressively administered the whole "land of Java" (Javabhumi) and held sovereignty over "other islands" *(nusāntara/dvīpāntara),* and whose authority was also recognized by all "other countries" *(desāntara).*[66] The state's monarchs justly ruled and protected their subject population, were well-informed of the affairs of their state, and stimulated their state's development. But while these records glorify the centralizing activities of Majapahit's fourteenth-century monarchs, these same records note that Majapahit's monarchs did not hold absolute authority over their domain.[67] Like the other great "classical" wet-rice plain states of the Southeast Asian mainland, Majapahit's state system still depended on a network of patron-client relationships that allied regionally based elites to the Majapahit court.

Majapahit-era inscriptions openly report the semiautonomous powers held by important regional elites, who were normally linked to the reigning monarch by blood or marriage, although these inscriptions carefully specify that the activities of regional elites were performed in the name of their Majapahit overlord. The *Nagarakĕrtagama* highlights the powers of administration that Hayam Wuruk (the most powerful among the poem's monarchs) shared with his father Kĕrtawardhana, who was known as the "Prince of Singhasari," and the king's uncle Vijayarājasa, who had administrative responsibilities in the eastern Java region and was called the "Prince of Wĕngker."[68] Remarkably, this same uncle maintained independent diplomatic contact with the Chinese court. When the Ming court received envoys in 1377 and 1379 from both the Wĕngker uncle, whom the Ming considered the "ruler of eastern Java," and Hayam Wuruk's Majapahit court, which was believed by the Chinese to hold authority in "western Java," the Ming court concluded that the Javanese realm was politically divided.[69] The Ming eunuch Cheng Ho held this perception when he visited the "eastern Java capital" with his fleet in 1405, and Chinese envoys were present when the Majapahit monarch of "western Java" invaded this "eastern capital" in 1406—170 Chinese residents were reported to have been accidentally killed in the fighting as the "eastern capital" was ravaged.[70]

While Majapahit inscriptions and other indigenous sources do not support the Ming view that the Majapahit population divided its loyalty between two sovereigns in the fourteenth century, they do demonstrate that there were rival branches of the royal family that resided in several regions of eastern Java.[71] Majapahit's monarchs tolerated the semiautonomy of their Wĕngker kinsmen until 1406, when apparently in response to the increasingly offensive actions of their relatives it became necessary for the Majapahit monarchy to confirm its supremacy over eastern Java.[72] Tolerance of regional semiautonomy was not unusual and, as noted above, was indeed necessary because of the Majapahit state's inability to directly administer all over which it claimed sovereignty. But dependence upon regional allies created a potential for fragmentation when the center showed signs of weakness or when regional subordinates were able to secure outside assistance to support their efforts to reestablish their autonomy from the center.

Modern historians have theorized about the demise of the Majapahit state that followed the 1406 "civil war."[73] In this age north coast ports that were dominated by commercial populations who were converting to Islam were breaking away from Majapahit's political authority. This drive for independence by the north coast commercial enclaves has been traditionally viewed as severely weakening the Majapahit political system. Deprived of their control over the north coast trade, Majapahit's monarchs could no longer depend on trade revenues to support their statecraft and instead had to depend on revenue collections from the land. The refocusing of state revenue demands brought a backlash from regional landed elites, who were already suspicious of the concentration of power in royal hands that was characteristic of the fourteenth century. The various subordinate regions of the state sought to reestablish their semiautonomy by shifting their support among various factions of the royal family who were competing for the Majapahit throne on a regular basis during the fifteenth century or by allying with one or another of the coastal commercial centers that willingly supplied military assistance in return for a region's commitment to provision the coast.

During this fifteenth-century era of supposed decline Majapahit's records (which are quite limited in comparison to those of the previous century) stress the state's cultural activities in the Javanese hinterland. They focus on the flourishing rural economy and its Hindu-Javanese culture rather than continuing to highlight the state's efforts to extend Majapahit's political authority.[74] The 1406 civil war appears to have been a watershed vis-à-vis the state's involvement in the commercial affairs of the coast.

The available evidence suggests that the 1406 civil war was fought in part to bring the populations of the Wĕngker prince's commercial center under control. The heavy concentration of Chinese residents in the "eastern capital" implies that the Wĕngker titleholder administered a commercial center of some importance. This view is consistent with the Wĕngker prince's dispatch of envoys to the Ming court in 1377 and 1379, which presumably was done to solicit commercial exchanges under the Chinese tributary system.[75] The Prince of Wĕngker was also promoting trade during the 1380s and 1390s when he issued the Biluluk Charters, which enhanced that region's commerce. These records suggest that the Wĕngker prince assumed a prominent role as a promoter of Majapahit's commerce, a role appropriate to his seeming regional administrative responsibility for the eastern Java coast.[76] Significantly, it was after Majapahit's conquest of the "eastern capital," which had been visited the year before by Cheng Ho's fleet, that north coast commercial centers began to establish their political autonomy from Majapahit's sovereignty.

These coastal centers and their populations were the Majapahit state's former allies, who had ironically gained their commercial stature largely due to the economic initiatives of Majapahit in the previous century. Majapahit's rulers had initially patronized trade and traders, encouraging the emergence of commercial specialists who were free from subsistence agriculture and traditional social structures, who were preoccupied with trade and commerce, and were members of a new, cosmopolitan, urban, commercial society. During the fourteenth century Majapahit monarchs had utilized trade-derived revenues to institute a new state order, but when the commercial populations began to challenge their authority the land-based rulers could not contain their initiatives. There seems to have been a conscious withdrawal of Majapahit from the coast and a refocusing of its statecraft on the ruler's spiritual rather than his economic and political leadership.[77] If such was the case, then Majapahit's elite intentionally let the coast develop as a separate zone of international trade beyond the Java hinterland and its rural traditions. Thereby Majapahit's fifteenth-century "decline" may actually reflect two corresponding movements: (1) the growing political autonomy of the formerly subordinate north coast ports and (2) the Majapahit state's conscious "internalization" of its statecraft.

Chinese sources support the contention that Majapahit was purposely withdrawing from the coast during the early fifteenth century. The Chinese reported that an agreement had been reached with Majapahit at the beginning of the fifteenth century, such that an enhanced Chinese role in the western archipelago—particularly in the Strait of Malacca region that Majapahit had previously claimed to be subject to its authority—was accepted without challenge by the Javanese. Cheng Ho, when he removed the pirate chief of the Palembang coastal enclave in southeastern Sumatra in 1407 as part of an attempt to rid the area of piracy, claimed to act in the name of the Majapahit monarch. This and other actions by Cheng Ho in the Strait of Malacca region until the 1430s do not seem to have been initiated to destroy Majapahit's authority but rather were the consequence of Chinese understanding that Majapahit's authority in the region by that time was in name only.[78]

The *Pararaton* also suggests that a transition had taken place. It reflects on Majapahit's past glory, highlighting the state's leadership in international commerce during the fourteenth century, but largely ignores the events of the fifteenth century.[79] This focus on the past suggests that the fourteenth-century image was no longer valid and seems to have been projected in retrospect to explain why the Majapahit state was no longer what it had been.

But while Java's ports developed during the fifteenth century as important commercial centers beyond the political authority of the Majapahit state, the ports still needed the hinterland's produce—especially its rice—to be commercially viable. Furthermore, the hinterland elite still required external trade goods to reinforce their legitimacy. The fact that each sector needed the other necessitated continued exchanges between the Javanese coast and its hinterland. The north coast port of Tuban, for example, established its political independence from Majapahit and its elite subsequently converted to Islam, but it retained its close exchange relationship with the Majapahit court.[80] Other ports cultivated economic contact with Majapahit's regional subordinates, who were interested in securing military assistance against Majapahit and pledged their trade in return. In some instances the hinterlands were reluctant to make such commitments and had to be "encouraged" to do so. Tomé Pires, writing at the beginning of the sixteenth century, described the repeated late fifteenth-century wars between the Java coast ports and their hinterlands.[81] Since the coastal-hinterland conflicts continued long after Java's indigenous populations converted to Islam, these hostilities do not seem to have been due to religious differences but are better explained as being the consequence of political and economic competition over the flow of rice and other products from the interior to the coast.[82]

Consistent with this view of the fifteenth-century transitions, the new Mataram state that rose to power in the late sixteenth century was dominated by landed elites based in central Java, who initially suppressed the commercial elite of the coastal ports in an attempt to reestablish the hinterland's control over coastal trade. But in the early seventeenth century the new Mataram state allowed the Dutch to dominate the coastal ports, while Mataram was content to rule the Javanese hinterland. In exchange for foreign commodities supplied by the Dutch, Mataram's rulers guaranteed the periodic delivery of Javanese rice and other hinterland products to the Dutch ports.[83] Mataram's victory effectively internalized Javanese commerce and ended the remaining control of Javanese merchants over the Java Sea trade. Henceforth control over the international trade was assumed by others. In the Strait of Malacca, in Aceh on the northern tip of Sumatra, and in Johor on the southern Malay Peninsula, there emerged successors to the Javanese; and in the eastern archipelago Malay seamen in Brunei and the Sulu Sea assumed control over the regional and Chinese trade with the Spice Islands.[84]

The Transition from Southeast Asia's Classical Age

The study of Southeast Asia's history is problematical in that the region's archaeological remains demonstrate the early development of complex and populous civilizations, but these civilizations produced few settlements that can be called urban centers in the modern sense until the post-1400 era. Discoveries at Ban Chiang and other northeast Thailand sites show some of mankind's earliest bronze metallurgy and developed rice agriculture, but the evolution of Southeast Asian state systems did not take place until the first centuries of the Christian era.[85] Sufficient technology (e.g., the domestication of animals, rice cultivation, metalwork, pottery manufacture, ship construction, and long-distance navigational skills) were available for the emergence of an Angkor or Majapahit in the second millennium B.C., but such development did not occur. When states did begin to come into existence between the third and sixth centuries A.D. they were unevenly distributed, and rather than evolving their own distinctly Southeast Asian cultural traditions, these states were largely influenced by alien ideas and models.

The period in which these early states began to emerge coincides chronologically with the inception of intensive maritime commerce between China and India, which appears to have set in motion the formation of these earliest state systems. By A.D. 700 state development intensified; numerous archaeological sites on the mainland and Java produce sophisticated Buddhist and Hindu statues and reliefs. Yet the sea empire of Śrīvijaya, which is most conspicuous in the accounts of Indian, Arab, and Chinese who had contact with the region during this era, has left few written records of its own, and its archaeological remains are so few that the location of its urban center is still being debated. Most of these early states were located in river plains where there were extensive tracts of land suitable for growing rice with the aid of simple techniques of water and soil management, but again the Śrīvijaya realm was different—it was based on the shores of the Strait of Malacca where fertility was limited.

This book has concluded that two types of early states developed in the

Southeast Asian region, one based on the extraction of the surplus wet-rice production from subject populations, and the other supported by cesses that were levied on long-distance commerce and less dependent upon the quality of local soils and water supplies. In either state type, however, although indigenous contributions to the emerging patterns of regional civilization were important, and despite the region's critical commercial ties to China, the use of Indian ideas and symbols was extensive and was unusual in that this conscious emulation was not the consequence of military conquest or of a subsequent period of imperialist rule by Indians. It appears that these Indian ideas were necessary to motivate peoples who, despite possessing a satisfactory infrastructure to support state development, were largely uninterested in becoming an urban dwelling, monument erecting, commercially motivated society.

Prior to these developments Southeast Asia's society tended to live in herding, hunting, and village settings. Family units usually lived together in clusters that formed the basis for primary social, economic, and political systems. Members of leading families became "chiefs"; some with impressive Indian ceremonial titles were endowed with the ultimate power to allocate goods and privileges authoritatively, while other members of their families discussed decisions with these leaders. The leaders' powers were limited; they were answerable to the community and could not make major policy decisions without community consent.

The autonomy of these local socioeconomic groups began to break down when some of their leaders responded to new opportunities afforded by the intensification of maritime trade that was passing through the region. Numerous regions of the South China Sea that were adjacent to the main international sea route developed, while those away from it—the upriver highlands of the island and mainland, the eastern Indonesian archipelago, and the Philippines (despite having a vast wet-rice basin in central Luzon) did not. Indian culture was localized to legitimize the concentration of power, the collection of grains, and the accumulation of goods by newly emergent "kings." These kings and their entourages usually lived together in a separate urban center. Despite this spacial separation from the locally based socioeconomic systems, the monarch and his elite supporters still shared the customs and traditions of their subjects, and the court-based elite's way of life and their value system were not radically different from their rural subjects; they ate the same food, wore the same clothing, and worshiped the same gods. There was still frequent physical contact between the court and its subject populations, as in the absence of an effective bureaucratic capacity these early states' rulers depended on a network of personal relationships to support them. Kings fulfilled their subjects' continuing expectations of reciprocity via ceremonial redistributions of accumulated material as well as symbolic capital. In exchange for their acknowledgment of the court's spiritual authority—through their participation in and reflection of, in varying degrees, the power of the center—the subordinate centers preserved a great deal of their internal autonomy. Basic decisions on land distribution, irrigation control, punishment of wrongdoers, organization of public functions, and the regulation of family affairs was still largely with the primary socioeconomic units.

The broad extension of trade in the fourteenth century changed all this. In response to the greater global demand for Southeast Asian spices the number of people who engaged in or derived their income from commerce greatly expanded; the repercussions of the intensifying trade even penetrated the local population clusters where farmers in the river-plain states responded to the multiplying demand for their rice, which flowed from the hinterland to provision the coastal centers of trade. Coastal populations in turn exported this rice surplus to new cosmopolitan centers of trade and to the spice production centers of the Indonesian archipelago, where the rice was consumed by the newly specialized populations who grew or collected the spices. The rulers of new expansionist states came to depend on the taxation of commerce rather than of their subject villages. But commercial elites who initiated independent trade relations with the village production centers could make the villages dependent upon them for food or goods instead of upon their royal courts—the villagers could make profits and acquire metals without the intervention of their king. All these developments had begun prior to the arrival of European traders in the sixteenth century.

As in chapter 8's examination of Samudra-Pasai, the Java case study in this chapter has shown the transitions that fourteenth-century Southeast Asian population centers were undergoing. The Majapahit state that came into existence at the end of the thirteenth century was different from those of the earlier age; its authority over its subordinate regions penetrated deeper. The increasing importance of the Indonesian archipelago's spices in international trade resulted in the need to control the flow of rice from the Javanese interior to the coast. Control over territory that produced rice became essential. Thus the loose federations among hinterland population centers that characterized traditional Javanese politics were assaulted by Majapahit's monarchs in an attempt to more effectively concentrate political and economic authority in one dominant center.

As a consequence of these initial transitions, during the fifteenth and sixteenth centuries new Southeast Asian urban centers emerged and assumed an enhanced economic and political role vis-à-vis their subject hinterlands and also accepted their traditional role as the source of cultural identity among subordinate populations. The classical Southeast Asian centers, although they attempted to maintain themselves economically and politically with regard to local-level alliance networks, were vulnerable. The local level, reinforced by kinship and economic ties, had permanence. Clients of local patrons or "big men"—for example, landed elites, tribal chiefs, or in the case of Burma, the Buddhist *saṅgha*—would remain loyal to their leader until the local civilization was destroyed.[86] When the center demonstrated the least sign of weakness, however, its clients rapidly began to express their independence. But the loss of a center was crucial to the local society, for the center provided unity among the various competing local units, if not on a political and economic level then at least in a cultural sense. When an old cultural center was lost regional units competed with each other to become the new center, building new networks of economic and political alliance and underscoring these relationships by establishing new sources of legitimacy—for example, by conversion from syncretic Hindu and Buddhist religious systems to the Theravāda Buddhist and Islamic religious traditions or by fabricating links with eras of past glory, as in the case of Malacca looking backward to the Śrīvijayan age and in Ayudhya and later Thai states where Thai monarchs saw themselves as the legitimate successors to Angkor's royal line. If they failed to initiate such new linkages they languished, and their populations became more isolated and internalized economically, politically, and socially.[87]

However, in looking at the peasant populations subordinate to these centers it would be wrong to view the local societies as being static. A return to the "good old days" might have been desired but was impossible to achieve because the structure of the societies, their economic organization, and their perceptions of the world had been affected by the penetration of more elaborate civilizations during the classical age. There were expectations that had to be fulfilled, for instance the maintenance of the standard of living to which the local peasantry had become accustomed during the glory years of indigenous participation in the supralocal patterns of trade, such as the continued redistribution of wealth from state centers and the provision of certain trade goods like ceramics, spices, and cloth that had become necessities of life. The collapse of one of the classical centers created disorder and had profound cultural consequences as the society attempted to rationalize its disorder. As an aftermath the society often found it necessary to restructure its very existence. New urban centers synthesized the new economic and political forces with the indigenous cultural heritage; their success or failure in making this synthesis in most instances determined their fate in the new commercial age.

It was within these new Southeast Asian urban centers that classical societies and foreign cultures continued to intersect, producing tensions that often precipitated open conflict. But it was also within such urban centers where the synthesis of traditional and "modern," if indeed the process of change can be reduced to this dichotomy, took place. Among some segments of the indigenous population foreign cultures were fully accepted, and traditional ways of doing things were rejected as being backward and the cause of economic and political instabilities. Others chose the opposite course, totally rejecting new opportunities or cultures while reaffirming their old cultural norms, explaining difficulties that arose as the consequence of foreign values that had in various ways corrupted the traditional system.[88] Defenders of the traditional society stressed the need to return to the "pure" cultural forms of some past golden age. A third group attempted to syncretize the other two, selecting the best of their own society while accommodating those foreign ways considered necessary to survival in the ever more complex world order. In such urban centers indigenous political and economic leaders came to terms with the past and present to articulate a future for Southeast Asia.

Abbreviations Used in Notes and Bibliography

ARE	*Annual Report on Indian Epigraphy.* Archaeological Survey of India (Madras, Delhi)
BEFEO	*Bulletin de l'École Française d'Extrême-Orient* (Hanoi, Saigon, Paris)
BKI	*Bijdragen tot de Taal-, Land-, en Volkenkunde (van Nederlandsch-Indië), uitgegeven door het Koninklijk Instituut voor Taal-, Land-, en Volkenkunde (van Nederlandsch-Indië)* (s'Gravenhage, Leiden)
BSOAS	*Bulletin of the School of Oriental and African Studies* (London)
EB	*Epigraphia Birmanica* (Rangoon)
EI	*Epigraphia Indica.* Archaeological Survey of India (Calcutta, Delhi)
EZ	*Epigraphia Zeylonica.* Archaeological Survey of Ceylon (Columbo)
IC	George Coedès, *Inscriptions du Cambodge*
ISCC	*Inscriptions sanscrites du Cambodge et Campa*—August Barth, *Inscriptions sanscrites du Cambodge;* Abel Bergaigne, *Inscriptions sanscrites de Campa*
JA	*Journal Asiatique* (Paris)
JAS	*Journal of Asian Studies* (Ann Arbor)
JBRS	*Journal of the Burma Research Society* (Rangoon)
JESHO	*Journal of the Economic and Social History of the Orient* (Leiden)
JMBRAS	*Journal of the Malay/Malaysian Branch of the Royal Asiatic Society* (Singapore, Kuala Lumpur)
JRAS	*Journal of the Royal Asiatic Society* (London)
JSEAH	*Journal of Southeast Asian History* (Singapore)
JSEAS	*Journal of Southeast Asian Studies* (Singapore)

JSS	*Journal of the Siam Society* (Bangkok)
MKAWAL	*Mededeelingen van de Koninklijke Akademie van Wetenschappen, Afdeeling Letterkunde* (Batavia)
TBG	*Tijdschrift voor Indische Taal-, Land- en Volkenkunde uitgegeven door het Koninklijk Bataviaasch Genootschap van Kunsten en Wetenschappen* (Batavia, s'Gravenhage)
VBG	*Verhandelingen van het Bataviaasch Genootschap van Kunsten en Wetenschappen* (Batavia)

Notes

Chapter 1

1. See Karl L. Hutterer, "Prehistoric Trade and the Evolution of Philippine Society: A Reconsideration," in *Economic Exchange and Social Interaction in Southeast Asia: Perspectives from Prehistory, History, and Ethnography,* ed. Karl L. Hutterer, 177–196.

2. See J. G. de Casparis, "Historical Writing on Indonesia (Early Period)," in *Historians of South-East Asia,* ed. D. G. E. Hall, 126.

3. See Paul Wheatley, "Urban Genesis in Mainland South-East Asia," in *Early South East Asia: Essays in Archaeology, History and Historical Geography,* ed. R. B. Smith and W. Watson, 288–303.

4. George Coedès, *The Indianized States of Southeast Asia,* ed. Walter F. Vella, passim. See Preface, and I. W. Mabbett, "The 'Indianization' of Southeast Asia: Reflections on the Prehistoric Sources," *Journal of Southeast Asian Studies* (henceforth *JSEAS*) 8, 1 (1977): 1–14; 8, 2 (1977): 143–161.

5. This is one of the themes of O. W. Wolters in *Early Indonesian Commerce: A Study of the Origins of Sri Vijaya.*

6. See Kenneth R. Hall and John K. Whitmore, eds., *Explorations in Early Southeast Asian History: The Origins of Southeast Asian Statecraft,* passim.

7. In some cases others were granted land to develop in the core—these might be royal service grants or religious endowments. See chap. 6.

8. Robert Heine-Geldern, "Conceptions of State and Kingship in Southeast Asia," *Far Eastern Quarterly* 2 (November 1942): 15–30; and Paul Mus, *India Seen From the East: Indian and Indigenous Cults in Champa,* trans. I. W. Mabbett and D. P. Chandler.

9. Buchari, "A Preliminary Note on the Study of the Old-Javanese Civil Administration," *Madjalah Ilmu-Ilmu Sastra Indonesia* 1 (1963): 122–133.

10. See Keith W. Taylor, "The Rise of Đai Viet and the Establishment of Thang-long," in Hall and Whitmore, *Explorations in Early Southeast Asian History,* 149–192.

11. See Clifford Geertz's model of the "theater-state" in *Islam Observed,* 36–39. A more recent application and discussion of the Geertz model is Clifford Geertz, *Negara: The Theater-State in Nineteenth Century Bali.* Geertz suggests the centrality of ritual, ceremony, and theatrical behavior generally in an Indianized Southeast Asian state:

> The expressive nature of the Balinese state was apparent through the whole of its known history, for it was always pointed not toward tyranny, whose systematic concentration of power it was incompetent to effect, and not even very methodically toward government, which it pursued indifferently and hesitantly, but rather toward spectacle, toward ceremony, toward the public dramatization of the ruling obsessions of Balinese culture: social inequality and status pride. It was a theatre state in which the kings and princes were the impresarios, the priests the directors, and the peasants the supporting cast, stage crew, and audience. . . . Court ceremonialism was the driving force of court politics; and mass ritual was not a device to shore up the state, but rather the state, even in its final gasp, was a device for the enactment of mass ritual. Power served pomp, not pomp power. (P. 13)

Although this suggests that ceremony constituted an end in itself, Geertz goes on to modify his position, describing ritual as a political instrument that established the court as a faultless image of civilized existence, an "exemplary center" that reflected the order of the universe—the world around it was encouraged to become a rough approximation of its own excellence—and thereby promoted the welfare of the state's subject population.

12. Stanley J. Tambiah, *World Conqueror and World Renouncer: A Study of Buddhism and Polity in Thailand against a Historical Background,* 9–72, provides a useful summary of recent theoretical discussion of divine kingship in both the Hindu and Buddhist traditions, and especially on their application to Southeast Asia. See also Paul Wheatley, *Nāgara and Commandery: Origins of the Southeast Asian Urban Traditions.*

13. John Stephen Lansing, *Evil in the Morning of the World,* reports on the synthesis of indigenous and Hindu/Buddhist conceptions of time and place in Bali.

14. Tambiah, *World Conqueror and World Renouncer,* and Frank E. Reynolds, "The Holy Emerald Jewel: Some Aspects of Buddhist Symbolism and Political Legitimation in Thailand and Laos," in *Religion and Legitimation of Power in Thailand, Laos, and Burma,* ed. Bardwell L. Smith, 175–193.

15. Tambiah, *World Conqueror and World Renouncer,* describes early Southeast Asian states as "galactic polities" (pp. 102–131). Early states were in theory a *maṇḍala,* a core region surrounded by outer regions, and enclosed within a whole—forming an earth-based reflection of the Hindu-Buddhist universe. The "galactic state" was a centered or center-oriented space (as opposed to bounded space), a capital with surrounding territory and manpower over which the state exercised jurisdiction:

> although the constituent political units differ[ed] in size, nevertheless each lesser unit [was] a reproduction and imitation of the larger. Thus we have before us a galactic picture of a central planet surrounded by differentiated satellites, which are more or less "autonomous" entities held in orbit and within the sphere of influence of the center. Now if we introduce at the margin other similar competing central principalities and their satellites, we shall be able to appreciate the logic of a system that is a hierarchy of central points continually subject to the dynamics of pulsation and changing spheres of influence. (Pp. 112–113)

16. J. G. de Casparis, *Prasasti Indonesia II: Selected Inscriptions from the Seventh to the Ninth Century A.D.,* 330–338.

17. Boechari, "Epigraphy and Indonesian Historiography," in *An Introduction to Indonesian Historiography,* ed. Soedjatmoko et al., 50–60.

18. Casparis, *Prasasti Indonesia I: Inscripties uit de Çailendra-Tijd,* and *Prasasti Indonesia II,* passim.

19. Michael Aung-Thwin, "Kingship, the *Saṅgha,* and Society in Pagan," in Hall and Whitmore, *Explorations in Early Southeast Asian History,* 205–256.

20. As opposed to a modern bureaucracy that is composed of specialists who deal with specific responsibilities.

21. George Coedès, *Inscriptions du Cambodge,* vol. 4, 149–150, and M. C. Ricklefs, "Land and the Law in the Epigraphy of Tenth-Century Cambodia," *Journal of Asian Studies* (henceforth *JAS*) 26, 3 (1967): 411–420.

22. With the dual responsibility of administrative function and ritual performance the royal administrators became a secondary force within the state, with their own hereditary rights. This was the case in Cambodia, Burma, and Java. See Coedès, *Indianized States,* passim, and chaps. 6 and 7.

23. Aung-Thwin, "Kingship, the *Saṅgha,* and Society in Pagan."

24. Only with the coming of the Europeans in the sixteenth century was there extended direct penetration by foreign merchants into the Southeast Asian hinterland. Previous to that time Southeast Asian society had successfully responded to the potential for foreign trade by assuming the role of middleman in meeting the demands from international maritime traders for goods and services and by representing the interests of Southeast Asians in facilitating international contacts. On the differing circumstances, see Anthony Reid, "Trade and State Power in 16th and 17th Century Southeast Asia," in *Proceedings, Seventh International Association of Historians of Asia Conference,* 391–419; and M. A. P. Meilink-Roelofsz, *Asian Trade and European Influence in the Indonesian Archipelago between 1500 and about 1630.*

25. Bennet Bronson, "Exchange at the Upstream and Downstream Ends: Notes Toward a Functional Model of the Coastal State in Southeast Asia," in Hutterer, *Economic Exchange and Social Interaction in Southeast Asia,* 39–52. For further discussion of the Bronson model see chaps. 7 and 8.

26. Bronson makes the particularly interesting suggestion that for riverine states wars of conquest and even "extermination" were not only predictable but actually made better economic sense than they would for an inland kingdom because the cost-benefit ratio was more favorable. To conquer a rival coastal center and profit from its commerce, a riverine state needed only to seize its rival's river-mouth center, not its hinterland, in order to dominate the communication networks of its rival's entire drainage basin.

27. See also O. W. Wolters' comments on the Bronson model in O. W. Wolters, "Studying Srivijaya," *Journal of the Malaysian Branch of the Royal Asiatic Society* (henceforth *JMBRAS*) 52, 2 (1979): 1–38.

28. O. W. Wolters, "A Note on the Capital of Srivijaya during the Eleventh Century," *Essays Offered to G. H. Luce by his Friends in Honour of his Seventy-fifth Birthday,* 225–239; O. W. Wolters, "A Few Miscellaneous *Pi-chi* Jottings on Early Indonesia," *Indonesia* 36 (October 1983): 49–64; and Bennet Bronson and Jan Wisseman, "Palembang as Srivijaya: The Lateness of Early Cities in Southern Southeast Asia," *Asian Perspectives* 14, 2 (1976): 220–239. The Bronson model of riverine system statecraft is less comfortably applied to the numerous islands between the Malay Peninsula and the east coast of Sumatra, especially the Riau and Lingga archipelagos and portions of Sumatra's eastern coast that con-

sist of mangrove swamps and coral reefs occupied by Malay seamen—sea nomads, fishermen, and pirates—which constituted centers of semi-independent power that were not based in a drainage system but were still participants in Śrīvijaya's alliance network (see chap. 4).

29. O. W. Wolters, *The Fall of Srivijaya in Malay History,* 39–48. Despite his references to local centers of power, Wolters seems to attribute a high degree of centrality, as well as stability and continuity, to Śrīvijaya. He depicts Śrīvijaya rulers as generous dispensers of wealth and honors to Malay chiefs, who eagerly abandoned their less exciting local centers of power to enjoy honorable and lucrative posts at the state's court: "[their] chief compensation was found in official service in the great capital city, where the court was staffed on an impressive scale and required high dignitaries to perform important ceremonies and duties" (p. 17). While generous redistributions of wealth secured the loyalty of these Malay chiefs, Wolters believes that the bestowal of honors was a more prized reward.

30. Jan Wisseman, "Markets and Trade in Pre-Majapahit Java," in Hutterer, *Economic Exchange and Social Interaction in Southeast Asia.*

31. Ibid., 202, and chap. 9.

32. For a list of goods traded in *wanua* markets, see ibid., 211. This discussion of marketing hierarchy owes much to the study of G. William Skinner, *Marketing and Social Structure in Rural China.* Although the structure of the Javanese marketing system exhibits distinctive features not found in other marketing systems, it is nevertheless instructive to compare Javanese commerce with the hierarchical structure of traditional Chinese marketing as analyzed by Skinner. According to Skinner, a Chinese market town constituted the center of a community of exchange consisting of approximately fifteen to twenty-five villages. This "cell" was an integrated economic system with its own transport, trade, artisan industry, and credit mechanisms, and was organized spatially and temporally as a network of periodic markets. This economic system also defined the social world of the area's inhabitants, since marriage networks, voluntary associations, and clientage relationships usually corresponded to the dimensions of the marketing area. Marketing centers thus facilitated the cultural homogeneity of the local system while simultaneously fostering cultural isolation and differentiation vis-à-vis other systems by minimizing the external contacts of individual households. Javanese data represent much earlier and less voluminous evidence than Skinner's, and the hierarchical marketing system reflected in this data appears to be less complex in structure than the multitiered system described by Skinner. There are, nevertheless, notable similarities. The Javanese *pkĕn* was a designated center of exchange where itinerant and local commercial networks intersected and through which the circulation of goods and services was channeled. By dominating the external trade of the *wanua,* the *pkĕn* reinforced the locality's social and political integration. Thus the centralization of trade was not only a convenience for all participants but also served as a mechanism for minimizing the penetration of the locality by outsiders and controlling their activities, thereby strengthening the social cohesion of the *wanua* by protecting the interests of local merchants and producers.

33. It is unclear if this official *(apkĕn)* was a member of the local community or an outsider appointed by Javanese monarchs. Wisseman notes that *apkĕn* were normally mentioned in lists of *maṅgilala dĕrwaya haji* ("collectors of the king's due"), showing a royal interest in local exchange, but that *apkĕn* clearly

belong to a class of *wanua* officials who were paid for their services in usufruct of *wanua* land (p. 201). There is reference, for instance, to *lmah kapkanan,* land attached to the office of the market official (p. 211).

34. Wisseman identifies communities of potters and their distribution—i.e., marketing—region (p. 203). See also chap. 9.

35. Paul Wheatley, "Geographical Notes on Some Commodities Involved in Sung Maritime Trade," *JMBRAS* 32, 2 (1959): 67–86.

36. Wisseman, "Markets and Trade in Pre-Majapahit Java," 205.

37. See discussion in chap. 9 of the Majapahit realm, where major trade was conducted at urban centers downriver from the royal court.

38. See chap. 5; F. H. van Naerssen and R. C. de Iongh, *The Economic and Administrative History of Early Indonesia,* and Wisseman, "Markets and Trade in Pre-Majapahit Java." One of G. William Skinner's findings *(Marketing and Social Structure in Rural China)* was that in China the tensions between the Chinese state and commerce came to be embodied in a cartographical disjunction: market towns and the boundaries of marketing areas regularly failed to correspond with administration centers and the boundaries of districts. The state tended to superimpose its own divisive pattern upon the various local socioeconomic constellations.

39. Manañjung inscription (A.D. 928), text and translation in H. B. Sarkar, *Corpus of the Inscriptions of Java (up to 928 A.D.),* 227–247.

40. Dhinanaśrama inscription, as translated by Wisseman, personal communication.

41. Kaladi inscription (A.D. 909), as translated and discussed by A. M. Barrett, "Two Old Javanese Copper-plate Inscriptions of Balitung," M.A. thesis, University of Sydney, 1968.

42. Kamalagyan inscription (A.D. 1037), as translated by Wisseman, "Markets and Trade in Pre-Majapahit Java," 206.

43. Wisseman, "Markets and Trade in Pre-Majapahit Java," 208, and Kenneth R. Hall, "International Trade and Foreign Diplomacy in Early Medieval South India," *Journal of the Economic and Social History of the Orient* (hereafter *JESHO*) 21, 1 (1978): 75–98. This was the *maṇigrāmam* itinerant trade consortium.

44. Keith W. Taylor, "Madagascar in the Ancient Malayo-Polynesian Myths," in Hall and Whitmore, *Exploration in Early Southeast Asian History,* 25–60; and Wolters, *Early Indonesian Commerce,* passim.

45. In O. W. Wolters' view, Malay sailors were doing most of the sailing between India and the Malay coast and between Funan and China during this era. See *Early Indonesian Commerce.*

46. Wolters, *Early Indonesian Commerce,* 55–58. Wolters initially placed Koying on the southeastern coast of Sumatra, but recently has argued in favor of its center existing on Java's west coast. Wolters, "Studying Srivijaya," 35.

47. Wolters, *Early Indonesian Commerce,* 34–36. See chaps. 2 and 3.

48. Wheatley, "Geographical Notes on Some Commodities Involved in Sung Maritime Trade," 67–86.

49. Wolters argues that Sumatra's "favored coast" benefited not only from its position vis-à-vis the international route, but also (and more importantly) because it faced western Java. A Bangka Strait passage connected the "favored coast" with the exciting cultural developments taking place in western Java (Koying's base). These Javanese cultural developments were drawn upon by south-

eastern Sumatra's riverine-based chiefs as they asserted their spiritual prowess and thereby mobilized their upriver and coastal populations' participation in the international maritime route. See Wolters, "Studying Srivijaya," 35–36; see also chaps. 4 and 5.

50. Wolters, *Early Indonesian Commerce,* passim; chap. 4; and Wolters, "Studying Srivijaya."

51. Wolters, *Fall of Srivijaya,* 39–48.

52. Boechari, "Some Considerations on the Problem of the Shift of Mataram's Centre of Government from Central to East Java in the 10th Century," in Smith and Watson, *Early South East Asia,* 473–491. See chap. 5.

53. Karl L. Hutterer, "The Evolution of Philippine Lowland Societies," *Mankind* 9 (1974): 287–299.

54. Karl L. Hutterer, *An Archaeological Picture of a Pre-Spanish Cebuano Community.*

55. Java's eminence as a maritime power in Southeast Asia in this era is attested to by the Mongols' 1292 maritime expedition against the Javanese. See chaps. 8 and 9.

56. Kenneth R. Hall, "Trade and Statecraft in the Western Archipelago at the Dawn of the European Age," *JMBRAS* 54, 1 (1981): 21–47.

57. Wolters, *Fall of Srivijaya,* 47.

Chapter 2

An earlier version of this chapter appeared as "The Expansion of Maritime Trade in the Indian Ocean and Its Impact upon Early State Development in the Malay World," *Review of Indonesian and Malaysian Affairs* 15, 2 (1981): 108–135.

1. J. Kennedy, "Early Commerce of Babylon with India," *Journal of the Asiatic Society of Bengal* (1898): 241–288. Babylon imported rice, peacocks, and woods from India in that era.

2. R. E. M. Wheeler, "Arikamedu: An Indo-Roman Trading Station on the East Coast of India," *Ancient India* 2 (1946): 17–124; M. P. Charlesworth, "Roman Trade with India: A Resurvey," in *Studies in Roman Economic and Social History in Honour of Allen Chester Johnson,* ed. P. R. Coleman-Norton, 131–143.

3. Horace Jones, trans., *The Geography of Strabo,* 2.5.12, 17.1.13.

4. W. Schoff, trans., *The Periplus of the Erythraean Sea.*

5. H. Rackham, trans., *The Natural History of Pliny the Elder,* 6.26, 6.1. Pliny claims to list "20,000 facts compiled from 2,000 books by nearly 500 writers," works that have been lost to our age.

6. G. E. Gerini, *Researches on Ptolemy's Geography of Eastern Asia.*

7. Rackham, *Pliny the Elder,* 12.14.

8. Schoff, *Periplus,* 270.

9. Ibid.

10. R. E. M. Wheeler, *Rome Beyond the Imperial Frontiers,* 129.

11. The trade winds blew north in the upper (northern) Red Sea, as opposed to the monsoon winds that seasonally reversed in the lower Red Sea. This necessitated the overland transport of goods from the Nile to Myos Hormos and Berenice, which were located at the point of the wind current's transition. Archaeologists have discovered a network of watering stations between the Nile and these two

Red Sea ports, which have produced quantities of artifacts that document the significant volume of commercial transport across this route as well as Roman inscriptions that attest to the route's importance in the eyes of the Roman state. Michael P. Speidel, professor of history at the University of Hawaii at Manoa, has generously shared this information on recent archaeological discoveries.

12. Schoff, *Periplus,* 19.

13. Ibid., 43–56.

14. Ibid., 52.

15. R. P. Kangle, trans., *The Kauṭilīya Arthaśāstra,* bk. 2. The *Arthaśāstra* was largely composed between the fourth century B.C. and the fourth century A.D.

16. Wheeler, "Arikamedu," 19.

17. Schoff, *Periplus,* 43–54.

18. Ibid., 54. There is no evidence that Barygaza attempted to hang onto its former subordinate ports on the southern coast.

19. Strabo (15.1.4) wrote in his first-century geography that only stray individuals had sailed around India to the mouth of the Ganges (present-day Bengal) and that their accounts were of no use as records of history or places they had seen. Pliny the Elder (bk. 6) had no recent knowledge of Sri Lanka (Ceylon) except that an embassy from the king of the island came to Rome in the time of Claudius (10 B.C.–A.D. 54) soliciting Roman trade. The work of Ptolemy, an astronomer, mathematician, and geographer, represented the height of Roman geographical writings on the India trade.

20. *Paṭṭiṇappālai,* a Sangam poem dating to the first centuries A.D., 1.129, as quoted in K. V. Subrahmanya Aiyer, "Largest Provincial Organizations in Ancient India," *Quarterly Journal of the Mythic Society* 65, 1 (1954–1955): 38. These goods were charged duty and marked with the tiger emblem of the ancient king of that land before they were carried to ships. Similar levies were made on the articles brought in ships, and these goods passed into the country with the royal emblem upon them as well. Excavations of Arikamedu's warehouses substantiate this literary reference. The Arretine ware pottery type found in heavy concentration at Arikamedu has provided cross-dating reference, allowing archaeologists to estimate the height of Roman trade with this port to have occurred between A.D. 30 and 50 (Wheeler, "Arikamedu," 18; Charlesworth, "Roman Trade," 141). Whether one reached Arikamedu, Kaverippumppattinam, or other east coast commercial centers by land or by sea, it is clear that these centers were part of the developing India-Rome trade network by the mid-first century at the latest.

21. Wheeler, *Rome Beyond,* 144–145.

22. Ibid., 138–139. Wheeler notes that the Kushāna empire of northern India was probably absorbing and reminting Roman coinage—on which they patterned their own—explaining the nonexistence of hoards in the north.

23. Rackham, *Pliny the Elder,* 6.101; 12.18/41.

24. Clarence Maloney, "The Beginnings of Civilization in South India," *JAS* 29, 3 (1970): 603–616.

25. See Kenneth R. Hall and George W. Spencer, "The Economy of Kāñcīpuram, A Sacred Center in Early South India," *Journal of Urban History* 6, 2 (1980): 127–151, and Kenneth R. Hall, *Trade and Statecraft in the Age of the Cōḻas,* 162–184.

26. F. Hirth, *China and the Roman Orient,* 42.

27. *Hou Han-shu* [History of the Former Han], as quoted in O. W. Wolters, *Early Indonesian Commerce: A Study of the Origins of Sri Vijaya,* 40. Western traders were careful to keep the Western market value of Chinese silk and Western glassware a secret from the Chinese.

28. Ibid. The high profits and unsatisfied demand for such goods among the Chinese brought attempted imitation, as for example a glass factory that is thought to have been established near Virapattinam on the eastern coast of southern India in the first century. Similarly, Wolters demonstrates that initially Southeast Asian merchants passed off indigenous forest products as *Po-ssu*—Persian or "Western," in origin.

29. George Coedès, *The Indianized States of Southeast Asia,* ed. Walter F. Vella, 20.

30. When Nero debased the metal content of Roman coinage, its prestige crumbled, and there appears to have been a consequent unwillingness to accept Roman coins in trade. Thus hoards of coinage from Nero's reign and after are rarely found in India (Wheeler, *Rome Beyond,* 140–141). Despite the reluctance of Indian traders to accept Roman specie, Roman trade continued to increase after Nero's reign, as evinced by Arikamedu archaeology. Thus trade must have been sustained chiefly by the import of manufactured goods and raw materials from the West, which replaced Roman coins as the medium of exchange.

31. The unwillingness of Indian traders to accept Roman coins in trade after Nero's reign would more adequately explain the decrease in Roman coins in India after the mid-century than do Roman efforts, in response to Pliny's concern, to prevent the export of precious metal. Paul Wheatley, "Satyānṛta in Suvarnadvīpa: From Reciprocity to Redistribution in Ancient Southeast Asia," in *Ancient Civilization and Trade,* ed. J. A. Sabloff and G. C. Lamberg-Karlovsky, 232–233, argues that gold was much more rare in that age.

32. See Sylvain Levi, "Les 'marchands de mer' et leur role dans le bouddhisme primitif," *Bulletin de l'Association Française des Amis de l'Orient* 7 (October 1929): 19–39.

33. Wheatley, "Satyānṛta," 234, 261 n. 4. Wheatley traces the source of the Dīpamkara cult to Sri Lanka, where he found that a group of Anurādhāpura bankers financing trade with Southeast Asia in the sixth century had taken Dīpamkara as their patron saint.

34. This information was supplied by John K. Whitmore of the University of Michigan Center for South and Southeast Asian Studies, summarizing Chinese and Vietnamese language sources.

35. Wolters, *Early Indonesian Commerce,* 42. No doubt a number of what the Chinese court chose to call tributary missions were in fact shrewdly organized commercial ventures by foreign merchants (including Southeast Asians) with no official diplomatic status at all.

36. Wang Gungwu, "The Nanhai Trade: A Study of the Early History of Chinese Trade in the South China Sea," *JMBRAS* 31, 2 (1958): 33.

37. Wolters, *Early Indonesian Commerce,* 157.

38. Ibid., 50–61. Wolters originally believed that Ko-ying was based on the southeastern Sumatra coast but more recently has argued that Ko-ying was based on the Java side of the Sunda Strait. See O. W. Wolters, "Studying Srivijaya," *JMBRAS* 52, 2 (1979): 35.

39. H. A. Giles, trans., *The Travels of Fa-hsien, 399–414, or Record of the Buddhist Kingdoms,* 79.

40. F. H. van Naerssen and R. C. de Iongh, *The Economic and Administra-*

tive History of Early Indonesia, 18–23. Giles *(Travels of Fa-hsien)* places Yeh-p'o-t'i on the Java coast; van Naerssen argues that Yeh-p'o-t'i was on the Borneo coast.

41. Coedès, *Indianized States,* 54; Wolters, *Early Indonesian Commerce,* 35.
42. Wolters, *Early Indonesian Commerce,* 154.
43. Wheatley, "Satyānṛta," 234.
44. Wolters, *Early Indonesian Commerce,* 154.
45. Wang Gungwu, "Nanhai Trade," 20.
46. When in the late thirteenth century the Mongols went against this tradition and sent their military against Java and other Southeast Asian states they became caught up in the various interstate rivalries, and their expedition bogged down. See Coedès, *Indianized States,* 189–201.
47. O. W. Wolters, *The Fall of Srivijaya in Malay History,* 38–48.
48. R. C. Majumdar, *Hindu Colonies in the Far East,* 23.
49. J. C. van Leur, *Indonesian Trade and Society: Essays in Asian Social and Economic History,* 98. I. W. Mabbett, "The 'Indianization' of Southeast Asia: Reflections on the Historical Sources," *JSEAS* 8, 2 (1977): 155, outlining the sources and interpretations, shows that the possibilities are endless, for conceivably Brahmans might have functioned as traders, and Kṣatriya might have been bearers of Sanskrit culture. See also chap. 3.
50. A case study of the "Indianization" process that asks these questions is John Stephen Lansing, "The 'Indianization' of Bali," *JSEAS* 14, 2 (1983): 409–421.
51. Hall, *Trade and Statecraft in the Age of the Cōḷas.*
52. Burton Stein, *Peasant State and Society in Medieval South India;* and Kenneth R. Hall, "Peasant State and Society in Cōḷa Times: A View from the Tiruviḍaimarudūr Urban Complex," *Indian Economic and Social History Review* 18, 3–4 (1982): 393–410.
53. George W. Spencer, "The Politics of Plunder: The Cholas in Eleventh Century Ceylon," *JAS* 35, 3 (1976): 405–419.
54. Stein, *Peasant State and Society.*
55. Noboru Karashima, "The Power Structure of Chola Rule," *Second International Conference Seminar of Tamil Studies,* 233–238.
56. I do not wish to imply, however, that south Indian kings were universally weak relative to their locally entrenched agrarian subjects and were subordinate at all times to the interests of a propertied local agrarian elite. See Hall, "Peasant State and Society in Cōḷa Times."

Chapter 3

An earlier version of this chapter appeared as "The 'Indianization' of Funan: An Economic History of Southeast Asia's First State," *JSEAS* 13, 1 (1982): 81–106.

1. Paul Wheatley, *The Golden Khersonese: Studies in the Historical Geography of the Malay Peninsula before* A.D. *1500,* 114–115, discusses the historical merit of the records of these envoys.
2. Paul Pelliot, "Le Fou-nan," *Bulletin de l'École Française d'Extrême-Orient* (hereafter *BEFEO*) 3 (1903): 252.
3. Louis Malleret, *L'archeologie du delta du Mekong.* Whether K'ang T'ai traveled to Oc-èo is unclear.
4. It must be remembered that in terms of modern scale Oc-èo would not be

considered a major urban center. Indeed, its smallness has led historians to question its identity as the initial urban center of Southeast Asia. See Paul Wheatley, "Urban Genesis in Mainland South East Asia," in *Early South East Asia: Essays in Archaeology, History and Historical Geography,* ed. R. B. Smith and W. Watson, 298; also Bennet Bronson, personal communication. Archaeological remains of Oc-èo include various articles dating to the second through fifth century A.D., including Indian rings, seals, and jewels; coins of the Roman emperors Antoninus Pius (138–161) and Marcus Aurelius (161–180); Sassanid cabochons; and Chinese bronzes of the later Han and Wei dynasties (25–550). See Malleret, *L'archeologie du delta du Mekong,* passim.

5. Not until the French undertook the reclamation of lands in the Mekong Delta in the nineteenth century was the delta region as fully under cultivation. See Charles Robequain, *The Economic Development of French Indochina.*

6. Malleret, *L'archeologie du delta du Mekong;* W. J. van Liere, "Traditional Water Management in the Lower Mekong Basin," *World Archaeology* 11, 3 (1980): 265–280.

7. Paul Pelliot, "Quelques textes chinois concernant l'Indochine hindouisée," *Etudes Asiatiques* 2 (1925): 243-263, especially pp. 246–249. The Kauṇḍinya myth seems to suggest that Indians were using Malay ships on their passage through Southeast Asia, since the myth does not specify that he was traveling on an Indian ship, but that a man from beyond the seas was on a ship of unremarkable and thus presumably local origin. Chinese records report that ships were built in Funan's ports, including those that the Funan monarch Fan Shih-man ordered constructed for his third-century expedition of conquest against Malay Peninsula entrepôts.

8. Jean Przluski, "La princesse a l'odeur de poisson et la nāgī dans les tradition de l'Asie Orientale," *Etudes Asiatiques* 2 (1925): 265–284.

9. Gabriel Ferrand, "Le K'ouen-louen et les anciennes navigations interocéaniques dans les mers du sud," *Journal Asiatique* (henceforth *JA*), July-August 1919: 15, as translated in George Coedès, *The Indianized States of Southeast Asia,* ed. Walter F. Vella, 22.

10. R. C. Majumdar, *Hindu Colonies in the Far East,* and *Ancient Indian Colonization in South-East Asia.*

11. J. C. van Leur, *Indonesian Trade and Society: Essays in Asian Social and Economic History.*

12. See J. G. de Casparis, "Historical Writing on Indonesia (Early Period)," in *Historians of South-East Asia,* ed. D. G. E. Hall, 126.

13. Coedès, *Indianized States,* 14–35.

14. O. W. Wolters, *Early Indonesian Commerce: A Study of the Origins of Sri Vijaya.*

15. Updating and applying Wolters' thesis to a variety of scholarship published in the 1970s, I. W. Mabbett concludes in his article "The 'Indianization' of Southeast Asia: Reflections on the Prehistoric Sources," *JSEAS* 8, 1 (1977): 1–14 and *JSEAS* 8, 2 (1977): 143–161, that the sea barrier between India and Southeast Asia was significant to the process of "Sanskritization" (see M. N. Srinivas, *Caste in Modern India and other Essays,* and J. F. Staal, "Sanskrit and Sanskritization," *JAS* 22 [1963]: 261–275) in Southeast Asia. Firstly, the Indian influences were not constantly maintained by migration or other contacts, thus Southeast Asian kingdoms initially may have outwardly exhibited a high degree of Indian style but over the centuries became less and less Indian and more indigenous in

character. Secondly, there was no dominant caste group (e.g., Brahmans) who migrated to Southeast Asia, but small numbers of individuals from different castes and regional origin; thus Mabbett finds Southeast Asia's Sanskrit lore emerging from the contact to be of a highly syncretic character, more so than that found in "Sanskritized" areas of the Indian subcontinent. Thirdly, the "Sanskritization" process in Southeast Asia was initiated by elites from the communities being Sanskritized rather than by agents (i.e., Indians) of Sanskritization, as is revealed in the fact that Southeast Asia never developed a hierarchical caste system with foreigners assuming high-order roles in relation to the indigenous population. Instead Sanskritization legitimized the elite status of the indigenous rulers. "There is therefore a false dichotomy between Indian cultural imperialism and local autonomy. . . . We should not demand that Indian dominance be represented by the extirpation of local genius . . . [the Indian tradition] merely influenced" (p. 161).

16. O. W. Wolters, "Khmer 'Hinduism' in the Seventh Century," in Smith and Watson, *Early South East Asia,* 427–441. Wolters' thesis is an extension of the theoretical work of Marshall Sahlins, "Poor Man, Rich Man, Big Man, Chief: Political Types in Melanesia and Polynesia," *Comparative Studies in Society and History* 5 (1963): 285–303. Mabbett, in " 'Indianization' of Southeast Asia," broadly applying Wolters' thesis to early Southeast Asia, argues that the earliest Southeast Asian "states" (e.g., Funan, Champa, and Śrīvijaya) do not fit the description of "a regular Indian-style centralized state on the model of the *Arthaśastra*" (p. 148), but may be better understood as "a conglomeration of principalities" (p. 154).

17. Wolters, "Khmer 'Hinduism,' " 454; O. W. Wolters, *History, Culture, and Region in Southeast Asian Perspectives,* 4–8.

18. Wolters, *History, Culture, and Region,* 9–12.

19. See Robert E. Revere, "Ports of Trade in the Eastern Mediterranean," in *Trade and Market in the Early Empires,* ed. Karl Polanyi et al., 38–63. In exchange for facilitating this trade Funan's rulers would have been permitted to collect fees from those using their port.

20. Malleret, *L'archeologie du delta du Mekong,* 3:324 and 4:131. Malleret's methodology has been criticized and his dates are subject to revision. The Funan origin myth as well as K'ang T'ai's report both stress a well-developed agrarian sector previous to the fifth- and sixth-century dates Malleret assigned to the remaining evidence of a hydraulic system. Malleret suggested that the canal network also provided passage for ships through the Bassac estuary to the South China Sea, allowing them to avoid the treacherous passage around Cape Ca-mau on the southernmost tip of the Vietnam coast, which would have also protected seamen from the typhoons of the South China Sea. By passing "through" the Funan realm sailors could have caught the monsoon winds off the southern Vietnam coast to navigate northward in relative safety to China. See also B. P. Groslier, *The Art of Indochina,* 56.

21. Mabbett, " 'Indianization' of Southeast Asia," 11, 145. "Let us remember that the port of Oc-èo, however highly organized and cosmopolitan, need not have been the hub of a dense population sustained by intensive irrigated rice cultivation as were some kingdoms [e.g., Angkor] much later . . ." (p. 148).

22. Louis Finot, "Les inscriptions de Mi-so'n (No. 111)," *BEFEO* 4 (1904): 923.

23. Van Liere, "Traditional Water Management in the Lower Mekong Basin."

24. See Fig. 2, "Reconstruction of the natural environment of the lower Mekong Basin at the dawn of history," in ibid., 268.

25. Van Liere's study argues that early delta populations began to control water by constructing moats that surrounded settlement centers, with canals and roads radiating from the settlements—a view consistent with Malleret's reconstruction of the Funan hydraulic system. However, van Liere believes these early systems to have been localized rather than the centralized systems of the Angkor period that Malleret characterized Funan's hydraulic system as being similar to (ibid., 271). Van Liere also believes that the inhabitants of these settlements lived in houses built on stilts that were partly placed over the water along the canal or riverbanks:

> Such living conditions are quite satisfactory from several points of view: easy transportation in both the wet and the dry season by boat or over land; fish in the canal and rice on the floodlands; coconut and other useful garden trees along the bank and aquatic vegetables in the canal. (P. 269)

Such a description of settlement in the early Mekong Delta is consistent with the reports of fifth- and sixth-century Chinese records of Funan (Pelliot, "Le Fou-nan," 261–262, 269–270, 284–285). The history of the Liang dynasty *(Liang shu)* —which officially recorded events between A.D. 502 and 556 but also includes a good deal of earlier material in its section on foreign countries—notes that "several scores of families have a pond in common where they draw water," providing evidence of a local hydraulic system of the sort van Liere proposes was typical of early village hydraulic systems (ibid., 284–285).

26. This was the case with Malacca in the fifteenth century, importing rice from Java because it had no hinterland producing rice. See M. A. P. Meilink-Roelofsz, *Asian Trade and European Influence in the Indonesian Archipelago between 1500 and 1630,* 36–38. In reply to Mabbett, it may be suggested that a matter of scale and timing is significant in evaluating this earliest era of Funan's existence. During the Funan era there was as yet little indigenous competition to undermine Funan's commercial leadership, and the maritime trade itself was not of the volume it was when the maritime passage totally replaced the overland caravan routes as the principal line of commercial intercourse between East and West. Oc-èo was not a large port in modern terms; there was in this age, as compared to later eras, limited travel along the maritime passage. Accommodations —including food stocks—for visiting merchants were not beyond the capacity of Funan's initial population base (see van Liere, "Traditional Water Management in the Lower Mekong Basin," 269). O. W. Wolters argues a similar case in his defense of southeastern Sumatra coastal centers as being the focus of Śrīvijaya's hegemony. See O. W. Wolters, "Studying Srivijaya," *JMBRAS* 52, 2 (1979): 1–38.

27. See Kenneth R. Hall, "An Introductory Essay on Southeast Asian Statecraft in the Classical Period," in *Explorations in Early Southeast Asian History: The Origins of Southeast Asian Statecraft,* ed. Kenneth R. Hall and John K. Whitmore, 1–24.

28. Paul Wheatley, "Satyānṛta in Suvarṇadvīpa: From Reciprocity to Redistribution in Ancient Southeast Asia," in *Ancient Civilization and Trade,* ed. J. A. Sabloff and C. C. Lamberg-Karlovsky, 227–283. Wheatley's economic transformation thesis is based on works by Marshall Sahlins *(Stone Age Economics)* and

Talcott Parsons (see Talcott Parsons and Neil J. Smelser, *Economy and Society: A Study in the Integration of Economic and Social Theory*).

29. Wheatley, "Satyānṛta," 228.

30. Chinese records document Funan's rulers' wealth. K'ang T'ai, as noted above, reports that taxes were paid in gold, silver, pearls, and perfumes (Pelliot, "Le Fou-nan," 254). But he also notes that the population was contented and was not inclined to commit theft. The *Liang shu* speaks of royal ritual, and especially that associated with burials (ibid., 269–270). The high incidence of ritual objects among the archaeological remains at Oc-èo and other Funan sites substantiates the importance of religious ritual in the Funan domain. Carvings in stone accentuate royalty and their role in ritual (Groslier, *Art of Indochina,* 56–65).

31. See Eric Wolf, *Peasants*.

32. Wheatley, "Satyānṛta," 247.

33. Bennet Bronson, "The Late Prehistory and Early History of Central Thailand," in Smith and Watson, *Early South East Asia,* 315–336. The Chansen archaeological site is located north of modern Lopburi in the Chao Phraya River system.

34. Malleret, *L'archeologie du delta du Mekong*.

35. Ibid. The dates of such trade goods must be used with caution, as these items of value might normally have made their way along the trade routes over the course of months, years, or centuries.

36. Groslier, *Art of Indochina,* 63.

37. Pelliot, "Le Fou-nan," 257–270, 294.

38. Bronson holds that external contacts between central Thailand and the Funan realm were of a commercial and religious rather than political nature—archaeological evidence will not support the conclusion that central Thailand was ever conquered or colonized by outsiders (ibid., 324). Goods from Funan would have reached this site via the Chao Phraya Delta, passing through the Tun-sun realm that was conquered by the Funan monarch Fan Shih-man in the third century. See H. H. E. Loofs, "Problems of Continuity Between the Pre-Buddhist and Buddhist Periods in Central Thailand, with Special Reference to U-Thong," in Smith and Watson, *Early South East Asia,* 342–351.

39. Pelliot, "Le Fou-nan," 265.

40. C. Jacques, " 'Funan,' 'Zhenla': The Reality Concealed by These Chinese Views of Indochina," in Smith and Watson, *Early South East Asia,* 371–379. Jacques argues that there is a need to understand what "Funan" really was instead of accepting the term as representing a well-ordered state system, as he thinks too many historians in the past have done. "Funan" was known to the Chinese but was not a "state" recognized in Khmer genealogical records that originate with the original Kauṇḍinya.

41. Loofs, "Problems of Continuity."

42. A. H. Christie, "Lin-i, Fu-nan, Java" in Smith and Watson, *Early South East Asia,* 283–284. Christie, too, is questioning the existence of a "Funan" state, preferring to consider the Funan realm as a cultural center.

43. Wolters argues for the use of the terms "localized"/"localization" to describe this process of cultural adoption/adaptation. See Wolters, *History, Culture, and Region,* 53 n. 58. Wolters thinks that the term "localization" better captures "the initiatives of the local elements responsible for the process [of localization] and the end product . . . while 'adaptation,' 'syncretism,' and 'synthesis'

give the impression of the outcome of the process [and the] . . . reconciliation of originally contradictory differences."

44. Chapter 1 discussed premodern marketing systems in Southeast Asia. The initial substitutions of Southeast Asian goods for those of international origin is discussed in Wolters, *Early Indonesian Commerce*.

45. Pelliot, "Quelques textes chinois." This was the era in which Roman empire merchants made their first diplomatic visits to the Chinese court (see chap. 2).

46. Coedès, *Indianized States,* 275 n. 5, discusses Coedès and Wolters' conversation on this issue.

47. Ibid., 36.

48. Pelliot, "Le Fou-nan," 263.

49. Jayavarman (d. 514), the last Funan monarch to rule from Vyādhapura, noted in a petition to the Chinese court presented by the Indian Buddhist monk Nāgasena that he reigned as Śiva's equivalent on earth (Śiva Giriśa) "dwelling on the mountain" (Pelliot, "Le Fou-nan," 260; Coedès, *Indianized States,* 61; Groslier, *Art of Indochina,* 49–50). This reinforcement of the ruler's supernatural powers was related to traditional views that the successful ruler could influence one's post-death status. In later times the Khmer capitals of Cambodia also had at their heart a mountain (an area higher than that surrounding or a temple mountain), which was constituted as a pantheon of the gods of the personal and regional cults practiced throughout the realm. Eleanor Moron's study of Angkor Wat bas reliefs (c. 1131) notes that on Angkor Wat's southern face the dead enemies of King Sūryavarman II are descending into the underworld to be judged. The eastern face shows Sūryavarman as Yama, the Hindu tradition's judge of the dead, which is also the Indian god Viṣṇu's role in a passage of the *Mahābhārata* epic (Eleanor Moron, "Configurations of Time and Space at Angkor Wat," *Studies in Indo-Asian Art and Culture* 5 [1977]: 217–267). O. W. Wolters notes that Khmer monarchs as early as the seventh century were also depicted as Yama, the judge of the dead, only at that earlier time Khmer monarchs (and thus Yama) were associated with Śiva, not Viṣṇu. "Merit-earning conduct on the ruler's behalf promoted the subject's prospects of spiritual rewards . . . obedience and disobedience to the king had consequences in the afterlife" (Wolters, *History, Culture, and Region,* 62).

50. In addition to its position near the sacred mountain, there were additional advantages to Vyādhapura's inland location. In this age an inland capital was easier to defend than was a coastal center. As noted, the Malay seamen who were essential to Funan's ports' economic vitality could have turned to piracy when the sea route was unproductive and might even have pillaged the land surrounding their port base. Southeast Asian oral tradition as well as Chinese chronicles are full of tales about piracy in Southeast Asia and the raids of Malay seamen upon coastal centers. By moving Funan's capital to the interior, Hun P'an-huang not only mystically integrated his rule over the realms of the land and the sea by focusing his legitimacy on Vyādhapura and its mountain-based cult, but this shift also placed his capital in a more secure position defensively away from the more vulnerable seacoast. Chapter 7 discusses the difficulties the Cham domain encountered from such maritime communities in a later era.

51. See Wheatley, *Golden Khersonese,* 286, fig. 46. The subjugation of the Cham domain is documented in the first-known Sanskrit inscription attributed to

Funan, issued in the late third century by Fan Shih-man's descendant Fan Ch'an and placed at Vo-canh within the Cham realm. See Coedès, *Indianized States,* 40 and 278, nn. 38, 39.

52. Pelliot, "Le Fou-nan," 265–266. Loofs, "Problems of Continuity," argues that Fan Shih-man died before he could conquer Chin-lin, a victory that would have given him control over the precious metals (silver) of lower Burma that were absent in the remainder of the Funan realm.

53. Wheatley, *Golden Khersonese,* 16.

54. Wheatley, "Satyānṛta," 243.

55. This consolidation of Funan's control over the coastline was of economic importance to Funan and demonstrates the significance of trade-related revenues to Funan's economic well-being. Traders at this time were few in number and were thus easier to control. As visitors, merchants were vulnerable to the reasonable revenue demands and controls of their host. Revenues the Funan state derived from trade would have been utilized for public works as well as for territorial expansion of the type undertaken by Fan Shih-man. By controlling the entire coastline between Funan and the Malay Peninsula the Funan rulers monopolized the contemporary maritime trade passing through Southeast Asia and the revenues associated with the trade. Bennet Bronson has pointed out that such efforts to control interregional commerce stimulated state formation in central Thailand (see Bronson, "Late Prehistory and Early History of Central Thailand"). A similar argument could be made in relation to Fan Shih-man's efforts to totally control the maritime channels.

56. Coedès, *Indianized States,* 29; Wheatley, *Golden Khersonese,* 252–272; O. W. Wolters, "Tāmbraliṅga," *Bulletin of the School of Oriental and African Studies* (henceforth *BSOAS*) 21, 3 (1958): 587–607.

57. Funan's followers among the land-based populations were attracted to serve under Funan's rulers because of the magical qualities of the ruler—the supernatural powers attributed to the Funan ruler that could be shared with his loyal subjects. The seamen's loyalty was more directly the consequence of trade prosperity alone. Thus, as is argued later, when Funan's monopoly over the sea channels collapsed the Malay seamen quickly shifted their loyalties to more prosperous ports.

58. Wheatley, *Golden Khersonese,* 47–51.

59. Coedès, *Indianized States,* 40, and George Coedès, "Le date de l'inscription sanskrit de Vo-Canh," *Indian Historical Quarterly* 16 (1940): 484–488.

60. That is, Fan Shih-man's sister had married someone sufficiently powerful to provide her son with a manpower base from which he could seize power from Fan Shih-man's son. As noted earlier, marriage alliances between one's family and subordinate groups were intended to solidify one's power. However, such marriages could enhance the prestige of the allied family, providing them with a legitimate claim to the throne as a member of the extended royal family. For comparison on the role of kinship in later Khmer society, see A. Thomas Kirsch, "Kinship, Genealogical Claims, and Societal Integration in Ancient Khmer Society: An Interpretation," in *Southeast Asian History and Historiography: Essays Presented to D. G. E. Hall,* ed. C. D. Cowan and O. W. Wolters, 190–202.

61. See Pelliot, "Le Fou-nan," 271–278. Chinese court records report the reception in 357 of tribute from a Funan king named Chan-t'an, who was noted to be a patron of the Indian Hindu religion. Significantly, "Chandan," in its

Sanskrit form, was a royal title of the Kushāna monarchs, suggesting that Funan had contact with northern Indian culture prior to the rise of the Gupta monarchs, ca. 320. Ibid., 252, 255, 269; and Sylvain Levi, "Kanishka et S'ātavāhana," *JA* (January-March 1936): 61-121. Levi proposes that Chan-t'an was an Indian usurper of the Funan throne, although his evidence of this is inconclusive.

62. Wolters, "Khmer 'Hinduism,' " 428.

63. Pelliot, "Le Fou-nan," 252, 268.

64. Ibid., 299, a passage translated from the *Liang-shu*.

65. Possibly he could have come from the Kushāna realm with which Fan Ch'an had entered relations. Artistic evidence from the fifth century does reveal Persian artistic influence in Funan. Statued figures wear short tunics, sashes, and the boots of horsemen, all reflecting a northwestern Indian source. It is unclear, however, whether these came to Funan via diplomatic or commercial channels. See Coedès, *Indianized States,* 46-47.

66. Most recently I. W. Mabbett notes in his general study of the patterns of Indianization that fourth- and fifth-century evidence is more convincing testimony of direct Indian political influence (Mabbett, " 'Indianization' of Southeast Asia," 147).

67. Wheatley, "Satyānṛta," 244-245, stresses the role of Brahmans in this Indianization process, but notes problems in determining their origin. Wheatley argues, as do other historians, that although all evidence of a Brahman presence is post-eighth century in date, it is reasonable to expect similar practice in early times.

68. The Fan prefix was used by the Chinese in their records of Funan history to designate the indigenous element of the Funan royal line, as opposed to other family prefixes; for example, the Chu prefix was used to identify people native to India. See Pelliot, "Le Fou-nan," 252 n. 4; Coedès, *Indianized States,* 276 n.16. This evidence is normally cited as proof that Funan was not being ruled by kings emphasizing an Indian heritage in pre-fifth-century Funan history.

69. Pelliot, "Le Fou-nan," 251-252.

70. See O. W. Wolters, *The Fall of Srivijaya in Malay History,* 39-48. While Wolters' emphasis is on embassies being sent during eras of upheaval in Southeast Asia, this study also takes into account political unrest in China to explain interruptions in tributary missions (e.g., see chap. 2).

71. This date is derived from a Ta Prohm inscription dated A.D. 478; see n. 72.

72. The identification of the Funan prince who issued the inscription is from George Coedès; see Coedès, "Deux inscriptions sanskrites du Fou-nan," *BEFEO* 31 (1931): 1-8; Coedès, "A New Inscription from Fu-nan," *Journal of the Greater India Society* 4 (1937): 117-121. Van Liere, "Traditional Water Management in the Lower Mekong Basin," notes that the Khmer artificial lakes at Angkor were intended more for the "service of the gods" than for the "service of man" and argues that these "theocratic hydraulic works" actually impeded irrigation agriculture. In this light—and consistent with van Liere's suggestion that elaborate irrigation projects were not necessary to support early wet-rice cultivation in the Mekong Delta during the era Malleret associates with the construction of Funan's hydraulic system—it may be that Funan's "water management system" had greater ceremonial than economic value, and the construction of the water management projects may better document the Indianization taking place in the Funan realm during the fifth and sixth centuries. See also Paul Wheatley's comments on Funan civilization, especially his discussion of the Oc-èo region's

hydraulic system, in *Nāgara and Commandery: Origins of the Southeast Asian Urban Traditions,* 119–163.

73. Coedès, "Deux inscriptions sanskrite du Fou-nan"; "A New Inscription from Fu-nan."

74. Georges Maspero, *Le Royaume de Champa,* 77.

75. Since Fan Shih-man's conquest around A.D. 200, Lin-yi had been a "vassal state" of Funan.

76. Ultimately both were replaced by the new Sumatra entrepôt of Kan-t'o-li and its successor Śrīvijaya as the dominant entrepôt in the Java Sea realm. See Wolters, "Studying Srivijaya."

77. Wolters, *Early Indonesian Commerce,* passim.

78. The earliest epigraphic evidence of Java's irrigation agriculture is provided in a fifth-century inscription from a site in western Java near present-day Jakarta (J. Noorduyn and H. Th. Verstappen, "Purnavarman's River Works near Tugu," *Bijdragen tot de Taal-, Land- en Volkenkunde uitgegeran door het Koninklijk Institut voor Taal-, Land- en Volkenkunde* (hereafter *BKI*) 128 [1972]: 298–307; see chap. 5). O. W. Wolters believes eastern Java's wet-rice civilization began around the fifth century as well (Wolters, *Early Indonesian Commerce,* 201). Interestingly, comparative studies of Java's and the mainland's systems of irrigation agriculture argue that while later Angkorian civilization used a system of wet-rice agriculture derived from Indian technology (Bernard P. Groslier, *Angkor, Art and Civilization,* 107–112) Java's basic methods of irrigation management were quite different (C. A. Fisher, *South-East Asia: A Social, Economic, and Political Geography,* 75).

79. The presence of an Indianized culture on the western Borneo coast was only temporary. Historians have proposed that this was due to the fluctuations of the maritime trade and the refocusing of the trade on rival commercial centers that brought the demise of early "Indianized" entrepôts on the Borneo coast. No further development of an Indianized base took place thereafter. See F. H. van Naerssen and R. C. de Iongh, *The Economic and Administrative History of Early Indonesia,* 18–23.

80. Pelliot, "Le Fou-nan," 267.

81. Wolters, *Fall of Srivijaya,* 39–48.

82. Maspero, *Le Royaume de Champa,* 77–78.

83. Pierre-Yves Manguin, "La traversée de la mer de Chine méridienale, des dètroits à Canton, jusqu'au 17e siècle (La question des Iles Paracels)," *Actes du XXIXe Congrès international des Orientalistes* 2 (1976): 110–115.

84. I. W. Mabbett characterizes both Funan and Lin-yi during this era as "a conglomeration of semi-piratical rival ports and lowland river valley populations . . ." (Mabbett, " 'Indianization' of Southeast Asia," 154). George Coedès' last reconstruction of late fifth-century Cham history argues that Fan Tang of Lin-yi was overthrown by a usurper (a rival faction?) one year after the 491 Chinese recognition by a descendant of Yang Mah, a great Cham ruler of the earlier (430s and 440s) fifth century, whose royal line had been usurped by Fan Tang. Lin-yi's new ruler, Chu Nong, reigned for six years, but was drowned in 498 while leading a naval expedition/raid against Ton-king (Chiao-chi). See Coedès, *Indianized States,* 59.

85. See R. Stein, "La Lin-yi," *Han-Hiue* (Bulletin du centre d'études sinologiques de Pekin) 2 (1947): 1–54. This also is a comment on the Chinese relationship with Ton-king. Research by Keith W. Taylor, *The Birth of Vietnam,* demon-

strates that Chinese interaction with the Red River Delta region during these times was minimal and was more concerned with extracting tribute and holding Ton-king as an outpost and port region to facilitate maritime contact with the southern China realm. Cham raids against Ton-king's lands, controlled by an indigenous Vietnamese elite, were of little concern to the Chinese, whose main interest was in keeping the sea channels open between Ton-king and Canton.

86. Coedès, *Indianized States,* 56–57. Considering this 431 date, the concerns of Ho-lo-tan/t'o for the safety of its shipping may best be seen as a response to the shift of Malay seamen to Cham ports and the initial attempts of Cham rulers to replace Funan as the dominant intermediary in the China trade. In the 430s Lin-yi was under the authority of Yang Mah, the strongest of Lin-yi's fifth-century rulers. Among Yang Mah's activities were numerous maritime raids against Ton-king, raids that necessitated the support of Malay seamen. Such plundering expeditions were no doubt an incentive for former Funan seamen to transfer their base to Cham ports.

87. A useful summary of Indian statecraft is provided by Louis Dumont, *Religion, Politics and History in India, Collected Papers in Indian Sociology,* 62–88.

88. Coedès, "Deux inscriptions sanskrites du Founan," references to *King* (Śrī) Jayavarman.

89. This clerical aspect of Brahman service is examined in an essay by F. D. K. Bosch, "The Problem of the Hindu 'Colonisation' of Indonesia," *Selected Studies in Indonesian Archaeology,* 3–22.

90. From the *Liang shu,* Pelliot, "Le Fou-nan," 270.

91. At his new capital Vaiṣṇava statues predominate that are similar in style to those being produced in the contemporary Gupta realm in northern India, but go beyond the late Gupta empire's icons in their harmony and balance, notably in their free-standing style. The archaeological remains of Phnom Da demonstrate local initiative and the refinement of the Indian models (Groslier, *Art of Indochina,* 60–65). Coedès, "Deux inscriptions sanskrites du Fou-nan," notes that Guṇavarman, the son of Jayavarman (also the father of Rudravarman) was also a patron of Viṣṇu, while in that same era at the end of the fifth century Pūrṇavarman, who was establishing his authority over western Java (see above and chap. 5) was also a Vaiṣṇava patron. Coedès notes the similarity of references to Viṣṇu's footprints in Guṇavarman's and Pūrṇavarman's inscriptions: Guṇavarman founded a temple that was said to contain the footprints of Viṣṇu, while Pūrṇavarman symbolized his authority by reference to the placing of Viṣṇu's (Pūrṇavarman's) footprints to mark the areas that were subject to his authority.

92. On the history of Chen-la and its legacy from Funan, see Wolters, "Khmer 'Hinduism,' " and "North-Western Cambodia in the Seventh Century," *BSOAS* 37, 2 (1974): 355–384.

93. Groslier, *Art of Indochina,* proposes that the shift of the Funan capital to the Angkor Borei region may have corresponded to a geological transition in the Mekong Delta as the river systems changed their course, making the former Funan agricultural core unfit for cultivation and necessitating the local population's movement to the higher grounds surrounding Angkor Borei (p. 61). Van Liere, "Traditional Water Management in the Lower Mekong Basin," also suggests that a climatic or geological transition might have brought the demise of the Funan area, noting the abandonment of the floodlands of the Mekong Delta by the tenth century (p. 271).

Chapter 4

An earlier version of this chapter appeared as "State and Statecraft in Early Srivijaya," in *Explorations in Early Southeast Asian History: The Origins of Southeast Asian Statecraft,* ed. Kenneth R. Hall and John K. Whitmore, 61–105.

1. O. W. Wolters, *The Fall of Srivijaya in Malay History,* 19–48.

2. Trade in the early centuries A.D. went across the Gulf of Thailand to Funan ports, then proceeded across the isthmus from the Bay of Bandon to various west coast points of disembarkation. By the fifth century Malays had shifted the route south to the Strait of Malacca. See O. W. Wolters, *Early Indonesian Commerce: A Study of the Origins of Sri Vijaya,* 30–48.

3. Wolters, *Fall of Srivijaya,* 9. Wolters has rethought his earlier focus on the external and coastal concentration of Śrīvijaya's power, however, agreeing with me ("State and Statecraft in Early Srivijaya") that the key to the Śrīvijaya ruler's authority was his ability to associate himself with spiritual prowess and supernatural qualities in promoting his legitimacy among both the upriver and downriver populations of the river systems of Sumatra. See O. W. Wolters, "Studying Srivijaya," *JMBRAS* 52, 2 (1979): 1–38. Concentrating on this internal aspect of Śrīvijaya's authority, Wolters argues that the Śrīvijaya ruler "promoted sensations of psychological well-being among his followers, for his person was the effective ceremonial centre" (p. 24). Wolters then uses this view of the Śrīvijaya monarch as an indigenously defined ruler to postulate that riverine settlements of Śrīvijaya's upriver hinterland were more closely linked than Bennet Bronson's model (discussed in chap. 1) suggests was true. Not by extracting riverine produce (Bronson's focus), but by redistributing treasures derived from foreign trade to maintain his "glittering court and honor his entourage" (p. 24), the Śrīvijaya monarch acquired control of a network of riverine settlements whose inhabitants participated in the ruler's adventures and provided him with the key members of his entourage. This upriver hinterland, Wolters postulates, was the highland Malāyu kingdom, the realm of the mountains attributed to the Śrīvijaya monarch by foreign sources, which eventually fell subject to the Javanese monarch Kĕrtanagara in the second half of the thirteenth century. See also O. W. Wolters, *History, Culture, and Region in Southeast Asian Perspectives,* 23.

4. Wolters, *Fall of Srivijaya,* 8 (quoting Chou Ch'u-fei).

5. K. A. Nilakanta Sastri, *The History of Srivijaya,* 113 (Malay text and English translation).

6. For a bibliography of early Dutch archaeological studies of the southeastern Sumatra area, see Wolters, "Studying Srivijaya," nn. 20, 45.

7. See F. M. Schnitger, *The Archaeology of Hindoo Sumatra,* and Stanley J. O'Connor, Jr., *Hindu Gods of Peninsular Siam,* assorted maps and discussions. As a participant in the 1974 Palembang archaeological expedition of the Lembaga Purbakala dan Peninggalan Nasional (The Indonesian Archaeological Institute), I was able to form my own impressions of the Palembang area. The terrain of this region is essentially low and flat. There is little topsoil in this part of Sumatra, and one quickly encounters a hard red clay when excavating. Despite this natural handicap, local rice agriculture is an important source of food, utilizing both wet-rice and dry-rice technologies. One of the major rice-producing areas lies between the two dated seventh-century inscriptions: Kedukan Bukit and Talang Tua. The Kedukan Bukit inscription was found near the Kedukan Bukit

River, which leads to the foot of Bukit Seguntang, the highest hill in the Palembang area and a major source of remains for the early Śrīvijaya period. Moving toward the interior (and toward Jambi), the next high ground is Talang Tua where, as the Talang Tua inscription states, the king of Śrīvijaya dedicated a deer park. Unfortunately, my survey of the area between did not produce remains dating to this early period (see map 4). One problem in identifying the pre-tenth-century culture is the lack of evidence—particularly of a walled city of the Oc-èo type, which the Buddhist pilgrim I-ching indicated Palembang to be in 671 when he reported that in "the fortified city of Fo-shih" there resided a thousand Buddhist priests (see J. Takakusa, trans., *A Record of the Buddhist Religion as Practiced in India and the Malay Archipelago*). Twelfth- and thirteenth-century Chinese accounts also describe Palembang as a city surrounded by a brick wall. While traders dealt inside the wall, the people lived either scattered about outside the city or on the water on rafts of boards covered over with reeds (F. Hirth and W. W. Rockhill, *Chau Ju-kua: His Work on the Chinese and Arab Trade in the Twelfth and Thirteenth Centuries, Entitled Chu-fan chi,* 60). Bukit Seguntang is the most likely place in the Palembang area to correspond with I-ching's description. See Schnitger, *Archaeology of Hindoo Sumatra,* 1–4, for a description of the various statues discovered at this site. For a discussion of the dating of the Bukit Seguntang Buddha, see Nik Hassan Shuhaimi, "The Bukit Seguntang Buddha: A Reconsideration of its Date," *JMBRAS* 52, 2 (1979): 40–49.

We also excavated a site called Sarangwaty, which is located southwest of Telaga Batu (now known as Sabokingking), where a standing Bodhisattva Avalokiteśvara (see p. 87) was recovered as well as hundreds of small clay Buddhist stupicas. The stupicas, which contain small clay punch-marked seals roughly the size of a dime, were deposited in a rounded hole under the statue site, seemingly to sanctify the ground under the statue. This same practice of depositing stupicas under Buddhist statues has been found at the Borobudur in central Java. Avalokiteśvara, whose ability to help mankind reached even to the deepest and most unpleasant of the Buddhist purgatories, was particularly appropriate as a symbol of the Śrīvijaya monarch and his claimed powers. Affinity for this Bodhisattva in southeastern Sumatra was still strong in the thirteenth century when Kĕrtanagara consecrated a tantric Avalokiteśvara (Amoghapāśa) there and proclaimed that it was to be worshipped as an incarnation of his father (see chap. 9). Further excavations in the immediate area contributed no supporting remains from the pre-tenth-century period.

Edward McKinnon has associated Chinese porcelain he collected in the Bukit Seguntang area with the T'ang period and argues that these sherds may be associated with Śrīvijayan settlement corresponding to the I-ching reference (see McKinnon, "A Note on the Discovery of Spur-Marked Yueh-Type Sherds at Bukit Seguntang Palembang," *JMBRAS* 52, 2 [1979]: 50–58). Chinese ceramics experts have demonstrated that the green glazed stoneware was manufactured in the kilns of south China's Chekiang province during the T'ang era (Wolters, *History, Culture, and Region,* 22–23, n. 14). Further, unglazed stoneware of the type I recovered at Śrīvijaya sites has been found in quantity in the archaeological remains of Siraf on the Persian Gulf, the T'ang era terminus for Middle Eastern trade with Asia (this information was shared by David Whitehouse of The British School at Rome, Italy, who is studying 'Abbāsid era ceramics). Our 1974 excavations at Palembang revealed limited data supportive of Śrīvijayan civilization.

While we were able to easily identify the fourteenth- and sixteenth-century population centers, we did not excavate a definitive pre-tenth-century site. The reasons for this are varied, including the possibility that Palembang was not the center of Śrīvijaya. For the present I will explain our failure as being due to the dense settlement patterns of modern Palembang and the expectation that evidence of the old city is hidden under a layer of asphalt. Also, it is likely that early settlement patterns were similar to those of today, with people living in wooden houses along the various small tributaries that flow into the Musi River. Indeed, the Kedukan Bukit inscription was found near one such waterway. As a result, decomposition, fire, and yearly floods have probably taken their toll on much of the early archaeological remains of the Śrīvijaya state. For a summary of the 1974 expedition, see Bennet Bronson and Jan Wisseman, "Palembang as Srivijaya: The Lateness of Early Cities in Southern Southeast Asia," *Asian Perspectives* 19, 2 (1978): 220–239.

8. Wolters, *Early Indonesian Commerce,* 87–138.

9. From the Arab geographer Abū Zaid; see G. Ferrand, "L'empire sumatrannais de Crivijaya," *JA* 20 (1922): 57; and G. R. Tibbetts, *A Study of the Arabic Texts Containing Material on South-East Asia,* 29, 33–34.

10. Ferrand, "L'empire sumatrannais," 57; Tibbetts, *Study of the Arabic Texts,* 29, 33–34.

11. Nilakanta Sastri, *History of Srivijaya,* 113–115; J. G. de Casparis, *Prasasti Indonesia II: Selected Inscriptions from the Seventh to the Ninth Century* A.D., 2–6, 10–11.

12. Casparis, *Prasasti Indonesia II,* 32–46; 6–15.

13. Nilakanta Sastri, *History of Srivijaya,* 115–116. An equivalent of the Kotakapur inscription has been discovered at Palas Pasemah, near the southern coast of Sumatra and across the Sunda Strait from Java. See map 4 for the locations of these inscriptions. Information on the Palas Pasemah inscription was generously supplied by the Lembaga Purbakala dan Peninggalan Nasional staff, Jakarta.

14. The Sanskrit text and English translation of the ninth- or tenth-century inscription from Karimum Besar is provided in B. R. Chatterji, *History of Indonesia,* 195–196. The inscription honors a local ruler who was a patron of Mahāyāna Buddhism, the school favored by Śrīvijaya's monarchs. Nilakanta Sastri, *History of Srivijaya,* 119–121.

15. Casparis, *Prasasti Indonesia II,* 15–46. One of the problems in defining the relationship of the Telaga Batu inscription to the Palembang area is the location where the inscription was found. Telaga Batu, now known as Sabokingking, was one of the residences of the post-1500 Palembang sultanate. Also found at this site were thirty inscribed stones (including the three seventh-century inscriptional fragments discussed by Casparis, pp. 6–15), which appear to have been collected elsewhere and brought to this site where they were deposited near a sultan's grave, possibly because they were considered to have some desirable magical power. This may have been the case with the Telaga Batu stone as well, which judging from its size would have required no small effort to move. A similar plight could have befallen the other Palembang inscriptions and remains. Geding Suro, a site between Sabokingking and the river, was a major Muslim *caṇḍi* complex in the sultanate period and was also the source of three pre-tenth-century Buddhist statues that are now in the Palembang museum. Bukit Seguntang, another major source for the earlier period, is now the site of a Muslim cemetery

and pilgrimage center. In the latter cases, either the Śrīvijaya remains were moved to these spots or Muslim religious complexes were built on land that was already known to have magical qualities.

16. Nilakanta Sastri, *History of Srivijaya,* 120.

17. In local tradition *nāga*s were spirits superior to man that inhabited subaquatic paradises, dwelling at the bottoms of rivers, lakes, and seas. They were keepers of the life-energy that is stored in these earthly waters; they had the power to attract or control rain and were the guardians of the riches of the oceans. *Nāga*s were thus widely believed to be the source of fertility, prosperity, and earthly health. Local belief emphasized the Śrīvijaya monarch's special relationship with water and thus with the *nāga* spirits that symbolized water. The seven-headed *nāga* that encompassed the Telaga Batu stone drew from this tradition and localized Mahāyāna Buddhist mythology:

> Now Muchalinda, a prodigious cobra, dwelt in a hole amongst the roots. He perceived, as soon as the Buddha had passed into the state of bliss, that a great storm cloud had begun to gather, out of season. Thereupon he issued quietly from the black abode and with the coils of his body enveloped seven times the blessed body of the Enlightened One; with the expanse of his giant snake-hood he sheltered as an umbrella the blessed head. Seven days it rained, the wind blew cold, the Buddha remained in meditation. But on the seventh, the unseasonable storm dispersed. . . . In this legend and in the images of the Muchalinda-Buddha a perfect reconciliation of the antagonistic principles is represented. The serpent, symbolizing the life force that motivates birth and rebirth, and the savior, conqueror of that blind will for life, severer of the bonds of birth, pointer of the path to the imperishable Transcendent, here together in harmonious union open to the eye a vista beyond all the qualities of thought. . . . It is said by some that when the Buddha began teaching his doctrine, he soon realized that men were not prepared to accept it in its fullness. They shrank from the extreme implications of his vision of the universal Void. Therefore, he committed the deeper interpretation of reality to an audience of nāgas, who were to hold it in trust until mankind should be made ready to understand. . . . Not until some seven centuries had passed was the great sage Nāgārjuna, "Arjuna of the Nāgas," initiated by the serpent kings into the truth that all is void. And so it was he who brought to man the full-fledged Buddhist teachings of the Mahāyāna. (Heinrich Zimmer, *Myths and Symbols in Indian Art and Civilization,* 67–68)

18. Another inscription found at Telaga Batu, also dating from the late seventh century, records a lengthy *prasasti* that had been issued on the occasion of a great victory by the king leading his troops against his revolting subject (Casparis, *Prasasti Indonesia II,* 6). An insurgent had led "an army of the king's proper slaves" against the king. This was stated to be *"adharmeṇa,"* employing a common Indian expression of being against the proper code of conduct for a certain person's status. As punishment for acting *adharmeṇa,* the enemy troops had been annihilated. The fighting mentioned in this fragment is alluded to in another fragment as well. Troops of the enemies *(ripugaṇam)* fled or surrendered "at the approach of my army" (ibid., 8).

19. Lines 8, 19, 21, and 22.

20. Casparis, *Prasasti Indonesia II,* 25.

21. Ibid.

22. Talang Tua, line 6, in Nilakanta Sastri, *History of Srivijaya,* 114; Kotakapur, line 7, ibid., 115–116; Kotakapur, line 6; Telaga Batu, line 28, in Casparis, *Prasasti Indonesia II,* 36; Kotakapur, line 7; Telaga Batu, line 26.

23. Line 25. Buddhists, like Hindus, believe that man has multiple lifetimes in which to purify his soul so that it may be reabsorbed into the cosmic absolute from which it originally came (achievement of *Nirvāṇa*). The aim of the Buddhist was thus to gain release from the cycle of rebirths. The Theravāda way stressed self-discipline and meditation—sometimes under the direction of a teacher *(thera)*—that led to the ultimate loss of individuality. That of Mahāyāna sought the same goal, but with the help of heavenly Buddhas and Bodhisattvas—those who had achieved enlightenment but like the Buddha had postponed their own ultimate *Nirvāṇa (pari-Nirvāṇa)* to assist their fellow man in his quest. The Vijrayāna, "The Vehicle of the Thunderbolt," was a third way that depended on the supernatural—release was achieved through the acquisition of magical powers. Vijrayāna's sacred literature were the Tantrās, textbooks of mystical experiences, secret documents that were written in a mysterious language that revealed magical formulas *(mantra),* symbols, rituals, and spirits—especially goddesses (Tārās) and the spirits of the dead—that could activate an energy force that allowed the devotee to achieve rebirth after death into a Buddhist heaven. A *tantrā-mala,* "immaculate as a consequence of Tantrā," offered access to this life beyond death.

24. Line 16, Casparis, *Prasasti Indonesia II,* 5, 34. In the Buddhist religious tradition these three vices caused human suffering and sorrow and bound man to the cycle of rebirths, prevented his achievement of salvation (*Nirvāṇa,* his release from the cycle), and thus forced man to remain an earth-dwelling being.

25. G. A. Wilken, *Handleiding voor de Vergelijkende Volkenkunde van Nederlandsh-Indie,* 80.

26. Line 2; Sujipto Wirjosuparto, "Shrivijaya and Majapahit," *Hemisphere* 14, 9 (1970): 29.

27. Jean Sauvaget, trans., *Les marveilles de l'Inde,* 302, from the *'Ajā'ib al-Hind* (ca. 1000); Tibbetts, *Study of the Arabic Texts,* 47.

28. William Marsden, *The History of Sumatra,* 301.

29. Ferrand, "L'empire sumatrannais," 57; Tibbetts, *Study of the Arabic Texts,* 33. See chapter 5 for a discussion of this reference to Abū Zaid.

30. Hirth and Rockhill, *Chau Ju-kua,* 61.

31. Nilakanta Sastri, *History of Srivijaya,* 114. In Buddhism, *bodhi* signifies enlightenment; "The Three Jewels" form the basic profession of faith of Buddhism: "I go for refuge to the Buddha; I go for refuge to the Doctrine *(Dharma);* I go for refuge to the [monastic] Order *(Saṅgha)*."

32. Casparis, *Prasasti Indonesia II,* 10.

33. Ibid. Casparis' translation is: "praising the absent king is like somebody trying to glorify the sun during an eclipse."

34. The *'Ajā'ib al-Hind* (ca. 1000), reports that the Śrīvijaya ruler demanded a levy of twenty thousand dinars, no small sum, as right of passage before he would allow a Jewish merchant to continue his voyage to China (Tibbetts, *Study of the Arabic Texts,* 44). Such extravagant levies not only brought wealth to the Śrīvijaya ruler and his loyal subordinates, but also could well have antagonized merchants, who may not have been displeased when the Cōḷas eliminated Śrīvijaya's control over the strait region's trade in the next century.

35. For a discussion of the Cōḷa raid and its meaning to Śrīvijaya's eleventh-century statecraft, see George W. Spencer, *The Politics of Expansion, the Chola Conquest of Sri Lanka and Sri Vijaya,* 100–150.

36. Line 9. Casparis, *Prasasti Indoensia II,* 33, 39.

37. Ibid., "to divide into small parts . . . to spend the gold and jewels in order to destroy my keraton [*kraton*] . . ."

38. This is indicated in the Arab legend and symbolized in the redistribution of wealth at the death of a king. Abū Zaid's reference states that a king was remembered for the number of gold bricks left behind. The days of his reign, remembered by the number of gold bricks available for redistribution to his people, symbolized the king's ability to keep the system prosperous. According to Abū Zaid, it was for leaving behind great wealth that a king was rewarded with a place in history. Ferrand, "L'empire sumatrannais," 57; Tibbetts, *Study of the Arabic Texts,* 33–34.

39. O'Connor, *Hindu Gods of Peninsular Siam,* 59. O'Connor notes a "Srivijayan style" Mahāyāna Buddhist iconography on the Malay Peninsula and suggests a connection between the statuary and the portraits of deified individuals. He connects this practice with the eastern Java bathing place at Jalatunda (977). See also W. F. Stutterheim, "The Meaning of the Hindu-Javanese *caṇḍi,*" *Journal of the American Oriental Society* 51 (1931): 1–15, who proposed that Javanese *caṇḍi* statuary was shaped to portray deceased kings in the form of a deity; and Alastair Lamb, "A Note on the Tiger Symbol in Some Southeast Asian Representations of Avalokitesvara," *Federated Museums Journal* 6 (1961): 89–90, who describes the distribution of Tantric Buddhist statuary that he believes symbolized Śrīvijaya's control over the eastern Malay coast.

40. Hirth and Rockhill, *Chau Ju-kua,* 60.

41. The word for "oath" *(sumpah)* in the inscription is Malay rather than Sanskrit, reflecting the extensive local content in this act of oath taking. The Sumatran tradition of oath taking is discussed in Hall, "State and Statecraft," 90.

42. Line 21, Casparis, *Prasasti Indonesia II,* 43–44; lines 25 and 26, ibid., 45–46.

43. His later account of the method of extracting camphor from trees in Sumatra's interior adds veracity to his description. Ferrand, "L'empire sumatrannais," 52–53; Tibbetts, *Study of the Arabic Texts,* 28.

44. "Fragment A," Casparis, *Prasasti Indonesia II,* 2–6.

45. L. C. Damais, "Études soumatranaises III. La langue B des inscriptions de śrī Wijaya," *BEFEO* 54 (1968): 523–566.

46. O. W. Wolters, "A Few Miscellaneous *Pi-chi* Jottings on Early Indonesia," *Indonesia* 36 (October 1983): 54.

47. From Chao Ju-kua's *Chu-fan chih* of 1225, which presents passages from the *P'ing-chou k'o-t'an,* compiled by Chu Yü, translated by Wolters, "A Few Miscellaneous *Pi-chi* Jottings," 52–53. This *sūtra* and the Buddhist Tantric tradition were still important in the Śrīvijaya realm during the late eleventh century, as reflected in the comments of Chu Yü, whose writings in 1118–1119 on Chinese material culture incorporated his personal experiences during the time his father had been the chief administrator of the Canton port from 1099 to 1102:

> In Canton I [Chu Yü] once attended a public feast. The foreigners assembled in the [government] office. The foreign headman introduced someone from San-fo-ch'i [Śrīvijaya] and said that he could recite the *K'ung-ch'ueh* [Pea-

cock] *ming wang sūtra.* My view is that Buddhist works which [contain] *dharani* [magical formulas] are incomprehensible. . . .

48. Casparis, *Prasasti Indonesia II,* 19, 29, and 37 n. 4.

49. The Śrīvijaya king's perception of his new state is represented in the Telaga Batu inscription's multiple references to *huluntuhāṅku,* "the domain of the conquered and common people [*hulun*] and the ruling class [*tuhāṅ*]" (Casparis, *Prasasti Indonesia II,* 26). One could make a case that the Śrīvijaya king described here was a member of an "alien aristocracy" who was able to adjust his ambitions to the local Sumatran environment. Even if this were the case, the Telaga Batu inscription clearly emphasizes that indigenous tradition was the basis for and defined the initial development of the Śrīvijayan state.

50. See Keith W. Taylor, "Madagascar in the Ancient Malayo-Polynesian Myths," in Hall and Whitmore, *Explorations in Early Southeast Asian History,* 25–60.

51. Casparis, *Prasasti Indonesia II,* 19. Casparis believes that the *rājaputra* were sons of concubines of the Śrīvijaya king.

52. Ibid. See fig. 3 for a reconstruction of the early Śrīvijaya political system.

53. Ibid. Casparis translates *hāji-pratyaya* "royal sheriffs," indicating that their responsibility was to keep peace among the commoners *(hulun).*

54. Ibid., 20, 32, 37. Casparis translates *mūrdhaka* "somebody at the head of some group," and its position in the Telaga Batu inscription suggests that the people they controlled were commoners *(hulun).* This is undoubtedly an example of assigning a respectable Sanskrit title to a previously existing group of indigenous elites who are best described as "chiefs."

55. See the discussion of bondage in early Southeast Asia in chap. 6; and Anthony Reid, ed., *Slavery, Bondage and Dependency in South-East Asia.*

56. F. D. K. Bosch, "The Problem of Hindu 'Colonisation' of Indonesia," *Selected Studies in Indonesian Archaeology,* 3–22. The organization of the earlier southeast Sumatra port of Kan-t'o-li included Buddhist advisors of the Brahman type (Wolters, *Early Indonesian Commerce,* 221–223). In the Śrīvijaya period a similar group supported the king of the new dominant port, but by that time their status, as reflected in the Telaga Batu inscription, was considered lower than that of many other administrative and military officials.

57. Wolters, *Early Indonesian Commerce,* 229–253, and "Srivijayan Expansion in the Seventh Century," *Artibus Asiae* 24 (1961): 417–424. With the discovery of the Palas Pasemah inscription and archaeological evidence of an early settlement on the southeastern tip of Sumatra, the possibility exists that the old Kan-t'o-li port was located at Palas Pasemah, and that this area was brought under Śrīvijaya's authority in a way similar to Malāyu.

58. Wolters, *Early Indonesian Commerce,* 229–250.

59. "Fragment A," Casparis, *Prasasti Indonesia II,* 2–6.

60. Ibid., 45 n. 73.

61. David E. Sopher, *The Sea Nomads,* 93.

62. Ibid., 321.

63. Wolters, *Fall of Srivijaya,* 15. The island in the Riau Archipelago known as Karimum Besar, as noted above, has an inscription dating to the Śrīvijaya period (see map 4). See also Tibbetts, *Study of the Arabic Texts,* 31.

64. Casparis, *Prasasti Indonesia II,* 42 n. 52.

65. "Fragment A," line 11, ibid., 5.

66. Ibid., 37.

67. "Charged by me with . . ." (line 15) ibid., 42.

68. Casparis, *Prasasti Indonesia II,* 44.

69. Ibid., 42. The oath administered in the Khmer empire also required more than the testimony of loyalty to the state, as one specifically swore to become the king's eyes, feeding local information back to the center. See L. P. Briggs, *The Ancient Khmer Empire,* 151.

70. In Indonesian inscriptions *vaṇiyāga* is used to distinguish long-distance or seafaring merchants. It may be derived from the Sanskrit *vaṇij/vaṇik,* "merchant." But *niaga* is a Malay word for "trade" and with its verbal prefix *ber-* becomes *berniaga.* Therefore, unless this is a back formation, the derivation from *vaṇij* seems unlikely.

71. Casparis, *Prasasti Indonesia II,* 2. The *Ling wai tai ta* (Hirth and Rockhill, *Chau Ju-kua,* 60) regarded Malays living on rafts of boards as Śrīvijaya's principal inhabitants, a people "scattered about" the local river. Such inhabitants could well have been alluded to by the hinterland populations as "migratory men."

72. The *'Ajā'ib al-Hind* (ca. 1000) notes the confinement of merchants to the Śrīvijaya capital, which was readily accepted because of fear of wild animals (e.g., crocodiles) that were said to attack those who attempted to penetrate the interior. This report describes the Śrīvijaya capital:

> Some houses are built on the land, but most float on the water, kept up by pieces of wood tied together in the form of a raft and last forever. They do this for fear of fire, for their houses, constructed of wood, are very inflammable, and when one catches fire all are burnt down. Placed on the water, the houses are well protected, and if fire is detected each owner cuts the cables, floats away and then ties up elsewhere far from the conflagration. Whenever they do not like a particular quarter they can always move. The houses in the bay are arranged in streets, and the water between the houses is very deep. It is fresh water which arrives from the high country, enters the estuary and flows on to the sea, as does that of the Tigris. (Tibbetts, *Study of the Arabic Texts,* 47)

73. Hirth and Rockhill, *Chau Ju-kua,* 68.

74. See Karl Polanyi et al., *Trade and Market in Early Empires.*

75. Tibbetts, *Study of the Arabic Texts,* 53.

76. Anker Rentse, "Gantang of Kelantan," *JMBRAS* 11 (1933): 242–244.

77. From the *P'ing-chou k'o-t'an* of Chu Yü, chap. 2, as translated by Wolters, "A Few Miscellaneous *Pi-chi* Jottings," 55. High-quality frankincense was a product of "the West" (the Middle East or India) although Indonesian substitutes were also categorized as frankincense by the Chinese. See Wolters, *Early Indonesian Commerce,* passim.

78. For a discussion of the geography of the Musi River Delta and the implications of this geography to Śrīvijaya's history, especially with regard to consistency with foreign references to Śrīvijaya's geography, see O. W. Wolters, "Landfall on the Palembang Coast in Medieval Times," *Indonesia* 20 (1975): 1–57; and Wolters, "A Note on Sungsang Village at the Estuary of the Musi River in Southeastern Sumatra: A Reconsideration of the Historical Geography of the Palembang Region," *Indonesia* 27 (1979): 33–50.

79. Śrīvijaya's involvement in this international dialogue is initially documented in the accounts of Chinese Buddhist pilgrims who regularly stopped at

Śrīvijaya on their way to and from India. The dated Ligor inscription from Nakhọn Si Thammarat attests that the Śrīvijaya kings were enthusiastic sponsors of Mahāyāna Buddhism and did not confine their patronage to Sumatra. The effort to create monastic centers far from the royal court—especially in the region of the eastern Malay Peninsula coast that was at the edge of the Śrīvijaya state where the Śrīvijaya ruler was least likely to have exercised day-to-day control—was perhaps intended to establish a spiritual dialogue among the scattered Malay trading centers that would provide a bond of loyalty to the Śrīvijaya ruler as the supreme benefactor. Later Śrīvijaya monarchs endowed Buddhist monasteries at Nālandā, the foremost international center of Buddhist scholarship in those times, and in southern India. The Indian ruler of the Nālandā area of northern India assisted in this donation, and the inscription from Nālandā recording the collaboration expresses the nature of the ideological tie that drew the Śrīvijaya and Indian monarchs and their realms together as participants in a cultural system that transcended political and geographical boundaries. See Hirandanda Sastri, *Nālandā and Its Epigraphic Material,* 101–102. See also chap. 8.

80. Bronson, in Bronson and Wisseman, "Palembang as Srivijaya: The Lateness of Early Cities in Southern Southeast Asia," argues that the Śrīvijaya realm did not have a continuous history as a consequence of these economic fluctuations and instead should be better understood as periodically coming into existence when the international trade route offered sufficient opportunities to acquire trade-derived revenues to facilitate the alliance networks necessary for Śrīvijaya's existence. Bronson further argues that Śrīvijaya's center, as a consequence, likely shifted among several rivermouth entrepôts in the Malacca Strait region. The fluctuating fortunes of a Malay riverine state are further discussed by Bronson in Bennet Bronson, "Exchange at the Upstream and Downstream Ends: Notes Toward a Functional Model of the Coastal State in Southeast Asia," in *Economic Exchange and Social Interaction in Southeast Asia,* ed. Karl L. Hutterer, 39–52, as discussed and applied to Śrīvijaya in chap. 1.

81. Nilakanta Sastri, *History of Srivijaya,* 80.

82. Wolters, *Early Indonesian Commerce,* 266 n. 33, and "A Note on the Capital of Srivijaya during the Eleventh Century," *Essays Offered to G. H. Luce by his Friends in Honour of his Seventy-fifth Birthday,* 225–239. The decay of Śrīvijaya may well have predated the 1025 raid. Three tenth-century inscriptions from western Lampung Province reflect the entry of the western coast as a participant in the patterns of Asian trade. See L. C. Damais, "Études d'epigraphie Indonesienne, III. Liste des principales inscriptions datées de l'Indonésie," *BEFEO* 46 (1952–1954): 98–103, no. 275 (Bawang), no. 283 (Batu Bedil), and no. 289 (Ulu Belu), and Damais, "Études Soumatranaises, I. La date de l'inscription de Hujung Langit ("Bawang"); II., L'inscription de Ulu Belu," *BEFEO* 50 (1960): 275–310. One of these inscriptions is in Old Javanese; one is in Old Malay, but seems to have a Javanese style; the third is in Sanskrit, but is written in Javanese script. All reflect a Javanese orientation to this early trade. Previous archaeological research has virtually ignored Sumatra's west coast, yet Bennet Bronson of the University of Pennsylvania Museum, who conducted a preliminary survey of potential sites during the summer of 1973, found a considerable amount of surface material in the Barus area—particularly pot sherds and Sung porcelain. In 1088, Tamil merchants were active at Lobo Tua near Barus (see K. A. Nilakanta Sastri, "A Tamil Merchant Guild in Sumatra," *Tijdschrift voor Indische Taal-, Land-, en Volkenkunde uitgegeven door het Bataviaasch Genootschap van Kunsten en Wetenschappen* [hereafter *TBG*] 72 [1932]: 314–327). Such evidence may

well indicate that by the eleventh century the Strait of Malacca was no longer the focal point of island trade, as alternative routes were available and were being used by the various maritime traders. See the discussion of this tenth-century evidence in chap. 5.

83. In contrast to the thriving and peaceful trade center depicted in Chu Yü's 1118–1119 account quoted above is that of Chou Ch'u-fei (1178):

> San-fo-ch'i is on an important thoroughfare in the southern ocean for all foreigners using the maritime route. . . . Traders from all . . . countries must pass through this area to reach China. The country [of San-fo-ch'i] has no products, but its people are skillful in warfare and attack. They digest medicine in their bodies, and weapons cannot wound them. They attack on land and sea and are foremost in both [forms of warfare]. . . . All neighboring countries therefore submit [to San-fo-ch'i]. If foreign ships traveling through this region do not enter the country, [San-fo-ch'i] is bound to send out an expedition to destroy them. . . . Among its dependencies is Fo-lo-an [Kuala Berang in Trengganu on the western Malay Peninsula coast], whose chief is chosen and appointed by San-fo-ch'i. . . . (From Chou Ch'u-fei's *Ling wai tai ta,* as noted in Chao Ju-kua and translated by Wolters, "A Few Miscellaneous *Pi-chi* Jottings," 56.)

Wolters argues that it is difficult to see why such force was necessary if Śrīvijaya's monarch received tribute as his share of customs duties and other profits from his network of ports, as had been the case in earlier times. Such control measures, Wolters holds, would have been applied only if the Śrīvijaya port did not constitute all the possible ports of call, and this reference suggests that in that late twelfth-century era Śrīvijaya did not exercise rigorous authority over the strait region. This Śrīvijaya, which had no products and relied on force to compel ships to use its port, was in a state of decline in a general era of transition in Southeast Asian commerce (see chap.8). Wolters also notes that in this commentary "foreign ships," not Chinese vessels, faced these actions (p. 57). In the twelfth century Chinese ships were sailing regularly to Southeast Asia and were even repairing their ships in Jambi's harbor on their way to Arab countries of the West.

84. Wolters, *Fall of Srivijaya,* 6.

Chapter 5

1. Soedjatmoko et al., eds., *An Introduction to Indonesian Historiography.*

2. W. J. Van der Meulen, S.J., "Ptolemy's Geography of Mainland Southeast Asia and Borneo," *Indonesia* 19 (April 1975): 16–22.

3. W. J. Van der Meulen, S.J., "In Search of Ho-ling," *Indonesia* 23 (1977): 87–111. Ho-lo-tan is associated with Java's northwestern coast. O. W. Wolters, *Early Indonesian Commerce: A Study of the Origins of Srivijaya,* 161–162, 212–213, 218, 340 n. 148.

4. P. Pelliot, "Deux itinéraires de Chine en Inde à la fin du VIIIe siècle," *BEFEO* 4 (1904): 274–275. The Lue Sung emperor dispatched a ship to bring Guṇavarman to China, but he had already left by the time the ship arrived. Wolters, *Early Indonesian Commerce,* 94–95 n. 33, discounts the Guṇavarman story as being recorded by the Chinese one century after the events, but Van der Meulen ("In Search of Ho-ling") holds that this was not unusual among Chinese annalists and thinks that most of the Guṇavarman story is realistic (pp. 94–95).

5. Pelliot, "Deux itinéraires de Chine en Inde," 286–288. See also Van der Meulen, "In Search of Ho-ling," 90. This information comes from a biography of Hui-ning written by the Chinese pilgrim I-ching in 685–695.

6. Pelliot, "Deux itinéraires de Chine en Inde," 271–274; Wolters, *Early Indonesian Commerce,* 151, 313 nn. 92, 95; from the *Liu Sung shu* [History of the Early Sung] (composed 470–478).

7. J. Ph. Vogel, "The Earliest Sanskrit Inscriptions of Java," *Publicaties van de Oudheidkundige Dienst in Nederlandsch-Indie* 1 (1925): 15–35; J. G. de Casparis, *Indonesian Palaeography,* 18–20; H. B. Sarkar, *Corpus of the Inscriptions of Java (up to 928 A.D.),* 1:1–12.

8. J. Noorduyn and H. Th. Verstappen, "Pūrṇavarman's River Works Near Tugu," *BKI* 128 (1972): 298–307.

9. Van der Meulen, "In Search of Ho-ling," 104, relates this information to the later inscription of Sañjaya (732), where the center of a monarch's power is said to be in his feet, which are placed over the heads of his enemies. Van der Meulen holds that Pūrṇavarman, ruler of Tārumānāgara, conquered Ho-lo-tan shortly after 452, the date of Ho-lo-tan's last embassy to China.

10. F. H. van Naerssen and R. C. de Iongh, *The Economic and Administrative History of Early Indonesia,* 28.

11. Noorduyn and Verstappen, "Pūrṇavarman's River Works."

12. The magical dwarf Viṣṇu in Vedic literature won the earth, the waters, and the sky realms for the forces of good in a competition with the forces of evil by taking three paces. See A. L. Basham, *The Wonder That Was India,* 235. In later Javanese statuary kings stand on the heads of their conquered enemies. This is especially true of statuary found in eastern Java. See A. J. Bernet Kempers, *Ancient Indonesian Art,* passim; see also p. 249.

13. Pelliot, "Deux itinéraires de Chine en Inde," 284. Corresponding to this expedition, Tārumā, a port said by the Chinese to be located on the Sunda Strait, sent an embassy to the Chinese court in 666–669, but the Chinese did not hear of this Javanese center again.

14. George Coedès, *Indianized States of Southeast Asia,* ed. Walter F. Vella, 83, proposed political domination of Java by Śrīvijaya until the 719–730 era, when the central Java-based ruler Sañjaya "liberated" the western coast's political dependencies, although the region continued as an economic subordinate of Śrīvijaya. See also L. C. Damais, review of *Riwajat Indonesia,* by R. Ng. Poebatjaraka, *BEFEO* 48 (1957): 639. Recently, O. W. Wolters has rethought his previous emphasis upon Śrīvijaya's singular economic authority, preferring to see the continued participation of northern Java ports in the international trade as demonstrated by the archaeological remains of Chinese ceramics scattered from the coast to the Java interior. See Wolters, "Studying Srivijaya," *JMBRAS* 52, 2 (1979): 1–38.

15. F. D. K. Bosch, "Een Maleische inscriptie in het Buitenzorgsche," *BKI* 100 (1941): 49–53.

16. L. C. Damais, "Études d'epigraphie Indonésienne, III. Liste des principales inscriptions datées de l'Indonésie," *BEFEO* 46 (1952–1954): 98–103, no. 275 (Bawang), no. 283 (Batu Bedil), and no. 289 (Ulu Belu).

17. N. J. Krom, *De Sumatraansche periode der Javaansche Geschiedenis.* The "Side B" inscription describes a ruler "who bears the aspect of Viṣṇu in his capacity to humble the pride of all enemies and is unrivalled in his powers, is called Śrī Mahārāja on account of his origin from the Śailendra family. . . ." The text and English translation of "Side B" and "Side A" of what has been known as

the "Ligor Stele Inscriptions," are provided in K. A. Nilakanta Sastri, *History of Srivijaya,* 44, 125. A Javanese inscription from Caṇḍi Kalasan dated 778 records the sovereignty of the Śailendra family, ibid., 45, 122–123; Sarkar, *Corpus of the Inscriptions of Java,* 1:34–40; and F. D. K. Bosch, "De inscriptie van Kĕloerak," *TBG* 68 (1928): 57–62. A seventh-century inscription containing the name "Selendra" was discovered in north central Java in 1962, which the Indonesian epigraphist Boechari has utilized to argue that the Śailendras were clearly an Indonesian family (Boechari, "Preliminary Report on the Discovery of an Old Malay Inscription at Sodjomerta," *Madjalah Ilmu-Ilmu Sastra Indonesia* 2–3 [1966]: 241–251), thus dispelling the earlier proposal of George Coedès that the Śailendras were the previous rulers of Funan (Coedès, "On the Origin of the Śailendras of Indonesia," *Journal of the Greater India Society* 1 [1934]: 61–70). The inscription mentions a "*ḍapunta* Selendra."

18. Nilakanta Sastri, *History of Srivijaya,* 125–128.

19. W. F. Stutterheim, *A Javanese Period in Sumatra History.*

20. J. G. de Casparis, *Prasasti Indonesia I: Inscriptie uit de Çailendra-Tijd; Prasasti Indonesia II: Selected Inscriptions from the 7th to the 9th Century* A.D.; and J. G. de Casparis, "Short Inscriptions from Tjandi Plaosan-Lor," *Berita Dinas Purbakala* 4 (1958): 25ff.

21. Nilakanta Sastri, *History of Srivijaya,* 122–123; Bosch, "De inscriptie van Kĕloerak," 57–62.

22. For text and translations into English, see Nilakanta Sastri, *History of Srivijaya* 117–119, and Sarkar, *Corpus of the Inscriptions of Java,* 1:15–24. Discussed in Nilakanta Sastri, *History of Srivijaya,* 122–123; Sarkar, *Corpus of the Inscriptions of Java,* 1:34–40.

23. Previous inscriptions were engraved in a south Indian Pallava Grantha script. The inscription invokes the three jewels of Buddhism (Buddha, Dharma, and the *Saṅgha*) and various Buddhist deities, as well as Brahma, Viṣṇu, and the Maheśvara. For an English translation of the text, see Nilakanta Sastri, *History of Srivijaya,* 45, 123–125, and Sarkar, *Corpus of the Inscriptions of Java,* 1:41–48.

24. Casparis, *Prasasti Indonesia I,* 50–73; Sarkar, *Corpus of the Inscriptions of Java,* 1:64–75. Casparis attributes two other inscriptions to the Śailendra realm that date to this interval. A Ratubaka Plateau inscription dated 792 seems to record the assignment of land rights to the Borobudur (see J. G. de Casparis, "New Evidence on Cultural Relations Between Java and Ceylon in Ancient Times," *Artibus Asiae* 24, 3–4 [1961]: 241–248, and Sarkar, 1:48, i–vii) and an Old Malay inscription from Caṇḍi Sewu that deals with the enlargement of a *vajnāsana* also dated 792 (J. G. de Casparis, "The Dual Nature of Barabudur," in *Barabudur: History and Significance of a Buddhist Monument,* ed. Louis Gomez and Hiram W. Woodward, Jr., 47–83).

25. Casparis, *Prasasti Indonesia II,* 219; Gandasuli inscription of 832, Casparis, *Prasasti Indonesia I,* 55–57, 107–111; Sarkar, *Corpus of the Inscriptions of Java,* 1:75, i–ii. Earliest reference to Patapān is the Munduan copper-plate inscription dated 826 found near the Gandasuli inscription of 832, which names Rakrayān Patapān Pu Manuku (see Denys Lombard, reporting on the second Seminar Sejarah Nasional, Jogjakarta, 1970, *BEFEO* 58 [1971]: 286). Casparis now concludes from this evidence that by the 820s the Śailendras held authority over the southern Kedu Plain. The original family base of the Śailendras was near the Borobudur; in that area older members of the family were buried in great

honor. By the 790s the center of Śailendra power had focused upon the more strategically located Ratubaka Plateau (Casparis, *Prasasti Indonesia I,* 294ff., and "New Evidence on Cultural Relations"), but in 856 Pikatan, Patapān's son, assuming the regnal title Kumbhayoni and claiming distinction as a victorious monarch, founded *lingas* on the Ratubaka Plateau (Casparis, *Prasasti Indonesia II,* 244–330, 341–343), which became the center of the Patapān line's authority.

26. Casparis, *Prasasti Indonesia I,* 24ff., 73, 79. Casparis attributes similar activities to the same principal queen of Rakai Pikatan in another inscription from the 840s (Casparis, "Short Inscriptions from Tjandi Plaosan-Lor," 25ff.), especially maintenance of the Borobudur.

27. Summarized in Coedès, *Indianized States,* 125–126.

28. Casparis, *Prasasti Indonesia II,* 289–297, and *Prasasti Indonesia I,* 107–109, 133. The Nālandā Charter was originally published in *Epigraphica Indica* 17 (1924): 310–327.

29. Casparis, *Prasasti Indonesia II,* 294–297, and *Prasasti Indonesia I,* 107–109, 133.

30. F. D. K. Bosch, review of *Prasasti Indonesia I & II,* by J. G. de Casparis, *BKI* 108 (1952): 191–199; 114 (1958): 306–320; see van Naerssen's reconstruction of the genealogical tables of this era, van Naerssen and de Iongh, *Early Indonesia;* 46–52.

31. G. R. Tibbetts, *A Study of the Arabic Texts Containing Material on South-East Asia,* 25–65, 104–117. For an earlier study of this material, see Gabriel Ferrand, *Relations de voyages et textes géographiques arabes, persans et turks relatifs à l'Extrême-Orient du VIIIe au XVIIIe siècles.*

32. Tibbetts, *Study of the Arabic Texts,* 57, 113.

33. Ibid., 44, 113. Buzurg ibn Shahriyar compiled the *'Ajā'ib al-Hind* at Rām Hurmuz, a port near the northern end of the Persian Gulf.

34. Ibid., 116–118.

35. See, for example, Wolters, *Early Indonesian Commerce.*

36. Wolters now holds Malāyu to have been the upriver Menangkabau hinterland of Sumatra at least in late Śrīvijaya times; previously he believed that Malāyu was associated with the Batang Hari estuary from Jambi to its upriver hinterland, which might relate to this Menangkabau realm. The Yuan do not mention San-fo-ch'i, but specify "Malāyu" and "Palembang" in their records, while the Ming in the second half of the fourteenth century return to the Sung nomenclature of San-fo-ch'i (Wolters, "Studying Srivijaya," 27). Recent revisions of interpretation by art historians studying early Southeast Asian art provide a better understanding of the importance of the Śrīvijaya and Java realms in early archipelago history. What had previously been considered "Śrīvijayan Art" from Sumatra and the Malay Peninsula is now viewed instead as reflecting significant Javanese artistic influence (H. G. Quaritch Wales, "The Extent of Sri Vijaya's Influence Abroad," *JMBRAS* 51, 1 [1978]: 5–12; Satyawati Suleiman, "The History and Art of Srivijaya," in *The Art of Srivijaya,* ed. M. C. Subhadris Diskul, 1–20). For instance, Satyawati Suleiman argues that there is a unity of ceramic evidence from the northern Java and southeastern Sumatra coasts dating from the pre-tenth-century era due to a close interrelationship between Javanese harbor princes and the rulers of Śrīvijaya; she views this area as a single trading region. Viewing the Sunda Strait region as a single economic unit explains the presence of central Javanese art influence in the Buddhist and Śaivite statuary and monumental art in the Musi and Batang Hari river basins as well as in other

areas subject to Śrīvijaya's authority. This counters earlier views that central Javanese art was a product of Śrīvijaya's influence. See Suleiman, "History and Art of Srivijaya," and F. M. Schnitger, *The Archaeology of Hindoo Sumatra*.

37. Coedès, *Indianized States,* 144–148.

38. Casparis, "Short Inscriptions from Tjandi Plaosan-Lor." At Śrīvijaya ports Javanese merchants received in exchange gold, silk, procelain, Indian cloth, and the incense of the Arabian countries. Also of interest is Hiram W. Woodward, Jr., "A Chinese Silk Depicted at Candi Sewu," in *Economic Exchange and Social Interaction in Southeast Asia: Perspectives from Prehistory, History and Ethnography,* ed. Karl L. Hutterer, 233–243, where Woodward demonstrates the incorporation of a Chinese silk cloth in the stone sculpture of Caṇḍi Sewu, a Śailendra temple associated with a 792 inscription (Casparis, "The Dual Nature of Barabudur"). Woodward argues that the Śailendra monarch, not merchants, controlled the distribution of foreign goods within Java at that time and that this fact is demonstrated as well as declared by the cloth's depiction on the *caṇḍi*. The Śailendra monarch was stating that it was he who controlled the world of merchants as well as their luxury goods. A royal monopoly over the distribution of such goods would have reinforced Śailendra power, as only by loyalty to the Śailendra monarch could one receive access to luxurious goods of foreign origin. The conclusion drawn from Woodward's thesis is that central Javanese monarchs were more involved in trade than many historians would believe, but it also supports the view that the Śailendra relationship with Śrīvijaya, whereby Śrīvijaya exercised a monopoly over foreign trade, facilitated the flow of foreign luxury goods to Śailendra monarchs. Thus the Śrīvijaya alliance reinforced Śailendra authority by providing special goods that could be redistributed in gift-giving ceremonies to those supportive of the Śailendras. Foreign merchants, thus, were important royal allies, since it was they who provided these goods for royal redistributions. This would also explain the numerous references to merchants of foreign origin who participated in royal *sīma* grant ceremonies and as donors to royal temples (Jan Wisseman, "Markets and Trade in Pre-Majapahit Java," in Hutterer, *Economic Exchange and Social Interaction in Southeast Asia,* 197–212, cites more than ten examples, a degree of reference unmatched in any other classical Southeast Asian state).

39. Añjukladang inscription dated A.D. 937, J. L. A. Brandes and N. J. Krom, "Oud-Javaansche Oorkonden," *Verhandelingen van het Bataviaasch Genootschap van Kunsten en Wetenschappen* (hereafter *VBG*) 60 (1913): xlvi, partially translated in Boechari, "Some Considerations on the Problem of the Shift of Mataram's Centre of Government from Central to East Java in the 10th Century," in *Early South East Asia: Essays in Archaeology, History and Historical Geography,* ed. R. B. Smith and W. Watson, 474.

40. Boechari, in "Some Considerations of the Problem of the Shift of Mataram's Centre," 473–475, disagrees that there was a century of conflict between Śrīvijaya and Java following the early tenth-century incursion, arguing that there is no Javanese evidence to substantiate Chinese reports of these hostilities.

41. F. H. van Naerssen, "Tribute to the God and Tribute to the King," in *Southeast Asian History and Historiography: Essays Presented to D. G. E. Hall,* ed. C. D. Cowan and O. W. Wolters, 297.

42. Ibid., 298.

43. See F. H. van Naerssen, "The Çailendra Interregnum," *India Antiqua: A Volume of Oriental Studies Presented . . . to Jean Philippe Vogel,* 249–253. Cas-

paris, too, has backed away from his earlier proposal that central Java's states were centralized political systems (J. G. de Casparis, "Pour une histoire sociale de l'ancienne Java principalement au Xeme s.," *Archipel* 21 [1981]: 125–154). He most recently proposed that an equilibrium existed (a "dyarchy," p. 136) between the central government and the villages during the tenth century. Contact between the two levels was facilitated by the periodic visits and residence of employees of the state at the village level; or the court assigned *watĕk* rights over villages, either giving responsibility for village clusters to court-based elites or to those descended from landed elites who already held local political rights; or monarchs assigned religious specialists to conduct rituals in local temples and integrated local priests into the ceremonies of the court (pp. 145–146). The state provided protection to the villages; the villages responded with periodic revenue and service payments to the royal court. Casparis concluded that institutional changes that brought the subordination of the Javanese villages to central government authority were more characteristic of the thirteenth and fourteenth centuries than of the previous age (p. 135).

44. Water management officials are thus conspicuous among lists of *watĕk* officials in central Java inscriptions. See, for example, the Old Javanese Caṇḍi Pĕrot inscription of Rakrayān Pikatan dated 850 (Casparis, *Prasasti Indonesia II,* 211–243, line 23), where the local "surveyor of water supply" and the "surveyor of dams" are listed among the officials of the *watĕk*. The view among many historians, including Casparis (see note 43), is that *watĕk* were imposed as regional units of administration from the top down, as *mahārāja*s assigned court-based allies or landed elites to assume administrative responsibility for *watĕk* units of regional authority. Emphasis in this chapter, as that of van Naerssen, is on the generation of *watĕk* from the bottom up, that is, as a natural development that responded to the changing needs of Java's agrarian system. Clifford Geertz in his study of Balinese society argues a similar theme, that the economic and religious as well as political integration of Balinese society emerged from early supralocal irrigation networks (see Geertz, *Negara: The Theater-State in Nineteenth Century Bali,* especially 68–85). Karl Wittfogel, *Oriental Despotism,* provides an important essay on the implications of water management networks in Asia's history to the development of centralized political systems (focusing upon Chinese civilization). Geertz's study questions the universal application of Wittfogel's thesis in a Southeast Asian context, suggesting instead that local water management networks can reinforce regional as opposed to supraregional loyalties to a political center.

45. Van Naerssen and de Iongh, *Early Indonesia,* 37.

46. F. D. K. Bosch, "The Problem of the Hindu 'Colonisation' of Indonesia," *Selected Studies in Indonesian Archaeology,* 3–22.

47. The text is published in W. F. Stutterheim, "Een belangrijke oorkonde uit de Kedoe," *TBG* 67 (1927): 172–215, as quoted in van Naerssen and de Iongh, *Early Indonesia,* 47; text and English translation appear in Sarkar, *Corpus of the Inscriptions of Java,* 2:64–81.

48. See L. C. Damais, "Epigrafische Aantekeningen," *TBG* 83 (1949): 18–20; and Casparis, *Prasasti Indonesia II,* 212, 218.

49. Van Naerssen and de Iongh, *Early Indonesia,* 76–81; Sarkar, *Corpus of the Inscriptions of Java,* 1:184, 199–201, 215–216. Ngabean near Kedu provides another inscription by the same *rakrayān* showing a different and more complete *kraton* administration than at Polengan, seemingly because the authority of the

Mahārāja Rakrayān of Kayuwangi was more direct at Ngabean than at Polengan, where the local *rakrayān,* ruling in the area called Sirikan, exercised a great degree of autonomy. For the text of this inscription, see L. C. Damais, "Études d'epigraphie Indonésienne, III," 34–43; text and translation are in Sarkar, *Corpus of the Inscriptions of Java,* 1:217–226.

50. For a discussion of *sīma* grants, see Boechari, "Epigraphy and Indonesian Historiography" in Soedjatmoko et al., *Introduction to Indonesian Historiography,* 50–60.

51. See van Naerssen and de Iongh, *Early Indonesia,* 76–81.

52. While the *rakrayān* controlled the temple as well as tribute from lands on which he held *watĕk* rights, he was not independent of the will of the land's producers; the *wanua* residents affected the *rakrayān*'s exercise of authority. Local produce would appear to have been for local consumption or trade or for tribute payments to *rakrayān*. In the latter instance, however, tribute payments were returned via a traditional network of gift-giving or mutual aid.

53. Geertz, *Negara,* demonstrates that in Bali temple networks assumed the role of economic and ceremonial centers for local irrigation networks. But in Bali temple networks appear to have emerged from the irrigation societies dominated by local farmers rather than from a political elite of the *rakrayān* type. That is, the Javanese economic system was more politicized than was true in Bali, where Geertz finds weak indigenous political institutions and leadership.

54. See, for example, Casparis, *Prasasti Indonesia II,* 211–243.

55. Pierre Bourdieu, *Outline of a Theory of Practice,* 172ff. Bourdieu argues that through the transformation of economic capital into "symbolic capital" the economic self-interest of a society's leadership can be imbedded within the traditional socioeconomy as that socioeconomy's institutions assume the leading role of limiting and disguising the play of economic interests and calculations. See chap. 6.

56. For an extended discussion of the system of "ritual sovereignty," see Burton Stein, *Peasant State and Society in Medieval South India,* passim, and chap. 2.

57. Van Naerssen, "Tribute to the God," 298. Van Naerssen points out that central religious complexes, *dharma*s, were widely known and survived despite several dynastic changes. He proposes that there was a Javanese pilgrimage network connecting Ḍihyang, Salingsan, Wulusan, Tigangrat, Raja, Jambi, Airbulang, Airasih, and Mangulihi, which is supported by early Javanese epigraphy as well as by later Javanese literature. Further, he identifies a second group of temples, the *dharma*s of deified rulers (*mahārāja*s), which further enhanced local images of royal status. In later practice, notably as evinced in the 907 inscription of Balitung, reigning monarchs invoked the spirits of the enumerated "previous gods" *(rahyangta rumuhum),* who were also drawn upon as "the accomplished gods who protect the realm *(dewata praśiddha)*." As shown in the *Nagarakĕrtagama,* there was a clear understanding of temple hierarchy among royal *dharma*s *(dharmahaji)* and local *dharma*s *(dharma swatantra* and *dharma lepas).* See Th. G. Th. Pigeaud, *Java in the Fourteenth Century,* passim.

58. See Clifford Geertz's model of the "theater-state" in Clifford Geertz, *Islam Observed,* 36–39. A glimpse of early Javanese court ritual is provided in the epigraphic proclamations of the foundations of temples and *sīma* grants, which report the participation of all important state elites, who are carefully recorded as being in attendance. In the era of the hegemony of central Java, *kra-*

ton court ritual was concentrated in the state's temples, and a select group of participants was allowed to partake in the court's sacred ceremonies. But after the tenth century, when the paramount court was based in eastern Java, massive state-sponsored public ceremonies were conducted in the capital and in other important urban centers, as is best shown in the court poetry and inscriptions of the Majapahit-based rulers that are discussed in chapter 9. While central Java monarchs stressed temple construction and ritual as their source of legitimacy, Majapahit kings seem to have placed more emphasis on organizing impressive public displays to promote their right to rule. Although there is limited documentation of earlier court ritual in surviving epigraphy, the archaeological remains of central Java *kraton* provide clues. On the Ratubaka Plateau, for example, one is still impressed by the elaborate network of water chambers that dominate the remains of a royal ceremonial complex that included hermitages, dance platforms, and a palace monastery. It is apparent that sacred water rituals were once performed at this site, which loomed over the king's subjects who lived on the plain below. A recent discussion of early Javanese state ritual within the context of the Geertz theater-state model is Jan Wisseman Christie, "Rāja and Rāma: The Classical State in Early Java," in *Centers, Symbols, and Hierarchies: Essays on the Classical States of Southeast Asia,* ed. Lorraine Gesick, 9–44.

59. Van Naerssen and de Iongh, *Early Indonesia,* 45.

60. On the implications of such "gift" relationships, see Marcel Mauss, *The Gift;* Henri Hubert and Marcel Mauss, *Sacrifice: Its Nature and Function;* Marshall Sahlins, *Stone Age Economics;* and Bourdieu, *Outline of a Theory of Practice,* 159–197.

61. Damais, "Études d'epigraphie Indonésienne, III," 36–37, 42–43, nos. 30, 35, 48, 64.

62. The text was originally published in H. Kern, *Verspreide Geschriften,* 7:115–118. The text and English translation appear in Nilakanta Sastri, *History of Srivijaya,* 117–119, and Sarkar, *Corpus of the Inscriptions of Java,* 1:15–24.

63. The *Tantu Panggĕlaran,* the fourteenth- to sixteenth-century encyclopedia of Śaivite tradition in Java, explains that Śiva created the Ḍihyang to be the scene of his first *yoga* practice on the soil of Java, in order to make Java fit for human habitation. Thereupon he gave the order to Brahma and Viṣṇu to proceed to the creation of the people of Java. See Th. G. Th. Pigeaud, ed. and trans., *De Tantu Panggĕlaran,* 57, 129, as quoted in van Naerssen and de Iongh, *Early Indonesia,* 96. There is also reference in the texts to Śiva's transfer of Mahâmeru-Mandara (Mount Meru) to Java, specifically to the Diëng Plateau (Pigeaud, 65–66, 136), in order to stabilize the universe. Later Javanese literature regards the Diëng Plateau as the Mĕḍang, the place of origin or first settlement of the Javanese state (Pigeaud, 60, 132). Van der Meulen, "In Search of Ho-ling," demonstrates the popularity of the worship of Gaṇeśa, Śiva's elephant-faced son, on the Diëng Plateau where roughly 30 to 45 percent of the remaining statuary is of Gaṇeśa—two to three times more than that of Śiva himself. Other historians have stressed the role of Agastya, the great Brahman sage and missionary who is closely associated with Śiva, in Sañjaya's Diëng Plateau cult. Agastya is said to have set out in Java with magic water in a pot, focusing upon his power to endow Java's water *(tirtha)* with magical properties *(āgama tirtha)* that would bring prosperity to Java's population. Rulers and their "Brahman" priests, themselves acting as Agastya in rituals that placed emphasis on the act of making magic waters, thus transferred the potent forces of the cosmos to the Javanese monarch. See K. A.

Nilakanta Sastri, "Agastya," *TBG* 76 (1936): 471–545, and Jean Filliozat, "Agastya et la propagation du Brahmanisme au Sud-Est Asiatiques," *Adyar Library Bulletin* 31–32 (1967–1968): 442–449.

64. Sañjaya's emphasis was upon Śiva the Destroyer (Bĕtara Kala), syncretizing earlier worship of a Black Ghost or Black Spirit of Indonesia. See Filliozat, "Agastya et la propagation du Brahmanisme."

65. The translation is modified from that given in Nilakanta Sastri, *History of Srivijaya,* 116–119.

66. Wolters, *Early Indonesian Commerce,* 216.

67. Ibid., 215. Su O, writing in the late ninth century, also records tribute missions from Ho-ling that were received by the emperor I-tsung at the T'ang capital of Ch'ang-an in 868 and 873 (Su O, *Tu-yang tsa-p'ien,* as translated by O. W. Wolters, "A Few Miscellaneous *Pi-chi* Jottings on Early Indonesia," *Indonesia* 36 [October 1983]: 61–62). Use of the toponym Ho-ling in Su O's account as well as in the *Hsin T'ang-shu* citation is problematical, in that the last Java tribute mission registered under the name Ho-ling came in 818:

> Thereafter Javanese missions were registered under the name of *She-p'o,* or "Java," and they came in 820, 831, and 839. The *Hsin T'ang-shu* states that there was another one in the 860–873 reign period, and this is probably the mission described by Su O as coming from *Ho-ling* in 868. . . . Su O is unlikely to have had access to court records and was probably using a name familiar to T'ang Chinese and famous because it is mentioned in accounts of Chinese Buddhist pilgrims in the seventh and eighth centuries. The compilers of the *Hsin T'ang-shu* in the eleventh century certainly understood *"Ho-ling"* and *"She-p'o"* to be equivalent names, though this does not mean that the royal centers in question were identical. Su O's jottings at least tell us that a Javanese mission arrived in China in 868, which is the reign of the Central Javanese ruler Kayuwangi/Lokapala whose dated inscriptions are from 860 to 882. 868 is five years later than the Pereng inscription of 863, which records the foundation of a Śivaite temple by the Rakai of Walaing, Pu Kumbhayoni. This person may have resigned his throne some years earlier. In 856 Pu Kumbhayoni is supposed to have overthrown the Śailendra princely family in Central Java.

Ibid., 62, citing L. C. Damais, "Études Sino-Indonésiennes, III. La transcription chinoise *Ho-ling* comme désignation de Java," *BEFEO* 52, 1 (1964): 93–141; Damais, "Études d'epigraphie Indonésienne, III," 32–43; Casparis, *Prasasti Indonesia II,* 249–254; and Casparis, "Dual Nature of Barabudur," 58.

68. Van Naerssen and de Iongh, *Early Indonesia,* 47–51. Casparis utilized the Balitung inscription to argue the equivalency of Śailendra *mahārāja*s and those in Balitung's list. See Casparis, *Prasasti Indonesia I,* passim.

69. J. G. de Casparis, "Nogmaals de Sanskrit-inscriptie op den steen van Dinojo," *TBG* 81 (1941): 499–513; Sarkar, *Corpus of the Inscriptions of Java,* 1:25–33.

70. Coedès, *Indianized States,* 89–91; Damais, "Études Sino-Indonésiennes, III," 130.

71. Damais, "Études Sino-Indonésiennes, III."

72. Van Naerssen and de Iongh, *Early Indonesia,* 56–57.

73. Casparis, "Nogmaals de Sanskrit-inscriptie"; Sarkar, *Corpus of the Inscriptions of Java,* 1:295–303.

74. Boechari, "Some Considerations of the Problem of the Shift of Mataram's Centre," 475.

75. Añjukladang inscription, Brandes and Krom, "Oud-Javaansche Oorkonden," xlvi, discussed in ibid., 474.

76. Casparis, "Short Inscriptions from Tjandi Plaosan-Lor."

77. Boechari, "Some Considerations of the Problem of the Shift of Mataram's Centre," 480.

78. B. J. Schrieke, *Indonesian Sociological Studies, II, Selected Writings,* 105–108.

79. The Mantyāsih inscription of this era mentions a big road *(hawān)* that had been protected by the elders *(patiḥs)* of Mantyāsih. See Boechari, "Some Considerations of the Problem of the Shift of Mataram's Centre."

80. Boechari alludes to Kublai Khan's attack against eastern Java in the late thirteenth century and the subsequent demise of Kaḍiri as another example of eastern Java's vulnerability.

81. Schrieke, *Indonesian Sociological Studies,* II, 292–300.

82. Casparis, *Prasasti Indonesia I,* 170–175; Casparis, "Dual Nature of Barabudur"; Casparis, "Short Inscriptions from Tjandi Plaosan-Lor."

83. Such use of the local labor force of a *rakrayān* reinforced the *mahārāja*'s powers vis-à-vis the *rakrayān*. Not only did the *rakrayān* thus recognize the *mahārāja*'s temple and cult of legitimacy focused therein but the use of the *rakrayān*'s labor dues prevented the *rakrayān*'s using this manpower service for his own economic ends; it was thus an indirect taxation of the *rakrayān* by the *mahārāja*. Local temple construction, too, was a means of indirectly limiting the powers of a subordinate *rakrayān* and forcing the redistribution of his economic capital. The *rakrayān* committed resources to the construction of temples that derived their legitimacy from the *mahārāja*'s central temples. The local temple ultimately enhanced the sacred capital of the *mahārāja* as well as of the local *rakrayān,* whose ritual status, a consequence of his temple's subordination to a central temple, was thus less than that of the *mahārāja*.

84. Men hoe, plough, and work an irrigation system, while women plant, weed, and often harvest. Children chase away birds to protect the maturing rice —at least this is the ideal. Unlike some areas of Southeast Asia, Javanese farmers did not have to spend large amounts of time keeping the forest cut back.

85. See also D. Kaplan, "Men, Monuments, and Political Systems," *Southwestern Journal of Anthropology* 19, 4 (1963): 397–410, who argues against the idea that temple construction was an economic drain in early societies. Kaplan also notes the psychological impact of temple construction. Workers—who derived religious merit for their efforts—willingly provided labor for temple construction and did not find the demand for their labor a threat to their existence. Quite the contrary, labor on the temple deity's behalf provided an emotional uplift that likely carried over into agrarian activities and could well have stimulated agricultural production. The focus of early Southeast Asian temples was upon fertility and prosperity, and the ceremonies conducted in the temples not only emphasized the religious prowess of the ruling elite who patronized these temples but also were intended to guarantee the productivity of the local socioeconomy. The fact that a farmer participated personally in the creation of such temples provided him with a sense of emotional well-being.

86. Boechari, "Some Considerations of the Problem of the Shift of Mataram's Centre," 485. Javanese workers happily gave their labor, as evinced by the

humorous reliefs at the Borobudur, Prambanan, and other central Java temple complexes.

87. Boechari notes a three-century cycle beginning with Dapūnta Selendra, founder of the Śailendra line, who ruled in the first quarter of the seventh century A.D.; Pu Siṇḍok, speaking of himself as Iśāna, interprets himself as the beginning of a new dynasty, the Iśānawangśa line, three centuries thereafter; three centuries later the Rājasawangśa line emerged at Singhasāri in 1222; Majapahit disintegrated in the first quarter of the sixteenth century, three centuries later. There is also a one-century cycle: in the first quarter of the eighth century the Śailendras shifted the Javanese *kraton* from Sañjaya's Diëng Plateau base to the Kedu Plain; in the first quarter of the ninth century the Śailendra line was being replaced by that of Patapān; in the first quarter of the tenth century Balitung began the shift of the Javanese royal *kraton* from central to eastern Java; in the first quarter of the eleventh century Śrīvijaya's devastating attack facilitated Airlangga's political consolidations of central and eastern Java. See Boechari, ibid., 487–491. In contrast, contemporary Cambodian Khmer rulers moved their courts and built a new state temple mountain with each new reign. See chap. 6.

88. Boechari holds that the focus of early Arab sources on a volcano associated with the Zābaj (Java) ruler's realm validates the possibility of such a cataclysmic eruption. The *Akhbar al-sin wa'l-Hind* (850) notes a great volcano in the kingdom of the *mahārāja,* information repeated by Mas'ūdi in the next century (Tibbetts, *Study of the Arabic Texts,* 27, 39). Abū Zaid's tenth-century account may be the most important in support of Boechari, noting that the land of Java is "one of continuous habitation and uninterrupted cultivated fields, except near the volcano, where the land was deserted for the distance of a parasang" (Tibbetts, 105). Supporting Boechari's thesis is the fact that the Borobudur and other central Java temple complexes were recovered from layers of ash by nineteenth- and twentieth-century Dutch archaeologists.

89. Van Naerssen and de Iongh, *Early Indonesia,* 76–81.

90. L. C. Damais, "Bibliographie Indonésienne, XI. Les publications epigraphiques du Service Archeologique de l'Indonésie," *BEFEO* 54 (1968): 506–507; van Naerssen and de Iongh, *Early Indonesia,* 52, 76–81; Sarkar, *Corpus of the Inscriptions of Java,* 1:278–287, 217–226, 266–275. Van Naerssen argues that there was unrest after this reign, a response to Kayuwangi's drain of his realm's economic productivity to build temples (i.e., converting economic capital into symbolic capital). But Boechari, questioning such a conclusion, says that there was no significant temple construction during this era. Casparis records that Pikatan assumed the regnal title Kumbhayoni in the mid-ninth century, an interpretation that van Naerssen does not share (see Casparis, *Prasasti Indonesia II,* 290; van Naerssen and de Iongh, *Early Indonesia,* 29–50). Casparis' view is that following conflict with Bālaputra of the Śailendra line, first Pikatan, who assumed the regnal title Kumbhayoni, and then Kayuwangi restored Śaivite kingship; van Naerssen's is that Kumbhayoni, Rakrayān of Walaing and great-grandchild of the Ratu of Halu, did not define his legitimacy from Sañjaya, but that Śrī Mahārāja Rakrayān Kayuwangi, who reigned from roughly 863 to 882, did. Further, van Naerssen finds Kayuwangi recognizing a "Rakrayān of Halu" in an inscription dated 882 (Damais, "Études d'epigraphie Indonésienne, III," 34–43; Sarkar, 1:278–287), as well as his other subordinate *rakrayān* of Hino, Wka, Sirikan, Tiruan, and Halaran (van Naerssen and de Iongh, 29–50). Van Naerssen argues that the incorporation of this former *ratu* as a subordinate *rakrayān* is

characteristic of Kayuwangi's reign and its policy of unification and gradual concentration of *kraton* administration. In his view, all previous monarchs reigned over regional units and may not be regarded as sovereigns ruling a territory as vast as central Java. In either instance, Kayuwangi's reign demonstrates a concern for economic development that may well relate to the immediate economic pressures of the post-Śailendra age. New temples on the Ratubaka Plateau and at Prambanan as well as regional temples in the image of the central temples were built under royal guidance. They became the focus of royal claims to legitimacy whether as a response to the disorders of the previous age and the replacement of the former Śailendra monarchs by a new royal line or because of the centralizing ambitions of Kayuwangi. Kayuwangi's efforts to elevate the status of his *kraton* vis-à-vis other *rakrayān*'s *kraton* may well have provoked a reaction by the other *rakrayān* following his reign; in essence such continuing competition effectively neutralized the evolution of a centralized polity in central Java.

91. Kamalagyan inscription (A.D. 1037), Brandes and Krom, "Oud-Javaansche Oorkonden," as discussed in F. H. van Naerssen, "De Brantas en haar waterwerken in den Hindu-Javaanschen tijd," *De Ingenieur* 53 (1938):A65–A66.

92. Airlangga's two dams, one at Waringin Sapta and another at Kĕlagyan in the Brantas Delta, were constructed to reestablish the old course of the river in the Brantas Delta and to protect local farmlands after a major flood that inundated the area in 1033 (at modern Mojokerto the Brantas curves sharply south and there uncontrolled floodwaters could have easily broken through; see N. C. van Setten van der Meer, *Sawah Cultivation in Ancient Java: Aspects of Development during the Indo-Javanese Period, 5th to 15th Century,* 18). Local villagers of Kamalagyan were required by Airlangga to settle by the dam at Waringin Sapta in order to guard against its damage or destruction (lines 15–16, Kamalagyan inscription, as translated by van der Meer, 80).

93. Coedès, *Indianized States,* 144–147. As noted, the earliest written inscriptions of Java were recorded in Sanskrit (Sañjaya's 732 Caṅggal inscription is the first dated epigraph), but while inscriptions in central Java continued to be written in Sanskrit, east Java epigraphy was the first to use Old Javanese (Kawi) script (Plumpangan Stone Inscription of 752) and by the ninth century was recorded in Old Javanese language and script (see Casparis, *Indonesian Palaeography*). O. W. Wolters, *History, Culture, and Region in Southeast Asian Perspectives,* 53, argues for the use of the term "localization" to describe the process of transition from "pure" Indian forms to forms in which the local tradition predominated (see chap. 3). Javanese literature provides a useful documentation of the process of "localization." By 856, landscape poetry was introduced into central Java epigraphy, written in Sanskrit verse, in which the beauty of nature was celebrated in a manner that goes beyond the poetry of India (P. J. Zoetmulder, *Kalangwan: A Survey of Old Javanese Literature,* 230; Casparis, *Prasasti Indonesia II,* 285). This poetic style was enhanced in later literature written in Old Javanese.

94. The remaining records of central Java wet-rice agriculture generally make reference to officials who were responsible for the administration of irrigation systems (e.g., the Caṇḍi Pĕrot inscription dated 850, Casparis, *Prasasti Indonesia II,* 211–243) or the conversion of lands to wet-rice cultivation (e.g., Sarkar, *Corpus of the Inscriptions of Java,* 1:278–287).

95. At Bakalan, for example, a 934 inscription issued by a *rakrayān* who was subject to the authority of Pu Siṇḍok records the initiation of wet-rice cultivation

after the construction of three dams and a local irrigation canal network "for the benefit of the *rakrayān*'s people." Local village elders were instructed by the *rakrayān* to see that farmers were fully aware of the significance of regulations affecting the use of this new irrigation system and that they were especially to abide by established rules applying to water distribution (Kromodjojo Adi Negoro, *Oud Javaansche Oorkonden op steem uit het afdeeling Modjokerto,* I, as summarized and discussed in van der Meer, *Sawah Cultivation in Ancient Java,* 51–52). Van der Meer argues that water distribution was difficult for a local community to administer, providing opportunities for outside political authorities to step in to punish those who took too much water). The Dinaya Stone Inscription of 760 (Sarkar, *Corpus of the Inscriptions of Java,* 25–33) provides the earliest evidence of political developments in this region where three major rivers flow to the Brantas from the Anjasmoro mountain range (see map 5). By the tenth century this well-established wet-rice producing center was under the authority of *rakrayān* claiming *mahārāja* rights over both central and eastern Java (e.g., Pu Siṇḍok's Sarangan Charter [929] and the Bakalan inscription of Rakrayān Mangibil [934], as discussed in van der Meer, 9). As a likely consequence of the periodic flooding of the lower Brantas and/or the threat of raids from the sea, eastern Java's population, like that of central Java that was more isolated from the coast, was so oriented toward the interior that post-tenth-century monarchs based in east Java had to undertake major recruitment campaigns to encourage hinterland peoples to populate the Java coast. See Wisseman, "Markets and Trade in Pre-Majapahit Java," 206.

96. Hariñjing "B" inscription (921), P. V. van Stein Callenfels, "De inscriptie van Sukabumi," *Mededeelingen van de Koninklijk Akademie van Wetenschappen, Afdeeling Letterkunde* (hereafter *MKAWAL*) 78 (1934): 116–122, as discussed in van der Meer, *Sawah Cultivation in Ancient Java.* The Hariñjing "B" inscription also appears in Sarkar, *Corpus of the Inscriptions of Java,* 2:196–197. Tuloḍong's orders were received by the *rakrayān* Mapatih Hino, who communicated the *mahārāja*'s determination to several named *rakrayān* that the area's water system should remain a freehold *(sīma)* of the area's landed elite (i.e., the named *rakrayān* were denied access to the area's land rights).

97. P. V. van Stein Callenfels, "De inscriptie van Kandangan," *TBG* 58 (1919): 359, as discussed in van der Meer, *Sawah Cultivation in Ancient Java,* 20. Van der Meer argues that the nearby Kelud volcano periodically erupted, creating the perpetual danger of consequent floods, and believes that the 1350 project was necessary because the 804 dam could not adequately handle the periodic floods.

98. Hariñjing "B" inscription (921), as discussed in van der Meer, *Sawah Cultivation in Ancient Java,* 116. The costs of this ritual were borne by the nearby village of Wulak. See chap. 9 for a discussion of the Caitra festival.

99. Ibid., 132.

100. F. D. K. Bosch, "The Old Javanese Bathing-place Jalatunda," *Selected Studies in Indonesian Archaeology,* 49–107, which describes a tenth-century eastern Java "bathing place" in the Brantas River system. A 943 inscription of Pu Siṇḍok speaks of sacred water that flowed past or through a temple (Casparis, *Prasasti Indonesia I,* 149), which the *rakrayān* Pikatan diverted: "After the Śiva sanctuary had been completed in its divine splendor, the (course of the) river was changed so that it rippled along the grounds . . . [of the sanctuary]" (Casparis, *Prasasti Indonesia II,* 328). The role of the bathing places can be compared to that of mountain temples and their irrigation network rituals in Bali, as discussed

in Geertz, *Negara,* and therein it may be possible to assume that irrigation ritual networks also played important roles as sources of regional integration in Java (see n. 102, below).

101. The sanctity of the Brantas River was widely recognized in literary and epigraphic references to the river as the "Lord of Waters" *(bangawan);* such records especially note a ceremonial relationship between eastern Java monarchs and the river. Eastern Java court ritual promoted the ruler's symbolic communication with his realm's river systems, which was portrayed as being important to the general prosperity of the state's economy (see chap. 9). In the fifteenth century this title was transferred to the Solo River—which in earlier inscriptions was also considered sacred—seemingly because of a shift in the course of the Brantas River in that time. See van der Meer, *Sawah Cultivation in Ancient Java,* 17; J. Noorduyn, "Further Topographical Notes on the Ferry Charter of 1358," *BKI* 124 (1968): 460–481.

102. Casparis, "New Evidence on Cultural Relations," argues that the Ratubaka Plateau inscription of 792 demonstrates that Śailendra homage was expressed not to the Lord Buddha, the Triratna, or Avalokiteśvara but to the "Cosmic Mountain of the Perfect Buddhas" *(samvuddha-sumeru),* that is, to the Borobudur itself:

> I pay homage to the Sumeru of the Buddhas, of lofty qualities and endowed with the awe-inspiring power of wisdom—whose profound caves are knowledge, whose rock is excellent tradition, whose brilliance is owing to its relic: the Good Word, whose streams are love, whose forests are concentration—truly the Mount of Few Desires, which is not shaken by the right horrible winds. . . .

Casparis, "The Dual Nature of Barabudur," 74. Broad Javanese cultural influence on all of Southeast Asia is stressed in Wolters, *History, Culture, and Region,* 16–33.

103. The Javanese state system described in this chapter differs significantly from that of its Balinese neighbor. In Bali, as noted in Geertz, *Negara,* local irrigation and religious networks confined to riverine drainage systems were the basis of regional interdependence, but there was minimal integration among regional irrigation and religious networks beyond their drainage systems. As each drainage system formed a self-contained exchange network, linkage normally took place via exchanges among the downriver ports at the edge of each system. As in other riverine economic systems in the island world, strong regional economic interdependency evolved in Bali, but integration of exchange networks into a hierarchical and interdependent economic system as a whole was weak. Because of this regional economic isolation, Bali did not develop a highly integrated polity; symbolic linkages connected drainage systems but religious ties were weakly institutionalized. Temple networks retained their autonomy vis-à-vis the political center and there was minimal economic and political integration that resulted from supraregional symbolic ties.

104. See, for instance, L. C. Damais, "Études Sino-Indonésiennes, I and II," *BEFEO* 50 (1960): 25–29, where a sea captain and overseas trader of importance, Ḍang Pu Hawang Gĕlis, and his wife in 827 donated several domestic utensils to a Ḍihyang temple patronized by the Gĕlis Patapān, the father of Pikatan who successfully challenged Śailendra sovereignty (in Casparis' reconstruction) shortly thereafter (text in Sarkar, *Corpus of the Inscriptions of Java,* 1:75, i–ii). Since

this Diëng Plateau complex established by Sañjaya as the basis of Śaivite legitimacy was drawn upon by Patapān's line as the source of their legitimacy, providing contact with earlier cults of legitimacy, the sea captain's gifts to the royal temple complex may have been intended to solicit the favor of the Patapān line and gain their support for the trader's commercial ambitions in the Javanese heartland.

Chapter 6

1. Paul Wheatley, "Satyānṛta in Suvarṇadvīpa: From Reciprocity to Redistribution in Ancient Southeast Asia," in *Ancient Civilization and Trade,* ed. Jeremy A. Sabloff and C. C. Lamberg-Karlovsky, 227–283. Wheatley draws especially from the work of Marshall Sahlins (e.g., *Stone Age Economics*) and Talcott Parsons (Talcott Parsons and Neil J. Smelser, *Economy and Society: A Study in the Integration of Economic and Social Theory*).
2. Ibid., 252.
3. I. W. Mabbett, "Kingship in Angkor," *Journal of the Siam Society* (hereafter *JSS*) 66, 2 (1978): 1–58, is a useful summary of past historiography on Khmer statecraft.
4. Pierre Bourdieu, *Outline of a Theory of Practice,* 172. Bourdieu argues that via the transformation of economic capital into "symbolic capital," the economy is not grasped *as* an economy, that is, as a system governed by the laws of "interested calculation, competition, and exploitation." "Symbolic capital" is a disguised form of physical "economic capital" and "originates in 'material' forms of capital which are, in the last analysis, the source of its effects" (p. 183). "Symbolic capital is always *credit* . . . i.e., a sort of advance which the group alone can grant those who give it the best material and symbolic *guarantees*. . . . Exhibition of symbolic capital is always very expensive in economic terms" (p. 181). He notes that as the "good-faith" (i.e., reciprocity) economy breaks up, the economic concept of "undisguised self-interest" takes hold, yet in this transition the society refuses to acknowledge this self-interest, devoting "as much time concealing the reality of economic acts as it expends in carrying them out." This movement away from the "good-faith" economy may be compared to Sahlins' (and Wheatley's) notion of a redistributive or mobilizative socioeconomy.
5. O. W. Wolters, "Jayavarman II's Military Power: The Territorial Foundations of the Angkor Empire," *Journal of the Royal Asiatic Society* (hereafter *JRAS*) (1973): 29–30.
6. The Buddhist concept was somewhat different: Mount Meru was the center of seven seas and seven mountain ranges, with four continents situated in an ocean beyond these seven mountain ranges—Jambudvīpa was the southernmost of these.
7. See Hermann Kulke, *The Devarāja Cult.*
8. Wolters, "Jayavarman II's Military Power."
9. Claude Jacques has retraced the early history of Angkor; see Claude Jacques, "Auteur de quelques toponymes de l'inscription du Prasat Tapan Run K. 598: la capitale Angkorienne, de Yaśovarman Ier a Sūryavarman Ier," *BEFEO* 65 (1978): 281–321.
10. L. P. Briggs, *The Ancient Khmer Empire,* passim.

11. O. W. Wolters, "Khmer 'Hinduism' in the Seventh Century," in *Early South East Asia: Essays in Archaeology, History and Historical Geography,* ed. R. B. Smith and W. Watson, 427–441.

12. See George Coedès, *Inscriptions du Cambodge* (hereafter *IC*), 2:151; 3:163; 1:15; 4:32; 6:8. Through the worship of the dead, ancestors who had attained eminence in life were accorded recognition; personal achievements in an individual's lifetime earned him ancestor status. Those who became prosperous thereby demonstrated that their contact with the ancestors was greater than that of others of their generation. Achievements and meritorious deeds were normally associated with superior spiritual prowess. Those with prowess were able to influence their fellow man's stature in this life as well as their hopes for recognition after death. Gifts to Hindu gods and local deities, as well as subordination to individuals who had by their personal achievements demonstrated superior prowess influenced one's prospects of achieving ancestor status. See chap. 3.

13. For example, Coedès, *IC,* 5:29.

14. In 685, for instance, a temple ceremony was performed by a local chief before no less than twenty-two witnesses, all political subordinates of their chief (Coedès, *IC,* 2:124); another seventh-century inscription recorded the gifts of twenty-five persons to the local cult temple as a display of homage to a chief (5:37–38). In yet another inscription a *liṅga* was set up in the name of a dominant local family by a brother-in-law; this gift denoted the subordination of his family to the religious prowess of his new in-laws, who thus became dominant over his family's lineage network (2:27–28).

15. The nature of Jayavarman's integration of the local and Hindu religious traditions is revealed in a seventh-century inscription in which Jayavarman ordered bondsmen to be conducted to a prominent chief and then allocated among the monarch's sanctuaries in a certain area (Coedès, *IC,* 2:117, as discussed by Nidhi Aeusrivongse, "*Devarāja* Cult and Khmer Kingship at Angkor," in *Explorations in Early Southeast Asian History: The Origins of Southeast Asian Statecraft,* ed. Kenneth R. Hall and John K. Whitmore, 115). In this inscription "Hindu" gods shared the "domain" of a tree spirit also named in a 611 inscription that recorded the merging of arrangements for maintaining a "Hindu" god's cult with those in honor of a sacred tree (*IC,* 2:21–23, as discussed in Aeusrivongse; the 611 inscription seems to distinguish the involvement of a political overlord). In these two instances, the local tree spirit acquired a direct relationship with a political overlord (Jayavarman) as well as with "Hindu" gods. This local spirit was thereby provided a place in the "Hindu" pantheon and also in the network of social and political relationships that defined seventh-century Khmer society in that early period of overlordship. The familiar local spirit became identified with the more abstract and universal Indian deities and was thus as well upgraded to an entity with greater distinction than was previously the case. Throughout Khmer history no single Khmer chief or "monarch" monopolized the "Hindu" materials. Khmer elites/chiefs as a whole were involved as early religious and political relationships overlapped. Seventh-century Khmer chiefs did, however, refer to themselves as "worshippers" *(bhakta)* of their overlords (see Wolters, "Khmer 'Hinduism' "). They explained this homage as being due to their overlord's special spiritual relationship with Śiva, which brought rewards to those who served him. Subordinate chiefs, with their own devotional cults, offered Śiva gifts as tokens of their devotion to powerful politi-

cal overlords such as Jayavarman. The "Hindu" cults in honor of Śiva heightened the political subordinate's devotion to Śiva and thereby called attention to a network of relationships in early Khmer society.

16. The *devarāja* cult continued to provide a source of unity among the Khmer, even after its direct importance in providing legitimacy to Khmer monarchs declined after the tenth century. The Sdok Kak Thom inscription of 1052, for instance, perpetuated the *devarāja* rites, proclaiming that the present and future kings could invoke additional supernatural protection from the deified ancestors (George Coedès and P. Dupont, "Les stèles de Sdok Kak Thom, Phnom Sandak et Prah Vihar," *BEFEO* 43 [1943–1946]: 56–154). Kulke, *Devarāja Cult,* distinguishes the *devarāja* cult from the personal cults of later Khmer monarchs.

17. I wish to thank Claude Jacques for pointing out the importance of the "protectors" of Angkor-era monarchs.

18. A. Barth and A. Bergaigne, *Inscriptions Sanskrites du Cambodge et Campa* (hereafter *ISCC*), 370.

19. Coedès, *IC,* 3:210.

20. Sūryavarman's association with the realm of the dead is further reinforced by his posthumous name "Nirvāṇapada," which indicated that he was the way to the abode of Nirvāṇa.

21. Eleanor Moron, "Configurations of Time and Space at Angkor Wat," *Studies in Indo-Asian Art and Culture* 5 (1977): 217–267. In Indian cosmology the *kṛta yuga* was followed by the age of decay *(treta yuga),* the age of dangerous balance between perfection and imperfection when spiritual perfection was lost *(dvāpara yuga),* and then the age of strife *(kali yuga),* which would be followed by a new *kṛta yuga* as the cycle repeated.

22. Wolters, "Khmer 'Hinduism'," discusses the importance of this association in Khmer tradition.

23. George Coedès, *The Indianized States of Southeast Asia,* ed. Walter F. Vella, 159–164. Vietnamese chronicles report three Khmer raids on the Vietnam capital at Nghệ-an during Sūryavarman II's reign, in 1127, 1128, and 1132. The last raid was joined by the Chams. See the *Đại Việt sũ-ký toàn thu',* as reported in O. W. Wolters, *History, Culture, and Region in Southeast Asian Perspectives,* 61 n. 15.

24. Briggs, *Ancient Khmer Empire;* and Bernard P. Groslier, *The Art of Indochina.*

25. Chou Ta-kuan, *Notes on the Customs of Cambodia translated from the Shuo-fu,* trans. Paul Pelliot (trans. from French into English by J. G. d'Avery Paul), 31.

26. Barth and Bergaigne, *ISCC,* 407.

27. Ibid., 473.

28. Ibid., 502; see also Wolters, *History, Culture, and Region,* 85–92, where Wolters discusses other Khmer inscriptions in which kings "spread everywhere and ceaselessly the *amrita* (ambrosia) of his immaculate glory" (quoting *ISCC,* 426).

29. W. J. van Liere, "Traditional Water Management in the Lower Mekong Basin," *World Archaeology* 11, 3 (1980): 274.

30. The waterworks around the Khmer capital at Angkor were dominated by two artificial lakes—the east and west *baray,* which connected with the Tonle Sap. Yaśovarman I's artificial lake, the east *baray,* constructed in the 890s at the

time when the capital was being established at Angkor, was the first. It has been estimated that the construction of the second *baray* to the west, probably initiated by Sūryavarman I in the eleventh century, at least doubled the amount of cultivated land in the Angkor region and provided the necessary economic wealth for the dramatic expansion of the Khmer state at that time (Bernard P. Groslier, *Angkor et le Cambodge au XVIe siècle d'après les sources Portugaises et Espagnoles,* 108–112). The resulting economic prosperity has been viewed as being responsible for the impressive urban development, recorded in Khmer inscriptions, that took place in the tenth and eleventh centuries (H. de Mestier du Bourg, "La première moitié de XIe siecle au Cambodge: Suryavarman Ier, sa vie et quelques aspects des institutions à son époque," *JA* 258, 3–4 [1970]: 308). W. J. van Liere, arguing against Groslier's view that the *baray* were critical sources of water for the region, notes that the *baray* did not contribute water to the region's agricultural production (van Liere, "Traditional Water Management," 265–280). Van Liere points out that Angkor-era agriculture was based on a bunded-field transplanted wet-rice method of cultivation. The Angkor *baray* were not designed to distribute water in this system, and when modern economic developers equipped the *baray* to do this, local farmers refused to use the *baray* water, preferring to connect their fields to the receding flood zone of the Tonle Sap from which they had traditionally drawn water (p. 279).

31. Van Liere, "Traditional Water Management."

32. Also important was a network of earth works that were concentrated downriver from Angkor on the edge of the Tonle Sap, which also were intended to retain floodwaters. Van Liere was impressed with the engineering of the Khmer hydraulic system and especially found that the Khmer well understood how to slope the waterfall from Phnom Kulen to the Tonle Sap (ibid., 277).

33. See discussion in chapter 1 of the importance of establishing a *maṇḍala* in early Southeast Asian states.

34. Chou Ta-kuan tells of Khmer people curing themselves from illness by bathing in the Siem Reap (river) that flowed from Phnom Kulen through Angkor to the Tonle Sap (Chou Ta-kuan, *Notes on the Customs of Cambodia,* 31).

35. Coedès, *Indianized States,* 100–103. After the establishment of Hariharālaya the *devarāja* cult was brought from Phnom Kulen to "reside" in the new Khmer capital.

36. See Wolters, *History, Culture, and Region,* 87.

37. Coedès, *IC,* 2:135.

38. Via the exchange of metals or goods for land. See, for example, ibid., 6:32.

39. Ibid., 5:7.

40. For example, in ibid., 3:180–192; 7:104–119; 5:143–146.

41. Ibid., 2:21; 2:22; 2:23; 2:37; 2:123; 2:135; 2:154; 2:200; 5:39; 6:47; 6:49; 6:52.

42. See, for example, ibid., 2:23; 2:200; 5:15; 5:87; 6:49.

43. See M. C. Ricklefs, "Land and the Law in the Epigraphy of Tenth-Century Cambodia," *JAS* 26, 3 (1967): 411–420.

44. See O. W. Wolters, "North-Western Cambodia in the Seventh Century," *BSOAS* 37, 2 (1974): 383, where Wolters argues that in early Cambodian history local chiefs dominated and that only Jayavarman I stands out as being able to hold together a large territory for a considerable length of time, although his achievement did not survive him. The early Khmer "state," Wolters holds, was a

temporary entity based upon the success of such independent leaders. See also Wolters, "Jayavarman II's Military Power," 21–30, where Wolters demonstrates that the reign of Jayavarman II marked the beginning of a unified Khmer political order.

45. Coedès, *IC,* 2:12; 2:39; 2:117; 2:199; 2:121; 2:45; Barth and Bergaigne, *ISCC,* 51, 60.

46. *Miśrabhoga* (Coedès, *IC,* 2:39; 2:117; 2:199), *paribhoga* (*IC,* 2:121), and the assignment of a pond (Barth and Bergaigne, *ISCC,* 1:58). Such consolidations were taking place at the regional level, initiated by regional elites. Sachchidanand Sahai finds three levels of Khmer state administration fully evolved in the Angkor era: the state, the region *(pramān* or *viṣaya),* and the village *(sruk)* (see Sahai, "Territorial Administration in Ancient Cambodia," *The South East Asian Review* 2, 1 [1977]: 35–50). Key in this system was the integration of the regional networks of villages. Sūryavarman I was especially conspicuous in recruiting the leaders of regions into his state's bureaucratic structure as provincial chiefs. See for instance *IC,* 6:273–274, where the "elected chief" of a region became a provincial or district chief in the royal administration. Further, Angkor kings did not permit *miśrabhoga* consolidations within their realm except with the formal approval of the monarch himself, seemingly to limit the additional growth of a regional elite's resources. In this light the *miśrabhoga* consolidations in pre-Angkor epigraphy may be seen as contributing to the establishment of a regional elite's power base.

47. Coedès, *IC,* 3:145; 5:25; 5:30; Barth and Bergaigne, *ISCC,* 42, 44.

48. Coedès, *IC,* 6:115.

49. Claude Jacques, " 'Funan,' 'Zhenla'; The Reality Concealed by these Chinese Views of Indochina," in Smith and Watson, *Early South East Asia,* 371–379, recently revised Jayavarman II's reign dates. As opposed to earlier opinions that Jayavarman's reign began in 802 (see Wolters, "Jayavarman II's Military Power"), Jacques demonstrates that Jayavarman emerged as Khmer monarch in 770 and ruled until 834. Wolters uses the Nakhọn Si Thammarat inscriptions discussed in chapter 5 to explain a seeming reference by Jayavarman II to Java in Khmer epigraphy (Wolters, "Studying Srivijaya," *JMBRAS* 52, 2 [1979]: 12) and thus dates the beginning of his reign shortly before the 775 date of the Nakhọn Si Thammarat "Side A" inscription.

50. Barth and Bergaigne, *ISCC,* 539.

51. Wolters, "Jayavarman II's Military Power," 22; George Coedès, "La stèle de Palhal," *BEFEO* 13, 6 (1913): 33; Pierre Dupont, "Les dèbuts de la royauté Angkorienne," *BEFEO* 46, 1 (1952): 148–149, 168–169.

52. The Palhal inscription states that Garyāk, given to the Angkor Borei brothers, had a temple *(tīrtha),* suggesting that it was already in the possession of previous occupants, presumably in a territory where the chiefs had decided not to accept Jayavarman's authority. See Wolters, "Jayavarman II's Military Power," 26-27; Coedès, "La stèle de Palhal," 33; Dupont, "Les dèbuts de la royauté," 148–149.

53. He was apparently successful; during the reign of Jayavarman's successor Jayavarman III (850–877) family members remained allies of the king and were said to be royal favorites (Coedès, "La stèle de Palhal," 34). Wolters notes that this wife of Jayavarman did not produce the heir, Jayavardhana, who reigned as Jayavarman III (Barth and Bergaigne, *ISCC,* 370, 541), suggesting that the Angkor Borei brothers' sister was not of "royal birth" (ibid., 370; Coedès, *IC,*

5:168). See Wolters, "Jayavarman II's Military Power," 25. Despite this seeming slight, the brothers' family remained allies, soothed by being "royal favorites."

On the significance of marriage alliances in Khmer kingship, see A. Thomas Kirsch, "Kinship, Genealogical Claims, and Societal Integration in Ancient Khmer Society: An Interpretation," in *Southeast Asian History and Historiography: Essays Presented to D. G. E. Hall,* ed. C. D. Cowan and O. W. Wolters, 190–202. Kirsch finds that regionally powerful Khmer families often gave daughters as wives to Khmer kings; Khmer monarchs in return enhanced the economic, social, or political status of their wives' families. For example, among the inscriptions of Jayavarman II there are at least seven instances of marriage alliances between Jayavarman and families supporting the king.

54. Wolters, "Jayavarman II's Military Power," 24; Coedès, *IC,* 7:133; Coedès, "La stèle de Palhal," 33.

55. Coedès, *IC,* 7:133; Wolters, "Jayavarman II's Military Power," 22; and Coedès and Dupont, "Les stèles de Sdok Kak Thom," 56–154.

56. L. A. Sedov, "On the Problem of the Economic System in Angkor Cambodia in the IX–XII Centuries," *Narody Asii i Afriki, Istoria, Ekonomika, Kul'tura* 6 (Akademija Nauk SSR, 1963): 73–81, trans. Antonia Glasse.

57. Philippe Stern, "Diversité et rythme des fondations royales Khmères," *BEFEO* 44, 2 (1951): 649–685. Stern coined the phrase "zone of imprecision," suggesting that omission of the proper sequence revealed the fundamental weakness of the state center during the era of "imprecision," until Jayavarman VII reestablished the center's supremacy.

58. Michael Vickery, "The Reign of Sūryavarman I and the Dynamics of Angkorean Development," *Proceedings, Eighth International Association of Historians of Asia Conference.*

59. Coedès, *IC,* 7:164–189.

60. Coedès and Dupont, "Les stèles de Sdok Kak Thom."

61. Ricklefs, "Land and the Law," 415.

62. In Khmer inscriptions from Phimai, which was an example of a peripheral area to Sūryavarman's core, there is evidence that this type of alliance was formed with the local elite. A Phimai inscription (1041) names a *khloñ viṣaya* for this area. Since the inscription makes no special reference to the chief's status, as was common when an individual with royal ties was appointed, it would seem to indicate that this figure was a chief of the local population whose traditions were being retained (Coedès, *IC,* 7:124–126). On the other hand, a Lopburi inscription from the same period, which registers the extension of the Khmer administration into the old Dvāravatī region, contains evidence that a *khloñ tamrvāc viṣaya,* a royal "inspector"—a person with ties to the center—was assigned by Sūryavarman to oversee this western area (George Coedès, *Recueil des inscriptions du Siam,* 13–18). Yet there is no evidence of a massive influx of Khmer administrators into Lopburi, indicating that the local Khmer government incorporated many of the indigenous elites. See also Milton Osborne's analysis of the integration of the Iśanapura and Sambupura areas into the Khmer realm in Osborne, "Notes on Early Cambodian Provincial History: Isanapura and Sambhupura," *France-Asie/Asia* 20, 4 (1966): 433–449.

63. The text is translated in Briggs, *Ancient Khmer Empire,* 151.

64. Robert Heine-Geldern, "Conceptions of State and Kingship in Southeast Asia," *The Far Eastern Quarterly* 2 (1942): 15–30.

65. Coedès, *IC,* 3:57–64; 4:140–150; 6:225–227.

66. This is consistent with the idea that Jayavarman VII's reign followed a period of disorder in which the Chams raided and looted the Khmer capital. Claude Jacques criticizes the reconstruction of George Coedès (*Indianized States,* 166, 169–171), which, using Chinese and indigenous sources, views the destruction of the Khmer capital in 1177 as the consequence of a Cham invasion. Jacques believes, based on his study of Khmer and Cham epigraphy, that the future Jayavarman VII was visiting in Champa when a major revolt broke out in the Khmer realm. With Cham assistance Jayavarman put down this civil strife and then assumed the Khmer throne. Jacques notes in personal communication that the twelfth-century prominence of Viṣṇu worship among Khmer monarchs (e.g., Sūryavarman II's dedication of Angkor Wat to Viṣṇu) was in some way related to a strong interrelationship between the Khmer and Cham kings, who confirmed their ties by a marriage alliance. Viṣṇu, not Śiva, was the traditional protector of Cham monarchs. When Jayavarman reestablished order in the Khmer realm he began to patronize Buddhism as a new source of legitimacy, but maintained his ties to the traditional "protectors" by surrounding the central Buddhist shrine of Angkor Thom's Bayon with images of Śiva, Viṣṇu, and indigenous protector deities. This helps to explain the prominence of Cham royalty as leaders of Khmer armies during Jayavarman's time (Coedès, 170). The major construction projects of Jayavarman's reign were part of his attempt to restore royal legitimacy and power, drawing attention to himself rather than to his subordinate "bureaucrats"—who may well have been opposed to his seizure of the throne—and thus reversing patterns typical since Rājendravarman's reign. Thus, too, it was Jayavarman VII who restored the patterns of Khmer kingship identified by Stern, but which had lapsed during the late tenth century when Khmer statecraft became more integrated. Supporting this proposal are the significant number of references to non-Khmer "bureaucrats" serving in Jayavarman VII's royal administration, a pattern that is unusual in earlier epigraphy. I wish to thank Professor Jacques for discussing his research on Jayavarman's reign with me.

67. On the application of the term "feudal" to Khmer statecraft, see Mabbett, "Kingship in Angkor." The ability of Khmer monarchs from the time of Jayavarman II to Sūryavarman II to wage apparently massive warfare demonstrates the strength and unity of the Khmer state, despite the impression that day-to-day government did not seem to be concerned with anything more extensive than securing the material needs of the center or mediating local disputes and interests. Mabbett notes that Khmer monarchs created special posts with ceremonial functions and prospects for future favors in order to attract members of the traditional landed elites. Khmer kings accommodated powerful kinship groups, each with its own network of relatives and dependents, by giving them administrative responsibilities, while the monarch monopolized divine authority. Subordinate Khmer elites thus flourished under a strong monarch. The Khmer system offset the absence of a strong centralized professional bureaucracy and dynastic institutions that were monopolized by a distinct "royal family." See also I. W. Mabbett, "Varṇas in Angkor and the Indian Caste System," *JAS* 36, 3 (1977): 429–442.

68. Coedès, *IC,* 6:254–272.

69. Coedès and Dupont, "Les stèles de Sdok Kak Thom."

70. Coedès, *IC,* 3:26–28; 3:29–33; 4:39–44; 5:125–242; 6:154–164; 3:148–156; 6:192–194.

71. Ibid., 7:94–98; 7:45–47; 5:182–185; 6:218–222; 5:306–313.

72. Ibid., 6:254–272. The pattern of such land assignment was: (1) a family applied to the king requesting "vacant land"; (2) the king decided whether to approve the request, while sending royal envoys to notify a local tribunal of the impending assignment; (3) villages in the settlement and neighboring villages were notified and were requested to state if there were conflicting claims (note that even the common man had rights in land transactions and that the king's authority over the land was certainly not absolute as has too often been argued about Khmer kingship; see, for example, Harry J. Benda, "The Structure of Southeast Asian History: Some Preliminary Observations," *JSEAS* 3 [March 1962]: 106ff.); (4) if the request was approved a ceremony formally enacted the assignment; normally a stone post was erected that was consecrated as a *liṅga* and became the center of a shrine/temple built around it; and (5) if the land was unpopulated the settlement of the land tract would then formally begin.

73. Ibid., 3:3–24.

74. Ibid., 5:125–142.

75. Ibid., 3:180–192: donations were subject to the authority of a relative versed in sacred lore (a *pandit*); workers associated with the land were subject to no other authority. But there is no similar specific restriction on property donated separately by others and such property was not subject to the donor's relatives. Ibid., 7:109–119: land donated remained under the authority of relatives of the donor who were "qualified in religion." Ibid., 5:143–146: the family of the donor was excluded from authority over the property except children and grandchildren who entered the priesthood.

76. Kulke, *Devarāja Cult,* passim.

77. See Clifford Geertz's model of the "theater state" in Geertz, *Islam Observed,* 36–39.

78. Bourdieu, *Outline of a Theory of Practice.* See Arjun Appadurai and Carol Appadurai Breckenridge, "The South Indian Temple: Authority, Honour, and Redistribution," *Contributions to Indian Sociology* (NS) 10, 2 (1976): 187–211, which points to the role of south Indian temples as centers of symbolic redistributions. Important articles on the economic functions of South Asian temples include Burton Stein, "The Economic Function of a Medieval South Indian Temple," *JAS* 19, 2 (1960): 163–176, and George W. Spencer, "Temple Money-Lending and Livestock Redistribution," *The Indian Economic and Social History Review* 3 (1968): 277–293.

79. Donors normally assigned a portion of the income from a parcel of land to a temple and often responsibility for the development and management of the land as well. Efficient land management supplied the temple with the revenues necessary to support the temple's various activities, usually a designated share of the land's production. But if the total productivity was increased by the temple's management then the donor's take from the land, the consequence of unassigned rights on a parcel's income retained by the donor, would also increase. See for instance Coedès, *IC,* 3:180–192; 7:104–119; 5:143–146. Among the temple's management force was the *khloñ karya,* the "superintendent of temple work" (ibid., 5:244), and the *khloñ kṣetra,* the "head of temple domains" (ibid., 3:180–192).

80. Appadurai and Breckenridge, "The South Indian Temple," 206–207.

81. For example, Coedès, *IC,* 2:82, 87. See Osborne, "Notes on Early Cambo-

dian Provincial History," 446, where a local deity of Sambupura was placed under the protection of the central shrine of Jayavarman VII's realm at Angkor's Bayon. See also *IC,* 3:170–171, where a *liṅga* to Śiva was erected in the temple of Amratakeśvara, a local family god of Sambupura, by a queen of Jayavarman II; there is another notice of a *liṅga* erected by Indravarman (877–889) in the temple of Amratakeśvara (*IC,* 1:31–35). Sambupura was an important Mekong River outpost on the western edge of the Khmer realm (Osborne, 445–446). Osborne demonstrates similar patterns of integration at Iśanapura, where regional and provincial gods were subordinated to central deities, but were integrated into royal cults in an important urban center within the Khmer heartland (pp. 436–439).

82. Bourdieu stresses the theoretical importance of establishing a comprehensive balance sheet differentiating between symbolic profits and material (economic) profits, where honor has greater value than the material and acquisition of "cultural capital" is preferred (Bourdieu, *Outline of a Theory of Practice,* 181–183). On the implications of such "gift" relationships, see Marcel Mauss, *The Gift;* Henri Hubert and Marcel Mauss, *Sacrifice: Its Nature and Function;* Sahlins, *Stone Age Economics;* and Bourdieu, *Outline of a Theory of Practice,* 159–197. Another aspect of the utilization of gift exchanges as the source of political integration was the marriage alliances forged by Khmer monarchs as discussed above and in Kirsch, "Kinship, Genealogical Claims, and Societal Integration."

83. Rather than a "hydraulic agricultural" network that demanded a centrality of control by a state (Karl Wittfogel, *Oriental Despotism*), the Angkor state developed regionally based hydroagricultural networks that facilitated the extension of wet-rice cultivation. Supervision of the construction and operation of these regional irrigational networks was vested with regional temples. See for example Coedès and Dupont, "Les stèles de Sdok Kak Thom," where the heads of a family and its branches acted—through their family temple—as managers of land, clearing forests, erecting dwellings for new inhabitants, building dikes and reservoirs, and setting "slaves" to work on land assigned for development.

84. Ricklefs, "Land and the Law," passim.

85. Recently enslaved laborers were unlikely to understand the technical requirements of the new irrigation system and had to learn when and how to execute, considering the fluctuating environmental conditions, the variety of tasks necessary in a wet-rice system. Carol Appadurai Breckenridge, "Land as Gift in the Vijayanagara Period," is useful for comparative purposes. Breckenridge views south Indian temples as centers of a "storage economy."

86. Breckenridge argues that in an era of change and uncertainty temples provided not only authority over the development of the agricultural sector, but also were cultural mediators providing psychological continuity to a potentially insecure and unstable social order facing an influx of new manpower, new agricultural technology, and new political alliances (ibid.).

87. Indeed, Khmer inscriptions describe agricultural productivity as "spiritual gain" and record the rights of monarchs and temples to a share of this "spiritual gain." See Sachchidanand Sahai, "Fiscal Administration in Ancient Cambodia," *The South East Asian Review* 1, 2 (1977): 123–138, especially 130. See also Bourdieu, *Outline of a Theory of Practice,* 171–183. Man's relationship with the land in traditional societies, Bourdieu argues, was a holy/sacred relationship. Land

was never treated as a raw material to be exploited but was an object of respect mixed with fear; bad treatment of the natural realm brought revenge (p. 175).

88. Coedès, *IC,* 3:180–192.

89. In the literature about Angkor, *kñuṁ* and most other references to Khmer agricultural laborers are translated "slaves," but this is misleading. In some instances "slaves" were given permanent lots of land and had rights over this land, in others they tilled fields that did not belong to them but received certain rights of security in exchange for their labor. See Mabbett, "Kingship in Angkor," 42ff.; also J. M. Jacob, "Pre-Angkor Cambodia: Evidence from the Inscriptions in Khmer concerning the Common People and their Environment," in Smith and Watson, *Early South East Asia,* 423–426, for differing views on the debate over the appropriateness of the translation of *kñuṁ* as "slave." In Khmer epigraphy, *kñuṁ* grind, spin, groom elephants, mold statues, sing, play musical instruments, sew leaves into mats, and assist in temple ceremonies, as well as till the soil (Mabbett, 409).

90. Other inscriptions demonstrate that land assigned to individual priests could be reassigned or the land and its *kñuṁ* sold. See, for example, Coedès, *IC,* 4:106–107.

91. This dating system was preserved in Thailand into the nineteenth century.

92. Coedès, *IC,* 3:3–24.

93. Sedov, "On the Problem of the Economic System in Angkor," calculates that the nineteen *kñuṁ* produced 5,715 kg. of rice annually, that is, 300 kg. per person, of which 85.6 kg. remained for personal consumption, the temple receiving 71.5 percent of the labor forces' productivity. In comparison the field assigned for the production of rice for the chief priest's personal consumption provided 553.4 kg. of hulled rice per year, or 1.5 kg. per day. Aside from the production of the land directly assigned to support the chief priest, Sedov argues that the chief priest undoubtedly received a share of the temple's "sacrificial rice." The implication is that these priests could use this additional daily rice allotment to secure other goods for their personal consumption. While there is little information on the functioning of Khmer marketplaces or of the specific role of temples or even the Khmer government as market supervisors or participants, temple priests could have had an impact upon market prices by withholding their allotments of surplus foodstuffs from the market or by exchanging this surplus within the marketplace, depending upon when in the agricultural calendar this was done.

94. See Coedès, *IC,* 4:107, where a certain amount of rice designated to support temple sacrifice was paid to the state.

95. The state may or may not have exercised its revenue rights over land, and often didn't. Its revenue demands were based on the land's capacity for production. As inscriptions recording land transfers normally note the land's productivity, it would seem that land surveys were conducted and that the state's revenue expectations were set accordingly. This does not mean that estimates of productivity were necessarily set by royal officials; they could equally have been established by the local elite, or derived through negotiation between the local elite and royal officials. Royal revenue officials received payments in kind or labor services, keeping a portion of their collections for their own benefit and passing a portion on to the king's treasury. The royal family thus derived income from such collections as well as from their own estates. See Sahai, "Fiscal Administration in

Ancient Cambodia," 123–138. Sahai believes that a Khmer monarch could rightfully claim between one-sixth to one-fourth of the "spiritual gain (i.e., the production) of his subjects" (p. 130). The phrasing of such royal claims, that is, taking a share in his subjects' "spiritual gains," well illustrates the mobilization of production under a religious pretext.

96. Coedès, *IC,* 5:229–234.

97. Ibid., 6:228–233. In addition, 6 kg. of vegetable oil, 25 kg. of sesame seeds, 25 kg. of chick peas, 2 banners, and 2 measures of cloth were annually provided by the local temple to the central temple.

98. George Coedès, "La stèle de Ta-prohm," *BEFEO* 6 (1906): 44–81.

99. Sedov, "On the Problem of the Economic System in Angkor," estimates that 366.8 tons of rice were supplied by roughly 66,625 villagers, each of the 3,140 villages providing roughly 117 kg. per year to the central temple.

100. Coedès, "La stèle de Prah Khan d'Angkor," *BEFEO* 41 (1941): 255–301. Despite this regional separation, there was a sense of belonging to a Khmer "state." O. W. Wolters argues that the Khmer sense of territorial identity was unlike that among other populations in early Southeast Asia. This sense is conveyed, for example, in an 868 inscription from the Korat Plateau that describes that area as being "outside *Kambudesa*" (Coedès, *IC,* 6:85; noted in Wolters, *History, Culture, and Region,* 31). Wolters believes that this attitude was confirmed by almost five hundred years of territorial integrity. Yet Khmer royal authority was often seen as limitless, as for instance in Yaśovarman I's (889–910) claim to have ruled from the Bay of Bengal to China, and Jayavarman VII's late twelfth-century records that he had received the homage of Vietnam and Java. See chap. 8.

101. By contrast, Cambodia's 3 million people during the early 1960s prewar era produced 1.2 million tons of rice annually, 400 kg. per person. Since the figure of 200 kg. of hulled rice is roughly equivalent to 400 kg. of paddy rice, Sedov, "On the Problem of the Economic System in Angkor," estimates the productivity of twelfth-century and twentieth-century Cambodian peasants to be equal. When one considers that Khmer monarchs could also claim one-sixth to one-fourth of a peasant's production, the degree of exploitation of Khmer workers is even more pronounced. In the Trapaeng Don An inscription noted above, by comparison, Sedov estimates that the local temple *kñuṁ* were allotted 86 kg. of their annual production of 300 kg. of rice, or about 30 percent of their total production, a figure consistent with those of the royal temple of Prah Khan.

102. See Michael Aung-Thwin, "Kingship, the *Saṅgha,* and Society in Pagan," in Hall and Whitmore, *Explorations in Early Southeast Asian History,* 205–256.

103. Boechari, "Some Considerations on the Problem of the Shift of Mataram's Centre of Government from Central to East Java in the 10th Century," in Smith and Watson, *Early South East Asia,* 473–491.

104. Hermann Kulke, "Early State Formation and Ritual Policy in Eastern Java," in *Proceedings, Eighth International Association of Historians of Asia Conference,* offers a similar thesis.

105. Buchari, "A Preliminary Note on the Study of the Old-Javanese Civil Administration," *Madjalah Ilmu-Ilmu Sastra Indonesia* 1 (1963): 122–133, and Boechari, "Epigraphy and Indonesian Historiography," in *An Introduction to Indonesian Historiography,* ed. Soedjatmoko et al., 50–60. *Sīma* grants were intended to develop economically peripheral lands, reward loyal followers, and extend the control of the throne.

106. Th. G. Th. Pigeaud, *Java in the Fourteenth Century: A Study in Cultural History,* 4:490.

107. See J. G. de Casparis, *Prasasti Indonesia I: Inscripties uit de Çailendra-Tijd,* 24ff., 73, 79; and Kulke, "Early State Formation."

Chapter 7

This chapter expands upon two earlier studies by Kenneth R. Hall: "Khmer Commercial Developments and Foreign Contacts under Sūryavarman I," *Journal of the Economic and Social History of the Orient* (hereafter *JESHO*) 18, 3 (1975): 318–336; and "Eleventh-Century Commercial Developments in Angkor and Champa," *JSEAS* 10, 2 (1979): 420–434.

1. H. de Mestier du Bourg, "La première moitié du XIe siècle au Cambodge: Suryavarman Ier, sa vie et quelques aspects des institutions à son époque," *JA* 258, 3–4 (1970): 281–314; and Michael Vickery, "The Reign of Sūryavarman I and the Dynamics of Angkorean Development," *Proceedings, Eighth International Association of Historians of Asia Conference.* Du Bourg notes in particular the intense religious and economic development of the Prāḥ Vihār region in the time of Sūryavarman I (p. 291), and also believes that the Angkor complex was constructed utilizing resources derived from lands assigned to and developed by temples (pp. 306–307).

2. Du Bourg, "La première moitié," 308.

3. The Mon region of Dvāravatī was absorbed by the Khmer in the mid-tenth century but reemerged as a recognizable cultural entity in the fourteenth century. See H. L. Shorto, "A Mon Genealogy of Kings: Observations on *The Nidāna Ārambhakanthā,*" in *Historians of South-East Asia,* ed. D. G. E. Hall, 163–172.

4. These are compounds of the Khmer words *khloñ* ("worker") and *jnvāl* ("Khmer"), resulting in the meaning "one who works for money" (George Coedès, *IC,* 3:14 n. 1), and the Sanskrit word *vāṇija* ("merchant"). Resident vendors had local roots that often included landholding rights. See for example *IC,* 3:11–16.

5. Ibid., 4:108–139. Here gold, precious stones, pearls, cloth goods, and "goods from China" were traded. Other Khmer inscriptions refer to silk, cotton, and other cloth goods; spices; animals such as cows, buffaloes, elephants, horses, and pigs; sandalwood; slaves; ceramics; precious stones; rice; and gold and silver as being among the commodities one could acquire from a merchant. The participation of itinerant merchants from foreign lands in the activities of Khmer commercial centers can be identified. A Cham merchant (Vāp Chāmpa) and a Vietnamese merchant (a *Yvan* of Kaṃvaṅ Tadiṅ) sold goods along with local merchants *(khloñ jnvāl)* in the eastern area of Phum Mīen in 984 (ibid., 6:183–186). A little farther west, at Tuol Pei (992), a China trader (Vāp China) was dealing in slaves, gold, silver, and other goods (E. T. Aymonier, *Le Cambodge,* 1:443).

6. Coedès, *IC,* 5:270–271.

7. Ibid., 7:94–98.

8. Aymonier, *Le Cambodge,* 1:443.

9. Coedès, *IC,* 6:225–227.

10. Ibid., 3:57–61.

11. Ibid., 4:140–150.

12. Ibid., 3:16–24.

13. Ibid., 3:16–24; 5:133–142.
14. See Du Bourg, "La première moitié," 307.
15. Coedès, *IC,* 5:133–142.
16. Ibid., 4:149–150.
17. Du Bourg, "La première moitié," passim.
18. Merchants may thus be seen as intervening on the Khmer elites' behalf, circumventing local autonomy relative to the centralizing ambitions of regional *(khloñ viṣaya)* and royal authorities. Merchants named in the inscriptions appear to have derived stature—which likely contributed to their commercial success—via the patronage of the Khmer elites whom they served. Similar use of merchants to extend royal authority is documented in Javanese epigraphy, as discussed in chapters 1 and 9.
19. Du Bourg, "La première moitié," 297.
20. Ibid., 298.
21. In the Beṅ Vien inscription of 946, it was noted that Rājendravarman was "victorious in combat against the powerful and wicked Rāmaṇya and Champa" (Coedès, *IC,* 5:97–104). Based on Burmese records that name the old Mon area at Pegu Rāmaññadesa, the Rāmaṇya in the Khmer inscription is identified as that of the Mons of eastern Dvāravatī. Two inscriptions from Thailand's Prachinburi province record activity in this area by Rājendravarman II. One was exhibited at the National Museum, Bangkok, in 1971; the other, from Aranna Pradesa district, was published in the Thai journal *Sinlapakon* 16, 1 (1972): 61–65. This information was generously supplied by Hiram W. Woodward of the University of Vermont, who has discussed the tenth-century evidence with me.
22. George Coedès, *Recueil des inscriptions du Siam,* 13–15.
23. Map 6 was constructed by plotting the locations of inscriptions that show clear evidence of commercial activity. Locations are based on E. Lunet de Lajonquière, "Carte archéologique de l'ancien Cambodge," *Publications de l'École Française d'Extrême Orient* 9 (1911): insert.
24. As previously noted, Prāḥ Vihār was the scene of intense religious and economic development in the reign of Sūryavarman (Du Bourg, "La première moitié," 291). For an idea of the geography of this area, see L. P. Briggs, *The Ancient Khmer Empire,* 111, fig. 19.
25. Coedès, *IC,* 7:94–98.
26. Louis Finot, "L'inscription de Ban That," *BEFEO* 12 (1912): 2.
27. Coedès, *IC,* 6:183–186. Evidence that this would be the case can be surmised from the 1128 attacks on Vietnam that followed this route. One of these attacks is even noted as having involved over seven hundred boats, an indication of the extent of travel in the upstream area on the Vietnamese side; see the Vietnamese chronicle *Đại Việt sũ-ký toàn thu',* 1: 263, 347. (Gratitude is extended to John K. Whitmore for an English translation of the appropriate sections of the chronicle.) See also Henri Maspero, "La frontière de l'Annam et du Cambodge," *BEFEO* 18, 3 (1918): 29–36.
28. See Milton Osborne, "Notes on Early Cambodian Provincial History: Isanapura and Sambhupura," *France-Asie/Asia* 20, 4 (1966): 447.
29. Coedès, *IC,* 7:63–70. L. P. Briggs, *Ancient Khmer Empire,* 178–182, credits Sūryavarman with bringing the upper Mun Valley into the Khmer administrative structure, dating the foundation of three temples in this region—at Phimai, Phanom Wan, and Phanom Rung—to his reign.
30. A Phimai inscription (1041) makes reference to the syncretic Śaivite cult

with which Sūryavarman was associated (Coedès, *IC,* 7:124–126; see Du Bourg's discussion of Sūryavarman's relationship with this cult in "La première moitié"), a cult that was also known to have been established at Lopburi (Coedès, *Recueil des inscriptions du Siam,* 10–12).

31. The Phimai (1041) inscription uses the twelve-year animal cycle associated with Thai rather than Khmer dating practice. The later development of a cultural center of the Thai-speaking peoples in the Lopburi region reflects the importance of these early communications between Phimai and Lopburi. An early nineteenth-century Thai map shows a well-developed road network connecting Phimai and Lopburi; see Victor Kennedy, "An Indigenous Early Nineteenth Century Map of Central and Northeast Thailand," in *In Memorian Phya Anuman Rajadhon,* ed. Tej Bunag and M. Smithies, 315–348.

32. By the late eleventh century Khmer kings were coming from this northern region. Jayavarman VI (1081–1107) first appears in a Phanom Wan inscription (1082), directing many high civil and religious officials to supervise the local monastery (Briggs, *Ancient Khmer Empire,* 178–179). The inscriptions of Jayavarman and his immediate successors are concentrated in the northern areas of Phimai, Prāḥ Vihār, and Bān Thāt, making a strong case for the development of consistent communication via the Mun River during the reign of Sūryavarman I.

33. It is no coincidence that modern roads from the Tonle Sap region follow this same route via Battambang and Sisophon to Thailand. The distribution of Khmer temple inscriptions indicates that an overland route from the Sisophon-Svay Chek region also connected the Phimai–Phanom Wan area to the Khmer "core."

34. Coedès, *IC,* 3:3–11. Briggs, *Ancient Khmer Empire,* 160, dates the construction of the temple to 1036, the date of this inscription.

35. Coedès, *IC,* 3:11–24.

36. Ibid., 3:13, 60.

37. The epigraphy from Bantāy Pṛāv records visits by the royal retinues *(kaṃsteṅ)* of Sūryavarman I and Harṣavarman III (1071). In the latter inscription, among those present was a man "of the caste from the West" *(varṇa anak pūrva),* who may be considered representative of the western contacts of this Khmer commercial center (ibid., 3:57–64).

38. Coedès, *Recueil des inscriptions du Siam,* 10–15.

39. As identified by O. W. Wolters, "Tāmbraliṅga," *BSOAS* 21 (1958): 587–607.

40. Alastair Lamb, "Kedah and Takuapa: Some Tentative Historical Conclusions," *Federated Museums Journal* 6 (1961): 76. Past literature has presented Tāmbraliṅga as the scene of eleventh-century conflict between the Śrīvijaya maritime empire and the expanding mainland power of the Khmers, as discussed in chapter 8. A political connection between the Khmers and Tāmbraliṅga has yet to be conclusively proved, although Chinese accounts from the Sung period considered Tāmbraliṅga to be within their pattern of geographical knowledge about Cambodia. The Chinese believed that mainland markets supplied Tāmbraliṅga with some of the best incense available. See Wolters, "Tāmbraliṅga," 593–594, 600; and F. Hirth and W. W. Rockhill, *Chau Ju-kua: His Work on the Chinese and Arab Trade in the Twelfth and Thirteenth Centuries, Entitled Chu-fan-chi,* 31–33.

41. Stanley J. O'Connor, *Hindu Gods of Peninsular Siam,* 60–62, and fig. 34.

42. David Wyatt of Cornell University has provided information on a Phattha-

lung chronicle reference to a Tamil inscription from Songkhla dated 983. In this account, a monk states that he is copying this inscription, which records an overland route to the west coast.

43. Alastair Lamb, "Takuapa: The Probable Site of a Pre-Malaccan Entrepot in the Malay Peninsula," in *Malayan and Indonesian Studies,* ed. John Bastin and R. Roolvink, 76–86.

44. Coedès, *IC,* 7:63–70.

45. Aymonier, *Le Cambodge,* 443.

46. Coedès, *IC,* 183–186.

47. Hall, "Khmer Commercial Development and Foreign Contacts under Sūryavarman I," 318–336.

48. See chapter 8.

49. G. H. Luce, *Old Burma, Early Pagan,* 1:21–23, 26, as discussed in chapter 8.

50. George Coedès, *The Indianized States of Southeast Asia,* ed. Walter F. Vella, 17.

51. Rolph Stein, "Le Lin-yi," *Han-Hiue* 2 (1947).

52. Coedès, *Indianized States,* 40.

53. Georges Maspero, *Le Royaume de Champa,* 54–55.

54. Ibid., 53.

55. As evinced by the travel itinerary of the fifth-century voyage of the Indian prince Guṇavarman, who was to have sailed from the Javanese coast to a Cham port on his way to China. See O. W. Wolters, *Early Indonesian Commerce: A Study of the Origins of Sri Vijaya,* 35, and chap. 3.

56. George Coedès, "Deux inscriptions Sanskrites du Fou-nan," *BEFEO* 31 (1931): 1–12.

57. Maspero, *Le Royaume de Champa,* 77–78.

58. George Coedès, *The Making of Southeast Asia,* 77. Earlier references to widespread piracy along the Cham coast—for example, the story of Nāgasena, an Indian monk who was shipwrecked on the Cham coast in the late fifth century and robbed of his possessions (see chap. 3)—suggests that this naval expedition was undertaken to deter piracy along the Cham coast, thus making the coast fit for trade. Fan Tang's title as "Pacifier of the South and Commander-in-Chief of the Military Affairs of the Seashore," reflected the Chinese court's view that he was responsible for maintaining control over Cham coast piracy. Fan Tang successfully engaged the loyalty of the Cham coast seamen. The necessity of a Chinese naval expedition to police the coast in the early seventh century suggests that in that era there was either an unstable relationship between the Cham state and its coastal inhabitants or that Cham monarchs actually encouraged raids as a means of providing their maritime allies with income when the international trade route was in a state of flux and even derived a share of the loot.

59. Wang Gungwu, "The Nanhai Trade: A Study of the Early History of the Chinese Trade in the South China Sea," *JMBRAS* 21, 2 (1958): 90–91. In 875 a new Cham dynasty came to power at Indrapura (Quang-nam), and reference in Chinese sources is henceforth made to Chan-ch'eng, "the Cham city," or Champapura (Maspero, *Le Royaume de Champa,* 6). That the Chinese thought of the Cham domain as principally a maritime state is reflected in *Annam Chí-lúo'c,* written in China in the early fourteenth century by a Vietnamese, Lê Tắc, which gives the following brief note on Champa (Chan-ch'eng-kuo): "(They) established

(their) state on the shore of the sea. Chinese merchant ships cross the sea. The outer barbarians who come and go all congregate here to take on fuel and water" (Lê Tắc, *Annam Chí-lúo'c,* 31). John K. Whitmore of the University of Michigan's Center for South and Southeast Asian Studies provided this translation.

60. See Maspero, *Le Royaume de Champa,* passim. Champa, like the Angkor state, patterned much of its statecraft on Funan, drawing upon its legacy as a former "vassal territory" of the Funan empire. See chap. 3. Early Cham epigraphy reflects the river valley focus of Cham agriculture. In these inscriptions Cham monarchs never assume a role as direct supervisors of agricultural activity, although their meritorious acts are considered responsible for the prosperity of their subject populations. The monarch's place was in the battlefield, where he protected the agrarian communities under his rule and thereby legitimized his ruling status. In return the Cham monarch was entitled to receive one-sixth of local agricultural production (also the official state share due to Khmer monarchs). But transfers of state income rights to property consistently emphasize that the state normally expected to collect only one-tenth of the income, which was assigned to temples, and report that because of the ruler's "benevolence" the state collected only one-tenth instead of its rightful one-sixth share. It is likely that the Cham monarch was largely incapable of collecting local land revenues and was thus assigning a token one-tenth in the hope that the temples might have better luck than he making collections. Instead of provoking hostility by collecting his share of local production, the monarch instead drew the symbolic merit that his "donation" bestowed. The growing importance of temples as economic centers—and as well as institutions of political consolidation—is shown in the numerous inscriptions that record the assignment to temples of management rights to public granaries by Cham monarchs and their direct political subordinates. Communal granaries played an important role as a source of unity among agricultural communities. Temples were also often responsible for bringing the lands of the Cham political elites under cultivation.

61. Champa was in a position to inherit the entrepôt position filled in earlier centuries by Funan to the south (Paul Pelliot, "Le Fou-nan," *BEFEO* 3 [1903]: 248–303). It was Śrīvijaya, however, that assumed Funan's former position as the chief entrepôt on the maritime route in the seventh century and maintained this position until the eleventh century. Champa's position, recognized by the Chinese, was that of a secondary port.

62. A. Barth and A. Bergaigne, *ISCC,* 253.

63. Aymonier, *Le Cambodge,* 1:191, and Barth and Bergaigne, *ISCC,* 217.

64. Wolters, *Early Indonesian Commerce,* and *The Fall of Srivijaya in Malay History*.

65. The Nakhọn Si Thammarat inscription from the eastern Malay coast dated 775 suggests that the Śrīvijaya monarch held political authority over the Southern Seas during the eighth century (K. A. Nilakanta Sastri, *The History of Srivijaya,* 120, provides the text and an English translation of the dated inscription). There is some debate, however, whether Śrīvijaya's authority during that period was being exercised from Sumatra or from Java (J. G. de Casparis, *Prasasti Indonesia II: Selected Inscriptions from the Seventh to the Ninth Century* A.D., 15–46, 258–261, 288–300, as discussed in chapter 5). Thai historians, however, propose a southern Thailand base, possibly Nakhọn Si Thammarat (M. C. Chand Chirayu Rajani, "Background to the Srivijaya Story," *JSS* 62, 1 [1974]: 174–211; 62, 2

[1974]: 285–324). The Chinese recognized Śrīvijaya's dominance over the Southern Seas until at least the twelfth century (Wolters, *Fall of Srivijaya,* 38), although Bennet Bronson has proposed that Śrīvijaya's hegemony was not constant but was intermittent; the center of authority probably shifted several times during the period when the Chinese were recognizing its dominance (Bennet Bronson and Jan Wisseman, "Palembang as Srivijaya: The Lateness of Early Cities in Southern Southeast Asia," *Asian Perspectives* 19, 2 [1976]: 220–239).

66. The Cham temples were said to have been desecrated in these raids, representing the destruction of the Cham king's legitimacy. As noted in the Po Nagar temple inscription recording these events, the temple's *linga* was carried off by the raiders but the Cham king followed with his navy. He was unable to recover the original *linga,* which was said to have been lost at sea in a battle between the Cham monarch and the raiders. The Cham king not only installed a replacement *linga,* the symbol of his legitimacy, but he also used the loot he acquired while defeating the marauders to reconstruct the damaged temple (Barth and Bergaigne, *ISCC,* 252).

67. See Bronson and Wisseman, "Palembang as Srivijaya."

68. Quoted in Wang Gungwu, "The Nanhai Trade," 81. In addition, the foreign merchant community themselves compounded the situation by sacking Canton in 763.

69. Quoted in ibid., 82. The Vietnamese ports were also subjected to similar raids during the 760s; this indicates their commercial importance in that age. See Coedès, *Making of Southeast Asia,* 79.

70. Wang Gungwu, "The Nanhai Trade," 90–91. T'ang records also show Cham ports to be a source of such local products as ivory, rhinoceros horns, tortoiseshell, amber, and manufactured gold and silver objects.

71. The fleet was destroyed by a gale and only the Cham king's vessel was spared. See Henri Maspero, "Le protectorat general d'Annam sous les T'ang," *BEFEO* 10 (1910): 678.

72. Vijaya, the Cham capital, was taken and five thousand prisoners were carried back to the Lý domain, where they were resettled in new villages. See Coedès, *Making of Southeast Asia,* 83.

73. E. Aymonier, "Première étude sur les inscriptions Tchames," *JA* 17 (1891): 29; see also Louis Finot, "Pāṇḍuranga," *BEFEO* 3 (1903): 634, 643, and Finot, "Nouvelles inscriptions de Po Klaun Garai," *BEFEO* 9 (1909): 205, 208.

74. Paul Ravaisse, "Deux inscriptions coufiques du Campa," *JA* 20, 2 (1922): 247–289. See also Pierre-Yves Manguin, "Études Cam II. L'introduction de l'Islam au Campā," *BEFEO* 66 (1979): 255–287.

75. Kodo Tasaka, "Islam in Champa," *Tohagaku* 4 (1952): 52.

76. The dating of this second effort is significant, since it coincides with the investiture of the new Sung emperor. See Edward H. Schafer, *The Vermilion Bird: T'ang Images of the South,* 75, quoting the *Sung shih* [History of the Sung] and *Wu tai shih* [Notes on military preparations], a series of charts and sailing directions prepared between 1621 and 1628, which report Southeast Asia as it was known to Chinese mariners in the early fifteenth century.

77. Maspero, *Le Royanne de Champa,* 29.

78. It would be useful if one could turn to the Vietnamese chronicles for insight. John Whitmore and I have explored this possibility, but aside from receiving affirmation of the existence of urban centers we have found all such references to the commercial centers of the north to be colored by later Confucian

historians and their general skepticism toward trade. While the Confucian overlay projects a negative attitude toward commerce, as yet limited archaeological evidence (see Jeremy N. C. S. Davidson, "Recent Archaeological Activity in Viet-Nam," *Journal of the Hong Kong Archaeological Society* 6 [1975]: 80–99) as well as Chinese and other external references generally evince a positive commercial stance by the Lý rulers. The Vietnamese chronicles also provide little evidence on the Chams other than references to Champa as being a "country inhabited by monkeys" and a source of manpower. Wars with the Chams are reported, but there is little interest in Cham lifestyle. It is hoped that more detailed analysis by Vietnamese historians may in the future provide further insight into these questions.

79. Maspero, "La frontière de l'Annam et du Cambodge," 29–36.

80. Coedès, *IC,* 6:183–186.

81. As noted, as early as the third century Cham navies were pillaging the northern Vietnam coast. The Cham ruler used a naval force in his unsuccessful attempt to recover the *liṅga* stolen from Po Nagar's temple during the eighth-century hostilities, although we are told that he did defeat the "wicked and vicious" plunderers in a naval battle. It is likely that in the eighth century he was also utilizing the seafaring population of his coastal ports and that the problems Cham rulers had with the seafaring groups predated the events of the tenth century. It is even possible, based upon the events of the eleventh century, that the eighth-century desecration of the Po Nagar temple was carried out by rebel seamen from the lower Cham coast whose loyalty to the Cham state in that earlier age was also subject to periodic lapses.

82. Coedès, *Indianized States,* 114. The inscription is reported in Barth and Bergaigne, *ISCC,* 492 n. 3.

83. See Philippe Stern, *L'art du Champa (ancien Annam) et son évolution,* 66–68, 109.

84. Edouard Huber, "L'épigraphie de la dynastie de Đong-du'o'ng," *BEFEO* 11 (1911): 299.

85. A. M. Barrett, "Two Old Javanese Copper-plate Inscriptions of Balitung," M.A. thesis, University of Sidney, 1968, 129. Regional trade was shifting away from Sumatra to the Java Sea region in the eleventh century, and in order to gain access to the valuable spices of the eastern archipelago traders had to deal directly with the Javanese. Thus it is reasonable to suppose that Javanese influence on Cham cultural patterns derived from Champa's participation in the international trade. There are political implications as well, as past historians have attempted to reconstruct the ninth- and tenth-century history of the mainland as being a period of Javanese hegemony. In support of this thesis they pointed to a Khmer inscription in which the Khmer king Jayavarman II (770–834) was said to have come from Java to reign over the Khmer domain and to have established his autonomy symbolically by throwing off his ties to the Javanese. See Coedès, *Indianized States,* 93, 97–98, 100, and chap. 5.

86. Coedès, *Indianized States,* 125, 139–140.

87. Maspero, *Le Royaume de Champa,* 29.

88. In 1050 the Cham monarch was also expanding, or reestablishing, his power over the eastern Khmer border, sacking Sambupura on the Mekong (Osborne, "Notes on Early Cambodian Provincial History," 449). Thus the Cham king's expedition against Pāṇḍuranga was part of a general expansion of his authority in 1050. In this instance, the conquest of Pāṇḍuranga was necessary

before the Cham king could expand along the Mekong. Overland access to Sambupura was difficult, so the Cham king probably launched his expedition up the Mekong from Pāṇḍuranga, utilizing the remnants of Pāṇḍuranga's maritime community, their loyalty newly restored, for this expedition of conquest (or plunder).

89. Aymonier, "Première étude sur les inscriptions Tchames," 29.

90. Anthony Reid, ed., *Slavery, Bondage and Dependency in South-East Asia.*

91. Maspero, *Le Royaume de Champa,* 138–139.

92. Ibid., 141–142.

93. Louis Finot, "Inscriptions du Quang Nam," *BEFEO* 4 (1904): 84.

94. Schafer, *The Vermilion Bird,* 76.

95. Consistent with Schafer's generalization, in the single epigraphic reference to Cham merchants—the 875 inscription from the site of a Buddhist monastery at Amarāvatī (present-day Đong-du'o'ng) in which merchants are included among those who were viewed as likely to take away the monastery's wealth—Cham merchants were not Muslims but were associated with a Buddhist rather than a Hindu temple complex. My research on epigraphy from other areas of Asia has convinced me that this attitude toward merchants was not characteristic of the Chams alone, but was a general attitude of agrarian states that were synthesizing Indic and Sinic cultural values. For example, see Kenneth R. Hall, *Trade and Statecraft in the Age of the Cōḷas.*

96. For example, Coedès, *IC,* 6:225–227; 3:11–16; 4:108–139.

97. Epigraphic evidence documents specialization among Khmer commercial centers, with several urban centers serving as the locus for supralocal exchange due to their strategic position on major communication channels or because the urban center was important as a hub for royal or regional administration or as a focus for religious ceremony. See, for example, Coedès, *IC,* 3:3–24, 57–64.

98. In making this application I do not wish to imply that the indigenous marketing networks of the Khmer realm were centralized or organized into a hierarchical system by a state or merchant elite. There is no evidence of such a purposeful integration of Khmer commercial centers.

99. See, for example, Maspero, *Le Royaume de Champa,* and Coedès, *Indianized States.*

100. R. Stein viewed early Cham civilization as characterized by shifting alliances among regional centers located among the river mouths of the Cham coast (Stein, "Le Lin-yi"); this view was reiterated by I. W. Mabbett, "The 'Indianization' of Southeast Asia: Reflections on the Prehistoric Sources," *JSEAS* 8, 2 (1977): 154. The Chinese characterized Champa as a maritime state; Lê Tắc's *Annam Chí-lúo'c* describes the Cham state as being "on the shore of the sea" (p. 31); earlier Chinese records name the Cham ruler as the "Commander-in-Chief of the Military Affairs of the Seashore." The Vietnamese also thought of Champa as a maritime state, as Vietnamese chronicles report the periodic maritime raids led by Cham rulers against the Red River Delta. Cham inscriptions, too, report the maritime adventures of Cham rulers. A maritime expedition led by the Cham ruler pillaged Angkor in 1177 (Coedès, *Indianized States,* 164); other maritime expeditions led by Cham rulers against the Khmer realm are noted above.

101. Coedès, *Indianized States.* An 1160 inscription from Pāṇḍuranga, for instance, reflects upon the current ruler's victories over the Khmers and Vietnamese but also against the people of Indrapura and Vijaya, the major rival political

centers to the north in the Cham riverine system. Barth and Bergaigne, *ISCC,* 282; Aymonier, "Première étude sur les inscriptions Tchames," 41.

102. Coedès, *Indianized States,* 311 n. 20.

103. See Kenneth R. Hall and John K. Whitmore, *Explorations in Early Southeast Asian History: The Origins of Southeast Asian Statecraft.*

104. Early Cham epigraphy places emphasis on land endowments to temples, but the endowed land is in every instance confined to the local river valley rather than in another river system. The inscriptions of Mi-so'n that record the endowment of this central royal temple, which one might expect to have received income endowments from beyond the immediate river system, holds true to the pattern of riverine system integration instead. See Louis Finot, "Deux nouvelles inscriptions de Bhadravarman Ier, roi de Champa," *BEFEO* 2 (1902): 187; and Finot, "Stèle de Çaṃbhuvarman a Mi-so'n," 3 (1903): 206. The irrigation networks in southern Vietnam, which fell under Cham authority and were redeveloped by the French in the nineteenth century, could have theoretically supported Cham ambitions, but were allowed to languish by Cham rulers, whose interests were channeled elsewhere. On the French development of southern Vietnam, see Charles Robequain, *The Economic Development of French Indochina.*

105. Cham monarchs were constantly interacting with Malay and other port-based seamen, for good reason. Chinese sources confirm Cham interests in its ports, noting the monarch's capable administration of his ports and indicating that port revenues collected by the ruler's agents were important royal income. Also, as pointed out at the beginning of this chapter, the classical states needed to diversify either their wet-rice or maritime base to achieve greatness. Without one or the other of these sources of support Cham monarchs and their state were doomed to secondary status in the classical age.

106. This autonomy may actually be regarded as a protective mechanism in the face of the center's weakness, insulating local regions against the periodic disorders associated with dynastic crises, wars, and unreasonable demands by state leaders upon the local population's economic productivity.

107. See Reid, *Slavery, Bondage and Dependency.*

108. Cham epigraphy consistently stresses the gift-giving redistributions of Cham monarchs and their subordinate military elite—for instance, the "male and female slaves, oxen, buffaloes . . . golden waistband, bracelet, anklet, diadems, jewels, pearls, corals, necklaces, and other ornaments; silver jug and dishes for rice, fans, umbrellas, pitchers for drinking water, chowries, shallow earthen dishes, and . . . other articles of enjoyment" that are listed in an early ninth-century inscription that records a royal gift to a temple near Pāṇḍuranga (Barth and Bergaigne, *ISCC,* 218). There are even specific notations that the donations were war plunder, as for example the 1056 inscriptions from Mi-so'n that report the gift of various war captives and spoils from the Cham victory over Sambupura (Louis Finot, "Les inscriptions de Mi-so'n," *BEFEO* 4 [1904]: 933, 943; see also Barth and Bergaigne, 275). Cham temples, too, were subject to plunder and had to be rebuilt—this was particularly true after the devastating Khmer and Vietnamese raids that became common in the eleventh century. For comparison, see George W. Spencer, "The Politics of Plunder: The Cholas in Eleventh Century Ceylon," *JAS* 35 (1976): 405–419.

109. In these raids sixty thousand people were killed and thirty thousand taken away as prisoners, among whom were the Cham monarch and fifty members of the royal family. See Maspero, *Le Royaume de Champa,* 237–239.

Chapter 8

Portions of this chapter were originally presented in Kenneth R. Hall and John K. Whitmore, "Southeast Asian Trade and the Isthmian Struggle, 1000–1200 A.D.," in *Explorations in Early Southeast Asian History: The Origins of Southeast Asian Statecraft,* ed. Kenneth R. Hall and John K. Whitmore, 303–340; and Kenneth R. Hall, "Trade and Statecraft in the Western Archipelago at the Dawn of the European Age," *JMBRAS* 54, 1 (1981): 21–47.

1. O. W. Wolters, *The Fall of Srivijaya in Malay History,* 42; E. H. Schafer, *The Empire of Min,* 75–78; and Wang Gungwu, "Early Ming Relations with Southeast Asia," in *The Chinese World Order,* ed. J. K. Fairbank, 47, 296 n. 27.

2. This activity is documented in several south Indian Tamil inscriptions that record the religious donations of the Śrīvijaya monarchs. See *Annual Report on Indian Epigraphy* (hereafter *ARE*) (1956–1957), nos. 161, 164, 166; and *Epigraphia Indica* (hereafter *EI*), 22: 213–281.

3. Wolters, *Fall of Srivijaya,* 1, 14; George Coedès, *The Indianized States of Southeast Asia,* ed. Walter F. Vella, 130, 142, 144.

4. For an extensive analysis of the 1025 Cōḷa raid, see George W. Spencer, *The Politics of Expansion: The Chola Conquest of Sri Lanka and Sri Vijaya.*

5. Paul Wheatley, *The Golden Khersonese: Studies in the Historical Geography of the Malay Peninsula before 1500 A.D.,* 63; O. W. Wolters, *Early Indonesian Commerce: A Study of the Origins of Sri Vijaya,* 251, quoting Chu'u-fei in his *Ling wai tai ta,* a work extensively incorporated into Chao Ju-kua's *Chu-fan-chih.* See F. Hirth and W. W. Rockhill, *Chau Ju-kua: His Work on the Chinese and Arab Trade in the Twelfth and Thirteenth Centuries, Entitled Chu-fan-chi.*

6. The Malay Peninsula ports attacked by the Cōḷas are named in the Tañjāvūr inscription of 1030. See *South Indian Inscriptions,* 2:105–109; this inscription has also been translated into English by K. A. Nilakanta Sastri, *The History of Srivijaya,* 80.

7. Paul Wheatley, "Geographical Notes on Some Commodities involved in Sung Maritime Trade," *JMBRAS* 32, 2 (1959): 16–17.

8. Ibid., 5–8; Hirth and Rockhill, *Chau Ju-kua,* 35–39.

9. Chao Ju-kua's record shows that this area, known later to the Westerners as the Spice Islands, sent cloves, nutmegs, lakawood, and tortoiseshell to the international route via Java and Sumatra in exchange for such goods as fermented liquor, porcelain, silk, and coarse salt. Wheatley, "Geographical Notes," 45, 61, 73, 83, 98, 100, 119, 124.

10. See Kenneth R. Hall, *Trade and Statecraft in the Age of the Cōḷas.*

11. G. R. Tibbetts, *A Study of the Arabic Texts Containing Material on South-East Asia.*

12. S. D. Goitein, *Letters of Medieval Jewish Traders.*

13. Jung-pang Lo, "The Emergence of China as a Sea Power during the Late Sung and Early Yuan Periods," *Far Eastern Quarterly* 14, 4 (1955): 497.

14. Wolters, *Fall of Srivijaya,* 42. Wolters believes that Chinese ships began to sail regularly to Southeast Asia during the last quarter of the eleventh century. He notes that by 1100, Chinese shippers were sailing to Arab countries in the West via Jambi, where their ships were repaired. In the tenth and early eleventh centuries, by contrast, the Sung government had to persuade foreign traders to visit Chinese ports. See Wheatley, "Geographical Notes," 24–25.

15. H. A. R. Gibb, trans., *The Travels of Ibn Battuta in Asia and Africa,*

1325–1354, 235–236. The Chinese junk itself was of remarkable craftsmanship for that era. It was superior to the Arab lateen, able to tack in a headwind with remarkable ease, and larger; its sails were also superior (see Auguste Toussaint, *History of the Indian Ocean,* 82). Ibn Battuta states that a junk could carry a thousand men and that Chinese junks were built only in Ch'uan-chou and Canton, from which they sailed southward (Gibb, 235).

16. B. Schrieke, *Indonesian Sociological Studies: Selected Writings,* 25. However, Chinese junks remained the chief transporters of goods to Chinese markets from Southeast Asia and retained the largest share of shipping in the South China Sea until the introduction of the European steamships in the nineteenth century.

17. Past literature has presented Tāmbraliṅga as the scene of eleventh-century conflict between the Śrīvijaya maritime empire and the expanding mainland power of the Khmer (see L. P. Briggs, "The Khmer Empire and the Malay Peninsula," *Far Eastern Quarterly* 9, 3 [May 1950]: 256–305). Tāmbraliṅga is believed to have made an attempt to free itself of Śrīvijaya's dominance in response to an expansion of the Sung China consumer market in the late tenth century. In 1001, a Tāmbraliṅga embassy brought a large quantity of sapanwood (a dye wood) to China in an attempt to impress the Chinese with the quality and quantity of local products (see O. W. Wolters, "Tāmbraliṅga," *BSOAS* 21 [1958]: 587–607. Embassies were also sent in 1014 and 1016, but in the latter year Tāmbraliṅga's hopes for recognition as a "first class" port were frustrated when the Chinese relegated the area to a "second class" status.

George Coedès has interpreted the dynastic controversy surrounding Sūryavarman's ascension to the Khmer throne as involving the ruling family of Tāmbraliṅga (George Coedès, *IC,* 7:164–189). In translating the Prasat Ben inscription (1008), Coedès suggested that Sūryavarman I had expelled the Malay prince of Tāmbraliṅga, Jayaviravarman, from the Khmer capital in 1008 (Coedès had earlier believed that Sūryavarman was a Malay and Jayaviravarman a Khmer). In general, it appears that Khmer expansion and Śrīvijayan decline coincided nicely and undoubtedly allowed Cambodian power to make itself felt more strongly in the area.

18. Stanley J. O'Connor, *Hindu Gods of Peninsular Siam,* 60–62, and fig. 34.

19. David Wyatt has provided information from a *Ligor Chronicle* reference to a Tamil inscription from Songkhla dated 983. In this account, a monk states that he is copying this inscription, which records an overland route to the west coast. Wyatt has discussed the sources for Nakhọn Si Thammarat's eleventh-century history in David K. Wyatt, trans., *The Crystal Sands: The Chronicles of Nagara Sri Dharmarāja,* 45–47, which include what seems to be an eleventh-century Tamil inscription from Vat Mahādhātu (see George Coedès, *Recueil des Inscriptions du Siam,* 38). A. Teeuw and D. K. Wyatt, *Hikayat Patani: The Story of Patani,* 2:263, notes a Phatthalung chronicle version of the Malay tale "Lady White-Blood" that apparently indicates such a transpeninsular route. See also Alastair Lamb, "Takuapa: The Probable Site of a Pre-Malaccan Entrepot in the Malay Peninsula," in *Malayan and Indonesian Studies,* ed. John Bastin and R. Roolvink, 76–86.

20. G. H. Luce, in his article, "A Cambodian (?) Invasion of Lower Burma—A Comparison of Burmese and Talaing Chronicles," *Journal of the Burma Research Society* (hereafter *JBRS*) 12, 1 (1922): 39–45, speculated that around 1050 there was a Cambodian invasion of lower Burma to check Burmese expan-

sion in the peninsula, but in a more recent work, *Old Burma, Early Pagan,* 1:21–23, 26, he asserts that the Burmese attacked to stop Mon-Khmer expansion westward.

21. See Milton Osborne, "Notes on Early Cambodian Provincial History: Isanapura and Sambhupura," *France Asie/Asia* 20, 4 (1966): 447.

22. Janice Stargardt, "Burma's Economic and Diplomatic Relations with India and China from Early Medieval Sources," *JESHO* 14, 1 (1971): 28–62. Michael Aung-Thwin's research indicates that the southern Burma commercial centers at Bassein (Kusumī) and Tala (a port near Pegu) became high priority administrative centers under Pagan rule. Important ministers were allowed "to eat" *(cā)* a percentage of the revenues (trade revenues?) of these commercial centers. In 1058, Aniruddha erected a statue of Gavaruputi, not only the patron saint of the Mons but also of merchants and seamen, at Pagan after his 1057 sack of Thaton. Michael Aung-Thwin, "Commercial Developments in the Pagan Era."

23. G. H. Luce, "The Career of Htilaing Min (Kyanzittha), the Unifier of Burma A.D. 1084–1113," *JRAS* (1966): 59.

24. G. H. Luce, "Some Old References to the South of Burma and Ceylon," in *Felicitation Volumes of Southeast-Asian Studies Presented to His Highness Prince Dhaninivat,* 2:270. Luce used the *Cūlavaṃsa,* the Sri Lankan Buddhist chronicle, as his principle source for this article.

25. Perumbur inscription, seventh year of Vīrarājēndra I, *South Indian Inscriptions,* 3, no. 84; and Charala Plates of Vīrarājēndra, Copper Plate no. 1 of *ARE* (1937–1938), sixth plate, as discussed in *EI* 25: 241–266.

26. Wilhelm Geiger, trans., *Cūlavaṃsa,* 58:8–9; Luce, *Old Burma,* 1:40.

27. Lamb, "Takuapa."

28. See the "Larger Leiden Grant," *EI,* 22:213–266; and *ARE* (1956–1957), nos. 161, 164, 166. There has been some controversy concerning the location of "Kaḍāram." General agreement places it on the western Malay coast, but many historians considered the words "Kaḍāram" and "Kedah" and the Arab geographers' reference to "Kalāh" to be the same and therefore placed "Kaḍāram" on the Kedah coast (see K. A. Nilakanta Sastri, *The Colas,* 217–218). Alastair Lamb's archaeological research has shown that the Kedah coast could not have been "Kaḍāram" in the south Indian references until the late eleventh century—a period dating later than all the inscriptions with reference to "Kaḍāram" (see Lamb, "Kedah and Takuapa: Some Tentative Historical Conclusions," *Federated Museums Journal* 6 [1961]: 84), and that, based on archaeological evidence, Takuapa had to be the "Kaḍāram" of these epigraphic and literary references. For a discussion of Arab references to the Kalāh realm, see Tibbetts, *Study of the Arabic Texts,* 118–128, and passim.

29. Coedès, *Indianized States,* 148.

30. Alastair Lamb, who conducted excavations at Kedah in the late 1950s, suggested that a temple he had excavated at Caṇḍi Bukit Batu Pahat in Kedah was similar in style to Caṇḍi Biaro Si Topajan at Padang Lawas in north central Sumatra, the center of a historically unidentified but seemingly important twelfth-century state (see Lamb, "Kedah and Takuapa," 2–9, 76). Lamb's view is supported with new evidence in B. A. V. Peacock, "Pillar Base Architecture in Ancient Kedah," *JMBRAS* 47, 1 (1974): 66–86.

31. Wolters, *Early Indonesian Commerce,* 266 n. 33, and "A Note on the Capital of Srivijaya During the Eleventh Century," *Essays Offered to G. H. Luce by his Friends in Honour of his Seventy-fifth Birthday,* 225–239.

32. Wolters, "Tāmbraliṅga," 595.

33. Wolters sees the Tāmbraliṅga mission of 1070, sent to inform the Chinese of its status as an independent port, as evidence of the shift of the Śrīvijaya center to Jambi. To him the mission symbolized the decline of Śrīvijaya's old economic control over the China trade. See Wolters, "Note on the Capital of Srivijaya."

34. Shwesandaw Pagoda Inscription, *Epigraphia Birmanica* (hereafter *EB*), ed. Charles Duroiselle and C. O. Blagden, 1:viii, 163.

35. *EI,* 11:(1911–1912): 119.

36. *EB,* 1:viii, 165, the Shwesandaw Pagoda Inscription.

37. Stargardt, "Burma's Economic and Diplomatic Relations," 52.

38. *EI,* 22:213–266. George W. Spencer, *The Politics of Expansion: The Chola Conquest of Sri Lanka and Sri Vijaya,* 134–135, argues that a breakdown in the Buddhist cultural dialogue between south Indian Cōḷa kings and Śrīvijaya during Rājēndra I's reign was one reason for the Cōḷa naval expedition against the Śrīvijaya realm in 1024–1025.

39. "The Smaller Leiden Grant," *EI,* 22: 267–281. Spencer, *Politics of Expansion,* 149–150, believes that Kulōttuṅga's renewal of the Nāgapaṭṭinam grant "signified a resumption of cordial relations that had been interrupted by Rājēndra's ambitions. . . . Kulōttuṅga's Nāgapaṭṭinam grant constituted a coded diplomatic statement, affirming the more modest and realistic aims of the [Cōḷa] court . . . [and] it was a way of announcing that the fever in the body politic had subsided, and that the Chōḷa state was now back to more peaceful and less threatening behavior toward its maritime neighbors to the east."

40. S. Paranavitana, "Negapatam and Theravada Buddhism in South India," *Journal of the Greater India Society* 11, 1 (1944): 17–25.

41. Luce, *Old Burma,* 1:63.

42. Tan Yeok Seong, "The Sri Vijayan Inscription of Canton (A.D. 1079)," *Journal of Southeast Asian History* (hereafter *JSEAH*) 5, 2 (1964): 17–24. Tan wrongly follows an earlier interpretation of Indian historians (see R. C. Majumdar, *Suvarnadvipa,* 182–190) that Kulōttuṅga had served in a high position in the conquered country of Śrīvijaya before ascending the Cōḷa throne. Neither this inscription nor other evidence that I have examined substantiates this claim. Such interpretations assume the Cōḷas to have exercised considerable control over Śrīvijaya's government on a continuing basis during the eleventh century. The Chinese themselves were not quite sure of the relationship between the two; some Chinese chronicles represent the Cōḷas as being subordinate to Śrīvijaya (see a passage from the *Sung Shih* that is quoted in Tan, 21). Noting that Cōḷa monarchs were incorporated as ancestors (Alexander the Great is also included) of fifteenth-century Malacca monarchs in the sixteenth-century court chronicle *Sejarah Melayu,* Spencer, *Politics of Expansion,* comments: "What seems significant is that the Malay chronicler-genealogists of the fifteenth century and later were so impressed by Malay memories of the Chōḷas that they regarded an ancestral connection with them to be worth bragging about" (pp. 148–149).

43. *EI,* 7:197–198.

44. K. A. Nilakanta Sastri, "A Tamil Merchant Guild in Sumatra," *TBG* 72 (1932): 314–327.

45. K. A. Nilakanta Sastri, "Takuapa and its Tamil Inscription," *JMBRAS* 22, 1 (1949): 25–30; Lamb, "Takuapa."

46. Hirth and Rockhill, *Chau Ju-kua,* 94, 98.

47. G. H. Luce, "The Early *Syam* in Burma's History: A Supplement," *JSS* 47, 1 (1959): 60–61.

48. David K. Wyatt, "Mainland Powers on the Malay Peninsula," paper presented to the International Conference on Asian History.

49. See S. Paranavitana, *Ceylon and Malaysia,* 80.

50. *Epigraphia Zeylanica* (hereafter *EZ*), 4:66–72, as cited by Wyatt, "Mainland Powers on the Malay Peninsula." The inscription also states that this same monk was instrumental in the establishment of the Buddhist religion in the Cōḷa country. See Paranavitana, "Negapatam and Theravada Buddhism," 24.

51. "Episode of the Tooth Relic," see Wyatt, *The Crystal Sands,* 26–28, 38–39, 42, 59, 66–71, 72–79; and Wyatt, "Mainland Powers on the Malay Peninsula," 13–14. The dating of Narapatisithu's reign is based on the research of Michael Aung-Thwin (see n. 55).

52. G. H. Luce, "Some Old References to the South of Burma," 276. The "Dhammarajika Inscription" of A.D. 1196 commemorates Narapatisithu's conquest of the south.

53. Geiger, *Cūlavaṃsa,* 76:10–75.

54. Ibid., 76:59–75.

55. Burma Archaeological Department, *She Haung Myanma Kyauksa Mya* 1 (1972): 33–37, the "Cañsū Maṅ Krī Inscriptions," and the "Mrat Krī Cwā Khai Toṅ Inscription of 1169." Michael Aung-Thwin has discussed these inscriptions and other evidence relating to the Singhalese raid in his article, "The Problem of Ceylonese-Burmese Relations in the 12th Century and the Question of an Interregnum in Pagan: 1165–1174 A.D.," *JSS* 64, 1 (1976): 53–74.

56. Sirima Wickremasignhe, "Ceylon's Relations with South-east Asia, with Special Reference to Burma," *Ceylon Journal of Historical and Social Studies* 3, 1 (1960): 48. See also C. E. Godakumbura, "Relations between Burma and Ceylon," *JBRS* 49, 2 (1966): 145–162.

57. *EZ,* 3:321, no. 34.

58. Geiger, *Cūlavaṃsa,* 80:6–8.

59. *EZ,* 2, no. 17.

60. Ibid., 74.

61. Geiger, *Cūlavaṃsa,* 76:35.

62. Thomas R. Trautmann, "Consanguineous Marriage in Pali Literature," *Journal of the American Oriental Society* 93, 2 (1973): 158–180. As explained in chapter 6, such marriage alliances were a common practice of Khmer kings.

63. Wolters, "Tāmbraliṅga," 600, translated from the *Ling wai tai ta* (1178).

64. Ibid., 605.

65. Ibid.

66. Ibid., 598 n. 5. Ports that were possibly Khmer have yet to be discovered. This fleet may well have been confined to river transport on the Mekong and other major rivers of the Khmer domain. In the eleventh century one of the main commercial routes to China seems to have gone north on the Mekong to a point near the Ha-trai pass, where goods passed to Nghệ-an on the Vietnamese coast. Nghệ-an in turn had contact with commercial developments of the Red River Delta and the Vietnamese capital at Thang-long. The 1128 Khmer attacks on Vietnam were launched via this route. One of these attacks involved over seven hundred boats, which may be an indication of the extent of travel in the upstream area on the Vietnamese side (*Đại Viêt sũ-ký tuàn thu',* 1:263, 347, translation by John K. Whitmore).

67. Wolters, "Tāmbraliṅga," 606 n. 5.

68. Ibid., 605.

69. Ibid., 598.

70. Coedès, *IC,* 2:178.

71. George Coedès, "La stèle de Prah Khan d'Angkor," *BEFEO* 41 (1941): 255–301.

72. E. Aymonier, *Le Cambodge,* 3:528. This inscription is undocumented.

73. See Pierre Dupont, "Le Buddha de Grahi et l'ecole de C'āiya," *BEFEO* 42 (1942): 105–113; J. G. de Casparis, "The Date of the Grahi Buddha," *JSS* 55, 1 (1967): 31–40; Coedès, *IC,* 7:124–126.

74. I wish to thank Hiram W. Woodward, Jr., for calling to my attention this inscription's use of the twelve-year animal cycle and its implications.

75. Michael Vickery establishes that the language of the Grahi Buddha is not linguistically Thai (Vickery, "The Khmer Inscriptions of Tenasserim: A Reinterpretation," *JSS* 61, 1 [1973]: 52–53 n. 8), and in his doctoral dissertation, Hiram Woodward argues on stylistic grounds that the Grahi Buddha does in fact date to this earlier period (Woodward, "Studies in the Art of Central Siam, 950–1350 A.D.," Ph.D. diss., Yale University, 1975, 1:91–102). Woodward presents evidence that the Grahi Buddha not only is a copy of a twelfth-century Khmer image but also incorporates stylistic influences from Burma and the peninsula.

76. S. J. O'Connor, "Si Chon: An Early Settlement in Peninsular Thailand," *JSS* 56, 1 (1968): 1–18.

77. Taw Sein Ko, *The Kalyāṇī Inscriptions,* 53. In 1181, according to this inscription, four monks returned to Pagan with the Burmese monk Chapatai: Śīvali from Tamalitthi; Ānanda of Kāñcīpuram; Rāhula, a Singhalese; and Tāmalinda, the son of the Khmer king.

78. J. Boisselier, *Le Cambodge,* 94, 275–276, and others, and in general Woodward, "Studies in the Art of Central Siam," 104–107.

79. R. H. Bautier, *The Economic Development of Medieval Europe,* 142–144, 205–209, 217–219. Meats were often dried or salted to preserve them; Southeast Asian spices were much desired to enhance the taste of such meat.

80. During the fourteenth century a Franciscan friar named Odoric of Pordenone who claimed to have visited Southeast Asia attributed all spices to the land of Java in his travel memoir. Odoric is likely to have acquired this information from Indian ports. Henry Yule, *Cathay and the Way Thither,* 1:88–89. Tibbetts, *Study of the Arabic Texts.*

81. Cloth was obtained from Bali and in addition to rice was another essential commodity of the interisland trade. Pepper was carried from Java's ports to Bali where it was exchanged for cloth, which was then transported to the Moluccas and exchanged for local spices. Chinese goods entering Java to be exchanged for the archipelago's products included porcelain, musk, "gold-flecked hemp silks," beads, yarns, gold, silver, iron, and copper coins (J. V. G. Mills, *Ying-yai Sheng-lan of Ma Huan [1433],* 97), and these also found their way to western and eastern archipelago spice centers (M. A. P. Meilink-Roelofsz, *Asian Trade and European Influence in the Indonesian Archipelago between 1500 and about 1630,* 83–84, 93–100, 105–115).

82. Java's coastal trade at the end of the thirteenth century was dominated by Tuban and Surabaya at the mouth of the Brantas River, which were the points of concentration for rice shipped to the eastern archipelago in exchange for various spices. Tuban was linked to its hinterland by a road network; both ports were adjacent to major rice-producing regions—rice was brought to the coast from internal market centers, which in return were supplied with spices and foreign

luxury goods (see chap. 9). What is striking about the economic organization of the coast at the beginning of the fourteenth century is that no one commercial center dominated trade. Ships sailed from Tuban as well as from Surabaya to eastern and western archipelago spice-producing regions.

83. Marco Polo, *The Travels of Marco Polo,* chap. 6 of Book III, 247–248.

84. Wheatley, "Geographical Notes," 100. In addition to pepper, eastern Java ports were also known in Sung times as the source of nutmegs and cloves (p. 32), products of the eastern archipelago.

85. See Jan Wisseman, "Markets and Trade in Pre-Majapahit Java," in *Economic Exchange and Social Interaction in Southeast Asia,* ed. Karl L. Hutterer, 197–212; and chaps. 5 and 9.

86. See Charnvit Kasetsiri, *The Rise of Ayudhya: A History of Siam in the Fourteenth and Fifteenth Centuries,* passim.

87. See Coedès, *Indianized States,* 204–207.

88. Ibid., 205.

89. F. M. Schnitger, *Forgotten Kingdoms in Sumatra,* 21. This does not necessarily indicate a Thai political presence but instead a commercial contact between the Thais and the southeastern Sumatra coast. "Thai" porcelain was discovered in 1974 excavations at Palembang; Edward McKinnon of Cornell University has informed me that there are substantial deposits of "Thai" ceramics at Jambi that he and O. W. Wolters surveyed during the summer of 1978.

90. A. H. Hill, trans., "The Hikayat Raja-Raja Pasai," *JMBRAS* 33, 2 (1960): 128–129.

91. P. Pelliot, "Deux itinéraires de Chine en Inde à la fin du VIIIe siècle," *BEFEO* 4 (1904): 398.

92. Wolters, *Fall of Srivijaya,* 78–79, 108–109, 115–117, drawing on Chinese sources, demonstrates fluctuating Thai and Javanese control over the lower Malay Peninsula from the late thirteenth century until the establishment of Malacca's independence from Thai and Javanese authority in the early fifteenth century. There was apparently a Thai "viceroy" in Tumasek for a short period prior to an attack by Parameśvara, the founder of Malacca, in the late fourteenth century. See also Coedès, *Indianized States,* 243, 245.

93. Tibbetts, *Study of the Arabic Texts,* 240.

94. See David Sopher, *The Sea Nomads.* Chinese and Western references to later hostilities between Malacca and the Thais note that Malacca met Thai forces on the peninsula but defeated a naval expedition of Patani-based Malay seamen who were acting in the name of the Thais.

95. Hall, "Trade and Statecraft in the Western Archipelago."

96. Wolters, *Fall of Srivijaya,* 45.

97. Coedès, *Indianized States,* 201; Nilakanta Sastri, *History of Śrīvijaya,* 96.

98. That piracy in the strait was a problem in this era is confirmed in Chinese sources; eliminating Southeast Asian piracy was one of the reasons for the early fifteenth-century expeditions into the south of the eunuch Cheng Ho. See William Willetts, "The Maritime Adventures of the Grand Eunuch Ho," *JSEAH* 5, 2 (1964): 25–42.

99. The economic interaction between the Yuan and Ming and Southeast Asia, as well as that of the T'ang and Sung adds a significant dimension to the understanding of Chinese Confucian statecraft, which is normally seen as taking a negative view toward commerce and either discouraging commerce or subjecting trade to a government monopoly (see Charles O. Hucker, *China's Imperial Past,*

187–192). On the contrary, Chinese dynastic records of Southeast Asian contacts show that Chinese rulers often directly solicited foreign trade and even sent official envoys to Southeast Asian courts to encourage such interaction while allowing Chinese seafarers ample latitude to participate in this trade beyond any government monopoly.

100. Indeed, Yuan warnings to the Thai and attacks against Java may well have been part of an overall effort to reestablish "traditional Chinese patterns" in the strait, including the restoration of "Śrīvijaya/Malāyu," centered in Jambi, to its former position of prominence as China's trading partner. This interpretation is also plausible based upon Yuan efforts to reestablish Chinese authority over Vietnam, which the Yuan mistakenly considered a part of the Chinese state order, given the idealized view of the Chinese world order found in classical Chinese texts. See Lê Thành Khôi, *Le Viet-Nam, Histoire et Civilisation,* 170–191.

101. Pelliot, "Deux itinéraires de Chine en Inde," 326.

102. Wolters, *Fall of Srivijaya.* In response to an imperial command presented to Palembang in 1370, a mission was sent to the Ming court in 1371, and subsequent missions were sent in 1373, 1374, 1375, and 1377 (W. P. Groeneveldt, "Notes on the Malay Archipelago and Malacca," in *Miscellaneous Papers relating to Indochina and the Indian Archipelago,* ed. R. Rost, 192–193). Wolters interprets this frequency as an attempt by Palembang's rulers to recapture the old position of Śrīvijaya in the China trade (Wolters, 49–76, 187–190).

103. By this time the Chinese could draw upon first-hand information supplied by Ming imperial expeditions into the south as the basis for their action. Groeneveldt, "Notes on the Malay Archipelago," 197.

104. After the Thai raid of the late thirteenth century the Jambi region became more internally focused; a 1347 inscription from a ruined Jambi temple reports that Ādityavarman, ruler over the highland-based Menangkabau realm, held authority over Jambi (Schnitger, *Forgotten Kingdoms in Sumatra,* 31).

105. Tibbetts, *Study of the Arabic Texts,* 138–140.

106. Hill, *Hikayat Raja-Raja Pasai,* 8.

107. Polo, *Travels of Marco Polo,* chaps. 9–11 of Book III, 249–255.

108. The emergence of Samudra-Pasai was connected to the decline of Ramni to the north. Thai movements into the peninsula in the twelfth and thirteenth centuries as well as the declining presence of Arab traders in Southeast Asian waters appear to have resulted in the dispersion of Indian Ocean traders from the Malay coast to northern Sumatra. Ramni was certainly one of the places that benefited and appears to have emerged as the leading Sumatra port before Samudra's rise to power. When Ramni diminished in commercial importance is difficult to determine since the only reports of it after the thirteenth century were written by the Chinese long after its decline. Yuan histories note the reception of envoys from La-mu-li (Ramni) and Samudra, and Cheng Ho visited La-mu-li on each of his first six expeditions (Mills, *Ma Huan,* 10–14). Samudra-Pasai alone sent envoys to the Ming court in 1403, responding to solicitation by China's new dynasty and especially to Cheng Ho's visit shortly thereafter. From 1405 to 1424 Samudra-Pasai sent missions to China annually. There is no record of such a vigorous response by La-mu-li. It was not until 1412 that La-mu-li began to send envoys to China (ibid., 120–121). La-mu-li then sent a mission to the Ming court annually until 1424, the same date that Samudra-Pasai ceased its embassies. This was the time when the Ming dynasty abandoned its policy of maintaining a closely supervised tributary system in the Southern Seas. Ming records suggest

that La-mu-li yielded to Chinese pressure and sent tribute missions only in the face of an obvious threat or when Samudra-Pasai's authority over the northern coast was neutralized by the Chinese presence. La-mu-li's seeming indifference to the Chinese in the Yuan and early Ming eras suggests that La-mu-li's profit in international trade was unrelated to the Chinese market, and it saw no need to establish a tributary relationship with China, or it was subject to Samudra-Pasai's commercial preeminence. Thus it was appropriate that Samudra-Pasai as the dominant entrepôt on the northern Sumatra coast established a tributary relationship with the Chinese; La-mu-li, as a commercial subordinate, would have traded with the Chinese at Samudra-Pasai.

109. Hill, *Hikayat Raja-Raja Pasai,* 12.

110. Gibb, *Travels of Ibn Battuta,* 274.

111. Ibid., 273–274.

112. Hill, *Hikayat Raja-Raja Pasai,* 9.

113. See Shelly Errington, "Some Comments on Style in the Meaning of the Past," *JAS* 38, 2 (1979): 231–244.

114. Hill, *Hikayat Raja-Raja Pasai,* 27; Phillip L. Thomas, "Thai Involvement in Pasai," *JSS* 66, 1 (1978): 89–101.

115. Scholars have argued that the conversion to Islam of Samudra-Pasai, Malacca, northern Java, and other Malay world entrepôts was to encourage Indian Ocean merchants, themselves in some instances recent converts to Islam, to frequent their ports. Malacca, however, became a commercial power in the early fifteenth century despite Samudra-Pasai's wider recognition as a center of Islamic scholarship. Indeed, Chinese sources record the shift of Java's spice trade to Malacca before Malacca's rulers converted to Islam (see the *Hsing-ch'a Seng-lan* [Description of the Starry Raft] (a ship carrying an imperial ambassador), composed in 1436 by Fei-hsin, a junior officer who accompanied Cheng Ho, as translated in Groeneveldt, "Notes on the Malay Archipelago," 210). It is apparent in the case of Malacca that the initial growth of this new port was due to Chinese patronage; but with the withdrawal of the Ming from Southeast Asia, Malacca's rulers quickly converted to Islam, as if this was necessary to maintain Malacca's status as a major entrepôt (see C. Wake, "Malacca's Early Kings and the Reception of Islam," *JSEAH* 5, 2 [1964]: 104–128).

116. For comparison, see the retelling of this story in the *Sejarah Melayu,* C. C. Brown, "Sĕjarah Mĕlayu or 'Malay Annals': A Translation of Raffles Ms. 18," *JMBRAS* 25, 2–3 (1952): 1–276.

117. Groeneveldt, "Notes on the Malay Archipelago," 214.

118. Mills, *Ma Huan,* 13.

119. Yule, *Cathay and the Way Thither,* 86.

120. Gibb, *Travels of Ibn Battuta,* 273.

121. See Schrieke, *Indonesian Sociological Studies,* 24. Chinese ships carried spices and pepper from Javanese ports, especially from Tuban, to China.

122. Nicolo Conti, *The Travels of Nicolo Conti in the East in the Early Part of the Fifteenth Century,* 8–9. Conti was a member of a Venetian noble family and spent twenty-five years surveying the trade of Asia, returning home in 1444. He also notes that gold and camphor were gathered at Samudra-Pasai.

123. Mills, *Ma Huan,* 118.

124. By the middle of the fourteenth century Javanese influence had reached beyond Palembang to Haru, Kampe, and Tamaiang on the south Sumatra coast (Wolters, *Fall of Srivijaya,* 43). A Javanese relationship with Samudra-Pasai is well reflected in the *Hikayat Raja Pasai* as well as in the external evidence noted

above. The *Hikayat* even records a major fifteenth-century maritime expedition against Samudra-Pasai attributed to Majapahit. This raid was explained as punishment by the gods for the misdeeds of the Samudra-Pasai rulers rather than as a result of economic competition; Java's economic and political influence on Samudra-Pasai thereafter remained considerable.

125. Mills, *Ma Huan,* 118.

126. This story is likely symbolic of the establishment of a gift-giving agreement between the adventurer and the local leadership signifying that the hinterland population would support the prince's ambitions if he would share future prosperity with the chiefs and their followers.

127. Gibb, *Travels of Ibn Battuta,* 274; Yule, *Cathay and the Way Thither,* 86.

128. Gibb, *Travels of Ibn Battuta,* 273.

129. Ibid., 274.

130. Yule, *Cathay and the Way Thither,* 468.

131. Hill, *Hikayat Raja-Raja Pasai,* 21–22. Pasai may be viewed as the successor to the Kedah coast as the dominant trade intermediary with Western traders. In this light, an early sixteenth-century reference to the residents of Pasai, among whom was a maritime trading community regarded as being tied to the Kedah coast, is important. See Armando Cortesão, trans. and ed., *The Suma Oriental of Tomé Pires,* 107.

132. Mills, *Ma Huan,* 120–121.

133. Ibid., 115–118.

134. Ibid., 119.

135. Given the potential for conflict among the competing foreign trade communities, the focusing of trade on a neutral port might have been preferable to the Javanese. Such an arrangement would have eliminated the necessity of providing port faciiities for a significant number of visiting merchants on the Java coast, thus avoiding friction between the indigenous Javanese populations and foreign seamen and as well preventing foreign populations from playing a role in local politics.

136. Cortesão, *Suma Oriental of Tomé Pires,* 142, 144.

137. From the *Tung hsi yang k'au* [Investigation on the eastern and western oceans], quoted in Groeneveldt, "Notes on the Malay Archipelago," 199. The *Tung hsi yang k'an,* composed in 1617 by the Fukien provincial official Chang Hsieh, is a study of trade routes and trade in areas of Southeast Asia and Japan with which the Chinese had commercial relations and includes documentary materials as well as long quotations from earlier written materials on the subjects.

138. Indeed, Chinese sources stress the high profits accruing to all who participated in Samudra-Pasai's pepper trade. See ibid., 214.

139. Cortesão, *Suma Oriental of Tomé Pires,* 145.

140. That such cesses were important to Malay rulers is indicated by the common penalty for evasion of port cesses: enslavement of the offender. See R. O. Winstedt and De Josselin de Jong, "The Maritime Laws of Malacca," *JMBRAS* 29, 3 (1956): 54.

141. Yule, *Cathay and the Way Thither,* 86.

142. Gibb, *Travels of Ibn Battuta,* 273. The *Hsing-ch'a Sheng-lan* (1436) reports the import of copper and iron (Groeneveldt, "Notes on the Malay Archipelago," 210). Conti, *Travels of Nicolo Conti,* 9, said gold was in abundance at Pasai.

143. China was in this age known to be exporting gold to Southeast Asia to

acquire Southeast Asian goods—a matter of some concern to Chinese officials. See John K. Whitmore, "Vietnam and the Monetary Flow of Asia," in *Precious Metals in the Later Medieval and Early Modern Worlds,* ed. J. F. Richards, 363–393.

144. If this is true it would suggest an early monetarization of international trade, whereby metal exchanges as well as exchanges in kind characterized Samudra-Pasai's commerce. Pires reports that Samudra-Pasai issued tin and gold coins bearing the name of the reigning ruler (Cortesão, *Suma Oriental of Tomé Pires,* 144).

145. Ibid., 98, 107, 145.

146. Commercial specialization and the consequent need to import food became a pattern in other fifteenth-century Southeast Asian commercial centers. Malacca, for instance, depended on rice imports from Java, Burma, and Thailand while its population concentrated their energies on international commerce. See Anthony Reid, "Trade and State Power in 16th and 17th Century Southeast Asia," *Proceedings, Seventh International Association of Historians of Asia Conference,* 397.

147. Cortesão, *Suma Oriental of Tomé Pires,* 143. He notes that despite these hostilities, "there is no disturbance whatever in the city or among the [port residents] and merchants whether their king be killed or alive," suggesting the autonomy of the commercial affairs of the coast from the numerous succession crises and struggles between the Samudra-Pasai monarchy and the hinterland.

148. Meilink-Roelofsz, *Asian Trade and European Influence.*

149. Pegu was also important in its own right as the source of precious gems, especially rubies. See Than Tun, "History of Burma, 1300–1400," *JBRS* 42, 2 (1959): 119–135; and J. S. Furnivall, "Europeans in Burma in the 15th Century," *JBRS* 29, 3 (1939): 236–249.

150. Wolters, *Fall of Srivijaya,* passim.

151. Kasetsiri, *The Rise of Ayudhya.*

152. C. N. Spinks, "Siam and the Pottery Trade of Asia," *JSS* 44, 2 (1956): 61–111.

153. O. W. Wolters, "The Khmer King at Basan (1371–1373) and the Restoration of the Cambodian Chronology during the 14th and 15th Centuries," *Asia Major* 12, 1 (1966): 44–64.

154. Karl L. Hutterer, "The Evolution of Philippine Lowland Societies," *Mankind* 9 (1974): 287–299. The first mission to the Chinese court from the Philippines arrived in 1003. In 1007, envoys were again sent by the ruler of Butuan in northwest Mindanao requesting that the Sung court bestow upon them the same class of flags that had been received by the Cham envoys in 1004. The request was rejected because Butuan, the Chinese reasoned, was beneath Champa in commercial importance. See O. W. Wolters, "A Few Miscellaneous *Pi-chi* Jottings on Early Indonesia," *Indonesia* 36 (October 1983): 58.

155. Hutterer (ibid., 297) notes that there has been considerable confusion about the exact nature of *barangays* and *dātus*: "*barangays* could not possibly have been lineages, and *datus* could not possibly have been lineage elders. In fact, there is every reason to believe that it was precisely the political organization of *barangays* and the institution of the political leadership in the form of *datus* that cross-cut organizational features based solely on kinship principles. There is also a consensus among the sources that *datu* enjoyed considerable economic prominence and that *datu*-ship could be attained on the basis of personal achievements,

i.e., wealth." Gordon C. Thomasson of Cornell University has examined the *barangay* social and economic networks in the Manila region during the pre-Spanish era, and has shared with me his preliminary maps, which demonstrate the heavy concentration of manpower in the Manila region that he attributes to the economic prosperity associated with the China trade.

156. Hutterer notes archaeological proof of the growth of coastal settlements accompanied by a decline of population densities in interior parts of islands (ibid., 296). Hutterer's excavations in the Cebu City region have revealed multiple levels of Chinese porcelains, indicating a fairly extensive coastal settlement prior to the sixteenth-century Spanish incursions (Hutterer, *An Archaeological Picture of a Pre-Spanish Cebuano Community*).

157. See Robert Nicholl, "Brunei Rediscovered, A Survey of Early Times," *JSEAS* 14, 1 (1983): 32–45.

158. See Wisseman, "Markets and Trade in Pre-Majapahit Java"; Th. G. Th. Pigeaud, *Java in the 14th Century;* and Soemarsaid Moertono, *State and Statecraft in Old Java: A Study of the Later Mataram Period, 16th to 19th Century.*

159. Wolters, *Fall of Srivijaya.*

160. Cortesão, *Suma Oriental of Tomé Pires,* passim.

161. Ibid., 139. Pedir was also at war with Aceh in the early sixteenth century. According to Pires, Pedir was more important than Pasai as a center of Sumatra trade in the late fifteenth century, but Pedir had become involved in a series of wars, a consequence of a succession crisis and subsequent attempts to reestablish Pedir's role as a commercial power. This period of upheaval was detrimental to Pedir's stature as an entrepôt; "it was always at war—which is against trade" (ibid.). While there are no references to the number of ships calling at Pasai, Pires reports two ships from Gujarat, two from Bengal, one from the Coromandel Coast, and one from Pegu entering Pedir's harbor annually, despite its "demise." This would indicate that, even though Malacca was the dominant international port in the strait region during the fifteenth century, both Pedir and Pasai were still substantial entrepôts before they became subject to Aceh's authority in the 1520s.

162. See also O. W. Wolters, "Studying Srivijaya," *JMBRAS* 52, 2 (1979): 1–38.

163. Ibid., 24.

164. A. Reid and L. Castles, eds., *Pre-Colonial State Systems in Southeast Asia.* This theme is further explored by Anthony Reid, who holds that between 1300 and 1600 commercial as well as political life was becoming focused on the palace, but this promising movement toward institutionalized government was challenged by the parallel development of *orang kaya* commercial elites and continued hostility among hinterland populations toward the coastal populations. See Reid, "Trade and State Power."

165. Leonard Y. Andaya, "The Structure of Power in Seventeenth Century Johor," in *Pre-Colonial State Systems in Southeast Asia,* ed. Reid and Castles; see also Andaya, *The Kingdom of Johor 1641–1728;* Anthony Reid, "Trade and the Problem of Royal Power in Aceh," 55.

166. Unfortunately the sources do not allow a full definition of the delivery mechanisms whereby goods flowed from the hinterland to the coast. A detailed analysis of the governmental structure of the Samudra-Pasai state may reveal further evidence of the movement toward a more structured "mobilizative" system. But such an analysis, which must be drawn from the *Hikayat Raja Pasai,*

must be carefully done considering the entire range of chronicles produced by Malay states in the strait region.

167. Brown, "Sĕjarah Mĕlayu," 40ff.

168. Ibid., 99–102.

169. See L. F. Brakel, "State and Statecraft in 17th Century Aceh," in *Pre-Colonial State Systems in Southeast Asia,* ed. Reid and Castles, 65–66.

170. James Siegel argues that Islam transcended the isolation of Aceh's regional chiefs *(uleebelang)* in northern Sumatra. The *uleebelang* themselves operated at the edge of society, controlling the marketing of local products and the flow of local goods to the outside world. See Siegel, *The Rope of God.*

171. The populations of urban centers such as Malacca and Aceh in the late sixteenth and early seventeenth centuries were as large as a hundred thousand while Ayudhya, Makassar, Banten, Demak, Surabaya, and Patani all numbered fifty thousand or more. This rate of urbanization was not surpassed by the colonial centers of Batavia and Manila until after 1800. There were two functions of these urban centers. They were in the first instance centers of government and commerce. Secondly, they were cultural centers influencing and integrating their surrounding hinterlands via such means as promoting the spread of Islam in the Malay realm and Theravāda Buddhism on the mainland, both emphasizing the direct concern of the rulers for the welfare and salvation of their subjects. A substantial group of Southeast Asians had emerged who were free from subsistence agriculture and traditional social structures, who were preoccupied with trade and commerce and were part of a new, cosmopolitan, urban, commercial society. See Reid, "Trade and State Power."

172. Kasetsiri, *Rise of Ayudhya,* passim, and Moertono, *State and Statecraft in Old Java,* 136.

Chapter 9

1. George Coedès, *The Indianized States of Southeast Asia,* ed. Walter F. Vella, 185–188, 198–201, 232–234, 239–242.

2. Jan Wisseman, "Markets and Trade in Pre-Majapahit Java," in *Economic Exchange and Social Interaction in Southeast Asia: Perspectives from Prehistory, History, and Ethnography,* ed. Karl L. Hutterer, 197–212.

3. Paul Wheatley, "Geographical Notes on Some Commodities Involved in Sung Maritime Trade," *JMBRAS* 32, 2 (1959): passim.

4. Wisseman, "Markets and Trade in Pre-Majapahit Java," 205.

5. A reconstruction of the traditional Javanese road network in the seventeenth century, with speculation about its character in Majapahit times, is supplied by B. Schrieke, *Indonesian Sociological Studies: Ruler and Realm in Early Java,* 103ff.

6. Canto 8, stanza 2 of the *Nagarakĕrtagama,* in Th. G. Th. Pigeaud, *Java in the Fourteenth Century: A Study in Cultural History,* 3:9.

7. Canto 23, stanza 3, ibid., 3:24; 4:55.

8. Canto 18, stanza 1, ibid., 3:23; 4:497.

9. Ibid., 3:25.

10. Canto 23, stanza 3, ibid., 3:24.

11. Ibid., 1:108–112; 3:156–162; 4:399–411 (Javanese text, English translation, and commentary).

12. This may be compared to a tenth-century reference to ferrymen of various central Java river-crossing districts in the Panambangan Ferry Charter of A.D. 903–904, which was discovered in the upper course of the Bengawan River (the eastern bend of the Solo River). This inscription provides for the institution and upkeep of a boatshed, houses for ferrymen, and boats, and for the free passage of all subjects of King Balitung without toll. Leading members of the local trade community (goldsmiths, ironsmiths, coppersmiths, and brass-smiths) received remitted royal taxes on deposit and were to pay for the above provisions out of the interest on these deposits. The inscription also discusses royal taxes imposed on members of the commercial community. The community's commercial leaders were granted freedom from tax on transactions up to specified levels, whereupon surplus sales above the designated level were subject to royal taxes. The inscription also lists the transactions of dealers in cloth, rice, sesame oil, salt, and other trades subject to royal taxes. The text and translation appear in H. B. Sarkar, *Corpus of the Inscriptions of Java (up to 928 A.D.),* 2:43–50. For comparison see the Palĕbuhan Copper-Plate inscription (ca. A.D. 927) that was discovered near Madiun and the Mananjung inscription (A.D. 928) that was issued near Malang, which record very similar tax arrangements with commercial communities that were subject to Siṇḍok (929–947). See ibid., 2:215–219, 227–247.

13. J. V. G. Mills, trans., *Ying-yai Sheng-lan of Ma Huan (1433),* 91.

14. Hardjowardojo, trans., *Pararaton,* 43, 58.

15. Sarkar, *Corpus of the Inscriptions of Java,* 215–219. For a discussion of the pre-Majapahit era *dĕrwaya haji* cesses, see Wisseman, "Markets and Trade in Pre-Majapahit Java." As noted above, the use of foreigners to collect *dĕrwaya haji* reflects several possibilities. It may simply have facilitated the movement of goods from the hinterland to the coast, or it may also be viewed as an attempt by Javanese monarchs to penetrate local political autonomy. Javanese monarchs, who had difficulty dealing with local powers, could have placed their trust in outsiders with no local connections. Such foreigners with few ties to the local political or social system could have enhanced their political, social, or economic status as a consequence of their royal service.

16. The concept of "symbolic capital" is drawn from Pierre Bourdieu, *Outline of a Theory of Practice,* 172ff., as discussed in chapter 6.

17. Pigeaud, *Java in the Fourteenth Century,* 3:160–162; 4:109.

18. Ibid., 4:400.

19. The *Nagarakĕrtagama* reports one such royal redistribution of textiles (along with bamboo and food) to workers who were responsible for the construction of viewing stands for those watching the games that took place at the Caitra festival (canto 87, stanza 3).

20. Pigeaud, *Java in the Fourteenth Century,* 1:115–117; 3:166–168. Pigeaud's assignment of a 1391 date to the second letter was revised to 1393 by L. C. Damais, "Études d'epigraphie Indonésienne, III. Liste des principales inscriptions datées de l'Indonésie," *BEFEO* 46 (1952–1954): 105, and "Études d'epigraphie Indonésienne, IV. Discussion de la date des inscriptions," *BEFEO* 47 (1955): 238.

21. It is not clear what a unit of "cash" was equivalent to, although Chinese accounts suggest that they were units of copper currency.

22. Pigeaud, *Java in the Fourteenth Century,* 3:166. The area in question was subject to the authority of the king's uncle (the Prince of Wĕngker, who plays a prominent role in the *Nagarakĕrtagama*) who independently issued a charter

around 1380 that was confirmed in the 1393 letter from the king to the local elite (ibid., 4:416).

23. Ibid., 4:426.

24. The court's right to a share of the *titiban* collections guaranteed the flow of locally produced trade commodities (salt, sugar, salted meats, cloth, oil, and a share of goods acquired in exchange for these products) to the court. The political implications of royal redistributions of these trade goods are discussed in Hiram W. Woodward, Jr., "A Chinese Silk Depicted at Candi Sewu," in *Economic Exchange and Social Interaction in Southeast Asia: Perspectives from Prehistory, History and Ethnography,* ed. Karl L. Hutterer, 233–244.

25. See F. H. van Naerssen and R. C. de Iongh, *The Economic and Administrative History of Early Indonesia,* 1–84.

26. Pigeaud, *Java in the Fourteenth Century,* 3:173; 4:449ff. While the *Nagarakĕrtagama* makes no mention of debt-bondsmen, the *Pararaton* lists many. A discussion of debt-bondsmen in early Southeast Asia is provided by Anthony Reid, ed., *Slavery, Bondage and Dependency in South-East Asia.*

27. He was assigned seven acres (one *jung*) of land that could be terraced *(pasawahan)* and one *kikil* (half a *jung*) of clearings. This territory was subject to the authority of the king's daughter's husband.

28. This consignment of fish *(acan)* was consumed in the great community meal that culminated the Caitra festival.

29. The importance of such marriage alliances is demonstrated in the case where the rejection of a marriage tie to the ruler of the Sunda Strait region led to armed conflict between the ruler's forces and those of the Majapahit state.

30. In the Angkor realm, peasants often retained only about 30 percent of what they produced on their lands, the remainder being due to elites or institutions (temples) that held rights to income from property (see chap. 6). Loss of control over surplus did not mean poverty for the peasant, however. With the percentage of local production due to those who held income rights to land fixed, increased productivity that generated additional surplus would have benefited the producer as well as those holding income rights to the peasant's land. Revenue was collected by the Majapahit state in three forms: cash, produce, and labor, with the latter two the most common. Rice was the principal means of payment in the fourteenth century (although cash settlements were becoming more common, especially among the nonagrarian population). Payments of rice due to the Majapahit government were collected by state ministers *(patih)* and were often stored until needed by the state (Pigeaud, *Java in the Fourteenth Century,* 4:386; see also Soemarsaid Moertono, *State and Statecraft in Old Java: A Study of the Later Mataram Period, 16th to 19th Century,* 85). "The Charter of Katiden" (1395) mentions a rice tax of *takerturun* ("a bundle of rice in the blade for every compound gate") (Pigeaud, 3:174; 4:456). The rice was collected from the fields at harvest time—the *Nagarakĕrtagama* mentions *prabherti,* the "first fruits of the harvest" that were payable to the government for use in the Caitra festival (canto 83, stanza 5). Writing in 1225, Chao Ju-kua, the commissioner of foreign trade at the China coast port of Ch'uan-chou, noted that the Javanese paid a "tithe-rent" rice tax; Javanese government officials received rice from this payment as their salary—these officials supervised cities, the state's treasury, and the state's granaries. See F. Hirth and W. W. Rockhill, *Chau Ju-kua: His Work on the Chinese and Arab Trade in the Twelfth and Thirteenth Centuries, Entitled Chu-fan-chi,* 76–77, 83.

31. These ceremonies converted the material capital derived from royal cesses into "symbolic capital." During the pre-Majapahit era Java's population was linked in a social and cultural order that focused on the court. In the Majapahit era new state ritual, such as that described in the *Nagarakĕrtagama* and in the three charters discussed above, broadened participation to include those who were of nonelite ("common") status. Majapahit rulers promoted the state's authority vis-à-vis local authority and encouraged ritual at the local level that "copied" that of the royal court. Various groups, not just landed elites as in former times, participated in local ceremonies and representatives of these groups attended ceremonies at the court. An extended discussion of ritual integration in early Javanese history is provided in Hermann Kulke, "Early State Formation and Ritual Policy in Eastern Java," in *Proceedings, Eighth International Association of Historians of Asia Conference.*

32. It is here implied that the Javanese peasant would have responded to such an opportunity to improve his income. This assumption is somewhat controversial, as scholars also argue that the typical Southeast Asian peasant had other priorities than economic goals in his life. See William C. Scott, *The Moral Economy of the Peasant,* and Samuel L. Popkin, *The Rational Peasant: The Political Economy of Rural Society in Vietnam.*

33. See Moertono, *State and Statecraft in Old Java,* 14–26. During the Majapahit era there was a shift of emphasis from the construction of colossal temples to more elaborate court ceremony. The Majapahit state built an impressive royal *kraton* and several strategic temples (e.g., Panataran); however, the *Nagarakĕrtagama*'s focus on the massive Caitra ceremonies indicates that lavish public festivals were considered more critical to the strengthening of ties between the state center and its outer regions.

34. Hirth and Rockhill, *Chau Ju-kua,* 78, 82–83.

35. Ibid., 78, 81–82 n. 16. Java also imported gold and silver vessels, silk, chemicals, lacquerware, and porcelain from China in Chao Ju-kua's time.

36. See John K. Whitmore, "Vietnam and the Monetary Flow of Eastern Asia, Thirteenth to Eighteenth Centuries," in *Precious Metal Flows in the Later Medieval and Early Modern Worlds,* ed. J. F. Richards, 363–393.

37. Mills, *Ma Huan,* 45–47, 88, 96, 97, 102, 107, 129–130, 136, 141, 151, 153, 156, 161, 167, 172.

38. Henry Yule, trans., *The Book of Ser Marco Polo,* 2:272–274.

39. Brian E. Colless, "Majapahit Revisited: External Evidence on the Geography and Ethnology of East Java in the Majapahit Period," *JMBRAS* 48, 2 (1975): 124–161.

40. The commander-in-chief of Majapahit's forces was said to have received 8,000 cash per diem from markets. Market merchants active near the court were obliged to relinquish part of their stocks to the "chiefs of trade," who shared this collection *(titiban)* with the court (Pigeaud, *Java in the Fourteenth Century,* 4:426). Chao Ju-kua reports that high government officials periodically received a supply of native produce to supplement their monthly salaries; soldiers and troop commanders received their salaries in gold (Hirth and Rockhill, *Chau Ju-kua,* 76).

41. The *Nagarakĕrtagama* (canto 16) implies that specific traders were under royal patent.

42. Chao Ju-kua reports that "traders going there (eastern Java ports) are put up in visitors' lodges, where food and drink . . . (are supplied to them)" (Hirth

and Rockhill, *Chau Ju-kua,* 77); traders were generously treated and were not charged for harborage or board—although the Java monarch received a return on foreign traders' exchange of gold and silver and other metals and produce for Java's spices (ibid., 83). The following quotation from Clifford Geertz's study of early Balinese civilization could well be describing the dilemma faced by Java's monarchs as they came to terms with their state's commercial interests:

> commerce in classical Bali, though definitely in [the state's realm of interest], was not altogether of it. Not only was the bulk of it in foreign hands (Chinese, Javanese, Buginese, on occasion European), but also it was connected to political life eccentrically—through a set of extremely specialized institutions designed at once to contain its dynamic and to capture its returns. The lords were not unmindful either that, in reaching for them, they risked the very foundations of their power. Grasping by habit, they were autarchic by instinct, and the result was a certain baroqueness of economic arrangement. (Geertz, *Negara: The Theater-State in Nineteenth Century Bali,* 87)

Geertz's study of nineteenth-century Bali holds that Balinese civilization generally looked away from the international trade centers ("politically insulated 'ports of trade' "); the state's elite mediated contacts with outsiders to the advantage of all (ibid.). In contrast, this study of Java shows less internal focus and greater interaction between the Javanese economy and the trade centers on Java's north coast, especially after the eleventh century.

43. Anthony Reid, "Trade and State Power in 16th and 17th Century Southeast Asia," in *Proceedings, Seventh International Association of Historians of Asia Conference,* 391–419; and Moertono, *State and Statecraft in Old Java.*

44. Pigeaud, *Java in the Fourteenth Century,* 3:105.

45. The state was also responsible for keeping public utilities in good repair (directly or indirectly through pressure on the local elite); they were specifically noted as being under government protection (ibid., 4:93–94). The royal government undertook such public works projects as the construction of dams, roads, bridges, fountains, and marketplaces, as well as the planting of trees (ibid., 4:103, 257).

46. Canto 83, stanza 4; canto 86, stanza 1–canto 87, stanza 3; Pigeaud, *Java in the Fourteenth Century,* 4:291.

47. Tradesmen and merchants brought tribute to the king at the annual Caitra festival ceremonies, the culmination of the Majapahit state's economic and social life. Here, too, representatives from China, India, Cambodia, Vietnam, Champa, and Thailand paid their respects to the king. They came to Java on merchant ships (it is unclear whose), arriving by the western monsoon before the beginning of the festival (February or March), and returned to the Asian mainland on the eastern monsoon. The same eastern monsoon brought traders from the eastern archipelago with spices (canto 83). Foreign Buddhist monks and Brahmans also participated in the Caitra festival (93.1). The view of Majapahit that these foreigners provided to their homelands is reflected in the following passage from the *Hikayat Raja Pasai:*

> The Emperor was famous for his love of justice. The empire grew prosperous. People in vast numbers thronged the city. At this time every kind of food was in great abundance. There was a ceaseless coming and going of people from the territories overseas which had submitted to the king, to say

nothing of places inside Java itself. Of the districts on the coast, from the west came the whole of the west, from the east came the whole of the east. From places inland right down to the shores of the Southern Ocean the people all came for an audience with the Emperor, bringing tribute and offerings. . . . The land of Majapahit was supporting a large population. Everywhere one went there were gongs and drums being beaten, people dancing to the strains of all kinds of loud music, entertainments of many kinds like the living theatre, the shadow play, masked-plays, step-dancing and musical dramas. These were the commonest sights and went on day and night in the land of Majapahit. (A. H. Hill, "Hikayat Raja-Raja Pasai," *JMBRAS* 33, 2 [1960]: 161)

48. The Phalguna-Caitra ceremonies began with the Bubat festival (*Nagarakĕrtagama,* cantos 86–87), continued with speeches on statecraft at gatherings of the royal family and its allies (88–89.5), and culminated with a community meal and dancing and singing performances in the royal compound (89.4–91.9).

49. The poem especially tells of the coming to power of the founder of the Singasari line, Ken Angrok (Rājasa).

50. In the *Pararaton* Tuban was identified as the Majapahit realm's most prosperous coastal port. Although it benefited from royal favor, it held no royal trade monopoly, and there was ample trade at other north coast ports.

51. The *Pararaton* tells most of this story; it was also made into a romantic poem entitled "Kidung Sunda," and the preamble to the Canggu Ferry Charter, as noted above, alludes to these events. The *Nagarakĕrtagama* omits reference to this event entirely, seemingly because it was considered a blight on the state's record that the rulers would rather forget.

52. Chao Ju-kua's 1225 report noted that the Sunda Strait region grew a superior variety of pepper but that "the people of the area are given to brigandage, on which account foreign traders rarely go there" (Hirth and Rockhill, *Chau Ju-kua,* 70).

53. According to the *Sejarah Melayu,* the Malacca court chronicle, after this raid the Palembang monarch, who was idealized as the legitimate heir to the Śrīvijayan rulers, moved away from Palembang. Malay authority over the strait was eventually reestablished at Malacca. See O. W. Wolters, *The Fall of Srivijaya in Malay History,* 113–114. Edward McKinnon believes that he has found archaeological evidence of a Majapahit sack of Muara Jambi in 1377. See O. W. Wolters, "A Few Miscellaneous *Pi-chi* Jottings on Early Indonesia," *Indonesia* 36 (October 1983): 60 n. 54.

54. This episode may well illustrate a manipulation of historical events in early Javanese literature to demonstrate the legitimacy of the state. In this light it is interesting that the *Pararaton* recorded the event while the *Nagarakĕrtagama* omitted reference to it. It would seem that the *Pararaton*'s emphasis on the trade sector, including extensive reference to ports that were totally ignored in the *Nagarakĕrtagama,* reflects a different concern from the magico-religious focus of the earlier work. While the *Nagarakĕrtagama* projects the image of a sanctified court that fulfilled earlier concerns for the state's "ritual sovereignty," the *Pararaton* recognized the importance of the nonreligious political and economic affairs of the Majapahit state. On the use of early Javanese literary sources for historical writing, see C. C. Berg, "The Javanese Picture of the Past," in *An Introduction to Indonesian Historiography,* ed. Soedjatmoko et al., 87–118.

55. The most recent English language summary of early Javanese history is

D. G. E. Hall (with M. C. Ricklefs), *A History of South East Asia,* 4th ed., 74–104.

56. A. J. Bernet Kempers, *Ancient Indonesian Art,* passim. Claire Holt, *Art in Indonesia: Continuity and Change,* depicts the Majapahit era as the peak of the cultural synthesis of Śiva worship and Buddhist tantrism, an era of the "Indonesianization" of classical forms in art, literature, and music (p. 72ff.). The Javanese *wayang* (puppet theater) and *gamelan* (orchestra) developed in the Majapahit court and was imitated throughout the realm.

57. Pigeaud, *Java in the Fourteenth Century,* 5, "The Centre of the Majapahit Complex in the Fourteenth Century According to Nagara-Kertagama Information," Outline Plan 1, insert.

58. Ibid., 3:3.

59. Ibid., 3:4; 4:468; and Anthony Johns, "The Role of Structural Organization and Myth in Javanese Historiography," *JAS* 24, 1 (1964): 93.

60. Pigeaud, *Java in the Fourteenth Century,* 4:528.

61. Moertono, *State and Statecraft in Old Java,* 1, speaks of the magico-religious principle that was the basis of Javanese kingship; Robert Heine-Geldern, "Conceptions of State and Kingship in Southeast Asia," *Far Eastern Quarterly* 2 (November 1942): 15–30, describes the cosmo-magic principle. See Stanley J. Tambiah, *World Conqueror and World Renouncer: A Study of Buddhism and Polity in Thailand against a Historical Background,* for a more recent discussion, and also chap. 1.

62. Pigeaud, *Java in the Fourteenth Century,* 3:4.

63. Cantos 42–43.

64. On the controversial reconstruction of the events of Kĕrtanagara's reign, see C. C. Berg, "Kertanagara, de Miskende Empire-builder," *Orientalie* 34 (July 1950): 3–32; and J. G. de Casparis, "Historical Writing on Indonesia (Early Period)," in *Historians of South-East Asia,* ed. D. G. E. Hall, 160–161. A more recent essay on the legacy of Majapahit in Javanese and Southeast Asian literature and the authenticity of Majapahit era literary sources, is S. Supomo, "The Image of Majapahit in Later Javanese and Indonesian History," in *Perceptions of the Past in Southeast Asia,* ed. Anthony Reid and David Marr, 171–185. Kĕrtanagara had previously divided the ashes of his father between two shrines; at one he was worshipped as an incarnation of Śiva, at the second as the Bodhisattva Amoghapāśa.

65. Supomo, "The Image of Majapahit."

66. Canto 4. 2. 4.

67. A useful discussion of Majapahit's state structure is Schrieke, *Indonesian Sociological Studies: Ruler and Realm in Early Java,* 25–70.

68. Cantos 79.2.2, 88.4; Kĕrtawardana was the husband of Hayam Wuruk's mother, who had reigned as queen of Majapahit prior to her son's ascension to the throne. Cantos 79.2.1, 88.2.4; the Wĕngker region was near Madiun—west of Kaḍiri on the upper eastern branch of the Solo River. Vijayarājasa's title associated him with the previous rulers of Kaḍiri (he was married to the Princess of Kaḍiri), while Hayam Wuruk's father's Singasari title associated him with the previous rulers of Singasari. The Majapahit monarch's sovereignty over these two princes symbolized the reigning dynasty's ties to the past. Vijayarājasa's administrative duties included responsibility for eastern Java and Bali, which was conquered by Majapahit in 1343 (see J. Noorduyn, "The Eastern Kings in Majapahit," *BKI* 131, 4 [1975]: 479–487). The *Nagarakĕrtagama* depicts the holder of

the Wĕngker title as being well-informed of peasant holdings; organizing the compilation of descriptions of the districts that were under royal authority; and stimulating the upkeep of roads, public buildings, and temples—the activities that were also associated with the king's father Kĕrtawardana (see Pigeaud, *Java in the Fourteenth Century,* 4:540–546).

69. From the *Ming-shih* ("History of the Ming"), as discussed in Noorduyn, "Eastern Kings in Majapahit," 481–482.

70. See Brian E. Colless, "A Note on the Names of the Kings of Java in the Ming History," *BKI* 131, 4 (1975): 487–489. The location of this "eastern capital" is unknown. Majapahit's apology for these deaths was accepted by the Ming court.

71. Pigeaud, *Java in the Fourteenth Century,* 4:537–546.

72. Ibid., see also Colless, "A Note on the Names."

73. Coedès, *Indianized States,* 239–242, following the lead of N. J. Krom, *Hindoe-Javaansche Geschiendenis,* 427–432.

74. J. Noorduyn, "Majapahit in the 15th Century," *BKI* 134, 2–3 (1978): 207–274.

75. See Wolters, *Fall of Srivijaya,* passim.

76. Noorduyn, "The Eastern Kings in Majapahit."

77. The Majapahit monarch could no longer guarantee that he could maintain the order necessary for his subjects' well-being—the most critical requirement of traditional Javanese monarchs—except in Java's hinterland; thus was statecraft legitimately refocused on the miniature cosmos that the monarch continued to rule in Java's interior.

78. See Mills, *Ma Huan,* passim.

79. Hardjowardojo, *Pararaton.*

80. Tuban and Gresik were the most important among the fifteenth-century ports on Java's north coast, largely because of their trade alliances with the Javanese interior (where they secured rice), the eastern archipelago (where they exchanged Java's rice for spices), and Malacca (where they provisioned the port population with Javanese rice and the eastern archipelago's spices). See M. A. P. Meilink-Roelofsz, *Asian Trade and European Influence in the Indonesian Archipelago between 1500 and 1630,* 103–115.

81. Armando Cortesão, trans. and ed., *The Suma Oriental of Tomé Pires,* 180–223.

82. Numerous fourteenth- through sixteenth-century Muslim gravestones discovered near the the Majapahit capital (the earliest dated 1368–1369), which appear to mark the graves of well-to-do Javanese not foreign Muslims, demonstrate that Islam did not initially represent a religious and political force that opposed Majapahit. See L. C. Damais, "L'epigraphie Musulmane dans le Sud-Est Asiatique," *BEFEO* 54, 2 (1968): 353–415. Tomé Pires noted that Muslim elites among the Java coast ports, especially those dominated by Southeast Asian populations, admired the Majapahit court and tried to emulate its manners and customs—and thus reflected the style of the Majapahit state to which they had previously been subject. This port elite *(orang kaya)* dominated trade by levying tolls, monopolizing the trade in specific staple products, and took an active part in maritime activities such as shipowning, piracy, and carrying on a personal trade.

83. See D. H. Burger, *Structural Changes in Javanese Society: The Supra-Village Sphere,* trans. L. Palmier; van Naerssen and de Iongh, *Economic and*

Administrative History, 102–104; and Moertono, *State and Statecraft in Old Java.*

84. Meilink-Roelofsz, *Asian Trade and European Influences.*

85. Chester Gorman et al., "Ban Chiang," *Expedition* 18, 4 (1976): 11–47.

86. Marshall Sahlins, "Poor Man, Rich Man, Big Man, Chief: Political Types in Melanesia and Polynesia," *Comparative Studies in Society and History* 5 (1963): 235–303.

87. Wolters, *Fall of Srivijaya;* O. W. Wolters, "The Khmer King at Basan (1371–1373) and the Restoration of the Cambodian Chronology during the 14th and 15th Centuries," *Asia Major* 12, 1 (1966): 44–64; Charnvit Kasetsiri, *The Rise of Ayudhya;* and Tambiah, *World Conqueror and World Renouncer.* For elaboration of this theme, see Geertz, *Negara.*

88. See, for instance, discussion of the hinterland population of Samudra-Pasai as reflected in the *Hikayat Raja Pasai* in chapter 8. This hinterland population assisted in the establishment of the Samudra-Pasai entrepôt but chose to retreat to their upriver homeland rather than convert to Islam and to become full participants in the new lifestyle of the entrepôt. Similar patterns were found in Malaysia by Diane Lewis, where upriver populations rejected the "civilization" of their fellow Malays who lived in downriver lowlands yet looked upon these downriver populations for political and economic mediation with the outside world. See Lewis, "Inas, A Study of Local History," *JMBRAS* 33 (1960): 65–94; and Kenneth R. Hall, "The Coming of Islam to the Archipelago: A Reassessment," in *Economic Exchange and Social Interaction in Southeast Asia: Perspectives from Prehistory, History and Ethnography,* ed. Karl L. Hutterer, 223–227.

Bibliography

Aeusrivongse, Nidhi. "*Devarāja* Cult and Khmer Kingship at Angkor." In *Explorations in Early Southeast Asian History: The Origins of Southeast Asian Statecraft,* edited by Kenneth R. Hall and John K. Whitmore, 107–148. Ann Arbor, 1976.

Andaya, Leonard. "The Structure of Power in Seventeenth Century Johor." In *Pre-Colonial State Systems in Southeast Asia,* edited by Anthony Reid and L. Castles. Kuala Lumpur, 1975.

Appadurai, Arjun, and Carol Appadurai Breckenridge. "The South Indian Temple: Authority, Honour, and Redistribution," *Contributions to Indian Sociology* n.s. 10, 2 (1976): 187–211.

Aung-Thwin, Michael. "Kingship, the Saṅgha, and Society in Pagan." In *Explorations in Early Southeast Asian History: The Origins of Southeast Asian Statecraft,* edited by Kenneth R. Hall and John K. Whitmore, 205–256. Ann Arbor, 1976.

Aung-Thwin, Michael. "The Problem of Ceylonese-Burmese Relations in the 12th Century and the Question of an Interregnum in Pagan, 1165–1174 A.D.," *JSS* 64, 1 (1976): 53–74.

Aung-Thwin, Michael. "Commercial Developments in the Pagan Era." Typescript.

Aymonier, E. *Le Cambodge.* 3 vols. Paris, 1900–1904.

Aymonier, E. "Première étude sur les inscriptions Tchames," *JA* 17 (1891): 1–86.

Barrett, A. M. "Two Old Javanese Copper-plate Inscriptions of Balitung." M.A. thesis, University of Sydney, 1968.

Barth, Auguste, and Abel Bergaigne. "Inscriptions Sanscrites du Cambodge et Campa." In *Académie des Inscriptions et Belles-Lettres, Notices et extraits des manuscrits de la Bibliothéque du roi et autres bibliothéques,* 27. Paris, 1885, 1893.

Basham, A. L. *The Wonder That Was India.* New York, 1959.

Bastin, John, and R. Roolvink, eds. *Malayan and Indonesian Studies: Essays Presented to Sir Richard Winstedt on His Eighty-fifth Birthday.* Oxford, 1964.

Bautier, R. H. *The Economic Development of Medieval Europe.* London, 1971.

Benda, Harry J. "The Structure of Southeast Asian History: Some Preliminary Observations," *JSEAH* 3 (March 1962): 103–138.

Berg, C. C. "Kertanagara, de Miskende Empire-builder," *Orientalie* 34 (July 1950): 3–32.

Berg, C. C. "The Javanese Picture of the Past." In *An Introduction to Indonesian Historiography,* edited by Soedjatmoko et al., 87–118. Ithaca, 1965.

Bernet Kempers, A. J. *Ancient Indonesian Art.* Amsterdam, 1959.

Boechari. "Epigraphy and Indonesian Historiography." In *An Introduction to Indonesian Historiography,* edited by Soedjatmoko et al., 50–60. Ithaca, 1965.

———. "Preliminary Report on the Discovery of an Old Malay Inscription at Sodjomerta," *Madjalah Ilmu-Ilmu Sastra Indonesia* 2–3 (1966): 241–251.

———. "Some Considerations on the Problem of the Shift of Mataram's Centre of Government from Central to East Java in the 10th Century." In *Early South East Asia: Essays in Archaeology, History and Historical Geography,* edited by R. B. Smith and W. Watson, 473–491. London, 1979.

Boisselier, J. *Le Cambodge.* Paris, 1966.

Bosch, F. D. K. "De inscriptie van Kĕloerak," *TBG* 68 (1928): 57–62.

———. "Een Maleische inscriptie in het Buitenzorgsche," *BKI* 100 (1941): 49–53.

———. Review of *Prasasti Indonesia I,* by J. G. de Casparis, *BKI* 108 (1952): 191–199; *Prasasti Indonesia II, BKI* 114 (1955): 306–320.

———. *Selected Studies in Indonesian Archaeology.* The Hague, 1961.

Bourdieu, Pierre. *Outline of a Theory of Practice.* Cambridge, 1977.

Brakel, L. F. "State and Statecraft in 17th Century Aceh." In *Pre-Colonial State Systems in Southeast Asia,* edited by Anthony Reid and L. Castles. Kuala Lumpur, 1975.

Brandes, J. L. A., and N. J. Krom. "Oud-Javaansche Oorkonden nagelaten Transcripties van wijlen Dr. J. L. A. Brandes uitgegeven door Dr. N. J. Krom," *VBG* 60 (1913): 134–136.

Breckenridge, Carol Appadurai. "Land as Gift in the Vijayanagara Period." Paper read at the Annual Meeting of the Association for Asian Studies, Toronto, Canada, March 1981.

Briggs, L. P. "The Khmer Empire and the Malay Peninsula," *Far Eastern Quarterly* 9, 3 (1950): 256–305.

———. *The Ancient Khmer Empire.* Transactions of the American Philosophical Society, no. 41. Philadelphia, 1951.

Bronson, Bennet. "Exchange at the Upstream and Downstream Ends: Notes Toward a Functional Model of the Coastal State in Southeast Asia." In *Economic Exchange and Social Interaction in Southeast Asia: Perspectives from Prehistory, History and Ethnography,* edited by Karl L. Hutterer, 39–52. Ann Arbor, 1977.

———. "The Late Prehistory and Early History of Central Thailand." In *Early South East Asia,* edited by R. B. Smith and W. Watson, 315–336. London, 1979.

Bronson, Bennet, and Jan Wisseman. "Palembang as Srivijaya: The Lateness of Early Cities in Southern Southeast Asia," *Asian Perspectives* 19, 2 (1976): 220–239.

Brown, C. C. "Sĕjarah Mĕlayu or 'Malay Annals': A Translation of Raffles Ms. 18," *JMBRAS* 25, 2–3 (1952): 1–276.

Buchari. "A Preliminary Note on the Study of the Old-Javanese Civil Administration," *Madjalah Ilmu-Ilmu Sastra Indonesia* 1 (1963): 122–133.

Bunag, Tej and M. Smithies. *In Memoriam Phya Anuman Rajadhon*. Bangkok, 1970.
Burger, D. H. *Structural Changes in Javanese Society: The Supra-Village Sphere,* trans. by L. Palmier. Ithaca, 1956.
Casparis, J. G. de. "Nogmaals de Sanskrit-inscriptie op den steen van Dinojo," *TBG* 81 (1941): 499–513.
———. *Prasasti Indonesia I: Inscripties uit de Çailendra-Tijd*. Bandung, 1950.
———. *Prasasti Indonesia II: Selected Inscriptions from the Seventh to the Ninth Century A.D.* Bandung, 1956.
———. "Short Inscriptions from Tjandi Plaosan-Lor," *Berita Dinas Purbakala* 4 (1958): 3–36.
———. "Historical Writing on Indonesia (Early Period)." In *Historians of South-East Asia,* edited by D. G. E. Hall, 121–163. London, 1961.
———. "New Evidence on Cultural Relations Between Java and Ceylon in Ancient Times," *Artibus Asiae* 24, 3–4 (1961): 241–248.
———. "The Date of the Grahi Buddha," *JSS* 55, 1 (1967): 31–40.
———. *Indonesian Palaeography.* Leiden, 1975.
———. "The Dual Nature of Barabudur." In *Barabudur: History and Significance of a Buddhist Monument,* edited by Louis Gomez and Hiram W. Woodward, Jr., 47–83. Berkeley, 1981.
———. "Pour une histoire sociale de l'ancienne Java principale au Xeme s.," *Archipel* 21 (1981): 125–154.
Charlesworth, M. P. "Roman Trade with India: A Resurvey." In *Studies in Roman Economic and Social History in Honour of Allen Chester Johnson,* edited by P. R. Coleman-Norton, 131–143. Princeton, 1951.
Chatterji, B. R. *History of Indonesia.* Delhi, 1967.
Chou Ta-kuan. *Notes on the Customs of Cambodia translated from the Shuo-fu,* trans. by Paul Pelliot (trans. from French into English by J. G. d'Avery Paul). Bangkok, 1967.
Christie, A. H. "Lin-i, Fu-nan, Java." In *Early South East Asia: Essays in Archaeology, History and Historical Geography,* edited by R. B. Smith and W. Watson, 281–287. London, 1979.
Christie, Jan Wisseman. "Rāja and Rāma: The Classical State in Early Java." In *Centers, Symbols, and Hierarchies: Essays on the Classical States of Southeast Asia,* edited by Lorraine Gesick, 9–44. Yale University Southeast Asian Studies Monograph no. 26. New Haven, 1983.
Coedès, George. "La stèle de Ta-prohm," *BEFEO* 6 (1906): 44–81.
———. "La stèle de Palhal," *BEFEO* 13, 6 (1913): 33.
———. "Deux inscriptions sanskrites du Fou-nan," *BEFEO* 31 (1931): 1–12.
———. "On the Origin of the Sailendras of Indonesia," *Journal of the Greater India Society* 1 (1934): 61–70.
———. "A New Inscription from Fu-nan," *Journal of the Greater Indian Society* 4 (1937): 117–121.
———. "Le date de l'inscription sanskrit de Vo-Canh," *Indian Historical Quarterly* 16 (1940): 484–488.
———. "La stèle de Prah Khan d'Angkor," *BEFEO* 41 (1941): 255–301.
———. *Inscriptions du Cambodge.* 6 vols. Hanoi, 1937–1942; Paris, 1951–1966.
———. *Recueil des inscriptions du Siam.* 2nd ed. Bangkok, 1961.
———. *The Making of Southeast Asia,* trans. by H. M. Wright. Berkeley, 1966.
———. *The Indianized States of Southeast Asia,* edited by Walter F. Vella, trans. by Susan Brown Cowing. Honolulu, 1968.

Coedès, George, and Pierre Dupont. "Les stèles de Sdok Kak Thom, Phnom Sandak et Prah Vihar," *BEFEO* 43 (1943-1946): 56-154.

Colless, Brian E. "Traders of the Pearl." *Abr Nahrain* 9 (1970): 17-38; 10 (1971): 102-121; 11 (1972): 1-21; 13 (1973): 115-135; 14 (1974): 1-16; 15 (1975): 6-17.

———. "Majapahit Revisited: External Evidence on the Geography and Ethnology of East Java in the Majapahit Period," *JMBRAS* 48, 2 (1975): 124-161.

———. "A Note on the Names of the Kings of Java in the Ming History," *BKI* 131, 4 (1975): 487-489.

Conti, Nicolo. *The Travels of Nicolo Conti in the East in the Early Part of the Fifteenth Century.* London, 1857.

Cortesão, Armando, trans. and ed. *The Suma Oriental of Tomé Pires.* London, 1944.

Cowan, C. D. , and O. W. Wolters, eds. *Southeast Asian History and Historiography: Essays Presented to D. G. E. Hall.* Ithaca, 1976.

Đại Việt sũ-ký toàn thu'. Nhà Xuât Bãn Khoa Học Xã Hội. Hanoi, 1967.

Davidson, Jeremy N. C. S. "Recent Archaeological Activity in Viet-Nam," *Journal of the Hong Kong Archaeological Society* 6 (1975): 80-99.

Damais, L. C. "Epigratische Aantekeningen," *TBG* 83 (1949): 18-20.

———. "Études d'epigraphie Indonésienne, III. Liste des principales inscriptions datées de l'Indonésie," *BEFEO* 46 (1952-1954): 1-105.

———. "Études d'epigraphie Indonésienne IV. Discussion de la date des inscriptions," *BEFEO* 47 (1955): 7-290.

———. "Études Sino-Indonésiennes, I. Quelques titres javanais de l'époque des Song; II. Une mention de l'ère śaka dans le Ming Che," *BEFEO* 50 (1960): 1-35.

———. "Études Soumatranaises, I. La date de l'inscription de Hujung Langit ("Bawang"); II. L'inscription de Ulu Belu," *BEFEO* 50 (1960): 275-310.

———. "Études Sino-Indonésienne, III: La transcription chinoise Ho-ling comme désignation de Java," *BEFEO* 52, 1 (1964): 93-141.

———. "L'épigraphie Musulmane dans le Sud-Est Asiatique," *BEFEO* 54, 2 (1968): 567-604.

———. "Bibliographie Indonésienne, XI. Les publications épigraphiques du service archaeologique de l'Indonésie," *BEFEO* 54 (1968): 295-521.

———. "Études Soumatranaises, III. La langue B des inscriptions de Śrī Wijaya," *BEFEO* 54 (1968): 523—566.

———. Review of *Riwajat Indonesia* by R. Ng. Poebatjaraka. *BEFEO* 61 (1975): 639.

Du Bourg, H. de Mestier. "La première moitié de XIe siècle au Cambodge: Suryavarman Ier, sa vie et quelques aspects des institutions à son époque," *JA* 258, 3-4 (1970): 281-314.

Dumont, Louis. *Religion, Politics and History in India: Collected Papers in Indian Sociology.* The Hague, 1970.

Dupont, Pierre. "Le Buddha de Grahi et l'ecole de C'āiya," *BEFEO* 42 (1942): 105-113.

———. "Les dèbuts de la royauté Angkorienne," *BEFEO* 46, 1 (1952): 148-169.

Duroiselle, Charles and C. O. Blagden. *Epigraphia Birmanica.* 5 vols. Rangoon, 1919-1936; reprinted Rangoon, 1960.

Ferrand, Gabriel. *Relations de voyages et textes géographiques arabes, persans et*

turks relatifs à l'Extrême Orient du VIIIe au XVIIIe siècles. 2 vols. Paris, 1913-1914.
———. "Le K'ouen-louen et les anciennes navigations interocéaniques dans les mers du sud," *JA* (July-August 1919): 5-68.
———. "L'empire sumatrannais de Çrivijaya," *JA* 20 (1922): 1-104, 161-246.
Finot, Louis. "Deux nouvelles inscriptions de Bhadravarman Ier, roi de Champa," *BEFEO* 2 (1902): 185-191.
———. "Stèle de Çaṃbhuvarman a Mi-so'n," *BEFEO* 3 (1903): 206-211.
———. "Pāṇḍuranga," *BEFEO* 3 (1903): 630-648.
———. "Inscriptions du Quang Nam," *BEFEO* 4 (1904): 83-115.
———. "Les inscriptions de Mi-so'n," *BEFEO* 4 (1904): 897-977.
———. "Nouvelles inscriptions de Po Klaun Garai," *BEFEO* 9 (1909): 205-209.
———. "L'inscription de Ban That, *BEFEO* 12, 2 (1912): 1-28.
Fisher, C. A. *South-East Asia: A Social, Economic, and Political Geography.* New York, 1964.
Furnivall, J. S. "Europeans in Burma in the 15th Century," *JBRS* 29, 3 (1939): 236-249.
Filliozat, Jean. "Agastya et la propagation du Brahmanisme au Sud-Est Asiatiques," *Adyar Library Bulletin* 31-32 (1967-1968): 442-449.
Geertz, Clifford. *Islam Observed.* New Haven, 1968.
———. *Negara: The Theater-State in Nineteenth Century Bali.* Princeton, 1980.
Gerini, G. E. *Researches on Ptolemy's Geography of Eastern Asia.* London, 1909.
Gibb, H. A. R. *The Travels of Ibn Battuta in Asia and Africa, 1325-1354.* London, 1957.
Giles, H. A. *The Travels of Fa-hsien, 399-414, or Record of the Buddhist Kingdoms.* London, 1956.
Godakumbura, C. E. "Relations between Burma and Ceylon," *JBRS* 49, 2 (1966): 145-162.
Goitein, S. D. *Letters of Medieval Jewish Traders.* Princeton, 1973.
Gomez, Louis, and Hiram Woodward, Jr., eds. *Barabudur: History and Significance of a Buddhist Monument.* Berkeley, 1981.
Gorman, Charles, James D. Mahly, Pisit Charoenwongsa, William Schauffler, Tamara Stech Wheeler, and Robert Maddin. "Ban Chiang," *Expedition* 18, 4 (1976): 11-47.
Gosling, L. A. Peter. "Contemporary Malay Traders in the Gulf of Siam." In *Economic Exchange and Social Interaction in Southeast Asia: Perspectives from Prehistory, History and Ethnography,* edited by Karl L. Hutterer, 73-95. Ann Arbor, 1977.
Groeneveldt, W. P. "Notes on the Malay Archipelago and Malacca, compiled from Chinese sources." In *Miscellaneous Papers relating to Indo-China and the Indian Archipelago,* edited by R. Rost, 126-262. London, 1887.
Groslier, Bernard P. *Angkor et le Cambodge au XVIe siècle d'après les sources Portugaises et Espagnoles.* Paris, 1958.
———. *The Art of Indochina.* New York, 1962.
———. *Angkor, Art and Civilization.* London, 1966.
Gunawardana, R. A. L. H. *Robe and Plough: Monasticism and Economic Interest in Early Medieval Sri Lanka.* Tucson, 1979.
Hall, D. G. E., ed. *Historians of South-East Asia.* London, 1961.
Hall, D. G. E. *A History of South East Asia.* 4th ed. New York, 1981.

Hall, Kenneth R. "Khmer Commercial Development and Foreign Contracts under Sūryavarman I," *JESHO* 18 (1975): 318–336.

———. "An Introductory Essay on Southeast Asian Statecraft in the Classical Period," and "State and Statecraft in Early Srivijaya." In *Explorations in Early Southeast Asian History: The Origins of Southeast Asian Statecraft,* edited by Kenneth R. Hall and John K. Whitmore, 1–38, 61–105. Ann Arbor, 1976.

———. "The Coming of Islam to the Archipelago: A Reassessment." In *Economic Exchange and Social Interaction in Southeast Asia: Perspectives from Prehistory, History and Ethnography,* edited by Karl L. Hutterer, 213–231. Ann Arbor, 1977.

———. "International Trade and Foreign Diplomacy in Early Medieval South India," *JESHO* 21, 1 (1978): 75–98.

———. *Trade and Statecraft in the Age of the Cōḷas.* New Delhi, 1980.

———. "Trade and Statecraft in the Western Archipelago at the Dawn of the European Age," *JMBRAS* 54, 1 (1981): 21–47.

———. "Peasant State and Society in Cōḷa Times: A View from the Tiruviḍaimuradūr Urban Complex," *Indian Economic and Social History Review* 18, 3–4 (1982): 393–410.

Hall, Kenneth R. and George W. Spencer. "The Economy of Kāñcīpuram, A Sacred Center in Early South India," *Journal of Urban History* 6, 2 (1980): 127–151.

Hall, Kenneth R. and John K. Whitmore, eds. *Explorations in Early Southeast Asian History: The Origins of Southeast Asian Statecraft.* Ann Arbor, 1976.

Hall, Kenneth R. and John K. Whitmore. "Southeast Asian Trade and the Isthmian Struggle, 1000–1200 A.D." In *Explorations in Early Southeast Asian History: The Origins of Southeast Asian Statecraft,* edited by Kenneth R. Hall and John K. Whitmore, 303–340. Ann Arbor, 1976.

Hardjowardojo, trans. *Pararaton.* Jakarta, 1965.

Heine-Geldern, Robert. "Conceptions of State and Kingship in Southeast Asia," *Far Eastern Quarterly* 2 (November 1942): 15–30; reprinted, Southeast Asia Program Data Paper no. 18. Ithaca, 1956.

Hill, A. H. "The Hikayat Raja-Raja Pasai," *JMBRAS* 33, 2 (1960): 1–215.

Hirandanda Sastri. *Nālandā and Its Epigraphic Material.* Memoirs of the Archaeological Survey of India, no. 66. Calcutta, 1942.

Hirth, F. *China and the Roman Orient.* Shanghai, 1888.

Hirth, F., and W. W. Rockhill. *Chau Ju-kua: His Work on the Chinese and Arab Trade in the Twelfth and Thirteenth Centuries, Entitled Chu-fan-chi.* St. Petersburg, 1911.

Holt, Claire. *Art in Indonesia: Continuities and Change.* Ithaca, 1967.

Huber, Eduoard. "L'epigraphie de la dynastie de Đong-du'o'ng," *BEFEO* 11 (1911): 269–299.

Hubert, Henri, and Marcel Mauss. *Sacrifice: Its Nature and Function.* Chicago, 1964.

Hucker, Charles O. *China's Imperial Past.* Stanford, 1975.

Hutterer, Karl L. *An Archaeological Picture of a Pre-Spanish Cebuano Community.* Cebu City, 1973.

———. "The Evolution of Philippine Lowland Societies," *Mankind* 9 (1974): 287–299.

———. "Prehistoric Trade and the Evolution of Philippine Societies: A Recon-

sideration." In *Economic Exchange and Social Interaction in Southeast Asia: Perspectives from Prehistory, History and Ethnography,* edited by Karl L. Hutterer, 177–196. Ann Arbor, 1977.
Jacques, Claude. "Auteur de quelques toponymes de l'inscription du Prasat Trapan Run K. 598: La capitale Angkorienne, de Yaśovarman Ier a Sūryavarman Ier," *BEFEO* 65 (1978): 281–321.
———. " 'Funan,' 'Zhenla': The Reality Concealed by These Chinese Views of Indochina." In *Early South East Asia,* edited by R. B. Smith and W. Watson, 371–379. London, 1979.
Johns, Anthony. "The Role of Structural Organization and Myth in Javanese Historiography," *JAS* 24, 1 (1964): 91–99.
Jones, Horace. *The Geography of Strabo.* Cambridge, 1949.
Kangle, R. P., trans. *The Kauṭilīya Arthaśāstra,* 2 vols. Bombay, 1963.
Kaplan, D. "Men, Monuments, and Political Systems," *Southwestern Journal of Anthropology* 19, 4 (1963): 397–410.
Kasetsiri, Charnvit. *The Rise of Ayudhya: A History of Siam in the Fourteenth and Fifteenth Centuries.* Kuala Lumpur, 1976.
Kern, H. *Verspreide Geschriften.* 15 vols. The Hague, 1913–1928.
Karashima, Noboru. "The Power Structure of Chola Rule." *Second International Conference Seminar of Tamil Studies,* 233–238. Madras, 1968.
Kennedy, J. "Early Commerce of Babylon with India," *Journal of the Asiatic Society of Bengal* (1898): 241–288.
Kennedy, Victor. "An Indigenous Early Nineteenth Century Map of Central and Northeast Thailand." In *In Memoriam Phya Anuman Rajadhon,* edited by Tej Bunag and M. Smithies, 315–348. Bangkok, 1970.
Kirsch, A. Thomas. "Kinship, Genealogical Claims, and Societal Integration in Ancient Khmer Society: An Interpretation." In *Southeast Asian History and Historiography,* edited by C. D. Cowan and O. W. Wolters, 190–202. Ithaca, 1976.
Krom, N. J. *De Sumatraansche periode der Javaansche Geschiedenis.* Leiden, 1919.
———. *Hindoe-Javaansche Geschiendenis.* 's-Gravenhage, 1931.
Kromodjoja Adi Negoro. *Oud Javaansche Oorkonden op steem uit het afdeeling Modjokerto.* Modjokerto, 1921.
Kulke, Hermann. *The Devarāja Cult.* Southeast Asia Program Data Paper no. 108. Ithaca, 1978.
———. "Early State Formation and Ritual Policy in Eastern Java." In *Proceedings, Eighth International Association of Historians of Asia Conference,* forthcoming.
Lajonquière, E. Lunet de. "Carte archéologique de l'ancien Cambodge." *Publications de l'École Française d'Extrême Orient,* 9. Hanoi, 1911.
Lamb, Alastair. "A Note on the Tiger Symbol in Some Southeast Asian Representations of Avalokitesvara," *Federated Museums Journal* 6 (1961): 89–90.
———. "Kedah and Takuapa: Some Tentative Historical Conclusions," *Federated Museums Journal* 6 (1961): 69–88.
———. "Takuapa: The Probable Site of a Pre-Malaccan Entrepot in the Malay Peninsula." In *Malayan and Indonesian Studies,* edited by John Bastin and R. Roolvink, 76–86. London, 1971.
Lansing, John Stephen. *Evil in the Morning of the World.* Ann Arbor, 1974.
———. "The 'Indianization' of Bali," *JSEAS* 14, 2 (1983): 409–421.

Lê Tắc. *Annam Chí-lúo'c* (in Chinese). Hue, 1961.

Lê Thành Khôi. *Le Viet-Nam, Histoire et Civilisation*. Paris, 1955.

Levi, Sylvain. "Les 'marchands de mer' et leur role dans le bouddhisme primitif," *Bulletin de l'Association Française de Amis de l'Orient* 7 (October 1929): 19–39.

———. "Kanishka et S'ātavāhana," *JA* (1936): 61–121.

Lewis, Diane. "Inas, A Study of Local History," *JMBRAS* 33 (1960): 65–94.

Lo Jung-pang. "The Emergence of China as a Sea Power during the Late Sung and Early Yuan Periods," *Far Eastern Quarterly* 14, 4 (1955): 489–503.

Lombard, Denys. "Reporting on the Second Seminar Sejarah Nasional, Jogjakarta, 1970," *BEFEO* 58 (1971): 286.

Loofs, H. H. E. "Problems of Continuity between the Pre-Buddhist and Buddhist Periods in Central Thailand, with Special Reference to U-Thong." In *Early South East Asia: Essays in Archaeology, History and Historical Geography,* edited by R. B. Smith and W. Watson, 342–351. London, 1979.

Luce, G. H. "A Cambodian (?) Invasion of Lower Burma—A Comparison of Burmese and Talaing Chronicles," *JBRS* 12, 1 (1922): 39–45.

———. "The Early *Syam* in Burma's History: A Supplement," *JSS* 47, 1 (1959): 59–101.

———. "Some Old References to the South of Burma and Ceylon." In *Felicitation Volumes of Southeast Asian Studies Presented to His Highness Prince Dhaninivat,* II, 269–282. Bangkok, 1965.

———. "The Career of Htilaing Min (Kyanzittha), the Unifier of Burma, A.D. 1084–1113," *JRAS* (1966): 53–68.

———. *Old Burma, Early Pagan*. 3 vols. Locust Valley, New York, 1969–1970.

Mabbett, I. W. "The 'Indianization' of Southeast Asia: Reflections on the Prehistoric Sources," *JSEAS* 8, 1 (1977): 1–14; 8, 2 (1977): 143–161.

———. "Varṇas in Angkor and the Indian Caste System," *JAS* 36, 3 (1977): 429–442.

———. "Kingship in Angkor," *JSS* 66, 2 (1978): 1–58.

Majumdar, R. C. *Suvarnadvipa*. Calcutta, 1937.

———. *Hindu Colonies in the Far East*. Calcutta, 1944.

———. *Ancient Indian Colonization in South-East Asia*. Baroda, 1963.

Malleret, Louis. *L'archeologie du delta du Mekong*. 4 vols. Paris, 1959–1963. Vol. 3: *La Culture du Fou-nan*. 2 pts. 1962.

Maloney, Clarence. "The Beginnings of Civilization in South India," *JAS* 29, 3 (1970): 603–616.

Manguin, Pierre-Yves. "La traversée de la mer de Chine méridienale, des dètroits à Canton, jusqu'au 17e siècle (La question des Iles Paracels)," *Actes du XXIXe Congrès international des Orientalistes* (Paris) 2 (1976): 110–115.

———. "Études Cam II. L'introduction de l'Islam au Campā," *BEFEO* 66 (1979): 255–287.

———. "The Southeast Asian Ship: An Historical Approach," *JSEAS* 11, 2 (1980): 266–276.

Marsden, William. *The History of Sumatra*. 3rd ed. London, 1811; reprinted, Kuala Lumpur, 1966.

Maspero, Georges. *Le Royaume de Champa*. Paris, 1928.

Maspero, Henri. "Le protectorat general d'Annam sous les T'ang," *BEFEO* 10 (1910): 539–584, 665–682.

———. "La frontière de l'Annam et du Cambodge," *BEFEO* 18, 3 (1918): 29–36.
Mauss, Marcel. *The Gift*. London, 1966.
McKinnon, E. Edward. "A Note on the Discovery of Spur-Marked Yueh-Type Sherds at Bukit Seguntang Palembang," *JMBRAS* 52, 2 (1979): 50–58.
Meilink-Roelofsz, M. A. P. *Asian Trade and European Influence in the Indonesian Archipelago between 1500 and about 1630*. The Hague, 1962.
Mills, J. V. G. *Ying-yai Sheng-lan of Ma Huan (1433)*. Cambridge, 1970.
Moertono, Soemarsaid. *State and Statecraft in Old Java: A Study of the Later Mataram Period, 16th to 17th Century*. Ithaca, 1968.
Moron, Eleanor. "Configurations of Time and Space at Angkor Wat," *Studies in Indo-Asian Art and Culture* 5 (1977): 217–267.
Mus, Paul. *India Seen From the East: Indian and Indigenous Cults in Champa*, trans. by I. W. Mabbett and D. P. Chandler. Clayton, Victoria, 1975.
Nicholl, Robert. "Brunei Rediscovered, A Survey of Early Times," *JSEAS* 14, 1 (1983): 32–45.
Nilakanta Sastri, K. A. "A Tamil Merchant Guild in Sumatra," *TBG* 72 (1932): 314–327.
———. "Agastya," *TBG* 76 (1936): 471–545.
———. *The History of Srivijaya*. Madras, 1949.
———. "Takuapa and its Tamil Inscription," *JMBRAS* 22, 1 (1949): 25–30.
———. *The Colas*. 2nd ed. Madras, 1955.
Noorduyn, J. "Further Topographical Notes on the Ferry Charter of 1358," *BKI* 124 (1968): 460–481.
———. "The Eastern Kings in Majapahit," *BKI* 131, 4 (1975): 479–487.
———. "Majapahit in the 15th Century," *BKI* 134, 2–3 (1978): 207–274.
Noorduyn, J., and H. Th. Verstappen. "Purnavarman's River Works Near Tugu," *BKI* 128 (1972): 298–307.
O'Connor, Stanley J. "Si Chon: An Early Settlement in Peninsular Thailand," *JSS* 56, 1 (1968): 1–18.
———. *Hindu Gods of Peninsular Siam*. Ascona, 1972.
Osborne, Milton. "Notes on Early Cambodian Provincial History: Isanapura and Sambhupura," *France-Asie/Asia* 20, 4 (1966): 433–449.
Paranavitana, S. "Negapatam and Theravada Buddhism in South India," *Journal of the Greater India Society* 11, 1 (1944): 17–25.
Parsons, Talcott, and Neil J. Smelser. *Economy and Society: A Study in the Integration of Economic and Social Theory*. London, 1956.
Peacock, B. A. V. "Pillar Base Architecture in Ancient Kedah," *JMBRAS* 47, 1 (1974): 66–86.
Pelliot, P. "Deux itinéraires de Chine en Inde à la fin du VIIIe siècle," *BEFEO* 4 (1904): 130–413.
———. "Le Fou-nan," *BEFEO* 3 (1903): 248–303.
———. "Quelques textes chinois concernant l'Indochine hinduisée," *Etudes Asiatiques* 2 (1925): 243–263.
Pigeaud, Th. G. Th., ed. and trans. *De Tantu Panggĕlaran*. The Hague, 1924.
Pigeaud, Th. G. Th. *Java in the Fourteenth Century: A Study in Cultural History*. 5 vols. The Hague, 1960–1963.
Polanyi, Karl, Conrad M. Arensberg, and Harry W. Pearson, eds. *Trade and Market in the Early Empires*. Glencoe, Ill., 1957.
Polo, Marco. *The Travels of Marco Polo*. Literary Guild of America Classic Series, n.d.

Popkin, Samuel L. *The Rational Peasant: The Political Economy of Society in Vietnam*. Berkeley, 1980.

Przluski, Jean. "La princesse a l'odeur de poisson et la nāgi dan les tradition de l'Asie Orientale," *Etudes Asiatiques* 2 (1925): 265–284.

Rackham, H. *The Natural History of Pliny the Elder.* Cambridge, 1960.

Rajani, M. C. Chand Chirayu. "Background to the Srivijaya Story," *JSS* 62, 1 (1974): 174–211; 62, 2 (1974): 285–324.

Ravaisse, Paul. "Deux inscriptions coufiques du Campa," *JA* 20, 2 (1922): 247–289.

Reid, Anthony. "Trade and the Problem of Royal Power in Aceh." In *Pre-Colonial State Systems in Southeast Asia,* edited by A. Reid and L. Castles. Kuala Lumpur, 1975.

———. "Trade and State Power in 16th and 17th Century Southeast Asia." In *Proceedings, Seventh International Association of Historians of Asia Conference,* 391–419. Bangkok, 1979.

Reid, Anthony, ed. *Slavery, Bondage and Dependency in South-East Asia.* London, 1983.

Reid, Anthony, and L. Castles, eds. *Pre-Colonial State Systems in Southeast Asia.* Kuala Lumpur, 1975.

Reid, Anthony, and David Marr, eds. *Perceptions of the Past in Southeast Asia.* Singapore, 1979.

Rentse, Anker. "Gantang of Kelantan," *JMBRAS* 11 (1933): 242–244.

Revere, Robert E. "Ports of Trade in the Eastern Mediterranean." In *Trade and Market in the Early Empires,* edited by Karl Polyani et al., 38–63. Glencoe, Ill., 1957.

Reynolds, Frank E. "The Holy Emerald Jewel: Some Aspects of Buddhist Symbolism and Political Legitimation in Thailand and Laos." In *Religion and Legitimation of Power in Thailand, Laos, and Burma,* edited by Bardwell L. Smith, 175–193. Chambersburg, Pa., 1978.

Ricklefs, M. C. "Land and the Law in the Epigraphy of Tenth-Century Cambodia," *JAS* 16, 3 (1967): 411–420.

Robequain, Charles. *The Economic Development of French Indochina.* New York, 1944.

Sabloff, J. A., and G. C. Lamberg-Karlovsky, eds. *Ancient Civilization and Trade.* Albuquerque, 1975.

Sahai, Sachchidanand. "Fiscal Administration in Ancient Cambodia." *The South East Asian Review* 1, 2 (1977): 123–138.

———. "Territorial Administration in Ancient Cambodia." *The South East Asian Review* 2, 1 (1977): 35–50.

Sahlins, Marshall. "Poor Man, Rich Man, Big Man, Chief: Political Types in Melanesia and Polynesia," *Comparative Studies in Society and History* 5 (1963): 285–303.

———. *Stone Age Economics.* Chicago, 1972.

Sarkar, H. B. *Corpus of the Inscriptions of Java (up to 928 A.D.).* 2 vols. Calcutta, 1971–1972.

Sauvaget, Jean. *Les marveilles de l'Inde.* Paris, 1954.

Schafer, E. H. *The Empire of Min.* Rutland, Vt., 1954.

———. *The Vermilion Bird: T'ang Images of the South.* Berkeley, 1967.

Schnitger, F. M. *The Archeology of Hindoo Sumatra.* Leiden, 1937.

———. *Forgotten Kingdoms in Sumatra.* Leiden, 1939.

Schoff, W., trans. *The Periplus of the Erythraean Sea.* New York, 1912.

Schrieke, B. J. *Indonesian Sociological Studies: Selected Writings* (pt. I). The Hague, 1955; *Ruler and Realm in Early Java* (pt. II). The Hague, 1957.
Scott, William C. *The Moral Economy of the Peasant*. New Haven, 1976.
Sedov, L. A. "On the Problem of the Economic System in Angkor Cambodia in the IX-XII Centuries," *Narody Asii i Afriki, Istoria, Ekonomika, Kul'tura* 6, Akademija Nauk SSR (1963): 73-81.
Shorto, H. L. "A Mon Genealogy of Kings: Observations on *The Nidāna Ārambhakantha*. In *Historians of South East Asia*, edited by D. G. E. Hall, 63-72. London, 1961.
Shuhaimi, Hassan Nik. "The Bukit Seguntang Buddha: A Reconsideration of its Date," *JMBRAS* 52, 2 (1979): 40-49.
Siegel, James. *The Rope of God*. Berkeley, 1975.
Skinner, G. William. *Marketing and Social Structure in Rural China*. Ann Arbor, 1974.
Smith, R. B., and W. Watson, eds. *Early South East Asia: Essays in Archaeology, History and Historical Geography*. London, 1979.
Soedjatmoko, Mohammad Ali, G. J. Resick, and George McT. Kahin, eds. *An Introduction to Indonesian Historiography*. Ithaca, 1965.
Sopher, David. *The Sea Nomads*. Singapore, 1965.
Spencer, George W. "Temple Money-Lending and Livestock Redistribution in Early Tanjore," *Indian Economic and Social History Review* 5, 3 (1968): 277-293.
———. "The Politics of Plunder: The Cholas in Eleventh Century Ceylon," *JAS* 35, 3 (1976): 405-419.
———. "When Queens Bore Gifts: Women as Temple Donors in the Cōḷa Period." Paper, Association for Asian Studies meeting, Toronto, 1981.
———. *The Politics of Expansion: The Chola Conquest of Sri Lanka and Sri Vijaya*. Madras, 1983.
Spinks, C. N. "Siam and the Pottery Trade of Asia," *JSS* 44, 2 (1956): 61-111.
Srinivas, M. N. *Caste in Modern India and Other Essays*. Bombay, 1962.
Staal, J. F. "Sanskrit and Sanskritization," *JAS* 22 (1963): 261-275.
Stargardt, Janice. "Burma's Economic and Diplomatic Relations with India and China from Early Medieval Sources," *JESHO* 14, 1 (1971): 28-62.
Stein, Burton. "The Economic Function of a Medieval South Indian Temple," *JAS* 19, 2 (1960): 163-176.
———. *Peasant State and Society in Medieval South India*. Delhi, 1980.
Stein, R. "Le Lin-yi," *Han-Hiue (Bulletin du centre d'études sinologiques de Pekin)* 2 (1947): 1-54.
Stern, Philippe. *L'art du Champa (ancien Annam) et son évolution*. Paris, 1942.
———. "Diversité et rythme des fondations royales Khmères," *BEFEO* 44, 2 (1951): 649-685.
Stutterheim, W. F. "Een belangrijke oorkonde uit de Kedoe," *TBG* 67 (1927): 172-215.
———. *A Javanese Period in Sumatra History*. Surakarta, 1929.
———. "The Meaning of the Hindu-Javanese *caṇḍi*," *Journal of the American Oriental Society* 51 (1931): 1-15.
Subrahamanya Aiyer, K. V. "Largest Provincial Organizations in Ancient India," *Quarterly Journal of the Mythic Society* 65, 1-2 (1954-1955): 29-47, 70-98, 270-286; 66, 1 (1955): 8-22.
Suleiman, Satyawati. "The History and Art of Srivijaya." In *The Art of Srivijaya*, edited by M. C. Subhadradis Diskul, 1-20. Kuala Lumpur, 1980.

Supomo, S. "The Image of Majapahit in Later Javanese and Indonesian History." In *Perceptions of the Past in Southeast Asia,* edited by Anthony Reid and David Marr, 171–185. Singapore, 1979.

Takakusa, Junjiro. *A Record of the Buddhist Religion as Practiced in India and the Malay Archipelago, by I-Tsing.* Oxford, 1896; reprinted, Delhi, 1966.

Tambiah, Stanley J. *World Conqueror and World Renouncer: A Study of Buddhism and Polity in Thailand against a Historical Background.* Cambridge, 1976.

Tan Yeok Seong. "The Sri Vijayan Inscription of Canton (A.D. 1079)," *JSEAH* 5, 2 (1964): 17–24.

Tasaka, Kodo. "Islam in Champa," *Tohagaku* 4 (1952): 52–60.

Taw Sein Ko. *The Kalyāṇī Inscriptions.* Rangoon, 1892.

Taylor, Keith W. "Madagascar in the Ancient Malayo-Polynesian Myths," and "The Rise of Đai Viet and the Establishment of Thang-long." In *Explorations in Early Southeast Asian History: The Origins of Southeast Asian Statecraft,* edited by Kenneth R. Hall and John K. Whitmore, 25–60, 149–192. Ann Arbor, 1976.

———. *The Birth of Vietnam.* Berkeley, 1983.

Teeuw, A., and D. K. Wyatt. *Hikayat Patani: The Story of Patani.* 2 vols. The Hague, 1970.

Than Tun. "History of Burma, 1300–1400," *JBRS* 42, 2 (1959): 119–135.

Tibbetts, G. R. *A Study of the Arabic Texts Containing Material on South-East Asia.* Leiden, 1979.

Toussaint, Auguste, *History of the Indian Ocean.* Chicago, 1966.

Trautmann, Thomas R. "Consanguineous Marriage in Pali Literature," *Journal of the American Oriental Society,* 93, 2 (1973): 158–180.

———. *Dravidian Kinship.* Cambridge, 1981.

Van der Meer, N. C. van Setten. *Sawah Cultivation in Ancient Java: Aspects of Development during the Indo-Javanese Period, 5th to 15th Century.* Canberra, 1979.

Van der Meulen, W. J. "Ptolemy's Geography of Mainland Southeast Asia and Borneo," *Indonesia* 19 (1975): 16–22.

———. "In Search of Ho-ling," *Indonesia* 23 (1977): 87–111.

Van Leur, J. C. *Indonesian Trade and Society: Essays in Asian Social and Economic History.* The Hague, 1955.

Van Liere, W. J. "Traditional Water Management in the Lower Mekong Basin," *World Archaeology* 11, 3 (1980): 265–280.

Van Naerssen, F. H. "De Brantas en haar waterwerken in den Hindu-Javaanschen tijd," *De Ingenieur* 53 (1938): A65–A66.

———. "The Çailendra Interregnum." *India Antiqua: A Volume of Oriental Studies Presented . . . to Jean Philippe Vogel,* 249–253. Leiden, 1947.

———. "Tribute to the God and Tribute to the King." In *Southeast Asian History and Historiography,* edited by C. D. Cowan and O. W. Wolters, 296–303. Ithaca, 1976.

Van Naerssen, F. H., and R. C. de Iongh. *The Economic and Administrative History of Early Indonesia.* Leiden, 1977.

Van Stein Callenfels, P. V. "De inscriptie van Sukabumi," *MKAWAL* 78 (1934): 116–122.

———. "De inscriptie van Kandangan," *TBG* 58 (1919): 359.

Vickery, Michael. "The Khmer Inscriptions of Tenasserim: A Reinterpretation," *JSS* 61, 1 (1973): 51–70.

———. "The Reign of Suryavarman I and the Dynamics of Angkorean Development," *Proceedings, Eighth International Association of Historians of Asia Conference,* forthcoming.

Vogel, J. Ph. "The Earliest Sanskrit Inscriptions of Java," *Publicaties van de Oudheidkundige Dienst in Nederlandsch-Indie* 1 (1925): 15–35.

Wake, C. "Malacca's Early Kings and the Reception of Islam," *JSEAH* 5, 2 (1967): 104–128.

Wales, H. G. Quaritch. "The Extent of Sri Vijaya's Influence Abroad," *JMBRAS* 51, 1 (1978): 5–12.

Wang Gungwu. "The Nanhai Trade: A Study of the Early History of Chinese Trade in the South China Sea," *JMBRAS* 31, 2 (1958): 1–135.

———. "Early Ming Relations with Southeast Asia: A Background Essay." In *The Chinese World Order,* edited by J. K. Fairbank, 34–62. Cambridge, Mass., 1968.

Wheatley, Paul. "Geographical Notes on Some Commodities Involved in Sung Maritime Trade," *JMBRAS* 32, 2 (1959): 5–140.

———. *The Golden Khersonese: Studies in the Historical Geography of the Malay Peninsula before A.D. 1500.* Kuala Lumpur, 1961.

———. "Satyānṛta in Suvarnadvīpa: From Reciprocity to Redistribution in Ancient Southeast Asia." In *Ancient Civilization and Trade,* edited by J. A. Sabloff and G. C. Lamberg-Karlovsky, 227–283. Albuquerque, 1975.

———. "Urban Genesis in Mainland South-East Asia." In *Early South East Asia,* edited by R. B. Smith and W. Watson, 288–303. London, 1979.

———. *Nāgara and Commandery: Origins of the Southeast Asian Urban Traditions.* University of Chicago Department of Geography Research Papers nos. 207–208. Chicago, 1983.

Wheeler, R. E. M. "Arikamedu: An Indo-Roman Trading Station on the East Coast of India," *Ancient India* 2 (1946): 17–124.

———. *Rome Beyond the Imperial Frontiers.* London, 1954.

Whitmore, John K. "The Opening of Southeast Asia, Trading Patterns through the Centuries." In *Economic Exchange and Social Interaction in Southeast Asia: Perspectives from Prehistory, History and Ethnography,* edited by Karl L. Hutterer, 139–153. Ann Arbor, 1977.

———. "Vietnam and the Monetary Flow of Eastern Asia, Thirteenth to Eighteenth Centuries." In *Precious Metal Flows in the Later Medieval and Early Modern Worlds,* edited by J. F. Richards, 363–393. Durham, N.C., 1983.

Wickremasignhe, Sirima. "Ceylon's Relations with South-east Asia, with Special Reference to Burma," *Ceylon Journal of Historical and Social Studies* 3, 1 (1960): 38–58.

Wilken, G. A. *Handleiding voor de Vergelijkende Volkenkunde van Nederlandsh-Indie.* Leiden, 1893.

Willetts, William. "The Maritime Adventures of the Grand Eunuch Ho," *JSEAH* 5, 2 (1964): 25–42.

Winstedt, R. O. , and De Josselin de Jong. "The Maritime Laws of Malacca," *JMBRAS* 29, 3 (1956): 22–59.

Wirjosuparto, Sujipto. "Shrivijaya and Majapahit," *Hemisphere* 14, 9 (1970): 26–31.

Wisseman, Jan. "Markets and Trade in Pre-Majapahit Java." In *Economic Exchange and Social Interaction in Southeast Asia: Perspectives from Pre-*

history, History and Ethnography, edited by Karl L. Hutterer, 197–212. Ann Arbor, 1977.
Wittfogel, Karl. *Oriental Despotism*. New Haven, 1957.
Wolf, Eric. *Peasants*. Englewood Cliffs, N.J., 1966.
Wolters, O. W. "Tāmbraliṅga," *BSOAS* 21, 3 (1958): 587–607.
———. "Srivijayan Expansion in the Seventh Century," *Artibus Asiae* 24 (1961): 417–424.
———. "A Note on the Capital of Srivijaya during the Eleventh Century," *Essays Offered to G. H. Luce by his Friends in Honour of his Seventy-fifth Birthday.* Artibus Asiae Supplementum 23, 225–239. Ascona, 1966.
———. "The Khmer King at Basan (1371–1373) and the Restoration of the Cambodian Chronology during the 14th and 15th Centuries," *Asia Major* 12, 1 (1966): 44–64.
———. *Early Indonesian Commerce: A Study of the Origins of Sri Vijaya.* Ithaca, 1967.
———. *The Fall of Srivijaya in Malay History.* Ithaca, 1970.
———. "Jayavarman II's Military Power: The Territorial Foundations of the Angkor Empire," *JRAS* (1973): 21–30.
———. "North-Western Cambodia in the Seventh Century," *BSOAS* 37, 2 (1974): 355–384.
———. "Landfall on the Palembang Coast in Medieval Times," *Indonesia* 20 (1975): 1–57.
———. "Molluscs and the Historical Geography of Northeast Sumatra in the Eight Century A.D.," *Indonesia* 22 (1976): 9–17.
———. "A Note on Sungsang Village at the Estuary of the Musi River in Southeastern Sumatra: A Reconsideration of the Historical Geography of the Palembang Region," *Indonesia* 27 (1979): 33–50.
———. "Studying Srivijaya," *JMBRAS* 52, 2 (1979): 1–38.
———. "Khmer 'Hinduism' in the Seventh Century." In *Early South East Asia,* edited by R. B. Smith and W. Watson, 427–442. London, 1979.
———. *History, Culture, and Region in Southeast Asian Perspectives.* Singapore, 1982.
———. "A Few Miscellaneous *Pi-chi* Jottings on Early Indonesia," *Indonesia* 36 (October 1983): 49–64.
Woodward, Hiram W., Jr. "Studies in the Art of Central Siam, 950–1350 A.D." Ph. D. diss., Yale University, 1975.
———. "A Chinese Silk Depicted at Candi Sewu." In *Economic Exchange and Social Interaction in Southeast Asia: Perspectives from Prehistory, History and Ethnography,* edited by Karl L. Hutterer, 233–244. Ann Arbor, 1977.
Wyatt, David K. "Mainland Powers on the Malay Peninsula." Paper presented to the International Conference on Asian History, Kuala Lumpur, 1968.
———. *The Crystal Sands: The Chronicles of Nagara Sri Dharmarāja.* Ithaca, 1975.
Yule, Henry. *Cathay and the Way Thither.* 4 vols. Revised by Henry Cordier. London, 1913–1916.
Yule, Henry, trans. *The Book of Ser Marco Polo.* 2 vols. London, 1903.
Zimmer, Heinrich. *Myths and Symbols in Indian Art and Civilization.* Princeton, 1972.
Zoetmulder, P. J. *Kalangwan: A Survey of Old Javanese Literature.* The Hague, 1974.

Index

About the Author

Kenneth R. Hall is currently assistant professor of comparative world history at North Adams State College (Massachusetts). He received his B.A. from Albion College in 1969, an M.A. from Northern Illinois University in 1971, and in 1975 he was awarded the Ph.D. in premodern South and Southeast Asian history from the University of Michigan at Ann Arbor. Hall has conducted field research in both Southeast Asia and India. In 1974 he was a member of the Sumatra Expedition of the Indonesian Archaeological Institute; during the summer of 1976 he was a fellow of the American Institute of Indian Studies in India; and in the summer of 1980, he was the American Council of Learned Societies delegate to the International Association of Historians of Asia Conference in Kuala Lumpur. In 1977, Elmira College (New York) recognized Hall as its Outstanding Junior Faculty Member. His publications include numerous articles on early South and Southeast Asian history that have appeared in such journals as the *Journal of the Economic and Social History of the Orient,* the *Journal of Urban History,* the *Journal of Southeast Asian Studies,* and the *Indian Economic and Social History Review.* He was co-editor (with John K. Whitmore) and contributor to *Explorations in Early Southeast Asian History: The Origins of Southeast Asian Statecraft,* and author of *Trade and Statecraft in the Age of the Cōḷas.* The preparation of this book was begun while Hall was a summer fellow of the National Endowment of the Humanities in 1979 and was completed with financial assistance from the Tufts University Faculty Research Fund.